preadolescent
development

preadolescent development

Hershel D. Thornburg
editor

THE UNIVERSITY OF ARIZONA PRESS
Tucson, Arizona

About the Author ...

HERSHEL D. THORNBURG has become widely known in the United States for his work in developmental psychology. His studies in child and adolescent psychology have helped bridge the gap between the areas of child development and adolescent development, and have set the stage for this present, precise focus on that bridge area. This focus had its roots in his six years of teaching and administrative duties at the junior high school level. Thornburg joined the Educational Psychology Department at the University of Arizona in 1967, having earlier earned his doctorate at the University of Oklahoma. He has authored several books and numerous journal articles in his field.

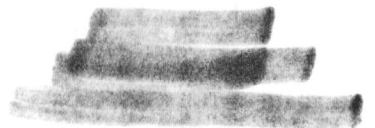

THE UNIVERSITY OF ARIZONA PRESS

I. S. B. N.-0-8165-0433-4
L. C. No. 73-87719

To
KRISTEN

contents

Contents

CHARTS

TABLES

preface

The two decades in American society since the mid-50s have brought increasing emotional and social pressures and awareness to our children and adolescents. In effect this period has caused our youth to become involved in social behaviors at an earlier chronological age than at any time previous in our society. This may mean that experiences once unique to the thirteen or fourteen year old may now be commonplace among ages eleven and twelve. In short, it has caused an increasing number of professionals in the behavioral sciences to consider the transitional period between childhood and adolescence — a period referred to herein as *preadolescence*.

Two major introductory sections within the body of the book itself set the stage for my presentation. The first, a general introduction, gives both rationale and organizational characteristics of the book. In addition it is designed to help the reader conceptualize what *preadolescence* is. The second introduction is transition — that is, it moves the reader from the issues of preadolescent development to the issues of preadolescent behaviors. In addition, each of the nine chapters has its own introduction which orients the reader to the specific chapter topic as well as integrating the articles reprinted within each chapter.

Throughout this book of readings, the author has interjected much of his own work. The eleven introductions and four of the 27 articles reprinted here constitute well over one-third of the entire book. This was intentional. The field of preadolescent development is relatively new. The author did not feel that a full text on preadolescence could be written without excessive extrapolation of scientific research. Nevertheless, the author holds and wants to share several definite viewpoints about preadolescence. Therefore, in some respects this book is a reader-text — a reader in the sense that the major portion reflects the published writings of individuals from several different scientific disciplines; a text in the sense that the integrated chapter introductions allow for continuity throughout the book.

Three factors affected my choice of articles. First, I chose those that present a contemporary viewpoint which is stressed within each introduction. Second, recency was a concern, and over 85 percent of the articles are post-1970. Finally, for a controversial or multi-faceted topic, articles that represent conflicting positions were selected.

I would like to give special thanks to Daniel Reschly, the University of Arizona, and Stephen Brown, Auburn University, for the critical analysis of my introductory materials. I would also like to thank reviewers for their evaluative comments and Elizabeth Shaw, University of Arizona Press, for her editorial counsel. Alice Schoenberger and Joan Nelson were most helpful in the manuscript preparation.

HERSHEL D. THORNBURG

General Introduction

A traditional, and somewhat overworked saying in the old West some one hundred years ago stated to the westward bound traveler, "You're now entering no-man's-land." To borrow that expression and use it to describe the uncertainty, ambiguity, and unpredictability of the outcomes for the child who enters preadolescence (nine to thirteen years) is not stretching the imagination too far. In fact, preadolescence at best is one of the most ill-defined and nebulous time periods in the developmental span. The accompanying diagram shows where the stage of preadolescent development fits into the overall developmental scheme.

The period preceding preadolescence (roughly the first eight years) is a very formative interval. In the first two years the infant, through development, begins learning social and intellectual behaviors that facilitate the eventual mastery of his environment. Learning to stand, crawl, walk, run, and climb are common motor behaviors he accomplishes. In addition, the child focuses on his mother and father and other significant people in his environment. This facilitates a sense of well-being, as such parental interaction is emotionally satisfying to the child. Furthermore, the infant intellectually develops as he begins identifying and reacting to people and objects in his environment. Toward age two he begins giving symbolic meaning to many of his environmental stimuli, which is representative of good intellectual development.

The preschool child becomes a more mobile being. Social adaptation and identification with similar age peers is basically facilitated by language acquisition. The child's vocabulary rapidly accelerates and such verbal mastery gives the child confidence to extend himself much further than he had done previously. In addition, the child's superego (conscience) emerges and most social behaviors are interpreted as acceptable (right) or unacceptable (wrong). The parents are the most profound influence on the child's

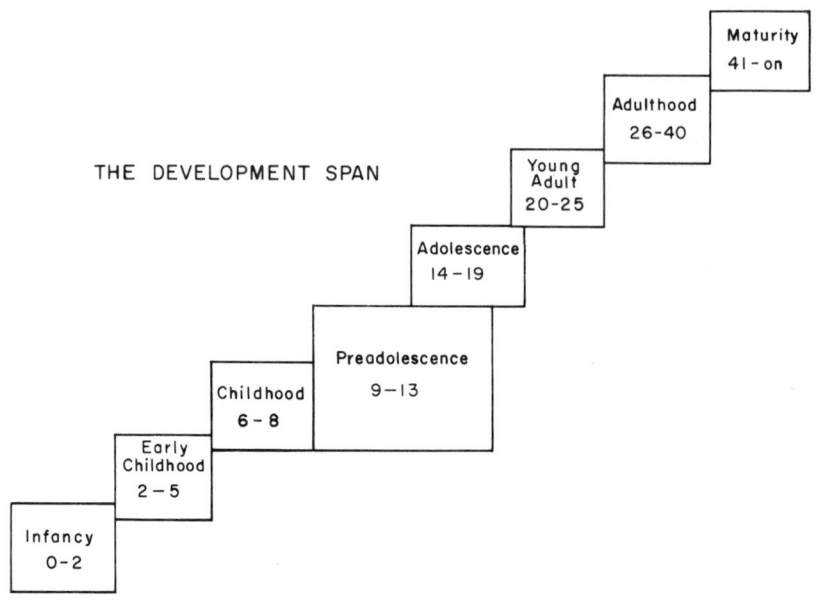

THE DEVELOPMENT SPAN

emerging attitudinal and value structures and often teach the child values that endure throughout one's lifetime.

The developmental period described as childhood (see chart) corresponds with grades one through three in school. Generally speaking, the primary grades in school are extensions of the home. The child continues learning acceptable social behaviors, both within a school environment, and outside the school framework. The teachings of the school commonly reinforce the earlier parental teachings which the child brings into the classroom with him. The need to get along with one's peers increases as each child is involved in longer periods of social interaction. Intellectually the child has the ability to conceptualize, learn logical rules, and apply such rules to a diversity of environmental and academic situations. One's intellectual ability is enhanced by the fact that he is required to focus on academic behaviors as his rational powers are not only tremendously increased, but accentuated.

The transitional period from childhood to preadolescence cannot be clearly delineated, although around nine years is the time in which the child now moves from a strong academic being to a social being. Many of his heretofore predictable behavioral patterns start becoming less predictable. Similarly, the well-defined values taught by parents may begin being challenged by the child as the focus on attitudinal and value sources moves more toward his peer group. The changes that the preadolescent undergoes are, in fact, distinct enough that the identification of preadolescence as a distinct developmental period seems warranted. It is, however, recognized that developmental psychologists may take issue with this viewpoint, as is attested to by the fact that this ambiguous developmental period is often referred to as late childhood or early adolescence in many well written psychology textbooks. It is the author's belief that the difficulties the preadolescent encounters are not solely transitional, however.

The organizational structure of this reader does, in fact, attempt to first isolate, then integrate major developmental problems and issues, both physiological and psychological in origin, which affect the child upon entering this developmental period. This book is organized into nine distinct chapters which deal with developmental, cultural, and social variables that are potential stresses for the emerging preadolescent. The nine areas of concern are briefly discussed herein.

Chapter One. The Preadolescent Years
The first chapter in the book presents definitive information as to what this age-range is all about and the nature of the child who is entering into it. Some theory as to normal growth patterns helps the reader not only better understand the period of preadolescence but makes this chapter an orientation chapter to the remaining eight chapters in the book. It focuses on this book's intent to explicate physiological, cultural, intellectual, and behavioral growth phenomena within the nine to thirteen year old.

Chapter Two. Physical Growth
In an attempt to better understand the changing child, this chapter deals with physical growth. The time of preadolescence includes glandular changes which are prerequisite to the occurrence of puberty. Some twelve to eighteen months preceding that physiological crisis is the period known as *pubescence*, which is very much a part of the preadolescent's life. This chapter acquaints the reader with that information as well as tracing growth through the crisis of puberty itself.

Chapter Three. Sex Differences
Through early parental interactions and many experiences in a child's early school life, distinct sex differences are drawn. This chapter examines sex differences that exist by preadolescence and the ongoing sources of learning sex roles, as well as experientially playing such roles. Changing societal sex role expectancies are also discussed.

Chapter Four. Preadolescent Intelligence
The design of this chapter is both theoretical and practical. In the chapter introduction and the first article consideration is given to the developmental nature of the preadolescent's intellectual structure. The basic theoretical notations come from the developmental psychology of Jean Piaget. The more practical approach in this chapter stresses the actual kinds of intellectual skills which the preadolescent can do. In addition, creativity and the ways in which the nine to thirteen year old expresses it are discussed.

Chapter Five. Emerging Values
A conceptual model of how an individual learns values and behaves in accordance with them gives some insight into the changing nature of attitudes and behaviors during this period. Using the prerequisite childhood value

teachings as a reference point, the chapter focuses on value conflicts, some of which occur through exercising varying behavioral patterns and others as a result of new outreach, vis-à-vis development.

Chapter Six. Discipline and the Preadolescent
To some extent this chapter is an adjunct to the discussion of values in chapter five. In addition, it focuses more strongly on functioning within structured environments, namely, the schools, than do the first five chapters. It is an important area to consider since the preadolescent is becoming a more active social being, and must, of necessity, learn socially acceptable ranges of behavior and their positive or negative consequences.

Chapter Seven. Drugs and the Preadolescent
This chapter and the succeeding one about sexual behavior consider relevant social phenomena with which the preadolescent is directly involved. The vulnerability of the preadolescent is due to his changing physical nature, his increasing peer interest, his increasing experiential curiosity, and his somewhat limited emotional growth. In addition to the identification of drugs and types of users, discussion also focuses on the educative aspects of drug use.

Chapter Eight. Sexuality in Preadolescence
The physiological changes that occur during pubescence stir a new awakening of sexual (libidinal) energy which causes the preadolescent to devote some time and attention to the nature of the opposite sex and his physical and emotional reactions. Emphasis is given to the normal growth sequences and the learning of sexual behaviors and feelings. Specifically, the nature of the preadolescent sexual being is discussed. Because of the vulnerability of the nine to thirteen year old in this behavioral area, some discussion as to the importance of systematic instruction on human sexuality is presented.

Chapter Nine. Toward Adolescence
If preadolescence is to be thought of as a distinct developmental period, then it is logical to discuss the transitional time between preadolescence and adolescence. This chapter is mainly interested in the changing perceptions of the preadolescent as he moves toward the close of this developmental stage and anticipates movement into adolescence. In addition to the transitional discussion, the reader briefly focuses upon some adolescent expectancies, especially in the area of establishing peer relations. Hopefully, such material will serve a guidance function, as it not only looks at the preadolescent in retrospect, but the emerging adolescent as well.

This brief overview of the book describes the range of change in the preadolescent from several dimensions. By looking at relevant developmental changes and the subsequent effects they have on behavior, it becomes easier to conceptualize the importance of the stage of preadolescent development.

It is important to consider the developmental nature of the preadolescent by age. While this author personally sees growth more as a continuous phenomenon than within distinct age segments, it is, nevertheless, of much value to see how, with age, the preadolescent changes. No one has done this any better than has David Elkind in his most provocative book *A Sympathetic Understanding of the Child Six to Sixteen.* The age profiles that follow are statements selected from his book.

Age Nine
A refinement of behaviors exhibited at age eight.
He gives the impression of steadfastness and responsibility that will be the benchmarks of his later maturity.
There is an increased awareness of sex and sex appropriate behaviors.
There is a tendency to organize and budget time.
His parental relationships are friendly and accommodating.
He begins strengthening close friendships with peers.
Academic achievement is of prime importance because it is a major way in which he is evaluated.

Age Ten
Girls are slightly more advanced sexually than boys.
Fears and anxieties are minimal at the age.
Increasing interest in parents, teachers, and peers is evidenced.
The ten-year-old is self-accepting.
Sex differences in friendship patterns begin emerging.
There is active participation in organized group activities.
He likes school and is a responsible student.

Age Eleven
The activity level shows a decisive increase.
He is anxious for new experiences and curious about the world around him.
Quarrelsomeness emerges.
He tends to be disciplined quite a lot.
The seeds of independence from parental influence show.
Friendships are formed around mutual interests and temperament.
More definite interest in the opposite sex is acknowledged.

Age Twelve
He is outgoing, enthusiastic, and generous.
He is beginning to assert that he is no longer a child.
Most youth this age relate successfully to peers and adults.
There may emerge a new competitiveness with parents, both in athletics and intellectual games.
Girls begin verbalizing their romantic interest in boys.
Boys still prefer interaction with same-sex peers to that with opposite-sex peers.
Restlessness and daydreaming are quite characteristic in school.

Age Thirteen
There is a turning inward and preoccupation with self.
Sulking and going to one's room when angry are common.
This age appears to be the least happy of the emerging adolescent years.
Attempts by adults to talk are often interpreted as prying.
There is an increase in dating by the girl.
Boys have decisively less interest in girls than when twelve.
There is a need for privacy and independent activity.

Figure 1 illustrates that beyond preadolescence there are still vital developmental periods, the first of which is adolescence. The range of adolescence has traditionally been thought of as the *teenage* years. Today the trend is thinking that the final two years of preadolescence (twelve-thirteen) and the early phases of adolescence overlap (Thornburg, 1971). This is one of the reasons that the final chapter in the book gears our thinking beyond preadolescence. The adolescent years are the final transitional years between an individual, the child, and an individual, the adult. In early adolescence (thirteen-fifteen), the ambiguities and uncertainties experienced in preadolescence only seem to have extended themselves. It is true though that when the adolescent is sixteen or seventeen he has reached nearly all his physical and intellectual growth, has learned the range of socially acceptable behaviors, and is actively coping with his ego identity crisis. In short, he is approaching adulthood.

The design of the chapter introductions that begin each of the nine chapters is to better orient you to the range of development and learning that the preadolescent has incurred. As you proceed through the book, the overview and age profiles presented here will take on additional meaning, and hopefully, facilitate a better understanding and appreciation of the developmental period known as preadolescence.

References

Elkind, D. *A Sympathetic Understanding of the Child Six to Sixteen.* Boston: Allyn and Bacon, 1971.
Thornburg, H. D. (Ed.) *Contemporary Adolescence: Readings.* Monterey, Calif: Brooks/Cole, 1971.

CHAPTER 1 the preadolescent years

Introduction

During the intermediate grade years and junior high school (ages nine to thirteen), our youth begin experiencing a period of steady developmental change. The most pronounced change is in physical growth as the preadolescent develops toward puberty. New social interactions and pressures are also indicative that the preadolescent is rapidly moving out of childhood. Other changes resulting from development are increased intellectual ability, a need for behavioral and emotional independence, and broad experiential opportunities.

Some writers call this period of life late childhood or early adolescence. It will be referred to as preadolescence within this reader for two reasons. First, this is a transitional period during which the individual is no longer a child, yet, not an adolescent. Secondly, this period of life is thought to be an important formative period for later adolescent behavior but has been tremendously limited in research and writing – to some extent because it has been tacked on to the discussion of childhood and/or adolescence. This reader will treat the preadolescent developmental period as an entity within itself, crucial to the ongoing development and behavior of the individual.

Throughout the history of development psychology, the individual has always been viewed as a child until hitting the magical age of thirteen, which ushered him into adolescence. This changed with the publication of the epochal article entitled "Preadolescents – What Makes Them Tick?" by Fritz Redl in 1943. Here, Redl, who describes preadolescence as the time when the nicest children begin to behave in the most awful way, discusses the changing nature of the individual and the dilemma felt by most adults in relating to the preadolescent.

Redl (1943) contends that the most peculiar phenomena of preadolescence is the child-adult relationship. The preadolescent, who heretofore had acquired most of his social learning from his parents, is now beginning to be skeptical of that relationship. Distrust and suspicion of parents is quite common, as is preadolescent irritability with one's parents. There are most likely two reasons for this. We should not lose sight of the fact that the first eight years of life are characterized by a well-defined, closely-knit pattern of behavior in which parents are the dominating influence. In addition, school focuses on the exhaustive presentation of factual material, and the beginning school child is often more concerned with learning and teacher approval than he is with peers.

Secondly, the preadolescent is beginning the gradual shift from parents towards peers. Jenkins et al. (1966) have shown that the shift of the preadolescent toward peers is primarily because of an increasing need for conformity. Another strong motive for peer involvement stems from the need to be in the environment of people who will accept the preadolescent, a perception often recognized in peers more than in parents (Harris and Tseng, 1957). The feeling of being important is crucial to the preadolescent, even to the extent that he may misbehave in order to gain attention (Peterson, 1961).

As the individual moves into preadolescence, he is still going to remain highly dependent on adult influences. But the nine-year-old rapidly gains a new maturity, self-confidence, and increasing independence of adults (Elkind, 1971). The peer group often assists the preadolescent in conforming or rejecting many behaviors learned in earlier developmental stages. Bledsoe and Brown (1965), for example, have observed that preadolescents become highly critical of peers who do not adhere to the rules of a game being played. Prior learning has established an appropriate way to do things. Failing to confirm such learning brings criticism toward peers. Still, it must be recognized that by the end of preadolescence, peers are vitally important and many earlier established behavioral patterns are of lesser importance.

The first article in this book by Elton McNeil provides us with an overview of today's preadolescent and analyzes the current rush toward adolescence which is felt by so many preadolescents. McNeil conjectures that today's society does not provide the preadolescent with a simple, uninvolved view of the world but one that is ambiguous, complex, and disconcerting. The author brings this point to bear on the topic of sex and the preadolescent. Here, somewhat dormant sexual interest is now encouraged and often capitalized upon. This same phenomenon has repeatedly been drawn out in the research of Broderick (1961, 1966a, 1966b, 1968).

It is McNeil's contention that the new social order makes it imperative for adults, especially educators, to look for new ways to listen to, understand, and guide our preadolescents into the world with some ability to meet it and individually cope with it. This can be accomplished by understanding normal developmental patterns, by accepting the preadolescent for what he is, and by recognizing the crucial developmental tasks confronting him.

The second article, written by Thornburg, describes six developmental tasks which are learned needs arising out of earlier developmental stages and highly important to successful emergence into adolescence. They are written within the framework of the middle school because of the author's belief that the new middle school organization should not fail to recognize the developmental and psychological needs of its students, some of which are expressed within the six developmental tasks. Briefly, they are:

1. *Developing and organizing knowledge and concepts necessary for everyday functioning.* The increasing capacity to think moves the developing youth out of the concrete thinking level and into an abstract, reflective thinking realm.
2. *Accepting increasing changes in one's physique.* The new growth pattern and changing physical characteristics begin to concern the preadolescent.
3. *Learning new social sex roles.* The movement toward clarifying one's masculine or feminine sex role has much emphasis here. This task is somewhat compounded by emerging alternative sex roles within our society.
4. *Developing friendships with peers.* The gradual and increasing need for peer affiliation is evidenced throughout preadolescence.
5. *Becoming an independent person.* Learning to become physically independent of parents is a preliminary independence to a more elaborate need expressed within adolescence.
6. *Developing elementary moral concepts and values.* A strong commitment to a self-system of values is an outcome of the interchange between youth during preadolescence.

The types of developmental tasks described in the Thornburg article (pp. 21-27) focus on the physical, intellectual, and social development necessary within the preadolescent years to successfully move out of childhood and into adolescence. To be sure, educators and psychologists must revise their concept of the preadolescent and find ways to meet the needs of this increasingly distinct group of youth. The final article in our discussion of these middle developmental years looks at ways to do this.

Fraser contends that within a formalized instructional setting it is imperative to begin individualizing the learning programs because of the varying needs expressed within the preadolescent ages. Fraser feels that the middle school movement illustrates the trend toward revising group teaching practices by considering flexible scheduling and innovative curriculum materials. He points to the opportunity that the middle school has of meeting the individual learning and emotional needs of these youngsters.

The Changing Children
of Preadolescence
(or The Questionable Joy of Being Pre-Anything)
ELTON B. McNEIL

Editor's Note:

McNeil expresses his concern (somewhat emotionally at times) about the ill-defined period of preadolescence in which the emerging adolescent is unclear as to how he should feel and behave and what societal or moral pressures may result. His comments are most pointedly made toward teachers of preadolescents, although what he is saying has relevance for parents and other adults.

The author challenges us to look at the changing preadolescent and the new social behaviors and pressures with which he must contend. In addition, McNeil sees increasing pressure on the preadolescent to be thinking about and looking forward to adolescence.

McNeil makes a special point about sexual interest in preadolescent youth. First, he contends that there is no defined latency period (which once bridged most of the preadolescent age range) and that upwards of 50 percent of our fifth and sixth grade children have definite interests in members of the opposite sex.

Can you think of some causative factors which might support McNeil's contentions about the preadolescent and sex?

Are there other comparable social pressures which these youth are likely to feel today?

H.D.T.

You have to be somewhat strange to enjoy being preadolescent since this condition seems to consist, in great part, of teetering precariously for four years on a slack wire strung loosely between childhood and adolescence. Had the fates been kinder, this stage of human development might have been

Reprinted with permission of the author and publisher from *Childhood Education*, 1970, 46 (4), 181-185.

designated as *Post Early Childhood* — a phrase that might have conjured up visions of a victorious soldier surveying the battlefield, a puzzle-solver fulfilled when the final piece falls into place, or an unscathed survivor dazed with relief as he stumbles free of the wreckage of an accident.

But, *pre* is the chosen designation. *Pre*, as in *preliminary*, connoting a minor match prior to the decisive contest, and *pre*, as in the motto we teach our ten- to thirteen-year-old Boy and Girl Scouts, *Be Prepared! Pre* what? *Be Prepared* for what? For adolescence, that's what. That's where the action is. The pre-ness of this stage of life may be the one communication of perfect clarity between adults and young persons in our society — to be preadolescent is to occupy space in an interminable limbo of social development, to be neither this nor that, to be only something that is becoming.

Which Preadolescent Are We Talking About?

Let's do an exercise together. Fix clearly in mind an image of a class of typical preadolescent boys and girls in a large city school. Now jot down the five adjectival phrases you feel are most descriptive of the young persons in that class. Take me seriously. Put a piece of paper over the rest of this page. Read no further until you have written down your five descriptions. Ready? Let's look.

Does your list contain *anxious to be an adolescent* or *sexually curious?* Does it include the words *black* or *poor?* If not, then you may be wearing an enormous set of cultural blinders — blinders of the kind they put on race horses to keep them from becoming aware of anything discordant that is happening in the pack they run with. If your image is that of a well-scrubbed, well-dressed, well-tamed, school-loving, middle-class, white child, then you may be exposed only to a restricted, narrow segment of American society. As a teacher, your tunnel-vision image of the preadolescent may make you an irrelevant appendage to a learning process that occurs outside the classroom.

It is important to note that each of us has a mental map of the terrain of preadolescence; i.e., each of us thinks he knows where it is, what it is all about, and how to reach it. But, if your mental map is drawn to a scale based solely on memory of personal experience, it may be outdated and useless. If the areas of race, poverty, social class, sex, and humanistic experiential education are not clearly indicated, you may, as the cartographers of olden days warned, sail blissfully until you fall off the edge of Earth.

Think honestly of the meager joys of being one of the lost millions of black, welfare-dependent, ghetto-dwelling, slum-housed, scruffily clothed, inadequately fed, discriminated-against preadolescents whose education takes place in an overcrowded firetrap dominated by punitive, second-rate teachers. The sanitized, rosy world of the affluent family is a way of life restricted to the precious, privileged few. If we are to speak of preadolescents at all, we need to talk about *all* preadolescents.

The Rush to Adolescence

Preadolescence is a pleasure primarily to those weary teachers and parents for whom it is a brief respite in the never-ending struggle to civilize the young in our society. For its victims, however, it is more like a fretful delay. Thus, many a preadolescent, feeling himself in a time of life whose prime motive seems to be the need to escape from ambiguity, appears in a hurry to leave his childhood and rush toward the apparently superior freedoms of the adolescent, who seems mysteriously to be privy to the adult pleasures and privileges of sex, smoking, driving, drugs and independence.

The thought that many preadolescents yearn fiercely for some change in their status understandably provokes outraged contentiousness among those convinced that all preadolescents are happy on the social plantation fashioned for them by adults.

Yet, it seems clear that these inbetweeners would be adolescents if they could, would seek drivers' licenses if they were legally available, and would stay out late cruising for the action if they could avoid parental wrath for so doing. And, if a miracle of modern nutritional chemistry happens one day to produce the unmistakable signs of physical adolescence at age ten, teachers and parents would be required to make a multitude of adjustments in our social, educational and psychological fabric.

Modern American society no longer enjoys the social luxury of preadolescents who resemble the picture psychologists once painted of them: "compliant, eager to learn, trainable, accepting of things-as-they-were, morally overzealous, and somewhat stuffy (McNeil, 1969b)." We can no longer expect our ten- to thirteen-year-olds to subscribe to a simplistic view of the world in which good and evil are easily identifiable and deftly mastered by a dictum of good deeds and clean living. The rush to adolescence has made this a new ball game — a game adults may be poorly equipped to play if they know only rules learned in their own childhood. Memory of eras long past may not be an adequate guide to the future.

Sex and Preadolescence

Right or wrong, the game was easier in the good old days when sex and preadolescence were rarely linked. Theorists of olden times insisted that, as far as sex went, there just wasn't any. We had the Latency Period in those days — a preadolescence in which sexual thoughts and actions were repressed from consciousness or, at least, sublimated into socially constructive activities. What sexual interests did exist in preadolescence were transformed, according to the theory then in vogue, into a harmless curiosity about the world or a pristine pure urge to explore and learn.

Current research literature in psychology suggests that the asexual latency period alleged to exist in the 1890s must indeed have been an event unique and somewhat peculiar in man's social history. Latency, historically, seems not to have been prevalent among primitive peoples, is regularly absent in lower-class children, and appears briefly, if at all, in upper-class children exposed to the permissive environment of some progressive schools in modern society. A thoroughgoing sexual latency, according to Freud, can only exist in a culture that is totally suppressive of things sexual — the so-called Victorian Era, perhaps, but not modern America. Certainly the American social scene of the last few years could hardly be described as rigidly prudish or suppressive of sexual stimulation. It has, rather, provided an unlimited, multimedia inundation of sexual stimulation for citizens of all ages (McNeil, 1969a).

Every educator who is not blind or deaf knows that suppression of sexual interest in children from ten to thirteen years of age is a phenomenon limited to a very few in our culture. Sarnoff (1962) noted, for example, ". . . in our society, the sexual milieu of the prepubescent child is rapidly changing in the direction of greater encouragement for heterosexual contacts — even among members of the middle class (Sarnoff, 1962, p. 363)." And, Gale (1969) reports that by the age of thirteen, 38 percent of boys have engaged in some form of homosexual play and are active sexually, at one level or another, prior to adolescence.

A host of reports of sexual expression among the young in our society indicate that the classic form of social relationships between young boys and girls is not the same as most of us recall it. Broderick and Fowler (1965) report that, among children in the upper, lower and middle classes (ages nine to thirteen), 52 percent of the children in the fifth grade and 38 percent of those in the sixth grade chose one or more friends of the opposite sex as the person they liked best of all among the children they knew. And, Broderick and Fowler recorded that the great majority of the children in the fourth, fifth and sixth grades claimed to have a sweetheart who reciprocated their romantic feelings.

Social Science and Salvation

If preadolescents are no longer the tame species they once were, a new formula must be discovered if education is to become relevant to the modern world. I agree with Postman and Weingartner (1969) that preadolescents have "built-in crap detectors," and that these devices readily sense the incredible gap between childhood education and the nature of real life. And, I insist that the bulk of the social education most vital to the welfare of our society no longer takes place in the classroom. If this gap is not bridged, the alienation of our young will continue with increasing speed and formal education may become even less relevant than it is today.

A great many seemingly rational persons are convinced that our continuing failure to comprehend the complexity of human development will one day magically dissolve in a flash of brilliant, insightful discovery by the social sciences. As a social scientist long concerned with the issues of education and human development, I feel some responsiblity to prick this roseate, fantasy-bubble of expectation. Social science will not be our salvation.

If I may again be allowed the immodest act of quoting myself, "Early adolescence bears the dubious distinction of being the least recognized, the least studied, and, until now, the least important of all the artificial slices of development invented by social scientists (1969a, p. 1)."

"The bulk of the literature devoted to preadolescence is useless to today's educator: it reports studies and theories of a past era; it is sanctimonious and moralizing about the way things ought to be rather than the way they really are; it is blind to color and social class status; and it is so generalized that it is inapplicable to the daily give-and-take that teachers have with individual students (1969a, p. 3)."

We are asking the impossible of social scientists if we ask them to compensate for the fact that so many of our educators are locked into (and silently assent to) a restrictive institutional system that studiously ignores the pressing issues of war, race, poverty, sex and injustice despite the fact their preadolescents attend, with greater enthusiasm, to a competing educational system (TV, movies, newspapers, books and real life) that tells it "like it really is." We cannot applaud the intellectual capacity of our preadolescents at the same moment that we punish them for putting two and two together to conclude that this is far from the best of all possible worlds even if their teachers seem oblivious to that fact.

We cannot wait for social science to solve the human problems of education. If the teachers of America cannot adapt the educational process to fit the changing demands of a rapidly evolving society, then the child's older peers will, for better or worse, rush in to fill the emotional and intellectual void.

The New Dropouts

The old-fashioned dropouts were easy to detect since, sooner or later, they removed their bodies from the irrelevant and intolerable situation called school. In contrast, the new dropouts faithfully deliver their physical beings daily into the hands of eager educators. But, emotionally and psychologically our brighter preadolescents have dropped out of the educational system. In sheer numbers their ranks may be slender but these capable, talented few have, historically, been the primary resource from which cultural invention, leadership, innovation and reform have issued. They are, thus, too valuable a resource to be squandered even for a single generation.

It is increasingly obvious that our unusually capable young persons are being "radicalized" by a social turmoil that cannot be shut out by the most rigid of curricula or the most disapproving of teachers adamant about maintaining the status quo at any cost. Our most promising preadolescents have begun the process of turning off the educational system as an irrelevant institution more concerned with the Mickey Mouse of dress codes and hair length than with the issues of death, destruction, and human misery.

Frankly, I don't blame them.

Don't Give Up the Ship

While this has been a prolonged tale of gloom and doom, it was not deliberately designed to drive educators into some other line of work. I have confidence in teachers — more confidence, perhaps, than they have in themselves — and I am convinced that they, and only they, hold the key to reconciling the generational value-clash of today.

There is, and always has been, a particular magic in the relationship of teacher and student — a magic parents cannot partake of and peers cannot possess, a magic that has changed the thrust of culture throughout history. This magic can regain its lost potency if teachers can learn to cease shaping students in the inappropriate image of a bygone age, face the reality of a changing society, and communicate to the young in more relevant ways.

This is not to suggest that bell-bottomed slacks, wide ties and mod styles are the answer. These external, superficial signs of independence and revolt are being worn by preadolescents who face age-old emotional and psychological dilemmas. In this case imitation may be a sincere but irrelevant form of flattery. As experienced adults we are the possessors of a fund of knowledge, wisdom and insight in sorely short supply among our young charges. We need only learn how to communicate this to the young. And, "learn" is exactly the right term.

How do we learn? In the same old way, of course. We listen, we reserve judgment, we don't panic, we accept youthful thoughts for what they are, and we support feelings at the same moment we attempt to feed our experience into that rational part of the young mentality that cries out for sensible answers to age-old puzzles. We sympathize, we tolerate, we respond wisely, and we do our best to lead the young to the joys of self-discovery. We act as models for the young and we open lines of communication with them by talking to them rather than lecturing at them.

Most important is the observation that it is much too early to entertain thoughts of abandoning ship. The young need us if they are not to go naked into the social world. It will be painful and difficult to again "turn on" the youth to education and it will be a task for which no teacher was prepared by a School of Education. But, it is a task that must be accomplished if our society is to survive.

If the teachers of America don't "get with it," their students will, in increasing numbers, take to the streets in a head-crashing attempt to earn their diplomas.

Learning and Maturation
in Middle School Age Youth
HERSHEL D. THORNBURG

Of all studied areas of human development, the stage of preadolescence has long been the most neglected. This age range, typically described as nine to twelve or ten to thirteen, is a uniquely awkward range that somehow bridges the gap between childhood and adolescence. It has been expressed as the period of time when the nicest children begin behaving in a most awful way (Redl, 1943).

Children of this age are difficult. Their unconventional mannerisms and their unpredictable behaviors make them a very difficult group to research. Teachers find them uncooperative. Parents find them annoying. In general, it is easier to deal with youth that are either younger or older than with the preadolescent. Yet, this should not fail to make us recognize the need for more knowledge about children within this age range.

Some hope for recognizing and meeting the needs of preadolescents may be found in the emerging middle school. By definition the middle school is a school built to cover the developmental range of late childhood, preadolescence, and early adolescence. It may best be thought of as a "phase and program of schooling bridging but differing from the childhood and adolescent phases and programs (Alexander et al., 1968).

Those who support the middle school feel that the failure of the junior high school to function as a bridging school between childhood and adolescence has forced educators to seek out an alternative. The faults inherent in today's junior high system appear to be twofold: (1) The ninth grade has tended to maintain its philosophical and practical ties with the high school. (2) Many seventh and eighth grades have still followed an elementary format such as the older 8-4 organizational plan used (Eichhorn, 1968). One additional

Reprinted with permission of the author and publisher from the *Clearing House*, 1970, 45, 150-155.

problem has resulted throughout the years of the 6-3-3 plan. The junior high school has tended to model after the high school. Extracurricular activities, interscholastic athletics, cheerleaders, bands, banquets, and proms, all activities enjoyed during high school, have become a way of life in many junior high schools. There is increasing support by several proponents of the middle school (DiVirgilio, 1969; Eichhorn, 1968; Oestreich, 1969) to have the middle school function as a transitional school and leave the above-described activities to the high school.

Eichhorn has tried to justify the middle school organization by advancing the concept of transescence.

Transescence is the stage of development which begins prior to the onset of puberty and extends through the early stages of adolescence. Since puberty does not occur precisely at the same chronological age in human development, the transescent designation is based on the many physical, social, emotional, and intellectual changes that appear prior to the puberty cycle to the time when the body gains a practical degree of stabilization over these complex changes (1968, p. 111).

Granted, there is no specific line separating childhood and adolescence. Rather there are gradual developmental and learning changes involving the physical, intellectual, and social life of youth. Through such maturation and learning, the well-knit pattern of childhood personality is considerably loosened as youths experience identifying behaviors with other youths, and thus move toward adolescence. Alexander (1968) found from a sample of middle school programs now in operation that 44.6 percent stated "to provide a program specifically designated for students in this age group" as a reason for establishing such a school. It is not the intent of this article to justify the middle school or describe reasons for its existence. However, since the concept of the middle school program is an increasing one, several developmental and learning tasks which youths encounter during preadolescence are presented to give proponents of the movement a basis to more realistically realize an educational program based on meeting student needs.

(1) *Developing and Organizing Knowledge and Concepts Necessary for Everyday Functioning.*

At ten and eleven years children develop interest in highly organizing and structuring their knowledge. The preadolescent develops a "mode of intellectual functioning (Flavell, 1963, p. 43)." The child initially operates toward the end of Piaget's stage of concrete operations. During this stage the individual is capable of reasoning about concrete objects experienced within his environment. By the fifth and sixth grade the preadolescent is not as dependent on immediate concrete objects in systematizing and understanding basic ideas about relevant phenomena and objects. Once the meaning of an object is established through experience, the ten- to eleven-year-old is capable of comprehending it without any current reference to the concrete object. Therefore, the intellect has developed to the point where it is increasingly independent of concrete objects, which suggests that the individual is ready for more advanced intellectual thought.

Within the structure of the middle school, learning experiences can be guided for youth so that there is easier transition to advanced stages of thought. Thus, by grades seven and eight, most students should be capable of reasoning about hypotheses and deducing conclusions, two characteristics of Piaget's stage of formal operations. Now all information which was ordered, organized, or structured within the mind is characterized by more flexible thinking and sets the basis for the ability to deal with reality.

One of the things that facilitates these increasing intellectual functions is an enlargement of interests within the preadolescent. Through his own intellectual curiosity, the preadolescent now becomes an experimenter. Particular academic subjects interest a youth and he has increasing tendencies to check them out. This promotes moving out of the realm of fantasy and questioning, and into the realm of experimentation and reality. Thus, his social and physical world take on increasing significance.

How may the middle school provide for a greater realization of this task with youth? First, ten- and eleven-year-old's intelligence functions on a junior high school level more so than on an elementary plane. Therefore, if students ages ten to thirteen fall within the same general period of intellectual development, it seems reasonable to develop an educational program in a manner more suitable to their needs and abilities. Thus, a middle school program with a more highly organized curriculum, staffed with teachers who are specialists in their discipline (DiVirgilio, 1969), can better realize student needs and abilities.

(2) *Accepting Increasing Changes in One's Physique.*

Preadolescents begin experiencing several physiological changes during the transitional period of childhood to adolescence. The term "pubescence" is applied to such changes and indicates that the body is rapidly approaching puberty which is characterized by sexual maturation.

Physically the average girl has her growth spurt after ten with the peak being reached around twelve. Girls experience the beginning of breast development about 10.5 years, pubic hair development around eleven, and menarche about twelve. Approximately 80 per cent of all girls reach menarche between 11.5 and 14.5 years (Meredith, 1967). Boys initially experience growth in the testes and penis around twelve and pigmented hair at thirteen. Involuntary rigidity of the penis and irregular seminal emissions may be experienced at this age. All such activities are part of the male growth spurt which begins about 12.5 and peaks around age fourteen (Winter, 1969).

Throughout the age range represented by the middle schools, virtually all youths will experience significant physical changes. To reduce anxiety, it is helpful if they have an awareness of what physiological changes will take place. Research has shown that they are concerned about their height, weight, fatness, thinness, and facial features. Of special concern to girls is largeness or smallness of the hips and breasts. Boys are similarly concerned about the largeness or smallness of the genitals (Angelino and Mech, 1955). If preadolescents are made aware that different rates of growth are not abnormal, they can learn to accept their physique better. The middle school could help them learn this if it can put physical and physiological changes into a normal developmental context for its students.

(3) *Learning New Social Sex Roles.*

Our culture sets patterns of accepted social behaviors throughout childhood and adolescence. In early childhood, this has meant aggressiveness in boys and dependency in girls. Boys are expected to be rough, active, adventurous, and rugged. On the other hand, girls are expected to be docile, ladylike, and interested in household or domestic type activities. Through perpetuation, the sex roles unfolded into the traditional work role for men and the wife-mother role for women.

In today's society, some varying social sex roles are being suggested. By preadolescence most youngsters have had exposure to role behaviors that are not as distinctly masculine or feminine as they once were. The hair of little girls is shorter and of little boys is longer. Both are playing with and accepting mannequin dolls, i.e., G.I. Joe and Barbie. In the case of girls, Barbie represents a sexy teen-ager who is involved in all types of social events as her diversified and descriptive wardrobe indicates. While it is hardly fair to give Barbie credit for accelerating female social interest, it is true that one's fantasies may later be transferred more readily to reality if such fantasies have been rewarding.

What today's ten- to thirteen-year-old is faced with is an increasing unisexuality, and an accelerated flexibility for women in American social structure. The effect has been felt in the emergence of one's sex role. Now less distinct masculine-feminine roles exist in our society. Most positively affected has been less emphasis on the developing girl to accept the traditional wife-mother role.

It is not intended to minimize the importance of identifying with contemporaries of the same sex. But, it is suggested that preadolescence is not the period of quietly accepting one's own sex role as it was once. Earlier socialization has brought about change. The most accelerated has been female aggressiveness (Reiss, 1960) and earlier heterosexual involvement. Havighurst (1952) suggested that around thirteen or fourteen most boys and girls become preoccupied with social activities with more intimate companionships, i.e., double-dating, with couple-dating following. Still, there are increasing indications that today group social activities begin around eleven or twelve with more selective dating following (Thornburg, 1970). Research indicates that many preadolescents are feeling pressures from their parents and peers to be involved heterosexually by grade six (Martinson, 1968). Perhaps the task of learning new social sex roles is more difficult for girls than boys. While it is quite obvious that learning appropriate social sex roles will not be totally realized during the middle school period, there is no doubt that what is learned during this period will have significant effects on the emerging adolescent and eventually emerging adult.

It is quite possible that the middle school movement may contribute to earlier adolescent socialization. While it is not possible to determine what the social impact might be, it is certainly possible that having ten- to thirteen-year-olds together will increase earlier socialization (Thornburg, 1970). This effect will be most likely determined by the philosophy of the school district. If the intent is to build a mini-high school, then it is most certain that earlier socialization will result. On the other hand, if the middle school emerges as a new school geared to the social, educational, and physical needs of its pupils, then early socialization will not be accentuated and emerging social sex roles may be more realistically realized.

(4) Developing Friendships with Peers.

Most peer relationships that are formed during preadolescence are with those of the same sex. Typically boys express a dislike for girls, and girls show a general lack of concern that boys are in their environment. Most close friends are of the same sex. With this group preadolescents learn to get along. On a general basis "they form teams, committees, and clubs and are very much aware of the personalities of people their own age (Havighurst, 1968, p. 121)." The importance of preadolescent peer groups should not be underrated. They, too, feel many of their behaviors being shaped by their peers. "Even though children may resist inwardly or feel threatened, they attempt to produce the behavior they think the group expects of them (Gordon, 1962, p. 223)."

The initial stage of peer development is formed among isolated unisexual cliques. It is considered isolated in terms of any relationship with corresponding groups of the opposite sex. Dunphy (1963) suggests that this represents the persistence of the preadolescent gang into the adolescent period. As preadolescents move into grades seven and eight, their peer associates may begin becoming heterosexual, although on a more limited basis than in later adolescence. Such heterosexual interaction is often done cautiously and is often only undertaken within the security of group settings where members of the same sex are also present.

The middle school could provide a structural framework where its students can develop meaningful and cooperative relationships with peers. This can be facilitated by (1) stressing the importance of socialization with members of the same sex and (2) by allowing heterosexual group activity to evolve out of the students' own natural development and personal interests. It seems important that in forming peer relations pre- and early-adolescents feel they are not being forced into such roles. Within the conceptualized middle school it may be possible to create this kind of environment better than in the existing junior high school where many social activities approximate high school behaviors.

(5) *Becoming an Independent Person.*

This task has been described by Havighurst (1968) as the time when preadolescent youth are expected to become physically independent. He stresses that this should not be equated with emotional independence but that it is strictly physical independence. Havighurst asserts that such independence is obtaining the ability to be away from home at night or go to a summer camp without being terribly homesick or needing mother in his environment.

The preadolescent should begin looking upon himself as a maturing individual and look upon adults as adults. He should see his parents in a new relationship. While maintaining such emotional dependency, the preadolescent should not exercise blind faith in his parents such as he did during childhood. In the process of normal development he gradually begins exercising his right to make choices. While his behavior may become increasingly independent of adults, such behavior should not be misconstrued by adults to think that he is independent and does not need guidance and continued support. Rather adults, i.e., teachers and parents, should recognize the preadolescent's growing concern for making choices and provide for him suitable experiences that allow the gradual acquisition of independence.

How might the middle school help its students with this task? First, by definition, it should provide a more independent and complex structure than the elementary school. Secondly, since its functions are transitional, it should provide a less complex model than the existing junior high school although it may be highly departmentalized. Havighurst (1968) makes an important point here. He has observed that not all youngsters ten to twelve years have enough self-control to get along in this structure. He sees the middle school requiring of its students the ability to adapt their behavior to a variety of situations. Therefore, quite realistically, Havighurst has pointed up one real test for the middle school — the ability to solve the problems of motivation and method so that this complex structure might aid in the process of becoming an independent person.

(6) *Developing Elementary Moral Concepts and Values.*

As the preadolescent begins identifying more with his peers, and adult identity declines, there is a shift in the way in which conscience develops. Children between the ages of ten and thirteen can make much progress in reasoning, sympathy, esthetic sense, love, and morality. These youth can now learn a greater regard for truth and fairness, especially within the activities of peer groups. Then as youths move out of preadolescence into adolescence, they can better begin assuming increasing self-responsibility and increasing responsibility to peer, school, and community activities.

In today's society much stress is being placed on individuality. Accompanying individuality should be self-responsibility. The middle school is in a good position to assist students in this task. Through departmentalization, students can learn responsibilities through many different academic and social approaches, since they are exposed to several different teachers and students in one day's time.

Probably the most detrimental factor to the student's learning this task is the effect of adult moralizing. Many teachers attempt to deal with stealing, lying, laziness, cruelty, and bullying by moralizing with the student. "Good" wins rewards and "bad" suffers consequences. If teachers are really interested in helping youths develop moral concepts and values, they might better help children "(1) make free choices whenever possible, (2) search for alternatives in choice-making decisions, (3) weigh the consequences of each available alternative, (4) consider what they prize and cherish, (5) affirm the things they value, (6) do something about their choices, and (7) consider and strengthen patterns in their lives (Raths et al., 1966, p. 47)." The flexibility of the middle school potentially makes this possible.

Conclusion

Discussion has focused on the physical, intellectual, and social development of ten- to thirteen-year-old youths during their transitional period from childhood to adolescence. Six maturational and learning tasks have been described as occurring during this age range. The ability for the middle school child to cope with these tasks and realize as many of them as possible should strengthen his ability to acquire increasingly more complex maturation and learning tasks during adolescence. Learning to cope with bodily changes, exercise a new mode of intellectual functioning, and taking steps to be a person in his own right present a tremendous challenge to the youngster from ten to thirteen. The challenge is significantly as great to the emerging middle school to develop and implement an educational program which will foster greater maturation and learning on the part of its students.

What's Ahead for Preadolescence?
DAVID W. FRASER

Editor's Note:

To some it may seem that Fraser's article here is more directed to the planner of educational programs than to the student of preadolescence. Granted the discussion of scheduling formats and curriculum materials is educationally based. However, there are two basic points made by Fraser that are relevant to the psychological development of the preadolescent as well.

First, Fraser calls for a revised concept of the preadolescent, a proposition similar to those advanced in the first two articles in this chapter. Emphasis is placed on increased cognitive skills, especially the fact that preadolescence bridges the transitional period of thought from concrete to abstract thinking. As we will see in chapter 4, this transition is based on development more than upon learning. Fraser contends that in order to meet the needs of each preadolescent, we must adapt our environment more toward the uniqueness and individuality of each person.

Second, the author asserts that within formalized educational settings, we must adapt our teaching styles so that the learner can progress at his own learning rate, a process that is psychologically sound. Adapting teaching to student needs infers that a deliberate attempt to understand developmental and learning stages within the preadolescent has been made.

H.D.T.

Background for Change

Are preadolescents (elevens and twelves) the forgotten element in our contemporary school society? Viewing the plethora of special, often federally funded, projects at the extremities of the school continuum, one might be led

Reprinted with permission of the author and publisher from *Childhood Education*, 1969, 45, 24-28.

to conclude that this is so. The thesis here, however, is that there is far more that is viable and innovative in education than Job Corps and Project Head Start. What is really afoot is a genuine and pervasive reform that is beginning to influence the educative experience of all learners, not the least of whom are preadolescents.

Substantiation for developing and changing learning patterns for preadolescents stems in part from a moderately revised perception of the preadolescent. There is more to this notion than the fact that puberty arrives at an earlier age in our society than it previously did. Implicit also is the realization that social sophistication, the background of information extracted from mass media, and the quality of emotional experience gleaned from urban living have quickened the pace and changed the character of the preadolescent stage of development.

Revised Concept
of the Preadolescent

Modern theories of child development depict the typical preadolescent as being on the threshold of a stage of "formal operations" where for the first time he begins to reason in genuinely hypothetical or abstract terms, unimpeded by the necessity to base his theoretical conjectures on reality. Some eleven- and twelve-year-olds, according to this point of view, may be well into this stage, while others may yet remain in a stage of "concrete operations" during which gaining sophistication in the manipulation of objects and symbols continues to be their basic orientation (Bruner, 1960).

The wide extent of differences implied by such a perception of preadolescence impels attention to individualization of the learning program. Accommodation of learners at a variety of stages of intellectual development, with a wide spread in terms of learning paces, styles and interests, implies a need for individualization of learning opportunity substantially beyond that conceived within the format of traditional, group-paced, school programs. A veritable smorgasbord of grouping, scheduling, materials utilization, and staffing practices are necessitated. These pose the frame around which future programs for preadolescents are being structured.

Grouping Practices

A broad variety of practices for grouping youngsters have evolved throughout the history of education in the United States. Vertical structures characteristically have accommodated learners in graded, nongraded or multigraded fashions. Horizontally, students have been grouped according to ability, sex, physical qualities, interest, achievement and a number of other criteria.

The major innovation in terms of grouping practices for today's preadolescents lies not in the identification of any new grouping technique. It lies rather in combining a number of such techniques to form a flexible, mutually reinforcing philosophy for grouping dedicated to the logical accommodation of specific, carefully defined, individual learning needs. Ideally, a comprehensive scheme for grouping preadolescents for learning activity includes a varied repertoire of grouping practices, lends itself to easy transition from one practice to another upon logical demand, and permits simultaneous accommodation of several horizontal and several vertical plans.

A variety of group sizes is also needed to accommodate instructional requirements. Large groups of a hundred or more may figure in the viewing of performance or expository activities. Small groups of a dozen or fewer students will be used widely to provide discussion opportunity. The independent studier, free to pursue his assigned or contracted study schedule in independent fashion, will predominate in many schools. More and more it seems apparent that the size of the group will be determined by the learning task to be achieved and that the preadolescent himself will have a hand in setting not only his learning tasks but also the social context in which he pursues them.

Any discussion of grouping practices relevant to the preadolescent learner of today would be incomplete without reference to the middle school concept. Born out of a desire to provide accommodation for logical maturity level groupings, most middle school formats suggest placing together all or most of the ten- through thirteen-year-old group. The Educational Facilities Laboratories publication, *Middle Schools*, says this of the middle school philosophy:

> In general, the proponents of the middle school envisage a school adapted to a range of children who, rampant individualists though they are, seem to have more in common with each other than with elementary-school children as a group, or high-schoolers as a group. The school would assume that, in general, its population had some mastery of the tools of learning but was not ready for the academic specialization of high school (and its attendant college-preparation pressures). The school could concentrate, then, on provisions for individual differences, so long touted, so little effected by American education, taking particular account of the increased sophistication and knowledge of today's ten- or eleven- to fourteen-year-olds over previous generations (Murphy, 1965).

The middle school concept, it would seem, is concrete manifestation of the trend toward revision of grouping practice for the early and preadolescent.

Scheduling Formats

A subject closely related to that of grouping is scheduling and, if grouping accommodations for the preadolescent are becoming more flexible and more closely identified with individual learning needs, the same might be expected of scheduling techniques.

Possibly the most noticeable trend at this time, one that holds substantial promise for influencing the schedule of the preadolescent, is abdication of the formal nine-month school year and six-hour school day. Both educators and laymen are asking the questions: Why permit expensive school facilities to lie idle for three months of the year? Why must all children take vacations in the summer months in a society that is no longer predominantly rural/ agricultural? Must all youngsters arrive and leave at the same hour each day? Indeed, do all learners require the same number of hours of learning experience? How much learning more appropriately may take place outside of the school facility than inside? These and similar questions are shaking the foundations of traditional scheduling practices and are serving as the basis for current functional change.

Another concept that serves to free scheduling practices of traditional restraints is that of the daily demand flexible schedule. The following excerpt from *The Guide*, a publication of the Thurston Intermediate School of Laguna Beach, California, provides a functional definition of this term:

Daily Demand Flexible Schedule. Students' and teachers' combined efforts develop a daily student schedule. Basing their decisions upon daily evaluation of student progress, teachers decide who should be called to their classes, what specific lessons should be taught, how long it will take, what teacher should teach the lesson, what size and type of group the class should be, what educational equipment should be used and what space is needed to contain the learners. These faculty decisions are submitted daily and the subject and time requests are placed on a master schedule. Students report to their counseling teacher each morning to make decisions regarding their school schedule for that day. Because teacher demands and student needs change daily there is a different schedule each day of the school year. Each student has modules committed for him by the teachers; however, the modules or time not so committed may be utilized by the student as he wishes. The student, therefore, can make decisions daily regarding subjects to be taken and time to be spent in the electives, the Learning Center, a study lab, or with selected teachers for special help (Thurston).

As the concept of the daily demand schedule becomes more widely tested and more effectively implemented, partly through the use of computer technology, there is little doubt that schools will begin to offer preadolescents substantial involvement in planning their own flexible, individualized schedules.

Curriculum Materials

If individualized curriculum materials are to free the preadolescent from the restrictions of a group-paced, comparatively evaluated format, they must satisfy two basic requirements: they must permit each individual learner *to progress at his own learning rate*; they must accommodate *individual learning styles and interests.*

Schools and publishers presently are producing such materials. Although many of these products already have met with enthusiastic reception, more often than not they are fledgling efforts that admittedly will require substantial refinement.

Ideally, the teacher of preadolescents in future years will have a nearly inexhaustible supply of "packaged" materials, which collectively will fulfill the following criteria:

- the materials will lend themselves to self-selection by learners
- the materials will come in small packages (groups of ideas taking from several hours to several days to consume will replace textbooks requiring a year or a semester to complete)
- the materials will contribute to realization of carefully stated, specific learner goals
- within the material, concepts will be clearly identified and related to companion concepts in the same and other disciplines
- instruments for evaluation of learning will be included as an integral part of the material
- the materials will accommodate specific learning styles or modalities
- sufficient variety of materials will exist so that drill, practice, or reinforcement activities will not become tedious
- the materials will lend themselves to efficient storage and retrieval procedures (possibly ultimate computerization)
- identification of occupational relevance of the content will be implicit in many materials
- participation in expansion or improvement of the material will be extended to the learner within the context of the material

In addition to description of such curriculum components, it is requisite to acknowledge the role of the teacher as a learning resource. Beyond the realm of fact, concept and skill acquisition lie normative concerns which programed learning packages may influence only superficially. Appropriately chosen human resources in well-calculated social context ever will be a prime curricular tool, especially in accomplishment of affective learnings. In this sense the teacher, as a guide to and participant in group process, becomes the most valuable of all curriculum ingredients, one who delegates the more mundane instructional tasks to packaged curriculum and paraprofessional and who assumes a fuller responsibility than ever before for motivation, exemplification and guidance of growth in humane understanding.

Staffing Accommodations

Similarly, staffing of schools attended by preadolescents will change. Students assuredly will assume greater responsibility for their own instruction as self-mediating and programed materials become available to them. Student peer helpers are a built-in feature of many individualized programs today. Increased use of secretarial and teaching aids will multiply the services rendered to teacher and student alike. Attention across the nation presently is focused on differentiating the functions and certification of elements within professional ranks. Generation of task-oriented teams of staff members currently is popular in schools that serve the preadolescent.

Such innovations clearly depict fresh opportunity for the preadolescent to experience independence in his opportunities to learn. The promise for maximum challenge for teacher and learner alike is increasing as shares in the learning management venture are distributed more widely than ever before.

Physical Accommodations

Future physical plant and equipment for preadolescents must reflect the need for flexibility, personal relevancy, and independence inherent in individualized programs. Convertible space and furniture that accommodate independent studiers, small discussion groups, or larger groups intent on an expositor or performance activities are being sought. Centers for the storage and consumption of learning resources must expand to house the explosion of multimedia materials. A nearly constant free flow of individuals will replace the traditional passing periods for classes of children. Acoustical control in the form of carpeting and sound insulation will obviate the need to insist on group silence, and the definition of "control" gradually will shift from predisposition with group discipline standards to concentration on the demonstrable learning achievement of individuals. The day of the nonschool-house, with children staying at home to view electronically mediated learning programs, may be distant, but a school purveying the ingredients of the complete society and embracing the community as its ultimate potential classroom is here today.

Conclusion

It seems desirable to make two observations. First, the insights described here may be biased or incomplete. They represent, after all, the observations of a single person. But they are based on *reality*. A live, functioning daily demand schedule is operating today at the Thurston Intermediate School, Laguna Beach, California. The Nova Schools, Fort Lauderdale, Florida; the Duluth, Minnesota Schools; the Oak Leaf School, Pittsburgh, Pennsylvania, all have produced and successfully used packaged learning materials with children. At least three states are making serious plans to implement differentiated staffing programs within the next few years. Innovative middle school plants have been built and are operational in Tiburon, California, and Amory, Mississippi. Year-round school is a reality in Atlanta, Georgia. Many of the innovations for individualizing learning for preadolescents are viable and demonstrable. To put them all together in a single operational unit — a venture currently planned by the Southeast Education Center of the Seattle, Washington, Schools — suggests achieving from the resultant system a whole far more productive than the sum of its parts.

Elizabeth Noon (1969) suggests two attributes that schools have a basic responsibility for helping children to attain — the ability to love and the ability to accept love. These are the kinds of ultimate ideals that, it seems to me, teachers always have labored to impart. Yet, these same teachers often become so preoccupied with teaching "basic skills" and with expositing factual knowledge that functional social learning is ignored. Is it possible that new curricula, new scheduling and grouping formats, new perceptions of teachers, children, schoolhouses and technology may release the preadolescent to enjoy an enhanced relationship with his teachers and a more vital infatuation with learning?

It is, of course, true that we can no more predict the future than we can forget the past. Just as true is the observation that the historical record of schools in our land is second to none. Because that record has been predicated on intelligent, relevant change, we should gain courage to examine current innovations with candor, anticipation and wisdom. To build creatively toward a quality of learning experience that truly will help youngsters live more nearly as brothers is a goal both worthy and timeless.

Combined References for Chapter 1

Alexander, W. M. The middle school movement. *Theory into Practice*, 1968, 7(3), 114-117.

Alexander, W. M., Williams, E. I., Compton, M., Hines, V. A., and Prescott, D. *The Emergent Middle School.* New York: Holt, Rinehart, Winston, 1968.

Angelino, H. and Mech, E. V. Fears and worries concerning physical changes: A preliminary survey of 32 females. *Journal of Psychology*, 1955, 39, 195-198.

Blair, A. W. and Burton, W. H. *Growth and Development of the Preadolescent.* New York: Appleton-Century-Crofts, 1951.

Bledsoe, J. C., and Brown, I. D. The interests of preadolescents: A longitudinal study. *Journal of Experimental Education*, 1965, 33, 337-344.

Broderick, C. B. Socio-sexual development in a suburban community. *Journal of Sex Research*, 1966a, 2, 1-24.

Broderick, C. B. Sexual behavior among preadolescents. *Journal of Social Issues*, 1966b, 22, 6-21.

Broderick, C. B. and Fowler, S. E. New patterns of relationships between the sexes among preadolescents. *Marriage and Family Living*, 1965, 23, 27-30.

Broderick, C. B. and Rowe, G. P. A scale of preadolescent heterosexual development. *Journal of Marriage and the Family*, 1968, 30, 97-101.

Bruner, J. *The Process of Education.* New York: Vintage, 1960.

DiVirgilio, J. Switching from junior high to middle school? *Clearing House*, 1969, 44, 224-226.

Dunphy, D. C. The school structure of urban adolescent peer groups. *Sociometry*, 1963, 26, 230-246.

Eichhorn, D. H. Middle school organization: A new dimension. *Theory into Practice*, 1968, 7(3), 111-113.

Eichhorn, D. H. *The Middle School.* New York: Center for Applied Research in Education, 1966.

Elkind, D. *A Sympathetic Understanding of the Child Six to Sixteen.* Boston: Allyn and Bacon, Inc., 1971.

Flavell, J. *The Developmental Psychology of Jean Piaget.* Princeton, N.J.: Van Nostrand, 1963.

Gale, R. F. *Developmental behavior.* New York: Macmillan, 1969.

Gordon, I. J. *Human Development: From Birth Through Adolescence.* New York: Harper and Row, 1962.

Harris, D. B. and Tseng, S. C. Children's attitudes toward peers and parents as revealed by sentence completions. *Child Development,* 1957, 28, 401-411.

Havighurst, R. J. The middle school child in contemporary society. *Theory in Practice,* 1968, 7(3), 120-122.

Havighurst, R. J. *Developmental Tasks and Education.* New York: McKay, 1952.

Jenkins, G. G., Shacter, H. S., and Bauer, W. W. *These Are Your Children.* (3rd. ed.) Palo Alto: Scott, Foresman, 1966.

McNeil, E. B. Sex education and the so-called latency period. SIECUS 1969. Washington, D.C.: Unpublished (L).

McNeil, E. B. *Human Socialization.* Monterey: Calif.: Brooks/Cole, 1969a.

McNeil, E. B. Early adolescence — fact and fantasy. In S. Dunning (ed.) *English for the Junior High Years.* Champaign, Ill.: National Council of Teachers of English, 1969b, pp. 1-13.

Martinson, F. M. Sexual knowledge, values, and behavior patterns of adolescents. *Child Welfare,* 1968, 47, 405-410.

Mead, M. Early adolescence in the United States. *NASSP Bulletin,* 1965, 49, (300), 5-10.

Meredith, H. V. A synopsis of puberal changes in youth. *Journal of School Health,* 1967, 37, 171-176.

Murphy, J. *Middle Schools.* New York: Educational Facilities Laboratories, 1965.

Noon, E. Editor's license. *The Instructor,* 1969.

Oestreich, A. H. Middle school in transition. *Clearing House,* 1969, 44, 91-95.

Peterson, D. R. Behavior problems of middle childhood. *Journal of Consulting Psychology,* 1961, 25, 205-209.

Postman, N. and Weingartner, C. *Teaching As a Subversive Activity.* New York: Delacorte Press, 1969.

Raths, L. E. Harmin, M., and Simon, S. B. *Values and Teaching.* Columbus, Ohio: Charles E. Merrill, 1966.

Redl, F. Preadolescents — what makes them tick? *Child Study,* 1943, 21, 44-48.

Reiss, I. L. *Premarital Sexual Standards In America.* Glencoe, Ill.: Free Press, 1960.

Sarnoff, I. *Personality Dynamics and Development.* New York: Wiley, 1962.

Sullivan, H. S. *The Interpersonal Theory of Psychiatry.* New York: Norton, 1953.

Thornburg, H. D. Adolescence: A re-interpretation. *Adolescence,* 1970, 5, 463-484.

Thurston Elementary School. *The Guide.* Laguna Beach, Calif.: Laguna Beach Unified School District (date unknown).

Winter, G. D. Physical changes during adolescence. In G. D. Winter and E. M. Nuss (eds.) *The Young Adult.* Glenview, Ill.: Scott, Foresman, 1969.

CHAPTER 2 **physical growth**

Introduction

There are several ways in which the growth of the preadolescent is assessed. (1) We use morphological age which gives normative data on height and weight. (2) We assess the emergence of secondary sex characteristics such as breast and penis development, and the growth of pubic and axillary hair. (3) We assess the age at reaching pubescence as indicated by menstruation or first ejaculation. (4) We use skeletal growth indexes. The preadolescent's growth patterns are sequential but often irregular as children move out of late childhood. For some preadolescents this means that physical maturation accelerates and the body grows rapidly, even disproportionately. For others, observable growth is not as rapid. Many internal physiological and glandular changes which occur are also indicators that the individual is approaching puberty.

The time of least growth in girls is from nine to ten and in boys from ten to eleven. After these ages accelerated growth is evidenced. For girls the growth spurt begins soon after age ten. Characteristics of this spurt are increased height, breast development, increased hip size, and pigmented hair (Bryan and Greenberg, 1952). Each development is a prelude to menarche, a physiological crisis which has been well researched. Most research indicates that menstruation starts between twelve and fourteen years (Milicer and Szczotka, 1966; Nicolson and Haney, 1953) which is the culmination of pubescent changes that also produce distinct sex characteristics in girls.

Boys usually experience their growth spurt twelve to eighteen months later than girls. This spurt is characterized by a change in height, enlargement of the testes and penis, and voice change. It is quite common for boys to experience seminal emissions and involuntary rigidity between eleven and twelve, phenomena which precede first ejaculation (Asayama, 1957). The preadolescent boy's pubic hair is usually evidenced by thirteen (Richey, 1937). The ages of nine to thirteen are active physical and physiological

[39]

change years for the male. While he may develop later than his preadolescent female counterpart, he, nevertheless, experiences numerous and profound body changes. A summary of preadolescent physical changes and ongoing adolescent changes for boys and girls is shown in Table 2A.

Table 2A
Changes During Adolescence by Sex*

Girls	Boys
Growth of pubic hair	Growth of pubic hair
Growth of hair under arms	Growth of hair under arms
Light growth of hair on face	Heavy growth of hair on face
Light growth of hair on body	Heavy growth of hair on body
Slight growth of larynx	Considerable growth of larynx
Moderate lowering of voice	Considerable lowering of voice
Eruption of second molars	Eruption of second molars
Slight thickening of muscles	Considerable thickening of muscles
Widening of hips	Widening of shoulders
Increase in perspiration	Increase in perspiration
Development of breasts	Slight temporary development of breasts around nipples
No change in hairline	Receding hairline at temples
Menstrual cycle	Involuntary ejaculations
No change in neck size	Enlargement of neck
Growth of ovaries and uterus	Growth of penis and testicles

*Reprinted from Winter, G. D. and Nuss, E. M., *The Young Adult*, 1969, p. 88 by permission of Scott, Foresman.

Chapter two focuses on these physical changes within the preadolescent. The first article by Howard Meredith is a synopsis of changes that occur in approaching puberty. It is reprinted here for three primary reasons: (1) The author provides a diversified explanation of physiological changes; (2) The author explains the events leading up to puberty and not just the puberal crisis itself; and (3) The article stresses the importance of realizing and recognizing the physiological changes youth go through, thus, the reader can be more sensitized to many problems which may manifest themselves in the preadolescent.

As boys and girls move toward puberty whether they are early or late maturers is determined by the relative position of their growth rate compared to their peers. Since the preadolescent boy or girl is aware of his or her own position vis-à-vis personal comparisons, their individual growth patterns usually have psychological implications as well. One such study, using a sample of sixth through ninth grade girls, was done by Margaret Siler Faust in an attempt to assess the effect that developmental maturity has on bringing prestige to girls. It is reprinted in this chapter as article two.

Faust points out that research has significantly shown that early maturation is advantageous for boys, especially as it relates to physical prowess and athletic skills. For girls, the relation between early development and prestige has not been as clearly established. In her study, Faust classified 731 girls within the developmental groups of prepuberal, puberal, postpuberal, and late adolescence. There were strong correlations between maturation and prestige traits such as "grown-up," "has older friends," at each grade level, which Faust interprets as indicative of girls having different traits assigned according to level of development. Upon reading this article it becomes clearer that the way in which an individual matures developmentally also affects the emergence of some personality and friendship traits.

An extensive research study comprises the final article in this chapter. Gertrude Lewis interviewed 5000 students, 2000 of which were preadolescents, about the special concerns they had in growing up. Three distinct observations can be made from the research. First, Lewis found that preadolescents were very much aware of factors which affect their well being. Secondly, Lewis found strong indications that such youth were attempting to cope with the present. Finally, the author found much concern about developing a preparedness for their future.

Lewis' research, which was conducted among students in grades five through eight, cogently points out several areas of concern among these youth, such as: (1) food — what are the best kinds to eat while developing; (2) physical exercise — concerns about physical fitness and the demands for exercise among girls as compared to boys; (3) personal health and grooming — attractiveness and cleanliness were quite important; (4) first aid and safety — concerns about personal safety needs were expressed; (5) diseases — some fear about body diseases was evidenced; (6) mental health issues — knowing myself, understanding others, peer and family relations; and (7) social concerns — drugs, smoking, drinking, etc. As you read through the article you will be interested in many of the actual questions raised by youth regarding their physical self which Lewis has reported in this study.

Increasing Personal Awareness

The prestige variables in the developing preadolescent cited by Faust and the mental health issues and social concerns listed in Lewis' research point to the increasing awareness among youth about changing body patterns and its implication for behavior. The preadolescent, perceiving increasing physical growth and intellectual ability, and being increasingly concerned with personal adequacy and peer affiliation, seeks ways to utilize new abilities for self-growth. It is common for boys to resort to games of skill at this age. Girls, because they begin preadolescence more physically advanced, may also be involved in quite active games. Toward the end of preadolescence, however, it is quite common for girls to turn to more dominant feminine interests and realize some self-enhancement through that expression.

A somewhat conflicting situation is faced by the preadolescent boy. First, his body is in the process of important physical changes, although such changes do not infer complete maturation. In addition, he is faced with an increasing social awareness, one aspect of which is the role of competition. The preadolescent soon learns that one's life is enhanced by success, a quality often interpreted as excelling in competitive situations. In addition, many adults see the preadolescent's changing physique to be indicative of new physical capabilities. This has been evidenced in the promotion of athletic activities within many preadolescents, such as organized football, basketball, and other contact sports. Interestingly enough, research by physical anthropologists indicates that participating in highly competitive games during preadolescence is subjecting the child to the vulnerability of bodily injury because of the still demanding and incomplete growth needs of the body (Krogman, 1954).

While it is true that the preadolescent's body takes on new meaning for him, it is likely that normal physical growth will in itself, be sufficient for most preadolescents. The exploitation of preadolescents physically at a time when their bodies are changing and not near completed maturation is to stress unnecessarily the urgency of growing up.

A Synopsis of Puberal Changes in Youth
HOWARD V. MEREDITH

Editor's Note:

Meredith's article is a review of known scientific evidence which indicates the actual changes and the process of change which occur in a youngster who is approaching puberty. Because the analysis is so detailed and representative of physical and physiological changes, it adequately serves the function of clarifying male and female crises at this critical point in growth and maturation.

Much writing about individual growth changes is concerned with the time preceding or following puberty. In the case of Meredith's article, he provides change information from approximately eight years of age through the puberal crisis. The effect of reading the article should be an awareness of normative data for growth expectancies in the preadolescent boy and girl. Will you have a better appreciation of some of the normal concerns our youth have about this period of life once you have read this selection?

H.D.T.

This article is addressed to school nurses and physicians, health instructors, physical educators, and other school health personnel who teach, appraise, or counsel pupils at the upper elementary and secondary school levels. The topics treated include adolescent increase in the size of genital and related structures, growth of pubescent hair, and advent of the female menstrual cycle. In addition to indicating the typical ages at which various puberal changes occur, the article discusses individual differences in the order and timing of puberal changes. There are provided: (1) up-to-date syntheses of knowledge, and (2) references for further study.

Termination of childhood is signified by increase in the growth rates for size of breasts, ovaries, and uterus in the girl; size of testes, scrotum, and penis in the boy; and, in both sexes, size of shoulders and hips, arms and legs, height, and total body mass. Other puberal changes include beginning

Reprinted by permission of the author and publisher from the *Journal of School Health*, 1967, 37, 171-176.

menstruation by the girl, voice change and growth of facial hair by the boy, and development by both sexes of moderately coarse pigmented hair in the armpit and groin regions. On the average, those puberal changes common to both sexes occur fully two years earlier in girls than boys. For individuals of a given sex, any particular change may vary in its time of occurrence by more than five years; further, the different sorts of change do not occur in the same sequence for all individuals.

Pubescent Hair Growth and Size Changes in Girls

The typical girl has an "adolescent spurt" in body height that begins shortly after age ten years and reaches its crest approximately at age twelve years; there follows a sharp velocity decline, so that by age fourteen years height is increasing much more slowly than in late childhood (Meredith, 1939). Similarly timed "puberal velocity humps" characterize average growth of trunk length, hip width, arm girth, leg girth, and body weight (Boynton, 1936; Shuttleworth, 1937). In individual girls these puberal changes commence, fairly simultaneously, at any age from eight years to thirteen years and, on rare occasions, both earlier and later (Meredith, 1939; Shuttleworth, 1939).

Average age of beginning breast enlargement in girls is approximately 10.5 years, individual girls commencing enlargement at all ages from 2.5 years earlier to 2.5 years later (Bryan and Greenberg, 1952; Lee et al., 1963). Length of time between beginning enlargement and full breast development is about three years (Nicolson and Haney, 1953; Reynolds and Wines, 1948).

Change in the size of anatomic structures during adolescence do not all fall in the categories of moderate acceleration (e.g., stature and hip width) or marked acceleration (e.g., uterus and mammary growth). There are no puberal spurts in dimensions of the central nervous system, pineal body, or adenoid mass (Scammon, 1930; Todd, 1936). Although a moderate velocity increase occurs in external width of hips, (Boynton, 1936; Simmons, 1944; and Tuddenham and Snyder, 1954) there is considerable resorption of bone at the rim of the pelvic inlet, with marked bone loss along both sides of this inner aperture mesial and anterior to the acetabula (Greulich and Thomas, 1944).

White girls typically show first appearance of a few pigmented hairs in the pubic region near age eleven years, (Nicolson and Haney, 1953; Reynolds and Wines, 1948) and a few pigmented hairs in the axillary regions shortly after age twelve years (Bryan and Greenberg, 1952; Hansman and Maresh, 1961). Individual variations normally extend below and above these averages approximately three years for beginning growth of pubic hair, and more than three years for beginning growth of axillary hair. Instances are known of pubic and axillary hair development in early childhood (Montagu, 1946; Seckel et al., 1949). The time from first appearance of some pigmented pubic (or axillary) hair to attainment of a fairly full density is roughly three years (Reynolds and Wines, 1948). Compared with the average white girl, growth of pigmented pubic and axillary hair in the average Chinese girl commences somewhat later and is more sparse (Knott and Meredith, 1966).

In relation to first appearance of pigmented pubic hair, breast enlargement may begin two years earlier, simultaneously, or two years later (Reynolds and Wines, 1948). Beginning growth of pigmented axillary hair occasionally precedes beginning growth of pigmented pubic hair (Priesel and Wagner, 1931).

Age at Menarche and Menarcheal Relationships

There have been many more investigations on age at menarche (occurrence of the first menstrual cycle) than on pubescent hair growth or breast development. A century ago, the average age at which menarche occurred in white girls was 14.5 years or later (Bowditch, 1877; Montagu, 1946; Tanner and O'Keeffe, 1962; Tanner, 1965). Recent studies on large samples of Australian, British, Hungarian, Polish and Russian girls indicate studies today the average age at which white girls reach menarche is approximately 13 years (Bottyan et al., 1963; Milicer and Szczotka, 1966; Scott, 1961; Towns et al., 1966; Tuddenham and Snyder, 1954; Vlastovsky, 1966). Averages from large collections of menarche records obtained during the decade 1955-65 on non-white girls are near age 13 years for Assamese, Burmese, Japanese, and Southern Chinese (Foll, 1961; Inoue and Shimizu, 1965; Lee et al., 1963), near age 14 years for Ibo girls in Eastern Nigeria and Mayan Amerindian girls in Guatemala (Sabharwal et al., 1966; Tanner and O'Keeffe, 1962), and near age 15 years for South African Bantu girls and Siberian Buryat Mongoloid girls (Boas, 1932; Oettle and Higginson, 1961; Tuddenham and Snyder, 1954).

Among present day white girls, variations are about as follows: fully 50 per cent reach menarche between ages 12 and 14 years (Bryan and Greenberg, 1952), approximately 80 per cent reach menarche between ages 11.5 and 14.5 years (Nicolson and Hanley, 1953; Scott, 1961), more than 95 per cent reach menarche between ages ten and sixteen years (Bottyan et al., 1963; Milicer and Szczotka, 1966), fewer than 2 per cent reach menarche between ages eight and ten years (Seckel, 1949), and fewer than 2 per cent reach menarche after age sixteen years (Heimendinger, 1964). Menarche variations for American Negro girls are similar to those for white girls (Michelson, 1944). Instances are on record of menarche occurring before school age and later than age twenty years (Montagu, 1946).

At the time menarche occurs a girl may be in any stage of puberal breast or hair development, i.e., breast variability at menarche extends from the infantile slight elevation of papilla to mature tissue enlargement with protruding nipple (Pyror, 1936), pubic and axillary variability extend from no evidence of pigmented hair to full density in each respect (Lee et al., 1963). In different individuals, breast and pubic hair growth may commence any time from more than four years before to shortly after menarche; the velocity increase in height may reach its crest at varying times from more than three years before to one year after menarche; pigmented axillary hair may begin to appear any time from four years before to two years after menarche; pigmented pubic hair may commence to grow at varying times from more than three years before to six months after the crest of velocity increase in height; and pigmented axillary hair may first appear any time from two years before to three years after age of maximum puberal velocity in trunk and limb dimensions (Hansman and Maresh, 1961; Shuttleworth, 1937).

Several attempts have been made to discover ways of predicting menarche. Moderately strong associations (r's .75 to .80) have been found for age at menarche with (a) age at beginning breast enlargement (Nicolson and Haney, 1953; Reynolds and Wines, 1948) and (b) age at beginning ossification of a small sesamoid bone near the lower end of the thumb (Flory, 1935). Somewhat lower relationships (r's .60 to .70) have been obtained between age of menarche and beginning of pigmented pubic hair (Reynolds and Wines, 1948), maximum puberal velocity in height (Nicolson and Haney, 1953; Shuttleworth, 1937), and height increase from age ten years to age eleven years (Nicolson and Haney, 1953; Simmons and Greulich, 1943). The last correlation denotes the tendency for large increase between ages ten and eleven years to be associated with early menarche, and vice versa.

The typical amount of increase in height after menarche is 2.5 inches, with only one girl in seven increasing four inches or more (Fried and Smith, 1962). Rarely does a girl have the ability to procreate at menarche; commonly there is a puberal sterility interval of three or more years between onset of menses and fertile ovulation (Mills and Ogle, 1936; Montagu, 1946).

Genital, Hair, and Other Puberal Changes in Boys

Usually the earliest externally observable indication of puberal change in boys is increase in size of the testes (Greulich et al., 1942; Stolz and Stolz, 1951). On the average, puberal enlargement of the male genitalia commences shortly before age twelve years for the testes, and near age 12.5 years for the penis (Kubitschek, 1932; Stolz and Stolz, 1951). Individual differences in age at onset of these changes extend from 9.5 years to 14.5 years for the testes, and from ten years to fourteen years for the penis (Schonfeld, 1943; Stolz and Stolz, 1951). The typical periods of time between initial increase in velocity and attainment of maximum size approximate five years for the penis and seven years for the testes; in most individuals puberal penis growth commences after the onset of testicle growth and ends before the termination of testicle growth (Stolz and Stolz, 1951). Quantitatively, average length of the penis almost doubles from ages 12.5 years to seventeen years, and average volume of the testes increases more than tenfold from ages twelve years to nineteen years (Schonfeld, 1943).

The findings reported in the foregoing paragraph are for white boys. Findings on the penis for Chinese boys are as follows: average age of beginning puberal increase near thirteen years, variation in time of beginning increase from eleven years to sixteen years, and average interval between puberal onset and full size less than four years (Chang et al., 1966).

The puberal velocity increase for body height typically starts near age 12.5 years and reaches its peak shortly after age fourteen years; rapid reduction in velocity ensues, and by age sixteen years the average boy is increasing in height much more slowly than in late childhood (Meredith, 1965; Shuttle-worth, 1939; Simmons, 1944; Stolz and Stolz, 1951). Individual boys vary from 10.5 years to sixteen years in age at onset of their height spurt, and from below twelve years to near seventeen years in age at attaining peak velocity (Meredith, 1939; Tuddenham and Snyder, 1954). Maximum increase in the height of an individual boy during the year extending from six months before to six months after peak velocity approximates five inches, or 8 per cent (Meredith, 1939). This increase is large in comparison with maximum gain for an individual during the year before puberal changes begin (roughly three inches, or 5.5 per cent), and small in comparison with average gain during the first year after birth (roughly 10 inches, or 50 per cent). As among girls, except shifted two years later among boys, "puberal velocity humps" are timed similarly for many measures of trunk size and limb size, average velocity crests occurring slightly earlier in leg length and hip width than in sitting height and body weight (Heimendinger, 1964; Shuttleworth, 1939; Stolz and Stolz, 1951).

Average age at which a few pigmented pubic hairs are first observable in white boys approximates thirteen years (Bryan and Greenberg, 1952; Dimock, 1937). Individual white boys normally manifest beginning pig-mented hairs near the base of the penis sometime between ages ten years and sixteen years, with 80 per cent of boys showing this stage of development at ages from eleven years to fifteen years (Dimock, 1937; Schonfeld, 1943). Pigmented pubic hair is not seen in the typical Chinese boy before age fourteen years and some Chinese boys do not have any pigmented hair until after age sixteen years (Chang et al., 1966). Instances are on record of pubic hair growth, also accelerated growth of the external genitalia, in early childhood (Seckel et al., 1949). Pubic hair growth is rapid in some boys, slow in others: one boy may remain at the stage of a few pigmented hairs for a period of two years, another may take less than six months in passing from first appearance of any pigmented hair to a moderately dense growth (Stolz and Stolz, 1951). The average time from beginning pigmented hairs to a dense growth is about three years (Chang et al., 1966).

A few boys exhibit sparse development of pigmented axillary hair by age eleven years, a few not until after age seventeen years, and most between ages twelve years and sixteen years (Richey, 1937). Approximately fourteen years is the average age of boys at first appearance of pigmented axillary hair (Kubitshek, 1932). This average age is similar to average age of initial pigmented hairs near each end of the upper lip (Kubitschek, 1932; Schonfeld, 1943), puberal voice unevenness and huskiness (Chang et al., 1966; Jerome, 1937; Kubitschek, 1932), and the puberal velocity apex for body height (Meredith, 1965; Nicolson and Haney, 1953; Shuttleworth, 1939; Stolz and Stolz, 1951; Tuddenham and Snyder, 1954). Beginning growth of axillary hair typically precedes modification of the contour of the hair line above the forehead, and development of pigmented hair on the chest (Greulich et al., 1942; Kubitschek, 1932).

Puberal changes in boys include small to moderate amounts of breast enlargement. A node of firm tissue, sometimes exceeding one-half inch in diameter, develops under each nipple. Nodes are present in a few boys by age eleven years and in most boys at age fifteen years (Jung and Shafton, 1935; Schonfeld, 1943; Stolz and Stolz, 1951). In late adolescence they frequently become too small to palpate.

In relation to onset of the puberal spurt in size of testes, the spurt in penis size may commence soon after in one boy and fully two years after in another; in relation to time at which full size of testes is reached, approximate full size of penis may have been attained two years earlier in one boy and only a few months earlier in another. Beginning development in pigmented pubic hair before noticeable increase in testicle size occurs in about 25 per cent of boys (Stolz and Stolz, 1951). In rare instances, boys show some growth of pigmented axillary hair prior to any appearance of pigmented pubic hair (Greulich et al., 1942; Priesel and Wagner, 1931). At the time boys reach the apex of the puberal velocity hump in height, they vary in amount of pigmented pubic hair from lack of any to practically a full density (Stolz and Stolz, 1951). Perceptible voice change occurs sometimes before penis acceleration or the presence of any pigmented pubic or axillary hair, and sometimes following full penis size, dense growth of pubic hair, and moderately dense growth of axillary hair (Chang et al., 1966; Greulich et al.,

1942). At the time spermatozoa are first discharged in the urine, a boy may be in any stage of pubic and axillary hair development from the prepuberal condition to almost full density in each region (Baldwin, 1928).

Among boys fourteen years of age: one may give no indication of puberal increase in penis size and another may show this organ to be near maximum size (Heimendinger, 1964); again, one may give no indication of pigmented pubic or axillary hair and another may show a dense growth of pubic hair and some axillary hair (Kubitschek, 1932). During the year between ages fourteen and fifteen years, three different boys may increase in height four inches, two inches, and one-half inch, respectively; the first boy is undergoing his puberal spurt, the second either is nearing his spurt or has recently passed it, and the third is close to his maximum adult height (Meredith, 1939). The combination of fully developed testes, scrotum, penis, pubic hair and axillary hair may be attained by age fifteen years, or may not be attained before age twenty years (Schonfeld, 1943).

Prediction of puberal changes has been investigated less extensively for boys than for girls. The early observation that boys tall in middle and late childhood tend to have their puberal spurt in height earlier than do the short boys (Baldwin, 1914) has been found a tendency too weak to have predictive usefulness. This is made explicit by noting that the correlation of height at age six years and age at maximum puberal velocity in height approximates $r = -.25$, yielding an index of forecasting efficiency below 4 per cent (Meredith, 1965). Moderate positive association (r near .65) has been found between age at beginning enlargement of the testes and age at reaching maximum puberal velocity in height (Nicolson and Haney, 1953).

There are other sorts of change during adolescence than those directed toward accelerated growth of body organs and segments; cumulative increase of moderately coarse pigmented hairs on regions of the face, trunk, and limbs; and development of additional physiologic functions. No puberal spurt occurs in volume of the brain, weight of the eyeballs, size of the bones of the inner ear, or number of erupting teeth (Knott and Meredith, 1966; Scammon, 1930). There is gradual decrease in weight of the cortex and medulla of the thymus (Boyd, 1936); also loss of head hair, causing gradual indentation of the male hair line on each side of the upper forehead superior to the eyebrows (Schonfeld, 1943). Average thickness of adipose tissue between the skin and muscles of the arm and leg, although increasing to a plateau at age fifteen years in girls (Boynton, 1936; Fry et al., 1965; Reynolds, 1950), progressively decreases in boys throughout adolescence (Fry et al., 1965; Meredith, 1939; Reynolds, 1950).

Developmental Maturity as a Determinant in Prestige of Adolescent Girls

MARGARET SILER FAUST

The factors involved in gaining and maintaining prestige during adolescence are still obscure, despite the numerous investigations which have sought to define them. Of the physical characteristics which have been studied in relation to prestige, level of maturity consistently has been found to be significant for boys (Jones, 1943, 1949*a*; Jones and Bayley, 1950). It has been clearly established that early-maturing boys command an advantage in social relations, not only during adolescence (Bower, 1941; Jones and Bayley, 1950), but in the later years of life, as well (Mussen and Jones, 1957). The gains in strength and physical ability which accompany puberty (Jones, 1943, 1949*b*; Stolz and Stolz, 1951) provide an advantage for the early-maturing boy in at least one important avenue for gaining prestige, i.e., athletics (Jones, 1943; Tryon, 1939, 1944).

For girls, however, the relation between developmental maturity and prestige is less evident and has not been clearly established. While early maturing provides no obvious prestige-gaining advantage for girls (such as competence in athletics brings for boys), it seems reasonable to expect that the rate and timing of physical changes at adolescence would have significant concomitants in the behavior and reputations of adolescent girls (Frank, 1953; Stone and Barker, 1939). One means of determining whether early puberty, with its concomitants, is advantageous or deleterious to the social status of girls would be to analyze Guess Who reputations of adolescent girls in terms of the girls' level of physical development during adolescence.

It is the purpose of the present research to determine for girls whether developmental maturity is a determinant in prestige during adolescence. The study is an extension of Tryon's *Evaluations of Adolescent Personality by*

From *Child Development* 31 (1960): 173-84. Reprinted with permission of the author and the Society for Research in Child Development.

Adolescents (1939), in which she noted differences between twelve-year-old and fifteen-year-old boys and girls in their evaluation of traits with respect to prestige. In the present study of adolescent girls four consecutive grades have been included in the analysis in order to see more clearly the relationship between developmental maturity and the evaluations of prestige and other traits during this phase of adolescence. The period from the sixth to the ninth grades is generally a time of rapid physical changes for girls, and it might be expected that developmental differences among girls would be systematically associated with certain trait scores of the Guess Who test. Some traits or reputations might be ascribed characteristically to the more mature rather than to the less mature girls. On the other hand, it is possible that, as the level of maturity of the girls changes from one grade to the next, their evaluations of traits and of developmental maturity may undergo progressive changes as well. In order to see more clearly the changing relationship between developmental maturity and the reputations of adolescent girls, the present analysis is undertaken for each grade separately. This may help to clarify the meaning which early and late development has for girls at various times during the adolescent period.

Subjects

The subjects were 731 girls enrolled in the sixth, seventh, eighth, and ninth grades in a suburban school community. Girls in the three upper grades attended junior high school, while the sixth graders attended various elementary schools, all of which were within the junior high school attendance area. The population represents roughly 96 percent of the girls enrolled in the classes selected for the study.

Procedure

The test used in this investigation was a duplication of the Guess Who test which Tryon (1939) employed, with the addition of the following pair of items, which were designed to measure prestige:

Here is someone whom everyone thinks a lot of who influences the group. What he (or she) says or does is important to the group.

Here is someone whom no one thinks much of; what he (or she) says or does matters little to the group.

The Guess Who test, comprised of twenty one pairs of trait descriptions, was administered in the natural classroom setting to both boys and girls, although only the scores of the girls were analyzed for the present purpose.

Following Tryon's procedure, the sixth graders were instructed to mention on the test anyone within their classroom, while in the three junior high school grades the pupils were instructed to mention anyone within their whole grade.[1]

Scoring the guess who test. For every girl the number of mentions received on the positive and the negative item of each trait pair was summed algebraically, following Tryon's procedure. A score of zero was assigned to anyone who was mentioned on neither item of a trait pair or who received an equal number of positive and negative mentions. Self-mentions were excluded.

For the sixth-grade girls each score was expressed as a proportion of the number of mentions received relative to the number of possible mentions (girls in the class). This gave scores which were comparable among the seven sixth grade classes, which varied considerably in size.

Scoring Developmental Maturity. Developmental maturity was assessed by means of menarcheal age scores, the data for which were obtained by the school nurses for the sixth grade girls and by the women's physical education staff for the three junior high school grades. The data were obtained at a time when the girls were in a health class or physical education class separate from the boys, and when it would seem very natural for the staff to obtain such developmental data.

Subsequently, the girls were classified into four developmental groups. Girls who had not reached menarche were considered "Prepuberal," while girls who had reached menarche within a year of the time of testing were classified "Puberal." Girls who had reached menarche more than one year and less than three years prior to the testing were called "Postpuberal." All others were considered "Late Adolescent." The distribution of girls in each developmental group is given in Table 2.1 for the four grades.

Analysis of data. Pearson product-moment correlations between *prestige* and each of the other Guess Who traits were computed for each of the four grades separately, and the findings are presented in Table 2.2. The close correspondence between Tryon's prestige-lending traits and the traits yielding the highest correlations with *prestige* by the present method is discussed elsewhere (Faust, 1957).

Before testing whether Guess Who scores were a function of developmental maturity, it was necessary to ascertain whether the various developmental groups within each grade were of comparable chronological age (CA). Analysis of variance revealed that, at each grade, the developmentally more mature girls were significantly older than the less mature girls. Therefore, it

---

1.See Faust (1957) for detailed description of administration, tabulation, and scoring procedures.

Table 2.1
Classification Into Developmental Groups

Grade	Prepuberal	Puberal	Postpuberal	Late Adolescent	Total
Sixth	96	29	5	0	130
Seventh	66	99	53	3	221
Eighth	17	45	104	27	193
Ninth	4	16	106	61	187
Total	183	189	268	91	731

Table 2.2
Correlations Between Prestige
and Other Guess Who Traits Within Each Grade

	Sixth $N = 130$	Seventh $N = 221$	Eighth $N = 193$	Ninth $N = 187$
Restless	-.42†	-.31†	-.15*	-.12
Talkative	-.01	.08	.15*	.05
Active—Games	.18*	.27†	.42†	.34†
Humor—Jokes	.23†	.34†	.29†	.35†
Friendly	.68†	.73†	.68†	.48†
Leader	.48†	.46†	.67†	.63†
Fights	-.27†	-.15*	-.10	-.05
Assured—Class	.43†	.33†	.55†	.34†
Daring	.47†	.39†	.41†	.50†
Tidy	.57†	.48†	.48†	.35†
Older Friends	.20*	.17*	.27†	.05
Humor—Self	.35†	.35†	.75†	.59†
Grown-up	.33†	.25†	.19†	.20†
Attention-getting	-.23†	-.09	-.18*	-.33†
Assured—Adults	.57†	.41†	.45†	.48†
Popular	.68†	.80†	.93†	.82†
Happy	.43†	.62†	.67†	.58†
Good-looking	.65†	.42†	.42†	.54†
Enthusiastic	.65†	.56†	.67†	.61†
Bossy	.15	-.01	-.03	-.12

*Significant at .05 level.
†Significant at .01 level.

became necessary to determine whether CA differences within a grade were related to Guess Who test scores. Twenty-one correlations between CA and Guess Who scores were computed for each grade. Of these 84 correlations, only one reached significance at the .05 level of confidence, and one is fewer than would be expected on a chance basis alone! Therefore it was unnecessary to use a covariance method of holding CA constant while analyzing the effect of developmental maturity upon Guess Who scores, since CA differences within a grade were found to be unrelated to trait scores. Thereupon, an analysis of variance (McNemar, 1955, p. 261 ff.) was conducted for each grade to determine whether any given trait was more closely associated with one level of development than with another. Some developmental groups in certain grades were not large enough to warrant their inclusion in the statistical analysis (*see* Table 2.1). Table 2.3 shows the mean scores of developmental groups on the Guess Who items upon which signficant differences among the developmental groups were revealed by this analysis.

Results

At every grade the more mature girls received progressively higher mean scores on the item *grown-up* than did their less mature classmates. Similarly, on the item *older friends* consistent differences among the developmental groups were observed at each grade, although only in the seventh and eighth

Table 2.3

Average Score for Individuals on Items Which Differentiated Significantly Among the Developmental Groups

	Prepuberal	Puberal	Postpuberal	Late Adolescent	p
Grown-Up					
Sixth	0.1	4.3	*	*	.05
Seventh	- 1.1	0.4	1.2	*	.001
Eighth	- 2.0	- 1.1	0.5	2.2	.001
Ninth	*	-0.8	0.2	0.8	.01
Older Friends					
Seventh	0.0	0.8	1.4	*	.001
Eighth	- 0.2	0.4	0.9	2.6	.001
Daring					
Ninth	*	-0.2	0.7	0.6	0.1

*Group not large enough to be included in the analysis.

grades did the differences reach statistical significance. While CA differences within a grade were unrelated to trait scores, developmental differences significantly affected the opinions which girls had of their peers on these traits.

On the other hand, the differences among developmental groups on the trait *daring* reached the .01 level in the ninth grade only. Since the differences on the trait *daring* were significant only in this grade and since they do not reflect a consistent trend in mean scores for the developmental groups, it is difficult to determine whether or not the differences might have resulted from chance alone.

Differences in mean scores among developmental groups were not great enough to reach significance on the other traits. However, the differences in mean scores for developmental groups on many of the items followed a consistent pattern within each grade. A consideration of the mean scores of developmental groups on the prestige-lending traits alone (see Table 2.2) suggests that level of development had some effect upon Guess Who evaluations. Considering only the item *prestige* and the items correlated significantly with *prestige*, it is apparent that one developmental group at each grade received more than a chance allotment of high scores on these favorable traits. At each grade the developmental group which received the highest mean score on *prestige* tended to receive high scores also on the items which correlated positively with *prestige* and to receive low scores on the items which were negatively correlated with *prestige* for that grade.

By means of the binomial test it was determined that at each grade one developmental group was attributed more of the prestige-related traits than was a likely occurrence on the basis of chance (see Table 2.4). For the three

Table 2.4
Distribution of Favorable Scores on
Prestige-lending Traits for Developmental Groups in Each Grade

Grade	No. of Traits Significantly Correlated with *Prestige*	Pre-puberal	Puberal	Post-puberal	Late Ado-lescent	p
Sixth	18	15	3	*	*	0.003
Seventh	17	4	3½	9½	*	0.035
Eighth	18	1	3	1	13	0.00003
Ninth	15	*	1½	5½	8	0.04

Note — When two developmental groups received the same high mean score, each was given credit for one-half.

*Group not large enough to be included in the analysis.

junior high school grades the most mature groups consistently received the highest mean scores on *prestige* and on items significantly correlated with it, such as *popular, friendly*, and *assured–adults*. While girls in the later stages of development were favored during the junior high school years, this was not the case for the sixth grade girls. Instead, the least mature girls, the prepuberal group, received favorable scores on most of the desirable traits in the sixth grade.

In the sixth grade a prepuberal girl is developmentally "in phase" with the majority of her classmates, and being at the prepuberal stage of development seems to be an asset in prestige in sixth grade. However, in the seventh grade the average girl is in the puberal group (see Table 2.1); yet the prestige-lending traits are most frequently ascribed to the postpuberal girls. In both eighth and ninth grades, when the average girl is in the postpuberal group, the desirable traits are most frequently ascribed to girls in the late adolescent group (four to six years beyond menarche).

Discussion

A girl's level of physical maturity is not the only determinant in her scores on the Guess Who items, but, together with associated emotional, social, sexual, and personality changes, level of maturity does contribute significantly to the reputation which a girl has in her social group. Although puberal development contributes only a small amount of variance to the Guess Who trait scores, it does seem to contribute enough to give slight but consistent direction to the mean trait scores.

Adolescents' awareness of developmental differences is clearly revealed in their evaluations on certain Guess Who traits. While CA bore no significant relation to scores on the items *grown-up* and *older friends*, at every grade the more mature girls received progressively higher mean scores than did their less mature classmates on these items. Thus, developmental differences were more significant than CA differences in affecting these scores. It is evident that the more mature girls are taller, on the average (Shuttleworth, 1937), and that they appear more "grown up" in terms of secondary sex characteristics (Greulich, 1944). These associated factors of development may be the basis for the girls' evaluations on the trait *grown-up*. The possible relation of developmental maturity to the scores on *older friends* is likewise evident. For the more mature girls to seek out comparably mature girl friends of a higher grade in school is reasonable and is consistent with Jones's (1948) finding that level of maturity is a factor in friendship selection. In addition, level of development is related to maturity of interests and activities (Stone and Barker, 1939), and common interests are known to be important in establishing friendships (Bonney, 1946). The evaluations on the trait *older friends* may indicate, on the other hand, that the more mature girls are judged as having boy friends in a higher grade in school. Since the boys of a given grade mature later than the girls, the girls of advanced physical maturity may find satisfaction of their heterosexual interest in dating older boys. However, by ninth grade, associating with older friends is no longer judged as being prestige lending ($r = 0.05$). Perhaps, as the discrepancy in physical maturity between boys and girls diminishes, the prestige-lending nature of dating older boys is concomitantly reduced to insignificance.

According to Jones and Bayley (1950), the traits *grown-up* and *older friends* were two of the Guess Who items upon which the early- and the late-maturing boys received significantly different scores. Consistently on six testings throughout the adolescent period the group of late-maturing boys were seen as less "grown up" and less likely to have "older friends" than were the early-maturing boys. These findings correspond with those found here among the girls: *grown-up* and *older friends* were characteristic of the more mature girls at each grade.

Although the scores of physically immature boys and girls are similar on these two traits, their score on the other Guess Who traits show a marked sex difference. Jones and Bayley (1950) report that the late-maturing boys received above average scores on *attention getting, restless, assured–class*, and *talkative*, while the evidence from the present study is that the less mature girls *in junior high school* were characterized by the traits *non-attention getting, quiet*, and *avoids fights*. According to Jones and Bayley, boys seem to defend themselves against the anxieties of late development by compensation for inferiority, expressed in attention-getting mannerisms. However, for girls the defense against immature physical status in junior high school seems to be more of a withdrawal and an attempt to be inconspicuous in the group. Both of these patterns seem to represent a perseveration of certain components of the respective sex-appropriate preadolescent pattern, which was prestige lending for neither boys nor girls at this level.

The findings of this study suggest that for girls level of development is a factor in the assignment of traits during adolescence. Although the single trait *prestige* is not significantly associated with level of physical maturity, the high scores on this item are consistent with the pattern of high scores on the other desirable traits; i.e., one developmental group at each grade received more of the favorable scores than would be expected on a chance basis. When all of the prestige-lending traits of a given grade are considered as a whole, it appears that prestige is more likely to surround those in the sixth grade who are developmentally "in phase" (prepuberal), whereas during the junior high school years being ahead of the group developmentally seems to be an advantage. While prepuberal status may be hazardous for girls in junior high school, it is not considered "immature" nor undesirable in sixth grade. A prepuberal girl in sixth grade is developmentally "in phase" with the great majority of her classmates, while a prepuberal girl in ninth grade is a "developmental isolate." A girl's level of physical maturity is not only relative to the development of others in the class, but it is seen against a background of developmental differences within the whole school. Being at the prepuberal level of development seems to lend different qualities to the composite picture of an individual in elementary school than it does to one in the junior high school grades.

Although the evaluations of traits in relation to *prestige* were much the same for sixth and for seventh grade girls (rho = .90), the actual traits were attributed to a developmentally different group of girls. In the one year from sixth to seventh grade, the prestige-lending qualities shift from the prepuberal to the postpuberal girls, a developmental difference of two to three years. Moreover, in the eighth and ninth grades it is the late adolescent group, girls from four to six years beyond menarche, who are at the favored developmental level. This discontinuity between rate of developmental change and rate of change in prestige-lending evaluations suggests that a girl who is prepuberal in sixth grade cannot remain in the favored developmental position in junior high school, because her level of maturity cannot keep pace with the *rate* at which peer evaluations change with respect to developmental maturity.

This discontinuity suggests that for girls neither physical acceleration nor physical retardation is consistently advantageous. It is not until the junior high school years that the early-maturing girl "comes into her own" and reaps the benefit of her accelerated development. Until that time her precocious development is somewhat detrimental to her social status. The adjustments which inevitably must be made to losses and gains in status during the adolescent period (Tryon, 1944) may be partly a function of this discontinuity in the relationship between developmental maturity and prestige during the adolescent period. Tryon alluded to this discontinuity and its significance when she described Case 29 (Tryon, 1939), a girl who commanded prestige at twelve years of age, but who at age fourteen or fifteen was still developmentally immature. Tryon noted that in the ninth grade "she is now one of the very few little girls; she seemed like a child in the midst of adults with a group of girls; tended to avoid large mixed groups of boys and girls and their activities" (p. 64). The emotional hazard of losing status during adolescence because of relative physical immaturity is not infrequently noted in case studies and observed in child guidance clinics. Contrariwise, as the findings of this study suggest, precocious physical maturity may possess its hazards, particularly in the period before entrance to junior high school.

After the transition to junior high school, girls begin to ascribe prestige to classmates who have been physically mature for a longer period of time and to girls whose interests and activities are undoubtedly more advanced. Perhaps these more mature girls satisfy a requirement for prestige in the group because of their "advanced standing" with respect to the new developmental tasks which the less mature girls are facing.

The significance of the present research is in its clarification of the changing relationship between developmental maturity and social prestige during adolescence. The findings of this study do not support Jones's assertion that "the very early maturing girl ... is in many respects in a disadvantageous position" (Jones, 1949*a*). From an unpublished study arising from the Adolescent Growth Study, Jones states that "*when we compared them* (italics the writer's) ... we found that the early-maturing (girls) were below average in prestige, sociability, and leadership; below average in popularity; below average in cheerfulness, poise, and expressiveness." Perhaps the discrepancy between the present study and the one which Jones reports lies in the phrase "when we compared them," for it is apparent that the present findings for *sixth* grade girls are not unlike the H. E. Jones quotation. However, the present findings indicate that early maturing is indeed advantageous in all three junior high school grades. By junior high school accelerated development has taken on a prestige-lending connotation. The favorable position of the early-developing girl is generally consistent with other of the California Growth Study findings, although not with the citation above of H. E. Jones. M. C. Jones and Mussen (1958, p. 497) report:

Although the differences were not consistent in all categories, the early-maturing girls tended to score more favorably than the slow-maturing on "total adjustment," and also on family adjustment and feelings of personal adequacy. These data from the self-report inventory seem to be generally consistent with the findings from the TAT.

The findings of the present research point out the complex nature of variables which interact in producing a girl's reputation during adolescence. The data support the hypothesis by Jones and Mussen (1958) that early and late development may mean different things at different times during adolescence. The discontinuity between rate of change in evaluations of prestige and rate of physical changes during adolescence means that, for girls, accelerated development is not a sustained asset throughout the adolescent period, as it is for boys. Accelerated development for girls is somewhat detrimental to prestige status before the junior high school years, while it places a girl in a very favorable social position throughout the junior high school years.

Summary

The purpose of the present study was to ascertain for girls whether level of physical maturity is a determinant in prestige during adolescence. Tryon's Guess Who test, including an additional pair of items designed to measure prestige, was administered to 731 girls in the sixth, seventh, eighth, and ninth grades. Correlations between prestige and the other twenty traits were computed for each grade separately, and the correlations were tested for significance.

Level of physical maturity was assessed by means of menarcheal age scores, which were obtained by the school nurses for the sixth grade girls and by the women's physical education staff for the three junior high school grades. On the basis of the menarcheal age data girls at each grade were classified into four developmental groups.

In order to determine whether CA differences within a grade were related to Guess Who scores, correlations between CA and each of the twenty one Guess Who traits were computed for each grade. No significant relation was found between CA differences within a grade and Guess Who trait scores.

An analysis of variance based upon developmental groups revealed that the developmentally more mature girls at each grade received significantly higher scores on the items *grown-up* and *older friends* than did their less mature classmates. Differences in mean scores among developmental groups were not great enough to reach significance on the other traits. However, one developmental group at each grade received the highest scores on more of the prestige-related traits than would be expected on the basis of chance. By means of the binomial test, it was determined that *prestige* and the significant prestige-related traits were more frequently ascribed to sixth grade girls who were developmentally "in phase" (prepuberal), while in all three junior high school grades girls who were physically accelerated and were in the most mature developmental groups received more of the favorable reputation scores. Thus, for girls precocious physical development tends to be a detriment in prestige status during sixth grade, while it tends to become a decided asset during the three succeeding years.

The findings indicate that level of development is not a single factor in determining a girl's status in the group, but it is an important part of a composite of factors in creating a girl's reputation during adolescence. A discrepancy between rate of developmental change and rate of change in prestige-lending evaluations during adolescence was noted and was interpreted in terms of the different meaning which early and late development have for girls at different times during adolescence. After the transition to junior high school, the more favorable reputation scores were ascribed to the physically accelerated girls.

"I Am—I Want—I Need"

Preadolescents Look at Themselves and Their Values

GERTRUDE M. LEWIS

Why do I act happy, sad, angry? Why can't I control my temper?
Why do I get blamed for everything?
I get so mad and feel like calling the person who angered me bad names.
When I try to do something right, it comes out wrong.
I would like to understand my personality.

Questions like these, asked by ten-year-olds in a recent study, indicate only a few of the deep concerns that haunt pre- and young adolescents as they grow up.

When Ruth V. Byler, health consultant in the Connecticut State Department of Education and leader in her field, decided to have the state health education guide revised, she determined to find a way to go to children and youth for some insights into modern-day interests, giving them opportunity to express their concerns and problems in their own words and without any structureu guide or checklist to influence their thinking. Under advisement of some of the nation's outstanding health-related experts, the department secured a director and an analyst and launched a study unique in many ways.

Project Design

Included in the project were more than 5,000 students in grades K-12 in four selected Connecticut school systems, representing inner city, suburban, rural, and high economic communities. By way of class and small group discussions, individual interviews, and free anonymous writing and teacher observations of real-life situations, selected coordinators and teacher-interviewers set the stage for students to express freely their *health interests,*

Reprinted by permission of the author and publisher from *Childhood Education*, 1970, 46 (4), 186-194.

concerns and problems. The complete account of the study reports a wide array of misconceptions, misinformation, half-truths and facts these young people had gleaned from their surroundings. Clues abound for teachers in all grades who wish to be of help to boys and girls in their "now" needs.

Focus of Partial Report

For the purpose of this article, evidence related to approximately 2,000 students in grades five to eight has been extracted from the total report. Hopefully, educators innovating in the "middle schools," where the purpose is to make the curriculum more relevant to the needs of today's ten- to thirteen-year-old young people, will find this partial report of especial use. For example, the sharp difference in questions raised by ten-year-olds and by eleven- to thirteen-year-olds raises some doubt about the advisability of grades five to eight grouping and indicates the care educators must take to make such a grouping profitable for ten-year-olds.

Summary of Responses

The responses indicate clearly the predominantly preadolescent character of fifth-graders, with a few students (usually girls) embarrassed by early maturation; the greater mixture of pre- and young adolescents in the sixth grades, with many concerned about indications of puberty; the greater number of young adolescents in the seventh grades, with a few worried and uncomfortable about late maturation; and the more homogeneous development in the eighth grades, but with a few very late maturers.

Interests and concerns reported here represent only some of the myriad problems that consume boys and girls in these highly significant years of development. The analysis of responses produced a clear pattern for organization that seems to fit all grades. Most questions relate to the body and its development and care, to mental health, and to peer and family relations. Some touch on social problems concerning the entire society.

The frequency with which young people of these ages voice interest in body development and function and in peer and family relations evidences that the desire to understand is not just one of mere interest but of real concern. Their drive for understanding causes them to seek answers actively wherever and however found, sometimes accruing to the seekers a formidable fund of fact and fiction. Within this melee the teacher-leader must identify clues enabling him to help each young person in his care to better understanding of self and of life-roles.

Interests Related to the Body,
Its Development and Care

General Concerns

Fifth-graders want to know *all about* the body, especially how it grows and develops, what is inside, how the mind works, why some people are smarter than others, how the heart beats, how the cells work, why we have hair, and a host of other things, chiefly about body mechanisms.

A sample poignant concern:

My mother started to tell me about my period, but she had to go out. I wouldn't know what to do if I get it. And what if I have a man teacher? I couldn't tell him.

They ask a few questions about babies:

Why do only girls have babies?
How is a baby formed?
How did our baby grow?
How do we stay alive in our mother's stomach?

Sixth-graders ask many more specific questions:

Why does everyone like me take on the human form and not some other form?
What makes the body go? You have everything you need but what pushes it so it will operate and you start living?
How did I start in my mother's stomach?
How does a baby come out of a woman?
What makes it a boy or girl?
Why can't you have a baby when you're not married?
Does smoking have anything to do with babies being formed wrong?
If your parents are small, will you be small?
Why do girls grow up faster than boys?

Interests of seventh-graders follow along similar lines but are expressed in more numerous and more expertly phrased questions – such as these two which point up the wide range of development in this grade:

Why do some girls in grade seven think they are so grown up?
Why do some kids in grade seven act so immature?

Interests about the body are:

How bodies are and how they grow; everything about the body.
How people grow, inside and out.
How the body changes.
The difference between men and women.
Why some people walk differently.
Why you perspire. What causes blindness.
Do humans have inborn instincts? If so, what are they?

What is sex? How can it affect you? What does it mean? Is it dirty? Are we wrong to be involved in it? Should kids be afraid of it? Adults should answer children's questions truthfully.

Some boys ask:

Why do some boys in this grade understand sex and giggle and laugh? What is so big about miniskirts and beautiful legs?

Some girls wish to "learn about menstruation, reproduction, pregnancy, birth, birth control, and how you get pregnant." Others ask:

What is a period? Does a boy get a period?
When does menstruation usually start?
How does a female get a baby? What causes reproduction?
Is there any other way to get a baby?
What about premarital sex relations?
You should know what happens if you have sex relations too young. You should know this before junior high school.
What is pregnancy? How do you know you have it?
What are X and Y chromosomes?
How are babies born? Why are some deformed?
Why are babies born without talk or teeth?
Can birth control pills affect a baby?
What is abortion?

Eighth-graders express interests even more comprehensively than do sevenths, and with evident restraint:

The school should teach about the whole body, about all parts; about growth of the body and mind.
It should teach how the parts function:
– how the mind affects the body
– what makes you grow
– how the blood system works
– what the glands and liver do
– how the body repairs itself
– how body weight can be controlled (This topic received much attention in this grade.)

Regarding sex education, eighth-graders almost unanimously agreed that it should be taught in the schools:

Parents won't help us; schools should.
Teach it before eighth grade so kids will know more than I do.
If we study it early, we will think of it as right and open; ignored, it is dirty.
A girl might do wrong with a boy just out of courtesy and become pregnant, so they need sex education, and protection against sex relations with boys.
Teach it early, but not too young. You learn much in the streets, but not enough.

They ask:

When are we susceptible to conception?

What is a virgin, reproduction, promiscuous, a Caesarian operation, a
lesbian, a homosexual, masturbation, etc.?
How can you get rid of a baby?
Are morals important today?
Why can't I get anything done because of thinking of sex and girls?

About Food

Fifth-graders ask:

What foods are best for a person to eat? What foods are bad for you?

Sixth graders:

What vitamins should you have?
What makes you fat?
Some people have no friends and they turn to food and get real fat. Some
turn to smoking or taking dope just to impress others because it's the only
way they can get recognition.

Seventh- and eighth-graders point their interest toward weight control.

About Physical Education and Exercise

Fifth- and sixth-graders want specific exercises for good health and for
keeping physically fit. Fifth-grade boys want to develop big muscles;
sixth-graders want a daily exercise program with a good gym and good,
well-trained teachers, large playgrounds, and track and sports.
Seventh-grade girls query:

Do we need as much as boys?
Suggest exercises for cramps.
Are gang showers sanitary, moral and healthy?
When you have a private shower, do you undress entirely?

In the eighth grade, some students question the need for physical
education; others want specific suggestions:

What exercises should teenagers do?
What exercises will help me
– build rock-like muscles
– reduce my waistline and upper thighs
– do the split
– make my chest fuller.

Some call for physical education in every grade, voluntary sports in junior
and senior high school.

About Personal Health and Grooming

Fifth-graders express little interest in appearance, although they make a
bow to general cleanliness, saying, "We should know how to keep clean."

Sixth-graders are more concerned, asking for information about care of fingernails, teeth, eyes, feet, and why hair gets oily. They add:

Kids think it's important to stay in style. Some kids dress the way they don't want to just so kids won't make fun of them. The school should have a uniform. Some pupils come to school looking like bums, long hair, dirty nails, shirt tails out, and so on.

Seventh-graders focus in two areas:

How much sleep do I need?
How can I look attractive, cute, and appealing all at once?

Eighth-graders also show intense interest in appearance and attractiveness:

Help us learn more about skin care, odors, cavities, germs, dress, hair styles.

About First Aid and Safety Education

These are considered important by fifth- and sixth-graders, "in case of accidents"; the records are grim with horror incidents. Seventh- and eighth-graders think both topics should be taught by specialists, saying:

We need to know about safety at home, on buses and on bicycles.
Have a fireman teach fire safety, and policeman self-defense.

About Diseases

Young people display fear about diseases of the body, especially in the seventh and eighth grades. Fifth-graders want to know what causes colds, measles, chicken pox and other common diseases and how to cure and prevent them. Sixth-graders show a growing scientific interest, asking how houseflies carry germs, how vaccines are made, and what besides smoking causes cancer.

Seventh-graders express deeper concern, especially about symptoms, causes, treatment and cure of innumerable diseases and ailments. Eighth-graders want to know about maladies to which they are vulnerable; symptoms of common diseases, including venereal diseases and "mono"; how diseases spread and can be prevented; possible cures for cancer and heart diseases; how babies get defects and how they can be helped.

Interests Related to Mental Health

Questions of these boys and girls reveal groping to establish basics for good mental health, especially self-understanding, relationships with others, and a philosophical code of beliefs to sustain and guide one.

"Knowing Myself"

Many fifth-graders want to understand themselves better, especially their uncontrollable moods and fears. Sixth-graders express many of the same concerns and add:

How are habits started? Stopped?
How do I know myself?
Why do I sometimes hate everybody?
Why do I sometimes feel like killing people and babies with ugly faces?
Why do my problems sometimes overrun me?
Why am I afraid of darkness, ghosts, falling from high places?
Everyone's afraid someone is going to make fun of them. That's the trouble. Everyone is afraid of being different. New kids in school are scared to death, especially if they're smart.
It's good to be rebellious because if we weren't, we wouldn't get ahead. Wearing long hair and other ways of rebelling, such as short skirts, is good, because kids might do something worse. It's an outlet for frustration. It's a lot healthier than some other things.

Seventh-graders seem to concentrate on the negative side of mental health:

What is mental illness? What causes it? Can it be cured?
Are there symptoms to tell if you are mentally sick?
How does mental illness differ from being just plain stupid?
Can you drive yourself into having mental illness? Is it the result of problems?

Eighth-graders show more introversion, such as was present in grades four and six. They ask:

How can I keep from yelling, lying, stealing, committing suicide?
How can you detect and prevent mental illness, cracking up, having a nervous breakdown?
How can you teach about teenagers' pressures without getting parents in? Unless they understand kids, it isn't going to do any good to talk about it. Couldn't they be invited to meet with small groups?
I would like to understand myself.

Understanding Others

Fifth-graders say:

I want to know about other people.
I would like to help others and understand them.
Height affects the way you act. John is the biggest boy and he bosses us around because we are smaller. I'm short. If I was tall, I'd act big, maybe. It's hard to say.
Why do boys and girls when they get older act so big and tell dirty things and steal?

Why are Negroes treated differently than white people?
Why does the teacher give my paper to another teacher when she said she wouldn't?

Sixth-graders want to know about psychology and retarded children:

I understand people's feelings, but sometimes I get stumped.
I should like to know what causes retardation and help find a cure for it.

Seventh-graders also want to understand retardation, its causes, treatment and cure. Eighth-graders add:

I hope some day we will have a real liking for each other; that we will understand people of different race and color.
Why do people judge others on superficial things, following fads, etc.?
Will today's generation of kids be able to take over from this generation of grown-ups well?

Fifth- and eighth-graders ask some philosophical questions:

Why did God make me if life is so terrible?
Who am I? What is life? What makes me tick?
What is thinking?
How can you be sure of what and who you are?
What is life all about?

Peer Relations

Friendships hold center stage in grades five and six, questions often revealing the capriciousness of group membership and the growing desire for "real" friends. Fifth-graders ask:

Why do my friends like me sometimes and sometimes not?
Can we prevent being disliked?

Annoyed by the attentions of several advanced fifth-grade girls, a boy confides to his small coterie of friends:

Why do girls call and send notes? If you tell them to cut it out, they call more.

Sixth-graders ask:

Why do I sometimes hate my friends?
What is a real friend? What can I do to make friends?

In seventh grade, the interest swings to dating:

Is there any solution to picking friends well?
How can you make a boy (girl) like you?
Do boys like girls who smoke and are gross?
Should seventh-graders have boy and girl parties?
What is petting?

Is eleven too young to "make out"? So many in the "cool crowd" are doing it. I wonder, "Is there nothing wrong with it?"
With a boy, how far is far enough?
Why do kids become hippies?

Peer relations rise to an absorbing emotion in the eighth grade. Most of the questions focus on attracting the opposite sex, dating and "going steady." They ask:

How can you attract the opposite sex?
Why are some kids so popular and others not? How can you get popular?
How can you get a boy to notice you and like you?
Is there such a thing as love at thirteen?
How do you know you're in love?
Is it wrong to go out with a boy a year or two older?
I am not going to marry. Should I date?
What does "going steady" mean?
Who should set the limit, the boy or the girl? Both should know how far to go and still love each other.

Family Relations

Questions and comments of ten- to thirteen-year-olds reflect the bickering and momentary jealousies that young people have expressed since third grade. Learning to cope with day-to-day emotions is not easy.

Nevertheless, relations with parents embrace at least two persistent concerns haunting today's young people, often putting upon them burdens for which they are unfitted: (1) concern that, in their own reaching for greater independence and for friendships outside the home, they will lose the love and support of their parents; and (2) concern for the stability of the home. They see their parents drifting apart and fear that they will lose one or both of them. Even as young as eight, a child agonized to her teacher, "My mother is getting a new husband. I don't think I have love enough for two fathers."

Fifth-graders ask:

Why does my mother get mad at me when I try to do something right? She spends more time with my sister.
Why do people fight between each other within the same family?

Sixth-graders, too, express concern:

Why can't I get along with my brother? Or sister?
Why don't married people be nice to each other?
Why does my father hit my mother for no reason?
Why do people get married if they don't love each other?
If a child has problems at home, who would she be able to talk to about them outside the child's family?

Seventh-graders ask:

How can you convince your mother you're old enough to make your own decisions?
Should I get upset when my parents fight?
Why do some parents let their kids smoke before they are sixteen?
Why do parents shut off their kids when they get drunk or take drugs? Avoid telling their children the facts of life?
If I told my parents I had a boy friend, would they laugh or take it seriously?

And eighth-graders, too, plaintively speak of strong desire for better understanding and communication with family members, especially parents:

How can I get along with my father?
How do you cope with your parents' fights?
What if there is intensive drinking in your family?
What do you do if your parents divorce and you have to go with one of them?
Parents have such different values from their children. How can you explain what's coming off and keep their trust?
Parents do not trust their children.
Why does sex ring such an awful bell in parents' minds?
Why do some parents disapprove sex education in the schools?

Social Concerns

Some upper-grade boys and girls extend their concern beyond the immediate environment, asking:

Why is there a scapegoat in every group?
Why do some people have love and understanding in their hearts and some have hatred?
Why are there different races of people? Why do people talk different languages; have different skin, traits and abilities?

Students are sufficiently concerned about smoking, drinking and drug abuse that they recommend teaching in grades five and six "the truth" about why people indulge, how body and brain are affected, how people become addicted, and how one can be helped to stop these habits.

My brother takes dope, so what should I do?
Tell me what drugs look like, so I can protect myself against pushers.

Some are infuriated that older people continue to smoke "when they know what it will do" and with newspapers, magazines and television in advertising them. They are impatient that the law, the "government," does not prohibit manufacture.

Proposed Timetables

In recommending early education in these and sex matters,
support of the grades nine to twelve groups, who think the high schoⁿ.
are too late to teach about any of these issues. Twelfth-graders say:

Attitudes of maleness and femaleness are formed by kindergarten.

Teach attitudes toward cliques, competition, dating, going steady, etc. Help students choose a good and trusty date.

The health program should begin at home and then be taken over by the school.

Parents should teach their children about sex, but most of them don't. They are embarrassed. Some don't know enough.

Parents don't tell us. There's no place except the school to help us students.

I hope the kids in the years to come will have it better than I did in the way of having education in the facts of life. This survey won't help me, but I sure hope something is done for the children in the years ahead.

In fact, the total report indicates, in charts based on the suggestions of young people and others drawn up by the analysts, that probably grades six to eight should carry the major responsibility for teaching students about human growth and development, including family life and sex relations, social-emotional development, and social problems in which they may soon become involved. A chapter that includes an account of the flow of interests in all topics from grades kindergarten to twelve should help teachers and curriculum builders locate points of high interest and reduce repetition in teaching.

Reprise

The evidence shows clearly that boys and girls of ten to thirteen are not placid and unconcerned but are keenly aware of situations threatening their well-being, eager to cope with the present and be ready to meet the future. They appreciate the worth of a good body and mind. They desire profoundly to have the persistent and faithful love and trust of their parents or, lacking that, of some understanding adult. They yearn for opportunities to talk with peers, to raise questions, and to have honest answers from a knowledgeable adult. They want very much to be assured of steady development as competent people. They say, in effect:

Here am I, help me to be all that I may become.

Combined References for Chapter 2

Asayama, S. Comparison of sexual development of American and Japanese adolescents. *Psychologia*, 1957, 1, 129-131.

Baldwin, B. T. Physical growth and school progress: A study in experimental education. United States Bureau of Education, 1914, Bulletin No. 10, Whole No. 581.

Baldwin, B. T. The determination of sex maturation in boys by a laboratory method. *Journal of Comparative Psychology*, 1928, 8, 39-43.

Boas, F. Studies in growth. *Human Biology*, 1932, 4, 307-350.

Bonney, M. E. A socioeconomic study of the relationship of some factors to mutual friendships in the elementary, secondary, and college levels. *Sociometry*, 1946, 9, 21-47.

Bottyan, O., Dezso, Gy., Eiben, O., Farkas, Gy., Rajkai, T., Thoma, A., and Veli, Gy. Age at menarche in Hungarian girls. *Annales Historico-Naturales Musei Nationalis Hungarici Pars Anthropologica*, 1963, 55, 561-572.

Bowditch, H. P. The growth of children. 8th Annual Report. Massachusetts State Board of Health, 1877, pp. 273-324.

Bower, P. A. The relation of physical, mental and personality factors to popularity in adolescent boys. Unpublished doctoral dissertation. University of California, Berkeley, 1941.

Boyd, E. Weight of the thymus and its component parts and number of Hasall corpuscles in health and in disease. *American Journal of Diseases of Children*, 1936, 51, 313-335.

Boynton, B. The physical growth of girls between birth and eighteen years. *University of Iowa Studies in Child Welfare*, 1936, 12, (4), 105.

Bryan, A. H. and Greenberg, B. G. Methodology in the study of physical measurements of school children. *Human Biology*, 1952, 24, 117-144.

Chang, K. S. F., Ng, C. K., Lee, M. M. C., Chan, S. J. Sexual maturation of Chinese boys in Hong Kong. *Pediatrics*, 1966, 37, 804-811.

Dimock, H. S. *Rediscovering the Adolescent: A Study of Personality Development in Adolescent Boys.* New York: Associated Press, 1937.

Faust, M. S. Developmental maturity as a determinant in prestige of adolescent girls. Unpublished doctoral dissertation. Stanford University, 1957.

Flory, C. D. Predicting puberty. *Child Development*, 1935, 6, 1-6.

Foll, C. V. The age of menarche in Assam and Burma. *Archives of Disease in Childhood*, 1961, 36, 302-304.

Frank, L. K. Personality development in adolescent girls. *Monograph of the Society for Research of Child Development*, 1953, 16, No. 53.

Fried, R. I. & Smith, E. Postmenarcheal growth patterns. *Journal of Pediatrics*, 1962, 61, 562-565.

Friedenberg, E. Z. *Dignity of Youth and Other Atavisms*. Boston: Beacon Press, 1965.

Fry, E. I., Chang, K. S. F., Lee, M. M. C., and Ng, C. K. The amount and distribution of subcutaneous tissue in Southern Chinese children from Hong Kong. *American Journal of Physical Anthropology*, 1965, 23, 69-80.

Greulich, W. W. Physical changes in adolescence. *NSSE Yearbook*, 1944, 43 (1), 8-32.

Greulich, W. W., Dorfman, R. I., Catchpole, H. R., Solomon, C. I., & Culotta, C. S. Somatic and endocrine studies of puberal and adolescent boys. *Monographs*, Society for Research in Child Development, 1942, 7 (3), 85.

Greulich, W. W., and Thomas, H. The growth and development of the pelvis of individual girls before, during, and after puberty. *Yale Journal of Biology and Medicine*, 1944, 17, 91-97.

Hansman, C. F. & Maresh, M. M. A longitudinal study of skeletal maturation. *American Journal of Diseases of Children*, 1961, 101, 305-321.

Heimendinger, J. Die ergehnisse von korpermessungen an 5000 basler kidern von 2-18 jahren. *Nelvelica Paediatrica* Acta, 1964, 19, Suppl. 13, 91-95.

Inoue, T. & Shimizu, M. *Physical and Skeletal Growth and Development of Japanese Children*. Tokyo: Japan Society for the Promotion of Science, 1965.

Jerome, E. K. Change of voice in male adolescents. *Quarterly Journal of Speech*, 1937, 23, 648-653.

Jones, H. E. *Development in Adolescence*. New York: Appleton-Century-Crofts, 1943.

Jones, H. E. Adolescence in our society. In *The Family in a Democratic Society*. New York: Columbia University Press, 1949a, pp. 70-82.

Jones, H. E. *Motor Performance and Growth*. Berkeley: University of California Press, 1949b.

Jones, H. E. & Bayley, N. Physical maturing among boys as related to behavior. *Journal of Educational Psychology*, 1950, 41, 129-148.

Jones, M. C. Adolescent friendships. *American Psychologist*, 1948, 3, 352.

Jones, M. C. & Mussen, P. H. Self-conceptions, motivations, and interpersonal attitudes of early- and late-maturing girls. *Child Development*, 1958, 29, 491-501.

Jung, F. T. & Shafton, A. L. The mammary gland in the normal adolescent male. *Proceedings*, Society for Experimental Biology and Medicine, 1935, 33, 455-458.

Kagan, J., Moss, H. A., and Sigel, I. E. The psychological significance of styles of conceptualization. In J. F. Wright and J. Kagan (Eds.) *Monograph of Social Research in Child Development*, 1962.

Knott, V. B. & Meredith, H. V. Statistics on eruption of the permanent dentition from serial data for North American white children. *Angle Orthodontist*, 1966, 36, 68-79.

Krogman, W. Some thoughts on football in pre- and early adolescence. (mimeographed) 1954.

Kubitschek, P. E. Sexual development of boys with special reference to the appearance of secondary sex characteristics and their relation to structural and personality types. *Journal of Nervous and Mental Disease*, 1932, 76, 425-451.

Landis, C. et al. *Sex in Development.* New York: Hoeber, 1940.

Lee, M. C., Chang, K. S. F., & Chan, M. C. Sexual maturation of Chinese girls in Hong Kong. *Pediatrics,* 1963, 32, 389-398.

McNemar, Q. *Psychological statistics.* New York: Wiley, 1955.

Meredith, H. V. The rhythm of physical growth: A study of eighteen anthropometric measurements. *University of Iowa Studies in Child Welfare,* 1939, 11(3), 128.

Meredith, H. V. Stature of Massachusetts children of North European and Italian lineage. *American Journal of Physical Anthropology,* 1939, 24, 301-346.

Meredith, H. V. Selected anatomic variables analyzed for interage relationships of the size-size, size-gain, and gain-gain varieties. In L. P. Lipsitt and C. C. Spiker (Eds.) *Advances in Child Development and Behavior.* New York: Academic Press, 1965, 2, 221-256.

Meredith, H. V. Synopsis of puberal changes in youth: *Journal of School Health,* 1967, 37, 171-176.

Michelson, N. Studies in the physical development of Negroes: IV. Onset of puberty. *American Journal of Physical Anthropology,* 1944, 2, 151-166.

Milicer, H. and Szczotka, F. Age at menarche in Warsaw girls in 1965. *Human Biology,* 1966, 38, 199-203.

Mills, C. A., and Ogle, C. Physiologic sterility of adolescence. *Human Biology,* 1936, 8, 607-615.

Montagu, M. F. A. *Adolescent Sterility.* Springfield, Ill.: Charles C. Thomas, 1946.

Mussen, P. H., Conger, J. J., and Kagan, J. *Child Development and Personality.* New York: Harper, 1963.

Mussen, P. H., and Jones, Mary C. Self-conceptions, motivations and interpersonal attitudes of late and early maturing boys. *Child Development,* 1957, 28, 243-256.

Nicolson, A. B. and Haney, C. Indices of physiological maturity: Derivation and interrelationships. *Child Development,* 1953, 24, 3-38.

Oettle, A. G. & Higginson, J. The age of menarche in South African Bantu (Negro) girls. *Human Biology,* 1961, 33, 181-190.

Priesel, R. & Wagner, R. Gesetzmassingkeiten in Auftreten der extra-genitalen sekundaren geschlechsmerkmale bie madchen. *Zeitschrift fur Konstitutionslehre,* 1931, 15, 333-352.

Pyror, H. B. Certain physical and physiological aspects of adolescent development in girls. *Journal of Pediatrics,* 1936, 8, 52-62.

Reynolds, E. L. The distribution of subcutaneous fat in childhood and adolescence. *Monographs,* Society for Research in Child Development, 1950, 15(2), 189.

Reynolds, E. L. & Wines, J. V. Individual differences in physical changes associated with adolescence in girls. *American Journal of Diseases of Children,* 1948, 75, 329-350.

Richey, H. G. The relation of accelerated, normal and retarded puberty to the height and weight of school children. *Child Development Monographs,* 1937, 2, No. 1.

Sabharwal, K. P., Morales, S., & Mendez, J. Body measurements and creatinine excretion among upper and lower socio-economic groups of girls in Guatemala. *Human Biology,* 1966, 38, 131-140.

Scammon, R. E. The measurement of the body in childhood. In J. A. Harris, et al. (Eds.) *The Measurement of Man.* Minneapolis: University of Minnesota Press, 1930, pp. 173-215.

Schonfeld, W. A. Primary and secondary sexual characteristics, study of their development in males from birth through maturity, with biometric study of penis and testes. *American Journal of Diseases of Children*, 1943, 65, 535-549.

Scott, J. A. Report on the heights and weights (and other measurements) of school pupils in the County of London in 1959. London: London County Council, No. 1961.

Seckel, H. P. G., Scott, W. W. & Benditt, E. P. Six examples of precocious sexual development. *American Journal of Diseases in Children*, 1949, 78, 484-515.

Shuttleworth, F. K. Sexual maturation and the physical growth of girls age six to nineteen. *Monographs*, Society for Research in Child Development, 1937, 2(5), p. 253.

Shuttleworth, F. K. The physical and mental growth of girls and boys age 6 to 19 in relation to age at maximum growth. *Monographs*, Society for Research in Child Development, 1939, 4(3), p. 291.

Simmons, K. The Brush Foundation study of child growth and development: II. Physical growth and development. *Monographs*, Society for Research in Child Development, 1944, 9(1), p. 87.

Simmons, K. & Greulich, W. W. Menarchael age and the height, weight, and skeletal age of girls age 7 to 17. *Journal of Pediatrics*, 1943, 22, 518-548.

Stolz, H. R. & Stolz, L. M. *Somatic Development of Adolescent Boys*. New York: Macmillan, 1951.

Stone, C. P. & Barker, R. G. The attitudes and interests of premenarcheal and postmenarcheal girls. *Journal of Genetic Psychology*, 1939, 54, 27-71.

Tanner, J. M. The trend towards earlier physical maturation. In J. E. Meade and A. S. Parkes (Eds.) *Biological Aspects of Social Problems*. London: Oliver and Boyd, 1965.

Tanner, J. M. & O'Keeffe, B. Age at menarche in Nigerian school girls, with a note on their heights and weights from age 12 to 19. *Human Biology*, 1962, 34, 187-196.

Todd, T. W. Integral growth of the face: I. The nasal area. *International Journal of Orthodontia and Oral Surgery*, 1936, 22, 321-332.

Towns, J., Johnson, J. M., & Roche, A. F. The age of menarche in Melbourne schoolgirls. *Australian Paediatric Journal*, 1966, 2, 67-69.

Tryon, Carolyn M. Evaluations of adolescent personality by adolescents. *Monographs of Social Research in Child Development*, 4, No. 4, 1939.

Tryon, Carolyn M. The adolescent peer culture. *Yearbook of the National Social Studies Education*, 1944, 3, 217-239.

Tuddenham, R. D. & Snyder, M. M. Physical growth of California boys and girls from birth to eighteen years. University of California Publications Child Development, 1954, 1(2), 183-364.

Vlastovsky, V. G. The secular trend in the growth and development of children and young persons in the Soviet Union. *Human Biology*, 1966, 38, 219-230.

Watson, E. H. & Lowrey, G. H. *Growth and Development of Children*. 3rd ed. Chicago: Year Book Publishers, 1958.

Zukowski, W., Kmietowicz-Zukowska, A., & Gruska, S. The age of menarche in Polish girls. *Human Biology*, 1964, 36, 233-234.

CHAPTER 3 **sex differences**

Introduction

The importance of the many physical changes encountered from nine to thirteen years cannot be minimized. As preadolescents move through this age period they move toward developing more complete sex roles and become increasingly aware of the basic sex differences with which they must learn to function. Recognition of such basic differences carries with it the clarifying pursuit of sex role identification. Lynn describes this as, "The internalization of the role considered appropriate to a given sex and to the unconscious reactions characteristic of that role (1962, p. 555)." It has also been suggested that youth should have a sex role preference, usually founded in parental identification, and, subsequently, adopt the appropriate sex role (Lynn, 1959, Rogers, 1972).

Traditionally, sex role preference has been interpreted to mean that boys should identify with males and girls should identify with females. The adoption of such roles meant accepting the work-provider role attitude among boys and the wife-mother role attitude among girls (Havighurst, 1952). In researching this hypothesis, Lynn found that "males tend to identify with a cultural stereotype of the masculine role, whereas females tend to identify with aspects of their mothers' own role specifically (1959, p. 130)."

Recent social changes however, have had significant effects on breaking down the stereotypes reported by Havighurst and Lynn. The effects of increased industrialization, the shift from a rural to an urban American, and the effects of World War II, have provided alternative roles in our society (Thornburg, 1971), a phenomenon described as depolarization by Winick (1968). Such alternatives are increasingly available for the female. While men may still find it easier to fit into a role expected by society, it is now challenged by women who are playing an increasingly competitive role as decreasing interest in the traditional wife-mother role becomes prevalent

(Dornbusch, 1966). This is repeatedly demonstrated by an increasing desire for advanced education among women, increasing community service, a female sexual precocity once characteristic of the male only, greater occupational involvement by women, more recognition in the performing arts, a greater movement toward unisexual appearance, and better planned child-rearing practices (Thornburg, 1970).

Yet, the developing preadolescent recognizes basic differences between the sexes in his search for identity. This poses a twofold question: (1) Are the changing sex roles so ambiguous and fluctuating that the preadolescent has no sex-type preference? and (2) Will the depolarization of male/masculinity and female/femininity have an effect on the developing preadolescent's role adoption? Winick (1968) seems to think so. He suggests that "multivalent, amorphous, and depolarized roles might theoretically lead to increased flexibility and options in behavior, but in actuality may tend to invoke uncertainty (p. 24)." He further asserts that it is not the kind of family structure that is as important as the distinct division of labor and responsibilities which determines the emerging sex role.

What is the desirability of modifying one's sex role? Is it likely that the developing preadolescent could better understand basic life processes and develop more effective interactions if some depolarization took place? Rogers contends that preadolescent boys adopt rigid masculine patterns, the effect of which is restrictive in their cognitive processes and interpersonal experiences. She states, "Either hypermasculinity or hypomasculinity, both of which may be related to underlying sex-role conflict, may produce problems in emotional and intellectual development, although more research is needed to verify this theory (1972, p. 124)." In addition, Bruce (1967) feels that the male is unnecessarily hemmed in by the restrictions imposed by his masculinity and, thus, denied some primary outlets for expression that are ordinarily considered to be the sole prerogatives of the feminine world. Also, there is a tendency in our society to judge a man who has unisexual appearances as being effeminate, a generalization without foundation. The conflict arising within the preadolescent is the fact that on the surface sex roles are externally represented as more depolarized, but functionally they reflect those standards long held to be exclusively masculine or feminine. Thus, the inner conflict leads to role confusion.

The three articles in chapter three will enlarge upon the issues presented here. In the first article (p. 83) Irene Josselyn discusses three major sources of sexual identity. First, she attributes sexual identity to inherent biological differences between the sexes, an idea which has already been suggested as a major awareness of the developing preadolescent. This, of course, is accentuated by the functional roles determined for each sex. Josselyn suggests that the second source of sexual identity comes out of the mores of the culture in which a person is reared. Josselyn uses cross-cultural data to establish this point. She feels that American culture is not well enough defined to clearly delineate identifying sex roles. Finally, Josselyn points to the attitudes of emotionally meaningful people in the preadolescents' environment as an identity source.

It is within the area of emotionally meaningful people (usually one's parents), where many writers feel the sources of sexual identity lie. This is especially true with parental identification. The second article on sexual identity is written by David Lynn and it focuses on parental influences on sex-role behavior. Generally, Lynn has found that boys attach to cultural expectations more than girls, while girls are more strongly attached to the mother's role than the cultural expectation for females.

Lynn cogently suggests several factors, thirteen in all, that are research supported which show the influence of parents upon the child's sex-role identification. Among those listed by Lynn are: (1) social learning experiences and their positive or negative effects; (2) the greater prestige given to the masculine rather than feminine role in our society; (3) greater ridicule among boys than girls for adopting the opposite sex role; and (4) greater difficulty among males than females in achieving the same sex-identification.

In contrast to Lynn, the work of Grambs and Waetjen (1966) stresses the importance of considering the classroom as a source for learning sex roles. They contend that learning proceeds according to individual differences and that instructional provisions are not flexible enough to meet such differences. Attention is drawn to the feminine-oriented school. If there is acceptance of the idea that sex role identity is gained from teachers as well as from parents, the feminization within the school will potentially lead to an imbalance in male-female sex role identification models. The authors assert that the schools should (a) have a more balanced male-female teaching staff, and (b) provide a broader base for interpreting the appropriate social-sex behavior of students.

The final article to be considered in this chapter focuses on the aforementioned comments about sources of sexual identity, considering their effects within the role behaviors expressed in contemporary society. Roessler discusses some of the problems within the masculine role and the constancy of the feminine role. This article distinguishes itself from the two previous articles in three ways. First, the author is convinced that the male role is more difficult to learn than the female role. This is advanced because Roessler holds that there is an inharmonious relationship between the required present role and the expected future role of the male. This differentiation perpetuates confusion rather than stability in sex role behavior.

Secondly, Roessler asserts that there is more constancy in the female's role and, thus, stability is demonstrated in her behavior. The author bases this statement around the supposition that even if the female is uncertain about some things, she is certain that she can be a wife and mother. Roessler thinks such constancy frees the female to help the male better realize his role, thus helping him shift from differentiation toward constancy.

It's not certain that Roessler's contentions can hold up under scientific research, and, in fact, this author (Thornburg, 1971) contends that changing social behavior may be causing as much confusion in female sex role adoption as it is in the male. Roessler does not preclude this possibility. He points to some of the alternative roles available to the female in our culture. It is likely that the increasing participation of females in sex role alternatives will change the supportive male-female interaction as we have known it traditionally. A deemphasis of subtleties and an increasing aggressiveness by females will force a new type of male-female relationship. Cross-sex roles and identity may help the traditional female play a modern role or it may create uncertainties in the role she should play. It cannot help but have effects on masculine identity, a factor which will likely be accepted by the more contemporary males but rejected by the traditional males in our society. And what about man? A capsule summary might read this way:

MAN! The rugged individualist who can start at the bottom and work to the top. The spirit of America personified on the moon. The consumer of *Playboy* and comparable literature. The sports car enthusiast who takes in Indy and dreams of LeMans. The individual who is theoretical head of the house. The girl watcher. The sloppy Saturday clothes chap who dresses neat and trim for his Sunday church appearance. The beer and peanuts man who is proud to announce he didn't miss a single pro-football game on TV. The lovable character whose occasional smile betrays his authoritarian facade. The money earner. The intimate character who sips cocktails while looking into the sexy eyes of a female. The masculine figure who projects masculinity on his son from birth through adolescence. The fighter and upholder of democracy. The individual who gets love confused with sex. MAN!

But what if you are a preadolescent and the prospect of coping with these social expectancies is overwhelming? Maybe football isn't really all that important. Besides, long hair is a way of expressing individuality. In addition, clothing and appearance are changing. Depolarization is occurring. Sex roles are becoming less distinctive. In analysis, it is logical to go back to Josselyn's three sources of sexual identity. If the preadolescent can be provided with a growing understanding of his changing body this will help him perceive emerging feelings about self. Equally important is the awareness of cultural factors that may affect his emerging role identity. In the case of the preadolescent boy this means that the previously described stereotype does not have to be perpetuated. For the preadolescent girl, greater self-assertion can be exercised. Finally, Josselyn pointed to adult identity. Today such identity models are varied, but are nonetheless effective in shaping the preadolescent's sex role identification; we must apprise him of the alternative roles available, the accepted social practices, and offer guidance in such sex role identification during the period of preadolescence.

The Sources of Sexual Identity
IRENE M. JOSSELYN

Editor's Note:
Josselyn's article was selected as the introductory article to this chapter on sex differences and identity because it essentially does just that – it introduces the reader to the concept of sexual identity and then discusses some of the sources from which ongoing sexual identity is derived.

Josselyn contends that within the United States there is no widely accepted social role for a man and woman. This has been heightened at different times in history, the most significant perhaps being immediately following World War I, a factor due primarily to industrial change and an accelerated living pace within our society.

The author sees the family as the primary identity source with children mainly identifying with the same-sex parent regardless of the logic or absurdity of the identification response. By keeping in mind Josselyn's statement about the family as a source of identity, a more defined concept becomes available for reading Lynn's article on learning parental and sex role identity.

H.D.T.

To deal psychologically with the questions of sexual differences, sexual roles, and the effect of external circumstances on the individual child's orientation to his own sexual identity, many factors must be considered. Some are universal; others are more specific to the culture in which the child is reared or are idiosyncratic to the particular child.

Of special significance are three major sources of sexual identity that determine a person's concept of himself and of others as male or female:

Reprinted by permission of the author and publisher from the *National Elementary Principal*, 1966, 46 (2), 25-29.

1) the inherent biological differences between the sexes; 2) the conceptualizations and mores of the culture in which he is reared; and 3) the attitudes of those emotionally meaningful in childhood — parents or, in some instances, other persons who may function in certain areas more effectively than the parents.

It is self-evident that the male and female in the human species are biologically different. This is true of the higher species generally. In the human species, the biological difference has been expanded as a result of the functional roles defined for each sex. It has been suggested that this has occurred partly because of the human being's long period of gestation and dependency. However, this is not the sole answer. There are other species in which both the gestation period and the dependency period of the infant are long. But, unlike some of these species which turned to the herd to handle the problems created by helpless young, human beings defined different functional roles for each sex in order to care for the young. The female was assigned the responsibility not only of nurturing the infant but also of providing general care for it. The male's role was to protect the mother and child from external harm and to bring them food. For this he was rewarded by sharing the home the mother created out of the shelter he provided. From this functional differentiation and the resulting interdependency, many related sex roles developed.

As different cultures evolved, the extension of the sexually defined roles did not follow identical pathways. Primitive tribes differ in defining the functions of the male and female in the tribal structure, but in any tribe there is a clear delineation between the tasks that are the responsibility of one sex and those which are the responsibility of the other. In less primitive cultures, there is less clarity of roles, but certain differences are discernible.

Thus, at the present time in some less primitive groups, the man is the authoritative person in the home and the mother is the loving and comforting one. In some advanced cultures, the senior members of the family continue to control the younger members even after they have formed families of their own. There are cultures in which the mother is the center of the family and the father depreciated or absent from the home. There are cultures in which the woman is sheltered from the outside world, incased in a golden cocoon if she is of the upper social groups or in a prison of drudgery if she is of the lower economic group. There are cultures in which the differentiation of the sexes' roles is limited to their biological functions, and the care of the child is relegated to the state.

A child brought up in a primitive culture that clearly structures the role of the man and woman does not have the responsibility for his future sexually determined self-concept. His environment defines it for him. His sole responsibility is to accept and fulfill the role that he is given because of his sex. To the extent that a more advanced culture defines his sex role less clearly, the child has some discretion about his sexual identity in adulthood.

A child reared in the United States lives in a society which does not sharply outline the significance of his sex. There is no predetermined, universally accepted social role for the man and for the woman. As a nation that has been a melting pot for a variety of cultures, we have not developed a culture of our own. There are few customs or taboos that offer the child guidelines in proceeding toward his adult identity as a man or woman.

It is the parent who interprets the culture to the child and first imposes conformity to it. Our children are reared by parents who often do not have a clear concept of male and female roles. Their attitudes are partly rooted in the past, determined by the national origin of their own parents or grandparents. Yet these old concepts have been blurred by contact with different cultures, without the new culture offering a sharp alternative.

For example, a refugee Jewish family with an orthodox background have within their family structure a clearly defined role for the man and the woman. They may live next door to a Jewish family who have had their home in the United States for several generations and to whom orthodox Judaism is as foreign as Catholicism. The man's and woman's roles in the two families would be quite in contrast. To find a place for themselves in the new world, the refugee family must make some changes. They may envy the ease with which their neighbors enjoy a different life but be tortured by the question of whether this new life is the good life. What should they accept? Inevitably, they will be confused; they will be unpredictable in their responses and will try to justify retaining some of the old life and accepting some of the new — depending on what they find satisfying.

I recall an orthodox Jewish couple who had been in the United States for several years. Their marriage was about to break up. The problems seemed to center around the man's insistence upon his own orthodoxy and his wife's objection. The most frequent quarrels concerned the Sabbath. He wished to obey the laws of the Sabbath and thus to come home from Temple to spend the day in appropriate discussions with men of equal religious erudition. His wife objected. Her objection, however, proved not to be over his wish to observe the Sabbath. It was because her husband insisted she clean the house while he went to Temple and then have a hot meal prepared for as many guests as he would invite to join him when he returned home. She suggested she prepare food that did not require cooking. To this he answered, "What would my friends think if you didn't give them a good meal? I'll be orthodox. You don't need to keep the Sabbath; you don't believe in it." It is not surprising that a child in this family showed marked confusion in many areas — not just about religion but also about the responsibilities and privileges of man and woman.

The confusion about sex roles has further been heightened by the fact that since about World War I, even the old, firmly established cultures have increasingly given way to change. Generally, in those countries with which the United States is most closely linked, the definition of the male and female role has become obscured. This shift lessens the value of the culture as a protection against the confusion created by lack of a current definition of roles. As a result, the little boy or little girl today grows up in an environment peopled by adults who do not know, beyond the facts of procreation, what the roles of the male and the female are!

There is an interesting parallel development which is in contrast to the apparent confusion of sex roles. Not so many years ago, all babies irrespective of sex, were garbed in "baby dresses"; their hair grew until the tragic time when the little boy's curls were cut off, perhaps not until his second or third year of life. Little Lord Fauntleroy was the prototype of the child every mother wished her young son to be.

Now, in contrast, the first strands of hair on the little boy's head that might exceed the masculine norm are clipped off. He is dressed from birth in boylike clothes. The little girl also has the privilege of wearing clothes easier to manage than the old dresses, and there is the possibility the baby girl will be misidentified as a boy. However, these new clothes have usually been given a feminine touch for her. Thus it is easier to recognize the sex of an infant than it was in the past. This may justify the conclusion that our society wishes to differentiate between males and females, even though in many areas it fosters confusion.

The Family's Part in Sex Differentiation

The typical family helps the small child to recognize his own sex and to contrast himself with a person of the opposite sex. The preschool boy is gradually introduced to boys' toys. To gratify his wish for something soft to cuddle, he is customarily given a huggable animal, while the little girl, even though she has fluffy animals, is presented also with a doll. The little boy is soon deprived of the pleasure of tears. He is reminded that boys are brave and do not cry. His mother may find it difficult to limit her comforting when her son is injured or unhappy, but if she overindulges herself, father soon protests that she will make a sissy of his son. The little girl is more typically encouraged to seek comfort; often her father most readily offers solace, her mother becoming, at times, a little suspicious that perhaps the tears exceed the pain.

In other subtle ways, the average parent helps the child in his attempt to find his role in the social world. On the whole, the little girl is encouraged to follow feminine interests — to "help" her mother cook and clean for example — and thus to play a game of being a housewife and mother. The little boy is encouraged to follow his father's interests and activities. He is encouraged to pretend he is a truck driver, an auto mechanic, a fireman, or a doctor — encouraged, in other words, to play at a vocation. He also "helps" with other tasks around the home defined as masculine — mowing the lawn, washing the car.

An interesting complication may follow this early emulation of the parent of the same sex — a complication that leads to recognition of the specific roles for each sex, but not to pleasure. The child is encouraged to pretend that he is doing sex-appropriate tasks, but they are often tasks for which the parents are quite free in expressing dislike. The jobs the parents don't like are often the ones that are passed on to the children once they are old enough to perform them. Mother complains of having to cook, wash dishes, and dust; father talks of his hard day at the office and wishes aloud that he did not have to mow the lawn. Then comes the day when the daughter can wash dishes and the son can mow the lawn! It is questionable whether many parents assign the child work to do around the home that they themselves really enjoy doing. They don't deprive themselves of their own pleasure in order to show the child that the role of a man or a woman in the daily routine of living is fun.

The Role of Identification in Self-Concept

As the child becomes aware of his sex, he typically identifies with the parent of the same sex. His attitudes toward his future role in society will be significantly affected by his impression of that parent and by the way the other parent responds to the parent with whom he identifies. To understand how the child sees himself in terms of this sexual identity, it is necessary to know how the sexual roles in the family are defined. Because of the lack of a cultural norm, it cannot be assumed that the role of either sex is defined with unanimity among a group of children.

Consider, for example, a boy of a minority group whose father has been gainfully employed only in irregular manual labor and whose mother holds a much respected position as secretary in the public school the child attends. The child may be uninterested in school achievement. This may be due to his self-concept as a male through identification with his father in the role assigned to the man in that particular cultural group or in the family. Or in contrast, the boy may be very much interested in academic achievement. This commendable point of view may have healthy roots; it may not. His father may be encouraging him to look toward a future of which the father himself can only dream. He accepts the father's dream as a possible reality. Or the boy may have found another, more successful, masculine figure with whom to identify and may have erased much of his identification with the father. He then will wish to gain an education in order to complete his identification with a successful male.

On the other hand, the child may have shifted the person with whom to identify and chosen his mother as his ideal. If this is limited to her academic interest, it will prove to be a positive factor in his life. However, it should be borne in mind that an unsatisfactory father can lead the little boy to seek a feminine answer for his role in life — a choice fraught with complications and frustrations.

As another example, a little girl may show little interest in academic work. Her father may be a person who, either because of his own cultural background or in order to feel he is important, insists that women must be subordinate drudges. The mother may have complied and shown no interest in learning. The little girl, in accepting herself as female, may identify with the mother and, like her, woo the father by being a dumb drudge. On the other hand, the little girl may strive hard to create a role for herself as a woman but, in contrast to her mother, do so by rebelling against her father. She will thereby free herself to fulfill her own potential and be eager to learn. However, the girl's intellectual interest may have a disturbing core. She may be identifying with her father and assuming that she has a right to the prerogatives of men. She will then struggle to deny her biologically determined role as a woman, a role she depreciates as her father depreciates her mother.

A child's self-concept as a male or female is also affected by other kinds of family patterns. Any family situation in which circumstances place a parent in a role more typically identified with the opposite sex can lead to serious confusion for the child. The effect will probably be most significant at two periods in the child's life: during the early years when he is first clarifying his biological identity, and in adolescence when he is intensely preoccupied with thoughts of whom he will become as an adult. Thus, whenever divorce, illness, death, or some other cause requires a parent to be both father and mother, the child does not receive a clear-cut picture of role differences.

Or if parents are constantly struggling to be dominant in the home rather than respecting the complementary roles a man and woman should have in the family, the child may internalize the conflict and within himself be a battleground for the battle of the sexes. He also may carry the struggle into his own social world, always seeing a person of the opposite sex as someone he must best.

There are certainly innumerable examples of the disastrous consequences to the developing character and personality of a child if, for any reason, he is unable or unwilling to recognize and accept his own sex identity and find constructive gratification in the role that identity creates for him.

There are many ways in which the child can be helped to attain a healthy and fulfilling self-concept, despite unfortunate family relationships or situations. It is obvious that a child reared in a family situation which does not foster healthy identification and recognition of the complementary role of the other sex needs to know other adults who will offer what the home lacks. There are many reasons why this is easier to outline in theory than to carry out in reality. However, recognition of the difficulty can lead to some positive steps that will be practical and helpful.

It should also be borne in mind that children have a remarkable capacity to surmount difficulties. Too often, we think of the child who has not surmounted such problems and generalize that no child could deal construc-tively with the situation. Actually, we can only say that certain children will be unable to grow up without serious psychological scars if reared under certain conditions. Since we cannot know which child will use an unfortunate situation constructively and which child will be seriously scarred by it, it is important that adverse circumstances be alleviated for all children to the extent possible.

The Future Cultural Pattern

At the beginning of this article, the lack of clear, cultural patterns for the role of man and woman was pointed out. The problems raised by this situation are not easily answered, even theoretically. It is important that an individual value himself in the framework of his sexual identity and that he see the role of the opposite sex as complementary, not as antagonistic or contemptible. But unless we can conceptualize what the sex-determined roles are and how they can be gratifying, how can we expect acceptance of a sex-determined identity? Any attempt to answer this question is far beyond the scope of this paper or the author's erudition, but I would like to explore briefly one facet of the problem.

It is frequently stated, explicitly or implicitly, that the woman's primary and most gratifying role is as a wife and mother. She should have an education because an education will make her a better wife and mother. She must also have an education so that if she doesn't marry, or if with marriage some exigency arises, she can be self-supporting. Her education must provide skills as well as abstract knowledge. In preparing the woman for these various possibilities, we open vistas that electric dishwashers, frozen foods, and drip-dry clothes can never match. The mother's daily, twenty-four hour care of the child is now often limited to the first two or three years. Day-care centers, once a blessing for the working mother, have become nursery schools which, many believe, are a growth-promoting experience for the child. They markedly shorten the daily hours of mothering. The mother's education has *not* prepared her to do "busy work," and automation has deprived her of the tasks that filled the hours for her grandmother.

At the same time, how are boys to find a sense of fulfilling their masculine roles when they have no unique future except to be the sole support of their family in the few years before the children are all in school? After that, the family's support could be assumed by the mother. And the male's role of providing physical protection for his family has long ago been taken over by other agencies.

And yet, a woman's ability to support herself or to supplement the family income is not of minor importance. Families are small these days and there may be no relatives to turn to for help. Aunts and uncles, if there are any, do not willingly support a widow with children. Parents, brothers and sisters do not willingly support a spinster for life. And families do want second cars, dancing and music lessons — all of the financially burdensome and supposedly essential aspects of the good life.

At one time, teaching at the elementary level, nursing, and social work provided the acceptable careers for women; other professions were for men. Men now have invaded the fields formerly the prerogative of women and have proved so valuable that those professions are no longer the sole province of women. And women are now admitted to professional schools to be trained for professions once considered to be for men only. As a result, the previously sex-determined professions are rapidly losing their sexual identity.

Women seek to develop interests and activities outside the home, as they taste aspects of life other than those identified with their primary roles of wife and mother and as these roles become less time consuming. Men, having enjoyed the asexual companionship of women with whom they share common interests, do not wish women to be confined solely to their biological functions. Is it not possible that the future differentiation between men and women will become increasingly limited to the biological differences and the specifics that are determined by the needs of the small child? This does not necessarily imply a narrowing of sexual identity. The woman who values her feminine identification will respond differently in many situations than a man who values his masculine identity. The difference in response need not lead to a battle of the sexes; it could lead to enrichment for both.

If this is the future cultural pattern, the challenge that must be met is to help children accept their own sex with a sense of fulfillment, value the complementary role of the opposite sex, and not contaminate those areas of activity and interest which are not sex-specific by attributing sexually determined implications to them. Fathers do not have to kill the wild animal in order to protect their families and provide food. Mothers do not have to cure the meat and prepare the hide for use as clothing. But no woman can be a good father; no man can be a good mother. . . . Either sex can write a book!

The Process of Learning Parental and Sex Role Identification

DAVID B. LYNN

Editor's Note:

This article by Lynn is one of the classic pieces of writing in the area of learning parental and sex role identification. The article is theoretical in nature, pointing to those two distinct identification systems.

An orientation that might be used in reading this article is to clearly delineate in one's thinking the difference in Lynn's definitions of parental identification and sex role identification. This, then, makes it more probable to read through his thirteen propositions as to how an individual learns identification, while using the two theoretical reference points he establishes at the beginning of his article.

H.D.T.

The purpose of this paper is to summarize the writer's theoretical formulation concerning identification, much of which has been published piecemeal in various journals. Research relevant to new hypotheses is cited, and references are given to previous publications of this writer in which the reader can find evidence concerning the earlier hypotheses. Some of the previously published hypotheses are considerably revised in this paper and, it is hoped, placed in a more comprehensive and coherent framework.

Theoretical Formulation

Before developing specific hypotheses, one must briefly define identification as it is used here. *Parental identification* refers to the internalization of personality characteristics of one's own parent and to unconscious reactions similar to that parent. This is to be contrasted with *sex role identification*, which refers to the internalization of the role typical of a given sex in a particular culture and to the unconscious reactions characteristic of that role.

Reprinted by permission of the author and the National Council on Family Relations from the *Journal of Marriage and the Family*, 1966, 28, 466-470.

Thus, theoretically, an individual might be thoroughly identified with the role typical of his own sex generally and yet poorly identifed with his same-sex parent specifically. This differentiation also allows for the converse circumstances wherein a person is well identified with his same-sex parent specifically and yet poorly identified with the typical same-sex role generally. In such an instance the parent with whom the individual is well identified is himself poorly identified with the typical sex role. An example might be a girl who is closely identified with her mother, who herself is more strongly identified with the masculine than with the feminine role. Therefore, such a girl, through her identification with her mother, is poorly identified with the feminine role (Lynn, 1962).

Formulation of Hypotheses

It is postulated that the initial parental identification of both male and female infants is with the mother. Boys, but not girls, must shift from this initial mother identification and establish masculine-role identification. Typically in this culture the girl has the same-sex parental model for identification (the mother) with her more hours per day than the boy has his same-sex model (the father) with him. Moreover, even when home, the father does not usually participate in as many intimate activities with the child as does the mother, e.g., preparation for bed, toileting. The time spent with the child and the intimacy and intensity of the contact are thought to be pertinent to the process of learning parental identification (Goodfield, 1965). The boy is seldom if ever with the father as he engages in his daily vocational activities, although both boy and girl are often with the mother as she goes through her household activities. Consequently, the father, as a model for the boy, is analogous to a map showing the major outline but lacking most details, whereas the mother, as a model for the girl, might be thought of as a detailed map.

However, despite the shortage of male models, a somewhat stereotyped and conventional masculine role is nonetheless spelled out for the boy, often by his mother and women teachers in the absence of his father and male models. Through the reinforcement of the culture's highly developed system of rewards for typical masculine-role behavior and punishment for signs of femininity, the boy's early learned identification with the mother weakens. Upon this weakened mother identification is welded the later learned identification with a culturally defined, stereotyped masculine role.

(1)* *Consequently, males tend to identify with a culturally defined*

---

*Specific hypotheses are numbered and in italics.

masculine role, whereas females tend to identify with their mothers (Lynn, 1959).

Although one must recognize the contribution of the father in the identification of males and the general cultural influences in the identification of females, it nevertheless seems meaningful, for simplicity in developing this formulation, to refer frequently to *masculine-role identification* in males as distinguished from *mother identification* in females.

Some evidence is accumulating suggesting that (2) *both males and females identify more closely with the mother than with the father.* Evidence is found in support of this hypothesis in a study by Lazowick (1955) in which the subjects were thirty college students. These subjects and their mothers and fathers were required to rate concepts, e.g., "myself," "father," "mother," etc. The degree of semantic similarity as rated by the subjects and their parents was determined. The degree of similarity between fathers and their own children was not significantly greater than that found between fathers and children randomly matched. However, children did share a greater semantic similarity with their own mothers than they did when matched at random with other maternal figures. Mothers and daughters did not share a significantly greater semantic similarity than did mothers and sons.

Evidence is also found in support of Hypothesis 2 in a study by Adams and Sarason (1963) using anxiety scales with male and female high school students and their mothers and fathers. They found that anxiety scores of both boys and girls were much more related to mothers' than to fathers' anxiety scores.

Support for this hypothesis comes from a study in which Aldous and Kell (1961) interviewed fifty middle-class college students and their mothers concerning childrearing values. They found, contrary to their expectations, that a slightly higher proportion of boys than girls shared their mothers' childrearing values.

Partial support for Hypothesis 2 is provided in a study by Gray and Klaus (1956) using the Allport-Vernon-Lindzey Study of Values completed by thirty-four female and twenty-eight male college students and by their parents. They found that the men were not significantly closer to their fathers than to their mothers and also that the men were not significantly closer to their fathers than were the women. However, the women were closer to their mothers than were the men and closer to their mothers than to their fathers.

Note that, in reporting research relevant to Hypothesis 2, only studies of *tested similarity*, not *perceived similarity*, were reviewed. To test this hypothesis, one must measure tested similarity, i.e., measure both the child and the parent on the same variable and compare the similarity between these two measures. This paper is not concerned with perceived similarity, i.e., testing the child on a given variable and then comparing that finding with a measure taken as to how the child thinks his parent would respond. It is this writer's opinion that much confusion has arisen by considering perceived similarity as a measure of parental identification. It seems obvious that, especially for the male, perceived similarity between father and son would usually be closer than tested similarity, in that it is socially desirable for a man to be similar to his father, especially as contrasted to his similarity to his mother. Indeed, Gray and Klaus (1956) found the males' perceived similarity with the father to be closer than tested similarity.

It is hypothesized that the closer identification of males with the mother than with the father will be revealed more clearly on some measures than on others. (3) *The closer identification of males with their mothers than with their fathers will be revealed most frequently in personality variables which are not clearly sex-typed.* In other words, males are more likely to be more similar to their mothers than to their fathers in variables in which masculine and feminine role behavior is not especially relevant in the culture.

There has been too little research on tested similarity between males and their parents to presume an adequate test of Hypothesis 3. In order to test it, one would first have to judge personality variables as to how typically masculine or feminine they seem. One could then test to determine whether a higher proportion of males are more similar to their mothers than to their fathers on those variables which are not clearly sex-typed, rather than on those which are judged clearly to be either masculine or feminine. To this writer's knowledge, this has not been done.

It is postulated that the task of achieving these separate kinds of identification (masculine role for males and mother identification for females) requires separate methods of learning for each sex. These separate methods of learning to identify seem to be problem-solving for boys and lesson-learning for girls. Woodworth and Schlosberg differentiate between the task of solving problems and that of learning lessons in the following way:

With a problem to master the learner must explore the situation and find the goal before his task is fully presented. In the case of a lesson, the problem-solving phase is omitted or at least minimized, as we see when the human subject is instructed to memorize this poem or that list of nonsense syllables, to examine these pictures with a view to recognizing them later (1954, p. 529).

Since the girl is not required to shift from the mother in learning her identification, she is expected mainly to learn the mother-identification lesson as it is presented to her, partly through imitation and through the mother's selective reinforcement of mother-similar behavior. She need not abstract principles defining the feminine role to the extent that the boy must in defining the masculine role. Any bit of behavior on the mother's part may be modeled by the girl in learning the mother-identification lesson.

However, finding the appropriate identification goal does constitute a major problem for the boy in solving the masculine-role identification problem. When the boy discovers that he does not belong in the same sex category as the mother, he must then find the proper sex role identification goal. Masculine-role behavior is defined for him through admonishments, often negatively given, e.g., the mother's and teachers' telling him that he should not be a sissy without precisely indicating what he *should* be. Moreover, these negative admonishments are made in the early grades in the absence of male teachers to serve as models and with the father himself often unavailable as a model. The boy must restructure these admonishments in order to abstract principles defining the masculine role. It is this process of defining the masculine-role goal that is involved in solving the masculine-role identification problem.

One of the basic steps in this formulation can now be taken. (4) *In learning the sex-typical identification, each sex is thereby acquiring separate methods of learning which are subsequently applied to learning tasks generally* (Lynn, 1962).

The little girl acquires a learning method which primarily involves (a) a personal relationship and (b) imitation rather than restructuring the field and abstracting principles. On the other hand, the little boy acquires a different learning method which primarily involves (a) defining the goal, (b) restructuring the field, and (c) abstracting principles. There are a number of findings which are consistent with Hypothesis 4, such as the frequently reported greater problem-solving skill of males and the greater field dependence of females (Lynn, 1962).

The shift of the little boy from mother identification to masculine-role identification is assumed to be frequently a crisis. It has been observed that demands for typical sex role behavior come at an earlier age for boys than for girls. These demands are made at an age when boys are least able to understand them. As was pointed out above, demands for masculine sex role behavior are often made by women in the absence of readily available male models to demonstrate typical sex role behavior. Such demands are often presented in the form of punishing, *negative* admonishments, i.e., telling the boy what not to do rather than what to do and backing up the demands with punishment. These are thought to be very different conditions from those in which the girl learns her mother-identification lesson. Such methods of demanding typical sex role behavior of boys are very poor methods for inducing learning.

(5) *Therefore, males tend to have greater difficulty in achieving same-sex identification than females* (Lynn, 1964).

(6) *Furthermore, more males than females fail more or less completely in achieving same-sex identification, but they rather make an opposite-sex identification* (Lynn, 1961).

Negative admonishments given at an age when the child is least able to understand them and supported by punishment are thought to produce anxiety concerning sex role behavior. In Hartley's words:

This situation gives us practically a perfect combination for inducing anxiety — the demand that the child do something which is not clearly defined to him, based on reasons he cannot possibly appreciate, and enforced with threats, punishments and anger by those who are close to him (1959, p. 458).

(7) *Consequently, males are more anxious regarding sex role identification than females* (Lynn, 1964). It is postulated that punishment often leads to dislike of the activity that led to punishment (Hilgard, 1962). Since it is "girl-like" activities that provoked the punishment administered in an effort to induce sex-typical behavior in boys, then, in developing dislike for the activity which led to such punishment, boys should develop hostility toward "girl-like" activities. Also, boys should be expected to generalize and consequently develop hostility toward all females as representatives of this disliked role. There is not thought to be as much pressure on girls as on boys to avoid opposite-sex activities. It is assumed that girls are punished neither so early nor so severely for adopting masculine sex role behavior.

(8) *Therefore, males tend to hold stronger feelings of hostility toward females than females toward males* (Lynn, 1964). The young boy's same-sex identification is at first not very firm because of the shift from mother to masculine identification. On the other hand, the young girl, because she need make no shift in identification, remains relatively firm in her mother identification. However, the culture, which is male-dominant in orientation, reinforces the boy's developing masculine-role identification much more thoroughly than it does the girl's developing feminine identification. He is rewarded simply for having been masculine through countless privileges accorded males but not females. As Brown pointed out:

The superior position and privileged status of the male permeates nearly every aspect, minor and major, of our social life. The gadgets and prizes in boxes of breakfast cereal, for example, commonly have a strong masculine rather than feminine appeal. And the most basic social institutions perpetuate this pattern of masculine aggrandizement. Thus, the Judeo-Christian faiths involve worshipping God, a "Father," rather than a "Mother," and Christ, a "Son," rather than a "Daughter (1958, p. 235)."

(9) *Consequently, with increasing age, males become relatively more firmly identified with the masculine role* (Lynn, 1959).

Since psychological disturbances should, theoretically, be associated with inadequate same-sex identification and since males are postulated to be gaining in masculine identification, the following is predicted: (10) *With increasing age males develop psychological disturbances at a more slowly accelerating rate than females* (Lynn, 1961).

It is postulated that as girls grow older, they become increasingly disenchanted with the feminine role because of the prejudices against their sex and the privileges and prestige offered the male rather than the female. Even the women with whom they come in contact are likely to share the prejudices prevailing in this culture against their own sex (Kitay, 1940). Smith (1939) found that with increasing age girls have a progressively better opinion of boys and a progressively poorer opinion of themselves. (11) *Consequently, a larger proportion of females than males show preference for the role of the opposite sex* (Lynn, 1959).

Note that in Hypothesis 11 the term "preference" rather than "identification" was used. It is *not* hypothesized that a larger proportion of females than males *identify* with the opposite sex (Hypothesis 6 predicted the reverse) but rather that they will show *preference* for the role of the opposite sex. *Sex role preference* refers to the desire to adopt the behavior associated with one sex or the other or the perception of such behavior as preferable or more desirable. *Sex role preference* should be contrasted with *sex role identification*, which, as stated previously, refers to the actual incorporation of the role of a given sex and to the unconscious reactions characteristic of that role.

Punishment may suppress behavior without causing its unlearning (Hilgard, 1962). Because of the postulated punishment administered to males for adopting opposite-sex role behavior, it is predicted that males will repress atypical sex role behavior rather than unlearn it. One might predict, then, a discrepancy between the underlying sex role identification and the overt sex role behavior of males. For females, on the other hand, no comparable punishment for adopting many aspects of the opposite sex role is postulated. (12) *Consequently, where a discrepancy exists between sex role preference and identification, it will tend to be as follows: Males will tend to show same-sex role preference with underlying opposite-sex identification. Females will tend to show opposite-sex role preference with underlying same-sex identification* (Lynn, 1964). Stated in another way, where a discrepancy occurs both males and females will tend to show masculine-role preference with underlying feminine identification.

Not only is the masculine role accorded more prestige than the feminine role, but males are more likely than females to be ridiculed or punished for adopting aspects of the opposite-sex role. For a girl to be a tomboy does not involve the censure that results when a boy is a sissy. Girls may wear masculine clothing (shirts and trousers), but boys may not wear feminine clothing (skirts and dresses). Girls may play with toys typically associated with boys (cars, trucks, erector sets, and guns), but boys are discouraged from playing with feminine toys (dolls and tea sets). (13) *Therefore, a higher proportion of females than males adopt aspects of the role of the opposite sex* (Lynn, 1959).

Note that Hypothesis 13 refers to *sex role adoption* rather than *sex role identification* or *preference*. *Sex role adoption* refers to the overt behavior characteristic of a given sex. An example contrasting sex role adoption with preference and identification is an individual who *adopts* behavior characteristic of his own sex because it is expedient, not because he *prefers* it nor because he is so *identified*.

Summary

The purpose of this paper has been to summarize the writer's theoretical formulation and to place it in a more comprehensive and coherent framework. The following hypotheses were presented and discussed:

1. Males tend to identify with a culturally defined masculine role, whereas females tend to identify with their mothers.
2. Both males and females identify more closely with the mother than with the father.
3. The closer identification of males with their mothers than with their fathers will be revealed most frequently in personality variables that are not clearly sex-typed.
4. In learning the sex-typical identification, each sex is thereby acquiring separate methods of learning which are subsequently applied to learning tasks generally.
5. Males tend to have greater difficulty in achieving same-sex identification than females.
6. More males than females fail more or less completely in achieving same-sex identification but rather make an opposite-sex identification.
7. Males are more anxious regarding sex role identification than females.
8. Males tend to hold stronger feelings of hostility toward females than females toward males.
9. With increasing age, males become relatively more firmly identified with the masculine role.
10. With increasing age, males develop psychological disturbances at a more slowly accelerating rate than females.
11. A larger proportion of females than males show preference for the role of the opposite sex.
12. Where a discrepancy exists between sex role preference and identification, it will tend to be as follows: Males will tend to show same-sex role preference with underlying opposite-sex identification. Females will tend to show opposite-sex role preference with underlying same-sex identification.
13. A higher proportion of females than males adopt aspects of the role of the opposite sex.

Sexuality and Identity
Masculine Differentiation and Feminine Constancy
RICHARD T. ROESSLER

To Erik Erikson, identity formation is an evolving configuration expressing both a persistent sameness with oneself and a persistent sharing of some kind of essential character with others (1959). Rolf Muuss interpreted Erikson's concept of identity as "the establishment and reestablishment of sameness with one's previous experiences and a conscious attempt to make the future a part of one's personal life plan (1962, p. 36)." Hence, a sense of constancy, the establishment and reestablishment of sameness, is one of the central processes of identity formation. DeLevita wrote of this process:

Every development within the personality presupposes both something that changes and something that remains the same, that which has remained the same stamping what has become different as a change; what in the one process constitutes what remains the same can however itself be the changing factor in another process. We think that here a concept would be useful which represents identity as a superpositioning of strata which all have something to do with "constancy", all the more so according as we are concerned with a deeper layer (1965, pp. 56-57).

To study identity from DeLevita's viewpoint suggests that one could spin off layers of identity, from fleeting fantasies to deeply significant identifications and aspirations. Therefore, the task is to trace through the strata various influences crucial to identity formation. One such pervasive element is the awareness that one is either male or female.

Margaret Mead placed sexuality deep within the identity spiral. For the woman, "Her femininity is concealed deep within her, nothing that she can touch and see, depend upon or flaunt (1949, p. 86)." Concealed, but not unknown, the female's sexuality is a basis for a universal understanding of her role. According to Mead, "The life of the female starts and ends with

Reprinted with permission of the author and publisher from *Adolescence*, 1971, 6 (22), 187-196.

sureness, first with the simple identification with her mother, last with the sureness that that identification is true, and that she has made another human being (1949, p. 156)."

Integration of one's sex role into the personality also results from a certain amount of differential treatment from others and the consequent social learning on the part of the individual. According to Bronfenbrenner, "Girls are more likely to be subjected to 'love oriented' discipline of the type which encourages the development of internalized controls. And, consistent with our line of reasoning, girls are found repeatedly to be 'more obedient, cooperative and in general better socialized than boys at comparable age levels (1961, p. 10).' "

From cross-cultural observations as well as from empirical research in our culture, one has some basis for proposing that femininity has certainty built into it, and that this certainty is often exaggerated due to oversocialization to the female role. This sureness of the feminine role which is often enhanced by oversocialization contributes constancy to the evolving feminine identity.

Margaret Mead recognized that "For the male, however, the gradient is reversed. His earliest experience of self is one in which he is forced, in the relationship to his mother, to realize himself as different, . . . (1949, p. 158)." Passing through phallic exaggeration into the realization that he is manlike, yet not manly, the young boy finds that he is neither like his mother nor wholly like his father.

Though he knows who he is not, the boy may have difficulties determining who he is. Certainly, he realizes that he is not female in a physical sense, but he may be uncertain as to how to translate this difference into aspects of self-definition and objective behaviors. Keniston has suggested several reasons for this difficulty.

His (the young boy's) close bond with the mother combined with the father's absence at work during most of the day, conspire to push him toward a deep early involvement with his mother. It is she who controls most of the things he wants: love, approval, security, material benefits and privileges (1965, p. 305).

Apparently, the young boy must learn the meaning of masculinity through indirect sources, e.g., from his own attempt to interpret what his father and other males do at work all day and from input he receives from females, e.g., his mother and school teachers. Hence, in part, the masculine identity reflects internalizations of female expectations for that role.

To give content to his role, the male may desperately need these female expectations. Mead noted that in some cultures the male role is uncertain, undefined and, perhaps, unnecessary. The initiatory cult for males is an admission that women hold the secrets of life, but that men possess the special knowledge and power required for transforming youth into men. If the male role is uncertain and undefined, it seems that he will be all the more open to expectations from the female. Consequently, the differentiation important to masculine identity seems less direct and sure than the constancy of femininity.

Since fewer realms of life exist solely for the male, this uncertainty in differentiation for the male is likely to increase. Traditionally, masculinity was expressed through achievement in society. Mead stated, "The recurrent problem of civilization is to define the male role satisfactorily enough . . . so that the male may in the course of his life reach a solid sense of irreversible achievement (1949, p. 160)." Whether a solid sense of achievement is possible in a specialized society is of itself debatable. But, it is less debatable that social achievement is today less a male prerogative. In higher education, males and females spend many years in a rather dependent state preparing for a later social role. Because both sexes share this state, it can be of little help to the male in his task of differentiating himself from the female.

Differentiation is the theme for another segment of the male's gradual social development. In moving from a filial role in the home to adult roles in society, the male may have difficulty in accommodating to the increased independence and impersonality. Regarding this issue, Keniston made the point that "the developmental discontinuities in our ways of raising children produce, to a greater or lesser degree, inner conflicts between the dependency needs exploited in childhood and the independence required in adulthood, . . . (1965, p. 307)." Resolution of this incongruity requires orientation away from the nurturant atmosphere of home and school. Because transition into many roles is no longer determined by sex, even this reorientation may not move the male into a sex exclusive domain.

Thus, the central theme is that masculinity is related to identity through the process of differentiation. According to Kurt Lewin, development through differentiation initially places one in an uncertain field.

The unfamiliar can be represented psychologically as a cognitively unstructured region. This means that that region is not differentiated into clearly distinguishable parts. It is not clear therefore where a certain action will lead and in what direction one has to move to approach a certain goal (1951, p. 137).

Because the relationship for the male between present and future roles may be inharmonious and because the male's model may be absent a significant amount of the time, the male seems almost abandoned in an uncertain field of many options and rapid changes.

For both male and female, events can come out of their most ameliorative sequence. But the likelihood of deviation seems more probable in a relationship between sexuality and identity that emphasizes differentiation rather than constancy. Yet, there must be reasons why this process, in so many cases, proceeds smoothly.

In his discussion of field theory and adolescence, Lewin states that being in an uncertain field heightens one's susceptibility to external influences, "cut loose from the region A, but not yet firmly established in the region B, puts him in a less stable position and makes him, as any object in 'statu nascendi', more formative (1951, p. 140)." Hence, the male would be open to external cues which at adolescence come more and more from the adolescent females around him.

Reaching adolescence, both sexes participate in more frequent and meaningful social contact with one another. The male meets the female who, if she is uncertain about some things, is certain that at some point she can become a wife and mother, a pattern which requires future stability in the male. Valuing this theme of constancy for herself, the female realizes that it must be woven into the male's conception of himself. To protect the certainty of her role, she must provide the male with certainty to his role. At this point, the female involves the male in a set of expectations which gradually provides the constancy for the link between masculinity and identity. To be specific, she will help the male become what our culture expects him to become.

Certain cultural expectations have grown up for masculinity and femininity. In their research, Bennet and Cohen showed that adult men and adult women view males as stronger, more competent, more aggressive and more daring than females. Adult women described themselves as weaker, warmer, more inadequate, more frightened, less aggressive and less mature than men (1959).

In our culture, these male and female stereotypes seem complementary in their interaction, each supporting the identity of the other. It is possible that the content of these roles is important only to the extent that it can provide this mutuality, this interaction in support of masculine and feminine identity.

But, this essay stresses that it is the constancy of the female role which introduces constancy into the male role. To realize her inner sense of certitude in the outer world, the female must support aspects of the male role. By her support, the female stabilizes aspects of masculine identity. For example, she would expect much of the male's aggressiveness to be channeled into the activities of a provider, one who nurtures wife and child. To be a provider, the male must be achieving, striving and decisive.

However, some women seem to feel that men are not fulfilling the expectations of the male role. In the following interchange, three coeds discuss this very issue.

May: Men are more frustrated than women.
Roberta: Yes, our generation is made for women. Women have always lived for the moment. But men have responsibility for the future.
Donna: Because of automation, men are looking for more in the home. There is a sense of failure. They are without means of self-recognition. They feel inferior. Woman is accomplishing in her

role; feeling secure-dominant. Man is without a feeling of accomplishment.

May: I'm discouraged with the boys and men I've met. I want them to grab hold of something. Their futures are undecided. They are pawns of the government. They don't have certainty they can do what they want to do.

Young college women recognize that men are confused, that men seem to be experiencing the frustration of trying to differentiate themselves from past experiences in order to relate to perceived future ones.

Recognizing this inconclusiveness in men, these women seem determined to help men recapture their masculine identity. Since it perpetuates the constancy of the female role, the content of this masculine identity will be that of our general cultural stereotype. In the following conversation, three female college students discuss their feelings about male-female relations.

Linda: I always see man as superior — shouldn't be domineering but I would choose to have my husband the superior one in the relationship. I feel I'm well prepared to face most challenges alone. I would want my husband to be able to take over — a feeling of security. He is always in control of the situation.

Mary: Every man wants to be a king. The man's word should always hold so he will feel he's the king. The women should make him feel like a king.

Linda: I guess I'm thinking of a king who is sort of democratic, a modern king; whose power is strong, but limited.

Betty: He is not wishy-washy (ideal man), but not domineering either. He doesn't make all the decisions and refuse to confer with his wife. You should (his wife) be an important part of making decisions; his role is to assert the decisions.

Traditionally, man has been the king, and, as has been mentioned earlier, such a role is a suitable context within which the female can express the certitude of her role. Among the women quoted, one finds the desire for a king, but a king in the modern sense. Possibly as an expression of their growing sense of individuality or of their disillusionment in not finding a male truly superior to them, women are attaching more and more qualifications and limits to masculine dominance.

To discover the origin of these female qualifications of masculine dominance, one must analyze other aspects of male-female relations, for example, the relationship of the sexes in school. Possibly, success in the competitive context of school is freeing women from viewing themselves as submissive to a domineering male. To be submissive, the female must be unrealistic; she must overlook past successes in school and probable future success in a career. College training only further develops her sense of possibilities. Hence, the submissiveness concept clashes with the ever-widening potential for women to perform in social roles outside the family.

Woman's theme of constancy may be torn at by career aspirations which would preclude prime allegiance to husband and children.

Increased education and widened social possibilities may also affect the female's concept of the male. In particular, the combination of these factors may heighten the female's expectation of how superior the male should be. Because relinquishing her own strivings has become an act of sacrifice, she is likely to relinquish them only to a man who is more likely to achieve what she would for herself. Herein lies the conflict; the male must be able to achieve and succeed in areas in which the female would be ineffective, yet the female has the training and aspirations to be more and more effective in just these areas. Though it is important for youth, male or female, to perceive continuity with future roles, the female can accept this continuity only when she finds a male who fits the image of a modern king.

Finding kings to be a scarce commodity, some women feel the need to create one. According to one high school student, this process is all too prevalent in American families. To quote him, "Maybe women want to see men dominant but they have a way of getting through it." Such a conflict might lead for different reasons to what Kenneth Keniston has called a "dangerous solution."

But perhaps the most dangerous "solution" is for a woman to transfer her own frustrated ambitions, needs for achievement and independence onto her husband and children, pushing them to the accomplishments from which her role blocks her. We see this solution among the mothers of our alienated subjects, who view their mother as pushing men to accomplishment, as the real centers of initiative in the family, as driving, ambitious, frustrated, and capable. This "solution" often places unbearable burdens on children, who are now required to achieve both for themselves and for their mothers (1965, p. 293).

All of these thoughts can be synthesized into several core concepts. Initially, the position is taken that the male role lacks the fundamental sureness of the female role. For the male, development must be through differentiation from a maternal matrix of home and school. This is not to make the male appear as a pawn, but to suggest that his development places him in an uncertain field. Thus, cultural cues, emanating in many cases from the females around him, have a great impact on how he defines his male role.

In order to understand masculine identity formation, the subtleties of the female role must also be considered. Femininity does include a biological function that fosters a continuity between identifying with the mother to becoming a mother at some future time. However, the development of our culture into a mass society has brought about a dissolution of certain male and female prohibitions. Not only is the female receiving increased training, but she is also experiencing a greater desire to utilize this training in career outlets.

The increased training and options open to the female may have several effects on male-female relationships. First, this educational preparation and resultant opportunity may become a function of the female's frustration as she attempts to work out the balance between her female constancy and her human potential. As this paper has suggested, one way she can maintain a balance is to cast the male in the role of a modern king.

But, as the female becomes more aware of her career potential, further disturbances in the equilibrium of male-female relations will occur. No longer will she need to cast the male in the provider or modern king role. However, it remains to be seen what she will expect from the male. One wonders what effect these unclear female expectations will have on masculine identity formation.

Combined References for Chapter 3

Adams, E. B. and Sarason, I. G. Relation between anxiety in children and their parents. *Child Development*, 1963, 34, 237-246.

Aldous, J. and Kell, L. A partial test of some theories of identification. *Marriage and Family Living*, 1961, 23, 15-19.

Bennet, E. and Cohen, L. Men and women: Personality patterns and contrasts. *Genetic Psychological Monographs*, 1959, 59, 101-155.

Bronfenbrenner, U. The changing American child: A speculative analysis. *Journal of Social Issues*, 1961, 17, 6-18.

Brown, D. G. Sex-role development in a changing culture. *Psychological Bulletin*, 1958, 55, 235.

Bruce, V. The expression of femininity in the male. *Journal of Sex Research*, 1967, 3, 129-139.

DeLevita, D. *The Concept of Identity*. New York: Basic Books, 1965.

Dornbusch, S. M. Afterward. In E. E. Maccoby (Ed.) *The Development of Sex Differences*. Stanford: Stanford University Press, 1966.

Erikson, E. The problem of ego identity. In M. Stein, A. Vidich, and D. White (eds.) *Identity and Anxiety*. New York: Free Press, 1959, pp. 37-87.

Goodfield, B. A. A preliminary paper on the development of the time intensity compensation hypothesis in masculine identification. Paper read at the San Francisco State Psychological Convention, 1965.

Grambs, J. D. & Waetjen, W. B. Being equally different: A new right for boys and girls. *National Elementary Principal*, 1966, 46(2), 59-70.

Gray, S. W. and Klaus, R. The assessment of parental identification. *Genetic Psychology Monographs*, 1956, 54, 87-114.

Hartley, R. E. Sex-role pressures and the socialization of the male child. *Psychological Reports*, 1959, 5, 458.

Havighurst, R. L. *Developmental Tasks and Education*. New York: McKay, 1952.

Hilgard, E. R. Introduction to psychology. New York: Harcourt, 1962.

Keniston, K. *The Uncommitted*. New York: Dell, 1965.

Kitay, P. M. A comparison of the sexes in their attitudes and beliefs about women: A study of prestige groups. *Sociometry*, 1940, 3, 399-407.

Lazowick, L. M. On the nature of identification. *Journal of Abnormal and Social Psychology*, 1955, 51, 175-183.

Lewin, K. *Field Theory in School Science.* New York: Harper, 1951.

Lynn, D. B. A note on sex differences in the development of masculine and feminine identification. *Psychological Review*, 1959, 66, 126-135.

Lynn, D. B. Sex differences in identification development. *Sociometry*, 1961, 24, 372-383.

Lynn, D. B. Sex-role and parental identification. *Child Development*, 1962, 33, 555-564.

Lynn, D. B. Divergent feedback and sex-role identification in boys and men. *Merrill Palmer Quarterly*, 1964, 10(1), 17-23.

Mead, M. *Male and female.* New York: W. Morrow, 1949.

Muuss, R. *Theories of Adolescence.* New York: Random House, 1962.

Rogers, D. *Adolescent: A Psychological Perspective.* Monterey, Calif.: Brooks/Cole, 1972.

Smith, S. Age and sex differences in children's opinion concerning sex differences. *Journal of Genetic Psychology*, 1939, 54, 17-25.

Thornburg, H. D. Adolescence: A re-interpretation. *Adolescence*, 1970, 5(20), 463-484.

Thornburg, H. D. *Contemporary Adolescence: Readings.* Monterey: Brooks/Cole, 1971.

Winick, C. The beige epoch: Depolarization of sex roles in America. *The Annals of the American Academy of Political and Social Science*, 1968, 376, 18-24.

Woodworth, R. S. and Schlosberg, H. *Experimental psychology.* New York: Holt, 1954.

CHAPTER 4 **preadolescent intelligence**

Introduction

The topic of intellectual development is important to discuss because of the increased capacity in the cognitive structure of the preadolescent. While learning may serve the purpose of exercising intellectual strengths, development has been thought to be a more profound influence on increasing capacity. The nature of such developmental influences has been discussed in the works of Jean Piaget (1950). Basically, Piaget views cognitive development as the progressive internalization of the forms of logic through periods or stages of growth (Flavell, 1963). Such stages are commonly accepted by many educators and psychologists as representative of the nature of man intellectually. It is fair to say, however, that some of Piaget's work is under question as educational researchers have raised the issue as to the accurateness of Piaget's classifications (Almy, et al., 1970; Anderson, 1965; Bryant, 1971; Leach, 1971; Milner and Bryant, 1970; Suppes, 1972).

Two periods described in the work of Piaget are evidenced throughout the preadolescent period. They are the periods of concrete operations and formal operations.

Concrete Operations Period. According to Piaget, this intellectual development period represents ages seven to eleven. Since preadolescence has been described as beginning at age nine, it is likely that most preadolescents are already operating in this intellectual stage. During this period thinking stabilizes and becomes more logical. Intellectual functions include the ability to master classes, relations, and objects (Elkind, 1967). Concepts may be learned through direct experience or instruction (Smedslund, 1964). As the preadolescent's thoughts become more systematized, they conform to rules, thus, appearing more logical. All of these functions are part of the preadolescent's attempt to focus on the reality of the world. Thus, intellectual operations are oriented toward concrete objects and environmental events that are *immediate.* Movement toward potential reality is virtually nonexistent, a point which Elkind discusses in his article reprinted here on page 114.

While the preadolescent's attention is still primarily centered around concrete objects, his internal cognitive function is distinguished by increasingly complex systems of action (Waller, 1969). Developmentally he arrives at the point where everything cannot logically be explained in concrete ways and he begins the search for more acceptable answers. This is characterized by the capability of hypothesizing, building abstract categories, and perceiving cause-effect relationships (Gordon, 1969), activities which are forerunners to moving into the formal operations period. Within Elkind's article there is a succinct description of the transitional modes of operation throughout the concrete operations period and into the formal operations stage. Elkind discusses three operations that are peculiar and distinct to the preadolescent. In addition, he shows the type of mental operations characteristic of the formal operations period. The clarity with which he sets forth these intellectual operations makes his article a logical choice for inclusion here.

Formal Operations Period. In the latter part of the preadolescent period, thinking shifts into Piaget's period of formal operations. During this period, which usually begins around age 11, the emerging adolescent acquires the capacity for abstract thought. Piagetians generally recognize that between 15 and 17 adolescent thought has reached its maximum growth potential and is similar in capacity to adult thought (Flavell, 1963; Inhelder and Piaget, 1958; Phillips, 1969).

For the preadolescent the shift from concrete to abstract thinking is clearly seen. In the classroom this becomes especially visible in mathematical and scientific concepts. This includes shifting from insoluble pieces of information to more integrated systems of thought. Flavell has expressed this shift by noting:

Piaget suggests that the route is similar in a general way to that by which the transition from preoperational to concrete-operational thinking was effected: As a child becomes more and more proficient at organizing and structuring problem data with concrete-operational methods, he becomes better and better able to recognize the latter's shortcomings as a device for yielding a completely and logically exhaustive solution. That is, as the child's concrete-operational analyses become sharper and more complete, they present him with gaps, uncertainties, and contradictions which a more impoverished analysis could never have brought to light. Faced with these new problems, the child gropes for new methods to attack (1963, p. 209).

Most preadolescents are in the early stages of the formal operations period. Yet, it is crucial to remember that at this developmental point the preadolescent's cognitive structure is still growing, thus, reorganizing. Movement away from concrete or environmental props occurs as experimentation, hypothesis-making, the testing of such hypotheses, reflective thinking, and analysis of cognitive materials with which one is acquainted, becomes characteristic of the changing intellect of the preadolescent.

The final two articles in this chapter are original essays written for this reader. The first article, by Michael McMahon, focuses on the intellectual capabilities of the preadolescent. The second article, by Sally Todd, is an analysis of the creative potential within the preadolescent. Both articles describe either cognitive or creative tasks which occur during middle childhood and preadolescence. McMahon discusses the interests of the preadolescent which are outcomes of continued growth. In addition, focus is placed on the in-school intellectual tasks and the preadolescent's growing ability to accomplish them throughout grades four, five, and six. Regarding creativity, after focusing on its nature, Todd expounds upon three issues relevant to creativity in the classroom. They are: (1) the stimulation and encouragement of creativity during the preadolescent years; (2) the threat to and discouragement of creativity in school; and (3) the teacher's role in challenging creative behavior. Both articles are highly readable and practical to contemporary school practices.

If we can gain an awareness that the preadolescent is a *changing intellect* then it will better facilitate helping preadolescents realize their potential while in the primary grades and the junior high school. There is little question but that Piaget's theory of intellectual development is not conclusive and will continue to change over the years. Continued research may show that many of his positions will not hold up. Undoubtedly, others will. However, it is true that Piaget's work at this point gives us a basic framework from which to observe the changing nature of the intellectual behavior and develop academic programs that will produce productive thinking.

Cognitive Structure and Experience in Children and Adolescents

DAVID ELKIND

Every affective experience whether it be a simple sensation, a general feeling or a complex emotion presupposes some form of cognitive structuring. For example, the recognition of the location of a simple sensation presupposes a general body schema. Similarly, the recognition of a general feeling as distinct demands a comparison with previous states, which at the very least engages judgmental and memory structures. The same holds true for emotions; the ability to recognize and label one's emotions requires the capacity to discriminate amongst the many possible emotions, and this in turn must engage cognitive structures.

From the developmental point of view, i.e., from the point of view which sees mental structures as manifesting a progressive evolution, we should therefore, expect to find changes in experience coincident with changes in cognitive structure. Put rather more directly, if the child lacks some of the cognitive structures he will have as an adult, he must of necessity lack some of the affective experiences he will encounter when he is mature. On a purely descriptive level this appears to be true. Prejudice, for example, rarely appears until adolescence, nor does the formation of cliques based on social class lines. It is also rare for a young child to bear a long-lasting grudge toward another young person. Depressive states are also rarely seen in preadolescents. Let us consider then the relation of cognitive structure to experience first in children and then in adolescents.

Reprinted by permission of the author and publisher. In D. Elkind *Children and Adolescents.* London: Oxford University Press, 1974, Chapter 7, pp. 96-104.

Cognitive Structure and Experience
In Children

The age of six to seven has long been regarded as the "age of reason," and Piaget's work on children's thinking (1952) has shown that this label was well-chosen. It is only at about elementary school age that children manifest the ability to move from premise to conclusion in their arguments, to nest smaller class concepts within larger class concepts (boys and girls equal the class of children), and to perform elementary arithmetical operations such as addition and subtraction. Moreover, as a consequence of concrete operations, children gradually come to appreciate, among other things, clock, calendar, and historical time; Euclidian, geographical, and celestial space; and the distinction between physical and psychological causality.

For our purposes, however, the latency-age child's attainments in the field of interpersonal communication and relations are of primary concern. Among these attainments, three are of particular note. First, the child at this stage can take another person's point of view and engage in true communication, with give and take about a particular subject. Second, the child at this level is capable of comparing what he hears and sees with what he knows, and is, therefore, able to make judgments regarding truth and falsehood and regarding reality and appearance. Third, the latency-age child is now able not only to reason from premise to conclusion but also from rule to particular instance — he can operate according to rules.

The ability to take another person's point of view and to engage in true communication makes possible the child's assimilation to the peer culture. Assimilation to this peer culture is facilitated by the existence of a large body of language and lore (which has been abundantly described by such writers as Opie and Opie [1959] and others) that provides the child with modes of peer interaction such as jokes, jeers, taunts, superstition, quasi beliefs, ritual, and so on. Adults, in effect, never teach children how to relate to peers and since these modes of interaction are not innate they must be acquired. The language and lore of childhood fulfills this function. Much of this language and lore is in the form of simple couplets such as

> Roses are red
> Violets are blue
> Onions smell
> And so do you

which resemble the syllogism and provide the child with material upon which to practice his budding reasoning abilities.

Coupled with this assimilation to the peer culture is a new estrangement from some forms of fantasy material attributable to the child's ability to compare what he knows with what he hears and sees. Among other things his new understanding of the difference between the real and the apparent brings about the deduction that there is no Santa Claus, and no such things as fairies, giants, and the like. The elementary school child may still enjoy such fictions but he makes it known that he is well aware that they are not real and are merely make believe.

Finally, the child's new ability to behave according to rules makes it possible for him to engage in organized play and to profit from formal instruction. With respect to play behavior, the child of elementary school age gets interested in every game from tic tac toe to chess. While initially he may have trouble learning and following the rules, the significant accomplishment of the period is his new recognition that the game must be played according to certain regulations. The ability to profit from formal instruction rests upon the same accomplishment. All formal education involves the transmission of rules whether these are the rules of phonics, grammar, or arithmetic. Concrete operational thought is a necessary prerequisite to formal education because it makes possible the comprehension of rules upon which all formal education is based.

These are but a few of the many new attainments of the concrete operational period. Perhaps these examples will nonetheless suffice to illustrate the extent to which the system of concrete operations brings the elementary school child closer to the intellectual level of adolescents and adults. Let us now look at the contribution of cognitive structures to adolescent experience.

Cognitive Structure and Experience in Adolescence

This section traces some of the experiences, which make their first appearance in adolescence, to the new cognitive structures which come to fruition at about the time of puberty. I do not wish to imply that these new structures *cause* the experiences in question but only to suggest that they are a necessary if not a sufficient condition for their occurrence. Indeed, the majority of adolescent experiences can only be fully understood within the context both of the new mental capacities which mark the advent of this age period and in the context of the new affective transformations which have been described by others (Blos, 1962; Erikson, 1959; Freud, 1946). If I here ignore the psychodynamics of adolescence it is for the purpose of emphasizing the role of cognitive structure and not to imply that motivational factors are unimportant.

Our knowledge about the cognitive structure of adolescents is due, in large measure, to the work of Piaget and Inhelder (1958). In their work on adolescent thinking, they have pointed out some of the ways that the thought of the adolescent differs from that of the child. The adolescent is, in the first place, capable of combinatorial logic and can deal with problems in which many factors operate at the same time. For example, consider the problem of arranging four differently colored poker chips into all possible combinations. There are 16 possible combinations in all. If the colors are red, blue, yellow and green the combinations would be: R; B; Y; G; RB; RY; RG; BY; BG; YG; RBY; RBG; BYG; RYG; RBYG; and none. Most adolescents can easily form all of these combinations; children cannot, and it is in this sense that the combinatorial reasoning of the adolescent goes beyond the more elementary syllogistic reasoning of the child.

A second feature which sets the thought of the adolescent off from that of the child, is his ability to utilize a second symbol system; i.e., a set of symbols for symbols. It is not without reason, for example, that algebra is never taught to elementary school children. The capacity to symbolize symbols makes the adolescent's thought much more flexible than that of the child. Words carry much more meaning because they now can take on double meanings, they can mean both things and other symbols. It is for this reason that children seldom understand metaphor, double entendre, and cartoons (Shaffer, 1930). It also explains why adolescents are able to produce many more concepts to verbal stimuli than are children (Elkind et al., 1969). For our purposes, the most significant result of this aspect of adolescent thought is that it enables the adolescent to take his own thought as an object which is to say that he can now introspect and reflect upon his own mental and personality traits.

Still a third characteristic of adolescent thinking is the capacity to construct ideals, or contrary-to-fact situations. The adolescent can accept a contrary-to-fact premise and proceed with the argument as if the premise were correct. Once again, the capacity to deal with the possible as well as the actual liberates the adolescent's thought so that he can now deal with many problem situations in which the child is stymied. Most importantly, for our purposes, the capacity to deal with the possible means that the future is now as much of a reality as the present and is a reality which can and must be dealt with.

In addition to expanding the adolescent's adaptive potentials, these aspects of adolescent thinking also pave the way for new experiences and reactions unknown to childhood. It is these experiences, for which the new cognitive structures of adolescence are necessary prerequisites, that we now need to consider.

The capacity to deal with combinatorial logic and to consider all possible factors in a given problem solving situation, lays the groundwork for some characteristic adolescent reactions. One consequence of the capacity for combinatorial logic is that, particularly in social situations, the adolescent now sees a host of alternatives and decision-making becomes a problem. He now sees, to illustrate, many alternatives to parental directives and is loath to accept the parental alternatives without question. He wants to know not only where a parent stands but also why, and is ready to debate the virtues of the parental alternative over that chosen by himself and his peers. Indeed, the adolescent's quarrels with parental decisions are part of his own indecisiveness. While he is having trouble making decisions for himself, at the same time he does not want others making decisions for him. Paradoxically, but understandably, the adolescent's indecisiveness also frequently throws him into a new dependence, particularly on his peers, but also on his parents. The adolescent demands that his parents take a stand if only so he can rebel against it.

Without denying the validity or importance of the dynamic factors, which lie beneath the adolescent's difficulties with his parents, the cognitive aspects of the struggle must be recognized. Were the adolescent not capable of grasping alternatives to parental directives and were he not in turmoil over making his own decisions, at least some of the storm and stress of this period would never appear or at least would appear in quite a different form. In primitive cultures, for example, where the more advanced mental structures may not be attained, there may be little storm and stress. In short, the presence of structures which enable the adolescent to construct multiple alternatives, sets the stage for characteristic conflicts between young people and their parents as well as for the increased dependence upon the peer group for final decision-making.

Another structural feature of adolescent thought with repercussions for adolescent experience, is the capacity to think about thinking, to introspect. For the first time, the adolescent can take himself as an object, evaluate himself from the perspective of other people with respect to personality, intelligence and appearance. The adolescent's self-consciousness about himself is simply a manifestation of this new capacity for introspection. Now that the adolescent can, so to speak, look at himself from the outside he becomes concerned about the reactions of others to himself. Many adolescents undertake a regime of physical or intellectual exercise because in examining themselves they find a discrepancy between what they are and what they wish to be, between the real and the ideal self. For the child, this discrepancy is seldom conscious but in adolescence, the capacity to introspect and examine the self from the standpoint of others brings it home in full force. It is for this reason, perhaps, that a child with a physical handicap (such as a deformed arm) who has been a happy optimistic child experiences his first real depression in adolescence.

This introspection has another consequence that might well be mentioned. The adolescent becomes secretive about his thoughts. He recognizes now that his thought is private and, more importantly, that he can say things which are diametrically opposed to his thoughts. When a child fabricates, he tends to believe the fabrication so that once it is constructed he defends it as the truth. This is not the case with the adolescent, who knows very well that what he is saying and what he is thinking are quite different and who doesn't believe his fabrications although he can make them sound entirely convincing. The adolescent thus begins creating the social disguises, so common in adults and so rare in children, behind which the young person conceals thoughts and wishes that are quite at variance with his verbal assertions. At one extreme these disguises are tact and politeness while at the other extreme they are deceit and exploitation. The potential for both is present as soon as the young person can say one thing and think another and be aware that he is doing so.

The capacity to construct ideals and to reason about contrary-to-fact propositions also plays a considerable role in adolescent experience and behavior. For one thing, the young person can conceive of ideal families, religions, and societies and when he compares these with his own family, religion, and society he often finds the latter wanting. Much of adolescent rebellion against adult society derives, in part at least, from this new capacity to construct ideal situations. These ideals, however, are almost entirely intellectual and the young person has little conception of how they might be made into realities and even less interest in working toward their fulfillment. The very same adolescent who professes his concern for the poor spends his money on clothes and records, not on charity. The very fact that ideals can be conceived, he believes, means that they can be effortlessly realized without any sacrifice on his part.

It is for this reason that young people feel that adults have compromised and sold out, that while adults profess justice, integrity, obedience to the law, they hypocritically fail to put these ideals into practice. In effect, the adolescent not only constructs ideal families, religions, and societies, he also constructs ideal persons. The short-lived adolescent crush is a case in point. It is short-lived just because no human person can match the ideal created in adolescent thought. The adolescent, moreover, tends to lack compassion for human failings both with respect to himself and to others. But while he is down on adults for ethical hypocrisy, he flails himself for personal shortcomings such as the control of masturbation, the making of social blunders, and academic or athletic failures. Perhaps it is because the adolescent is relatively uninvolved with serious issues of justice, integrity, and obedience to the law, that he feels so superior to adults in these regards.

These exaggerations of adolescence come gradually to an end as the young person is forced to adapt to the realities of adult life. As he begins to engage in productive work, he reassesses the adult world as well as his own limitations and becomes more accepting of both.

Intellectual Capabilities of the Preadolescent
MICHAEL P. McMAHON

The preadolescent period of development encompasses the school grades between the primary years of elementary school and high school, namely the fourth through the eighth grades.

The concept of intelligence has been defined in a variety of ways by educators and researchers. This article posits a definition that deals with what an intelligent person is capable of accomplishing — not an abstract definition of intelligence. Therefore, let us consider intelligence or intellectual capacity as the effective adaptation to situations in the individual's environment. This capability is present, in some degree, in all individuals. A definition of this ability is more concrete than many explanations proposed by other theorists in the field and is easier to understand.

Developmental Characteristics

During the preadolescent period, the physical growth of the individual is steadier than earlier in his life. Most children in this age range gain an average of two to three inches each year (Elkind, 1971). In addition to height and weight gains, there are also changes in body proportions. As the body enlarges the head finally becomes proportionate to it. The trunk and limbs are also growing, the chest is becoming broader and flatter, and the arms and legs become elongated, giving an appearance of gawkiness. The somewhat differential growth rate among body parts accounts for some children's sensitivity about their bodies. This sensitivity or embarassment can cause the child great concern during this part of his life (Elkind, 1971).

This is an original article written especially for this volume.

In the area of psychosocial development there are very well defined differences between the sexes. Boys tend to play highly active and organized games that demonstrate their physical prowess. Girls, however, usually participate in activities that are more socially acceptable for their sex, such as dressing up and cooking. The male of the species is also becoming more dominant and quarrelsome than his female counterpart. This dominant and aggressive behavior has been evidenced by research and observation in child guidance clinics and juvenile courts across the nation (Elkind, 1971).

Interests and Abilities

If it were completely possible to separate the physical, social, and intellectual interests and abilities of the preadolescent, it would then be possible to isolate the various factors that exist in the formation of the child. Since this separation is not possible, we must deal with each and its interrelation with the others.

As stated earlier, among boys and girls in this period there is a distinct tendency to partake in activities that are deemed socially acceptable for each of the sexes and a certain amount of disfavor is felt by those children whose interests or abilities, whether they be physical, social, or intellectual, deviate from these socially acceptable norms. Therefore, we would expect the normal preadolescent boy to have interests and abilities in sports of various types, games that require teamwork, and aggressive bodily contact types of activities. Preadolescent girls have a tendency to emulate those aspects of the female role that they will become part of in their later life (Lynn, 1962). In many cases the games favor noncompetitive types, and play appears to focus around the home life. The girls in this period apparently are preparing for their role in later life as wife and mother, which is still an aspired goal for many young girls in this society, although several alternative roles are emerging within the contemporary social structure.

A general definition of ability is given by Gagne and Fleishman (1959). This definition states that an ability is a general trait of an individual which determines the limit of performance he attains on many different tasks. Physical abilities are dependent on the level of an individual's manual dexterity and motor coordination. These, in turn, are dependent upon the individual's developmental progress. It would be absurd to assume that an eight year old is as mature as a fifteen year old. Therefore, it is increasingly recognized that physiological factors play an important role in determining one's basic abilities. The role of genetic factors has not been fully determined, except in the extreme cases. It is thought, however, that the genetic combinations fix limiting conditions, within which a wide range of variation is still possible (Gagne & Fleishman, 1959).

Since this article focuses on the intellectual abilities of the preadolescent it would be proper, at this point, to delve into the developmental stages proposed by Jean Piaget that include this age period. According to Piaget the child enters the concrete operations stage of development at roughly the seventh year of life and by the twelfth year has left this stage and is moving into the stage that Piaget labels the formal operations period (Elkind, 1970). During the concrete operations period the preadolescent child becomes capable of internalizing ideas and concepts that previously had to be coupled with real actions. The child becomes able to "think" about things. During this period the individual is also able to learn the relationships among classes of objects. This ability to classify and to internalize makes the child, by the end of this period of development, remarkably adept at doing thought problems and at combining and dividing class concepts.

The period labeled as formal operations by Piaget is the developmental stage when the child is able to think about his own thoughts, to be able to construct ideals, and to realistically reason about the future. During this stage, the preadolescent is able to accept assumptions that are contrary to previously learned facts and to reason with them. Piaget states that no new mental systems emerge after the formal operations stage, but that mental growth takes the form of an increased depth of understanding (Elkind, 1970).

Piaget's age ranges for his developmental stages should not be taken too literally. The age ranges and the transition points will vary with the concept being learned, the method of learning, and the cultural and experiential background of the individual (Braine, 1959). However, even if the age ranges for the two stages that encompass the preadolescent period are not entirely accurate they do give a good estimate of the capabilities of the average child in that period. For example, a child of nine years of age is able to differentiate the number of objects being counted (quantity) from the actions he performs upon the objects and the configuration in which he perceives the objects (quality). This concept of quantity and quality, and the distinction between them, is clearly observed by the fact that the individual no longer believes that there are more points in one configuration than in another because the distances between the points are different (Elkind, 1970).

These concepts, advanced by Piaget and his followers, assume that development is an interaction process between organismic and environmental factors. However, they emphasize the organismic factors and tend to underestimate the environmental ones. For this reason, much research has been undertaken in the past decade to examine Piaget's developmental stages. One of Piaget's main contentions is that his developmental stages are specific to certain age groups and that the developmental tasks of each of his stages cannot be learned at an earlier stage. Goldschmid (1968) demonstrated in his research that the concept of acquisition, one of Piaget's intellectual developmental tasks found in the concrete operations stage, could be facilitated by special training procedures. If we were to accept this study at its face value, we would have to seriously question all of the Piagetian principles and to examine them in the light of these research findings. If it is the case that certain of Piaget's concepts can be facilitated by special training, we would have to assume that the environment plays a more important part than is stated by Piaget and his followers.

However, since the work of Piaget has contributed much to the study of development, his concepts will be presented in some detail in this article. In the early stages of preadolescence, the individual has attained certain capabilities that were not possible for him before entering this period. Functioning at the concrete operations level, he is no longer bound to the particular phenomenal state of events, but is able to begin to take into account successive transformations, reversals, and detours in his thought processes. The thought patterns of the preadolescent change from those of egocentrism to one of perspectivism (Elkind, 1970). He is now able to accept differing points of view than his own. He is also acquiring the ability to judge the differing viewpoints and is able to realize that the nature of things is not absolute but relative to the viewpoint from which it is considered (Langer, 1969). These general areas are further expounded by Gordon (1962), who states that the growth in intellectual ability is steady and continuous during the preadolescent period. Research in the area of IQ score changes (Bayley, 1956; Sontag et al., 1958) points out that as age increases so do the intellectual capabilities of an individual.

While still in preadolescence the individual enters into the formal operations period. This developmental period begins around twelve years of age and is the last stage of cognitive development before adulthood. During this period, the preadolescent becomes increasingly capable of hypothesizing, building abstract categories, and perceiving cause and effect relationships. Another important aspect of development found in the latter part of the preadolescent period is the development of the concept of historical time. This historical time development is a crucial factor in the education of the child as many social concepts are based upon its development (Gordon, 1962).

This brief summary of intellectual development from a Piagetian viewpoint is by no means complete. However, since the intent of this article is to elaborate on the intellectual capabilities of the preadolescent it should help in the understanding of those capabilities.

For the sake of organization and clarity in showing the preadolescents' increasing intellectual capabilities the next section of this article will examine the following subject matter areas: science, mathematics, and social studies. Comparisons and contrasts will be drawn between the various grade levels associated with this developmental period.

Science

One of the most important aspects found in any science curriculum is the ability of the student to classify. In the fourth grade, the preadolescent is developing the abilities to distinguish between living and nonliving objects and also to classify animals into the various species. An illustration of this ability is a student who has the capability of realizing that all dogs belong to the same class regardless of their size or shape. By the time the student enters the sixth grade this ability to classify has progressed to the point where the student can classify various species of the animal kingdom into their respective phyla on the basis of the similarities of their anatomy. Another segment of the capability to classify is the subordering of the various phyla into class, order, family, genus, and species. By the time the student reaches the eighth grade he is capable of taking various parts of the body − heart, lungs, kidneys, etc. − and classifying them as to their functions. It is obvious that as the preadolescent progresses his ability to classify objects becomes more sophisticated.

Another concept that is closely related to that of classifying is the ability to discriminate. Discrimination in its simplest form is nothing more than the capability to note differences between two objects. A fourth grade student is expected to have a basic capability to discriminate between various nonliving and living things. In addition to this broad discrimination a typical fourth grade student will be able to demonstrate his discriminatory abilities by noting the similarities and differences between various types of minerals and animals. At the eighth grade level the preadolescent's power of discrimination has reached a relatively sophisticated form. At this level, the child can discriminate between such abstract topics as matter and energy. Discrimination at the eighth grade level is also found in the area of earth sciences. Under this topic the student must be able not only to classify the basic minerals but to discriminate between their varied origins.

Both of the previously mentioned capabilities that are developing during the preadolescent period are leading to a higher order ability or learning stage, that of concept formation (Gagne, 1970). The use of concepts is a most important process in this period. By the use of his capabilities to classify and discriminate the preadolescent is developing his capability of responding to common or abstract properties of various things. This pattern of classifying and discriminating enables the student to apply his knowledge to the abstract reasons behind the need for classification and discrimination. A fourth grader can classify and discriminate between various cloud formations, whereas the eighth grader can tell why the clouds are different and the functions of the various types of clouds. This may seem a minor point, but this ability to understand the concepts that underlie certain classifications and discriminations becomes even more important as the preadolescent progresses through school and life.

Since the area of science is stressed so highly in our society it is important that we realize the capabilities of our children in this area. Just as important, however, is the need to insure that each important area is capable of being understood by the learner. Classification and discrimination schemes and concepts that are not firmly imbedded in the learning repertoire of the individual are apt to cause difficulty later on when more difficult problems arise that depend upon these areas.

Mathematics

An academic area requiring similar intellectual operations as science is that of mathematics. During the fourth grade the child has the capabilities of classifying various numbers into their proper place value – hundreds, tens, ones – and properly group categories of measurement. An ability to classify is of importance in mathematics because if this capability were not present the student would have no direction as to which operations were appropriate for the given problem. Since the fourth grader's intellectual development is still incomplete and he cannot be expected to have the capability of accomplishing higher order mathematic skills, he is held responsible for the refinement of previously learned skills that will be important in developing the necessary concepts that will be called for in higher order mathematics. Whereas the fourth grade student is concentrating on addition, subtraction, multiplication of simple numbers, and division of simple numbers, the sixth grader has taken these abilities and applied them to the more complex problems of fractions, basic algebra, and geometry. By the time the child reaches the eighth grade he has intellectually developed sufficiently enough to be capable of classifying various types of number systems – decimal system, factors, and duo-decimal system. This ability to classify at a higher level than at the fourth grade is still based on the premise that there are logical methods for assigning objects to the proper classifications.

In the fourth grade the introduction of word type problems enables the student to use his discriminatory abilities to examine the problem and decide what type of mathematical operation he is being asked to perform. This form of discrimination can be, at times, extremely frustrating for a fourth grader if his previously learned skills are not sufficiently refined for him to discriminate between various mathematical operations. By the time the eighth grade is reached these powers of discrimination have been refined to the point where the student is able not only to choose the proper operation, but to discriminate among various types of geometric figures. Overall, there appears to be a logical progression of the child's power to discriminate, from simple to complex tasks. It should be stressed, however, that each step in the progression is dependent upon the previous step being adequately learned.

Probably the most important area of mathematics is in the field of concept formation. It is of extreme importance that students, at the various grade levels, develop the appropriate concepts. Most emphasis in this subject area should be placed on the formation of conceptual thinking in the preadolescent. A fourth grader, for instance, can grasp the concepts behind the simple mathematical operations, but is not yet ready for more complicated ones. The introduction of inappropriate concepts at too early a grade may result in the child not learning the concepts.

If the proper teaching techniques are used, the preadolescent is able to comprehend the conceptual relationships between the various aspects of mathematics and the part that each plays in the overall mathematics schema. The ability to understand these conceptual relationships enables the student to apply these concepts in the solving of mathematical equations, i.e., Area = Length x Width. This chaining together of concepts is described as rule learning by Gagne (1970) and Thornburg (1973).

Social Studies

The area of social studies as it is commonly taught in the fourth through eighth grades encompasses a very broad segment of the curriculum. The primary years of elementary school focus mainly on the local community, whereas the content of the fourth grade and above deals with broader topics. In the first stage of the preadolescent period, the fourth grade, the student is capable of classifying into the proper categories various aspects of his surrounding physical environment and acknowledging how each aspect is important to his culture. This classification task enables the student to assess the importance of the different cultural heritages found in American society. A more general intellectual capability of the fourth grader is his ability to list, group, and label the various topics found in the fourth grade curriculum such as natural resources, uses of different aspects of the environment, products of different regions, and types of careers found in various businesses. Of course the preceding capabilities are dependent upon the teacher making the necessary materials available to the student. This ability to classify is an important step in the acquisition of other cognitive skills since before the student can proceed to a more abstract level of thinking certain facts and their order must be firmly established in the student's learning repertoire.

Where the fourth grade student is capable of classifying his own society into the logical groups the fifth grader is delving even deeper into American culture. During this year the student is applying his previously learned knowledge to the area of current problems found in our society. Here again, it is necessary for the child to demonstrate his capabilities of classification; however, the student is now classifying on a more abstract level than before. He is expected to be able to classify problems of various types into a logical sequence that can be studied in a meaningful manner by him. To do this it is necessary for the preadolescent to draw on the various aspects of the social studies curriculum, such as history, geography, and community life. This amounts to the student accomplishing a double classification task and therefore increasing his capabilities in this area of intellectual development.

The preadolescent is still refining his classification skills by the time the eighth grade is reached. During this year, the last one of the preadolescent period, the student is not only capable of classifying things on a local, state, and national level but also on an international one. The same cognitive capabilities are being used but the intellectual powers have increased to the point where he is becoming capable of conceptualizing cause and effect relationships and their effect on classification schemes. At this grade level the student is able to classify historical events that had an impact on today's social problems and norms.

It is evident that this ability to classify objects, history, and societal standards is very dependent upon the teacher presenting the lessons in a sequence that is capable of being understood by the students at the various grade levels. This seems to require that the teacher have the ability to classify at the various levels also.

As in other subject matter areas the preadolescent's discriminatory capabilities are of importance. If the fourth grader cannot properly discriminate between the various aspects of his physical and social environment he will find it extremely difficult to properly classify the environment into its proper groups. This same principle holds true for the eighth grader who is required to discriminate between the various historical forces and their effects on present day life.

Once the basic classifications and discriminations have been made at the various grades, the student becomes capable of forming concepts and applying them to solve either problems that may be posed by the teacher or to actual problems found in his local community, state, or national government. The formation of concepts in the fourth grade is limited by the intellectual development of the child at that time, but certain concepts are capable of being developed by the student. These could be the realization that his locality is not the center of the universe and that his country is not the only country in the world. The upper grades of the preadolescent period, the seventh and eighth, require that the student has increased his capabilities of conceptualization to a higher degree. During these years the students must be capable of seeing relationships between the facets of the different cultures and to recognize some of the causes of the differences and similarities found in the cultures of the world. Another aspect of the eighth grade curriculum in the social studies area is the necessity for the student to be capable of forming generalizations about cause and effect relationships. To accomplish this type of task the student must be operating at a normal developmental pace and have retained the knowledge of the subject matter that has been covered in earlier years.

Conclusion

The three subject matter areas mentioned in this paper, science, mathematics, and social studies, have all demonstrated commonalities between them. All required the same basic capabilities from the students: the ability to classify, discriminate, form concepts and rules, and to apply the knowledge in solving the problems called for. The five grade levels, fourth through eighth, have also used these same intellectual capabilities in an increasing level of complexity as the grade level increased. It is important to note that even though these capabilities are a part of the preadolescent's intellectual development it is very necessary for the teacher to actively guide the student in the proper sequential development of these intellectual capabilities and to insure that the proper presentation of concepts is accomplished.

Creativity and the Middle School Years
SALLY M. TODD

Editor's Note:

Several plausible definitions of creativity can be found in literature. Guilford (1965) defines creative thinking which pertains to less structured situations in which the individual's thinking is free to go in different directions. Guilford includes in his divergent thinking category the factors of fluency, flexibility, originality, and elaboration. Ghilsen (1952) similarly describes creativity as an act which restructures our universe of understanding.

Mednick and Mednick state "creative thinking consists of forming new combinations of associative elements, which combinations either meet specific requirements, or are in some way useful. The more mutually remote the elements of the new combination, the more creative is the process or solution (1965, p. 54)." Their definition is related to that of Koestler's. He writes that the central thesis in all areas where thinking tends toward the production of creative insights, is that the bisociations of different patterns of logic, both conscious and unconscious, will lead to fresh perceptions. Association, he maintains, occurs within a single pre-existing matrix while bisociation brings together two frames of reference into a new revealing relationship. He claims the associative routine is the creative act superceded by bisociative originality (1964).

This is an original article written especially for this volume.

Getzels and Jackson propose the Freudian approach to creativity in the following manner (1962):

(1) Creativity has its genesis in conflict, and the unconscious forces motivating the creative solution are parallel to the unconscious forces motivating the neurotic solution.
(2) The psychic function and effect of creative behavior are the discharge of pent-up emotion resulting from conflict until a tolerable level is reached.
(3) Creative thought derives from the elaboration of the freely rising fantasies and ideas related to childhood and daydreaming.
(4) The creative person accepts these freely rising ideas, the noncreative person suppresses them.

H.D.T.

A creative person is said to have some of the following qualities: sensitivity to problems; fluency, both verbal and nonverbal; novel ideas frequently exhibited; flexibility of mind — ease of changing mental set; synthesizing ability — easy organization of ideas and analyses; reorganization or redefinition of organized wholes; complexity or intricacy of conceptual capability; and conception based on reality.

Guilford postulated that creative persons are original, although it is only one part of creativeness. Originality of response should be viewed in terms of quality of goodness vs. quantity of number. He found that those who were most fluent in suggesting new solutions tended also to come up with the better ones.

Creative persons are independent in thought and action. These persons often prefer to be alone. The problem derives from their high level of energy which they seek to channel into independent, nongroup coordinated strivings for extremely high goals of achievement — goals which they generally set for themselves and which may well conflict with goals that have been set for the group.

Creative persons are open to experience both of the inner self and of the outer world. The perceptive attitude expresses itself in curiosity and is the hallmark of an inquiring mind. Without curiosity or exploratory behavior creativity is impossible. The open mind can, of course, become cluttered and may reveal a good deal of disorder unless it goes to work ordering the multiplicity of experiences which has entered it. This can be sufficient cause for anxiety in preadolescents, and until they find some higher-order integrating and reconciling principles they will need help. Parents, teachers, and friends can be of invaluable help in communicating an emphathetic understanding of the turmoil going on in the young person's mind and in conveying to him a quiet confidence that whatever anxiety he is experiencing will pass.

Creative persons are intuitive. This ties in with sense perception and the immediate grasping of the real as well as the symbolic bridges between what is and what can be.

A strong sense of destiny is another attribute that Aschner and Bish (1965) included in describing the creative person. They felt that with resoluteness and a measure of egotism, the creative person considers himself to be destined to do what he is doing, or intends to be doing, with his life. There is a steady, unquestioning commitment of these individuals to their own creative endeavors. Another characteristic noted in the creative adult is that he knows who he is, where he wants to go, and what he wants to achieve. The creative adult person has solved the problem of his own identity.

Intelligence may not be significantly correlated with creativity. Certainly intelligence is required for creativity; but being highly or lowly intelligent does not determine the level of a person's creativeness. What is more important than the level of intelligence as measured by an intelligence test is the effectiveness with which one uses whatever intelligence one has.

According to Cattell and Butcher (1968) there is evidence that teachers prefer and rate more highly the child of high intelligence than the creative child. Getzels and Jackson (1962) compared a group of highly intelligent children with a group of highly creative children. Despite a mean difference of 23 points in IQ and no ascertainable difference in motivation, the highly creative group was not equally favored by teachers. Aschner and Bish (1965, p. 160) state that creativity fulfills three conditions:

1. It involves a response that is novel or at least statistically infrequent.
2. It must to some extent be adaptive to, or of, reality. It must serve to solve a problem, fit a situation, or accomplish some recognizable goal.
3. True creativeness involves a sustaining of the original insight, an evaluation and elaboration of it, a developing of it to the full.

From this point of view, creativity is a process extended in time and characterized by originality, adaptiveness, and realization.

The general psychological conviction seems to be that all individuals possess creativity to some degree. Creative acts can therefore be expected, no matter how feeble or infrequent, of almost all individuals.

Negative Influences on Intelligence

There are many things that are purposefully or inadvertently done in a classroom that stifle creativity. On top of the list is the strong push for conformity. Conformity calls for restriction, order, direction, and control; creativity on the other hand calls for freedom, experimentation, expression, and facilitation. Teachers may take their choice. But if they choose creativity, they need not expect their classrooms to be neat, quiet, and orderly.

There is evidence that differences between boys and girls should be given more attention in educational planning and programming. Torrance feels that the creative development of boys and girls suffers in different ways because of culturally misplaced emphasis on sex role differences. This faulty emphasis creates pressures that needlessly restrict the behavior of some boys and girls in school. As Torrance stated (1971, p. 211):

Creative behavior, by its very nature, requires both sensitivity and independent thinking. In the United States, sensitivity and receptiveness are feminine virtues while independence in thinking is a masculine one.... There is much that schools can do to reduce the tyranny of this misplaced emphasis. One way is through activities that approve independence in thinking and judgment as well as sensitivity and receptiveness. Training in the arts for boys and in science for girls through science and art camps and various kinds of co-curricular and curricular activities is one approach.

Charles H. Clark (1971) indicated that even by our words in conversation we can stifle creativity. Do any of the following sound familiar?

We've never done it that way before . . .
It won't work . . .
We haven't the time . . .
We've tried that before . . .
We're not ready for it yet . . .
Let's discuss it at some other time . . .
You don't understand our problem . . .
We have too many projects now . . .
What bubble head thought that up?
I just know it won't work . . .
Let's form a committee . . .
Let's think it over for a while and watch developments . . .
Let's wait and see . . .
Let's put it in writing . . .
I don't see the connection . . .
We've got to finish this first . . .
It's not in the book . . .
No one else wants to . . .
Your brother wouldn't have . . .
Please not now . . .

We will not spend much time dwelling on the factors preventing our schools from fully encouraging creativity, but a few might be listed briefly and then we will go on to more positive approaches to the nurturing of creativity.

In the 1962 yearbook of the Association for Supervision and Curriculum Development is found a list of factors that stand in the way of openness and creativity (Combs, pp. 145-146):

1. A preoccupation with order. Much of our practice seems to worship order, categorization, classifying, description and pigeonholing of one sort or another. Such a preoccupation is likely to discourage breaking loose and finding new solutions.

2. Overvaluing authority, support, evidence and the "scientific method." Such rigid, tight concepts often permit no question or exploration. They are, by definition, so.
3. Exclusive emphasis upon the historical point of view. This seems to imply that those things that have been discovered in the past are always good; change or the present is bad.
4. Various forms of "cookbook" approaches – the "filling in the blanks," "color the picture correctly" approach. This is an ever-present danger of teaching machines, also, if they permit only "given" answers.
5. The essentially solitary approach to learning often emphasized in some classrooms – creativity is very highly dependent upon communication.
6. The elimination of self from the classroom.
7. The school which is ruled almost entirely by adult concepts.
8. Emphasis upon force, threat and coercion. The use of "guilt" and "badness" as means of control; also severe forms of punishment, ridicule and humiliation. Anything which diminishes the self interferes with openness and creativity.
9. The idea that mistakes are sinful and that children are not to be trusted. Where mistakes are not permitted, there can be no experimentation. Teachers who fear youngsters and the possibilities that they may get out of hand cannot permit the kind of movement and freedom required by creativity.
10. School organizations which emphasize lock-step approaches, rules and regulations, managerial and administrative considerations, rather than human ones.

The Encouragement of Creativity

Guilford's 1964 study on productive and creative thinking in the classroom was an attempt to cultivate creative thinking abilities in the classroom. During his study, at one recess time, when the students went into the hall, he followed them out there, too. He found that all the things he had been trying to have happen in the classroom were occurring spontaneously in the hall. This left him wondering how he could ever get that intellectual liveliness into the classroom that was happening rather spontaneously in the hall. This is a question that we might ask ourselves as we consider the encouragement of creativity.

Mary Broderick (1966) feels that an environment that is conducive to creativity needs to be based on trust in others and faith in one's self. It gives the student courage to try, hope for change, and respect for the needs and interests of others. Students in this type of learning environment have freedom to make mistakes as they try new ideas. They have materials that are available for immediate use, a class schedule that permits some independent study and the pursuit of individual interest, a long range plan for a semester's or year's work, and a cooperative relationship with teachers and other students.

An environment that is conducive to creativity requires creative teacher-student relationships. These teachers provide students with an opportunity to communicate their ideas and to evaluate possible results. Good teachers provide thinking time for their students as part of scheduled activities in order to develop student self-awareness. They arrange the classroom environment so that there are lessons for the whole class which are enriching and stimulating, lessons for small groups because of their special interests or needs, and individual conferences with students to motivate further work, diagnose problems and give satisfaction for work well done.

To nurture the fullest creativity in active minds, greater emphasis should be placed, for the student, on seeking the implications, deeper meaning, and possibilities inherent in his ideas. This is a matter of pursuing ideas in depth and in scope, not of criticizing and rejecting the idea, which is easy to do and which is so crippling to creativity. Creative solutions to problems are not achieved unless their consequences are tested in application and revised and extended to meet the requirements of the situation for which they were originally conceived.

For the creative young people there need to be wise and reasonable limitations. It is helpful to all concerned if the students help in the establishing of reasonable rules and limitations for the classroom. They need the opportunity to consider the value of cooperative efforts and the learning of self discipline, while they are also afforded the time and freedom necessary to pursue their own interests and creative direction.

At one time or another each of the known learning and thinking processes should be experienced by students while they learn subject matter content. This is especially important during the middle childhood years as the cognitive skills are being internalized.

Teacher Influence

One cannot talk about encouragement of creativity in the schools without looking closely at the teacher and the role he plays in the classroom.

There are many studies that have shown that teacher attitudes are manifest in their behavior and that this behavior affects student achievement and classroom atmosphere. Yamamoto (1963) found some indications that creative teachers show certain characteristic reaction patterns toward the world within and around themselves and, hence, affect their pupils in a different way than that of their less creative colleagues. Creative teachers offer greater support and influence to creativity in their students.

Teachers who are sincerely interested in nurturing creativity must be prepared to grant more autonomy to their students and even reward them for some behaviors which at times may be disturbing to classroom norms.

A teacher may aid creativity by introducing items and topics to spark the curiosity of her students. In a study by Maw and Maw (1970) it was found that high-curiosity boys showed significant positive loadings for these factors and a low positive loading for a factor named Concrete Creativity. This study indicated that boys who differ in curiosity also differ in creativity.

Another important facet to creativity, as mentioned earlier, is that the student needs the command of a large body of facts, and he needs a wide variety of experiences and exposure to really think creatively and to express new relationships. These experiences provide a needed intellectual base for the cognitive aspects of creativity.

The teacher, by his dedication to his fields of study, by exhibiting the excitement and satisfaction which accompany a deep absorption in the problems and challenges of a field of study, by stirring the imagination of the student with a clear exposition of the structure of knowledge in the subject, and in his own seeking to respond creatively to its unsolved problems, offers the student a model with which he can identify. Often it is not with the profession of teaching that the identification is made but with the field of study that is taught with so much skill, dedication, and excitement, or with the professional field to which it may later lead.

Training students for creativity, however, is more a personality than a cognitive matter. It is based on one's values and way of life. Cattell and Butcher (1968) stated that creative individuals could probably be helped by teachers in education toward: (1) Learning how to manage their nonconformity without being delinquent. (For example, for a child who grasps a principle at once it would be reasonable to do only ten out of forty examples set for homework and to show that he has independently read further afield by doing examples in more advanced or specialized principles.) (2) Avoiding being dragged into race-track competitiveness. (Competition is said to bring all participants into the same track or race channel, instead of favoring exploration.) This independence requires a high degree of inner security. (3) Learning to spend time alone, reading and thinking, despite the constant social temptations. This would include breaking the habit of sitting for hours passively before the television. (4) Developing certain purely cognitive techniques, such as (a) the habit of intensive study and discussion of the principles involved; and (b) declining to take too seriously popular or conventional verbal terms to the exclusion of divergent thinking and logic.

The findings of several research programs indicate that an out-going optimism, creatively intelligent independence, and a certain amount of self-discipline are essential elements of emotional learning as well as of freedom to become a creative or talented individual. The lives of creative students need this discipline and self-control. These abilities must be learned if one is free to be truly creative, and self-discipline and control should be flexibly used, not rigidly or compulsively.

It is not uncommon to find teachers who pride themselves on teaching students to think and yet give examinations that are almost entirely a matter of knowledge of facts. The kinds of examinations we give really set the objectives for the students, no matter what objectives we may have stated. Our methods of evaluation as well as teaching have a role in the creative or noncreative environment.

The teacher has the decisions to make regarding the emphasis and the atmosphere for learning that the students in his class will experience. It is he who decides which qualities he wishes to develop in his students, and he must consider whether or not he is prepared to accept the problems that creative people make. Certainly our society wants people who have ideas and who can see new ways of doing things, new solutions to problems, and new relationships between things. We need people who are flexible and adaptable, ready and willing to learn, and part of our task as teachers is to see that children do develop these qualities. There is a limit however to how much nonconformity the society can tolerate. Nonconformity sometimes means unwillingness to cooperate. The strength of our society depends on people working and creating together in respectful cooperation. So, we must teach children balance in creativity, self-discipline, and cooperation. The task is not an easy one, but we have considered several relevant aspects of the creative process, and they should be worth testing.

Combined References for Chapter 4

Almy, M. C., et al. *Logical Thinking in the Second Grade.* New York: Teachers College Press, 1970.

Anderson, R. C. Can first graders learn an advanced problem-solving skill? *Journal of Educational Psychology*, 1965, 56, 283-294.

Aschner, M. J. and Bish, C. E. (Eds.) *Productive Thinking in Education.* Washington, D.C.: National Education Association, 1965.

Bayley, N. Individual patterns of development. *Child Development*, 1956, 27, 64-65.

Blos, P. *On Adolescence.* New York: Free Press, 1962.

Braine, M. D. S. The ontogeny of certain logical operations: Piaget's formulation examined by non-verbal methods. *Psychological Monographs*, 1959, 73, No. 5.

Broderick, M. Creativity in children. *National Elementary Principal*, 1966, 46, 18-24.

Bryant, P. E. Discrimination learning and the study of transfer learning in young children. *British Journal of Psychology*, 1971, 62, 1-11.

Cattell, R. B. *The Prediction of Achievement and Creativity.* New York: Bobbs Merrill, 1968.

Cattell, R. B. and Butcher, H. J. *The Prediction of Achievement and Creativity.* New York: Bobbs-Merrill, 1968.

Clark, C. H. How to squelch ideas. In G. A. Davis & J. A. Scott (eds.) *Training creative thinking.* New York: Holt, Rinehart, Winston, 1971, pp. 106-109.

Clark, K. B. The pathos of power: A psychological perspective. *American Psychologist*, 1971, 26(12), 1047-1057.

Combs, A. W. *Perceiving, Behaving, Becoming.* Washington, D.C.: National Education Association, 1962.

Elkind, D. Egocentrism in adolescence. *Child Development*, 1967, 38, 1025-1034.

Elkind, D. *Children and Adolescents: Interpretive Essays on Jean Piaget.* New York: Oxford University Press, 1970.

Elkind, D. *A Sympathetic Understanding of the Child Six to Sixteen.* Boston: Allyn and Bacon, 1971.

Elkind, D., Barocas, R. B., and Johnsen, P. H. Concept production in children and action in adolescence. *Human Development*, 1969, 12, 6-21.

Erikson, E. H. Identity and the life cycle. *Psychological Issues*, 1959, 1(1).

Flavell, J. H. *The Developmental Psychology of Jean Piaget.* New York: Van Nostrand, 1963.

Freud, A. *The Ego and the Mechanisms of Defense.* New York: International Universities Press, 1946.

Gagne, R. M. *The Conditions of Learning* (2nd Ed.). New York: Holt, Rinehart and Winston, 1970.

Gagne, R. M. and Fleishman, E. A. *Psychology and Human Performance.* New York: Holt, Rinehart and Winston, 1959.

Getzels, J. W. and Jackson, P. W. *Creativity and Intelligence: Exploration with Gifted Students.* New York: Wiley, 1962.

Ghilsen, B. *The Creative Process.* Berkeley: University of California Press, 1952.

Goldschmid, M. L. The role of experience in the acquisition of conservation. *Proceedings of the 76th Annual Convention of the American Psychological Association*, 1968, 361-362.

Gordon, I. J. *Human Development: From Birth Through Adolescence.* New York: Harper and Row, 1962.

Gordon, I. J. *Human Development* (2nd Ed.) New York: Harper and Row, 1969.

Guilford, J. P. Creativity. In W. B. Barbe (Ed.) *Psychology and Education of the Gifted.* New York: Appleton-Century-Crofts, 1965, pp. 455-472.

Guilford, J. P. Creativity: Yesterday, today and tomorrow. In *Exploring Human Development: Interdisciplinary Readings.* Boston: Allyn and Bacon, 1972.

Inhelder, B. and Piaget, J. *The Growth of Logical Thinking from Childhood to Adolescence.* New York: Basic Books, 1958.

Koestler, A. *The Act of Creation.* New York: Macmillan, 1964.

Langer, J. *Theories of Development.* New York: Holt, Rinehart and Winston, 1969.

Leach, G. Children scupper Piaget's law. *The Observer* (London), August 22, 1971.

Lynn, D. B. Sex-role and parental identification. *Child Development*, 1962, 33, 555-564.

Maw, W. H. and Maw, E. W. Nature of creativity in high and low curiosity boys. *Developmental Psychology*, 1970, 2, 325-329.

Mednick, S. and Mednick, M. T. An associative interpretation of the creative process. In C. Taylor (Ed.) *Widening Horizons in Creativity.* New York: Wiley, 1965, pp. 54-68.

Milner, A. D. and Bryant, P. E. Cross-modal matching by young children. *Journal of Comparative and Physiological Psychology*, 1970, 71, 453-458.

Opie, I., and Opie, P. *The Lore and Language of School Children.* London: Oxford University Press, 1959.

Phillips, J. L., Jr. *The Origins of Intellect: Piaget's Theory.* San Francisco: W. H. Freeman, 1969.

Piaget, J. *The Psychology of Intelligence.* London: Routledge and Kegan Paul, 1950.

Piaget, J. *The Child's Conception of Number.* New York: Humanities Press, 1952.

Shaffer, L. F. *Children's Interpretation of Cartoons.* New York: Teachers College, Columbia University, 1930, No. 429.

Smedslund, J. Concrete reasoning: A study of intellectual development. *Child Development Monograph,* 1964, 29, No. 2.

Sontag, L. W., Baker, C. T., and Nelson, V. L. Mental growth and personality development: A longitudinal study. *Child Development Monograph,* 1958, No. 73.

Suppes, P. The relation of research to facts and fantasies of education. AERA-Phi Delta Kappa Address, American Educational Research Association Meeting, Chicago, 1972.

Thornburg, H. D. *School Learning and Instruction.* Monterey: Brooks/Cole, 1973.

Torrance, E. P. Nature of creative talents. In *Training Creative Thinking.* New York: Holt, Rinehart and Winston, 1971.

Waller, P. F. Intellectual skills. *National Association of Secondary School Principles Bulletin,* 1969, 53(336), 65-96.

Yamamoto, K. Creative thinking and teacher effectiveness: A review. *Gifted Child Quarterly,* 1963, 7, 66-71.

CHAPTER 5 emerging values

Introduction

As the preadolescent moves into the intermediate grades of the elementary schools, he not only takes with him increasing intellectual skills but an increasing social awareness which makes him view his school as more than just an academic institution. Interests broaden. One student becomes interested in science, another history, still another math. Other students recognize the need for peer approval and actively engage in the behaviors that will bring about such approval. Some still attach to strong teacher affiliation. What becomes increasingly clear is that preadolescents are no longer characterizing earlier learning or behavioral patterns, but are impelled by new energies which result in increasing personal awareness, intellectual curiosity, value formations, and social behaviors.

The preadolescent brings into this stage of development attitudes and values which have been learned primarily from his parents. With new experiences, new sources of value teaching are presented to the preadolescent. The increased socialization at school allows the student to also view the teacher as a value source. Increasing involvement with peers constitutes another source. The result is that many accepted and heretofore unchallenged parentally-learned values may now be questioned for the first time. In addition, alternative values may be presented as a direct challenge to existing values.

Preadolescents form their system of value after considering those of peers and parents. Typically, they think that maintaining parental values will put them out of step behaviorally with their peers. Therefore, if peer behaviors or values are adopted, parental conflict may arise.

Attempts at showing the family to be the primary value unit have been made in the past few years primarily through the works of writers such as Aronfreed (1968), Hoffman (1964, 1967), Kohlberg (1964, 1966), and Piaget (1948). Hoffman analyzed the behaviors of some 450 preadolescents to determine the effects that parental behaviors had on the internalization of moral values. Hoffman felt that there were three basic ways in which the family exerted itself:

1. *Power Assertion.* This category includes physical punishment, the deprivation of material objects or privileges, the direct application of force, or threat of any of these.
2. *Love Withdrawal.* This includes techniques whereby the parent more or less openly withdraws love by ignoring the child, turning his back on the child, refusing to speak to him, explicitly stating that he dislikes the child, or isolating him.
3. *Induction Regarding Parents.* Includes appeals to the child's guilt potential by referring to the consequences of the child's action for the parent.

Hoffman and Saltzstein (see p. 148) found that power assertion was the least effective means of parental control in promoting the development of moral standards and the internalization of controls. The primary reason for this is that power assertions elicit hostility in the child and also provide him with a model (the parent) for expressing hostility outwardly.

In contrast, the researchers found that induction was the most effective way of teaching moral standards since it avoids the deleterious effects of power assertion. In addition, it is the technique most likely to optimally motivate the child to focus his attention on the harm done others as the salient aspect of his transgressions, and thus to help integrate his capacity for empathy with the knowledge of the human consequences of his own behavior.

Love withdrawal was found to provide a more controlled form of aggression by the parent than power assertion, but less than induction. It uses the affectionate relationship between the preadolescent and parent to a greater extent than the other two techniques, but may be more likely to produce disruptive anxiety responses in the preadolescent. A more complete discussion of parental effects on the preadolescent's moral development is found in the Hoffman and Saltzstein article reprinted here in this chapter.

It is this author's contention that adequate adult functioning occurs when there is consistency between what an individual believes and how the individual behaves. Thus, when behaviors represent the outcomes of one's values, consistency exists. However, when one behaves differently than the way one believes, inconsistency is present. An extensive discussion of emerging value systems is found in the second article in this chapter.

It is written by Thornburg and is an attempt to show how an individual works through his behaviors and values in becoming one's self. As one focuses on the preadolescent, the hypothesized movement toward incon-sistency is generated out of the realization of (a) more active social involvement in the middle age child, and (b) more diverse environmental influences on value development. The increasing inconsistency may best be viewed as a natural social growth outcome (Grinder, 1964; Medinnus, 1966).

Conflicting Values

The second article discusses value-behavior inconsistencies, and, in so doing, recognizes the potential for conflict. In the final article reprinted here (see p. 175) Charles Glatt has presented several ideas which might throw the learner into dilemmas regarding value formation. First, Glatt discusses the learning of values, a series of ideas quite comparable to those discussed in the Thornburg article. Glatt feels that most values are learned indirectly, usually prior to school age. The modification or unlearning of values is usually more difficult than the confirmation of values during preadolescence.

Glatt asserts that the middle class value system is the most common and the most perpetuated system in our society. Emphasis is placed on the cultural stereotypes which must be acceptable to middle class people. This often means playing a suggested role rather than expressing one's real behavioral desires. Glatt sees much confusion now being generated in our society because of the suggested alternatives to many stereotypes. The alternatives usually exclaim that the perpetuated stereotypes are not necessarily true. The generalization of some stereotypes to all or certain segments of our population in actuality represents prejudice, a subtle value taught to many children and preadolescents.

Examples of prejudicial statements were reported by Steinberg (1971) after conducting a national survey. His findings in Table 5.1 point to the continued belief and adoption of such beliefs as values. Much of the confusion in value formation today stems out of an increasing refusal to accept stereotyped values and a demand for the right to develop one's own values and behavioral forms. The existing social structure is challenged and many traditional, middle-class values are being discarded as irrelevant and noncontemporary to existing life style.

Teaching Values

Out of the increased activity in formulating value alternatives has come the fear that America morally, ethically, and behaviorally, may be in the process of disintegrating and on the verge of social chaos. In reaction to this fear, a strong plea has come for value teaching and value education.

Table 5.1
Percent at Each Educational Level Who Give Intolerant Answers
to Questions Dealing With Social and Cultural Diversity

(Based on a 1964 National Sample of Adults)

Amount of Education	Grade School	High School	Some College	College Graduates	Total
Do you think Jews have too much power in the United States? (yes)	18%	10%	4%	5%	12%
Jews are just as honest as other businessmen (disagree)	34%	28%	24%	14%	28%
Jews are more willing than others to use shady practices to get what they want (agree)	54%	42%	36%	21%	42%
In general, do you think that Negroes are as intelligent as white people — that is, can they learn things just as well if they are given the same education and training? (no)	21%	18%	22%	16%	19%
Do you think white children and Negro children should go to the same schools or to separate but equal schools? (separate)	55%	38%	24%	17%	38%
Generally speaking, Negroes are lazy and don't like to work hard (agree)	49%	41%	31%	23%	40%
Persons who insist on wearing beards should not be allowed to teach in public schools (agree)	39%	23%	16%	12%	25%
Suppose a man admitted in public that he did not believe in God. Should he be allowed to teach in a public high school? (no)	78%	58%	46%	38%	60%
America owes a great deal to the immigrants who came here (disagree)	30%	26%	16%	12%	24%
Nothing in other countries can beat the American way of life (agree)	86%	71%	54%	41%	70%

Reprinted by permission of the National Education Association.

We tend to look at values in three ways: (1) we look at our own values, how we obtained them, and their particular relevancy to us now; (2) we look at societal values and society's expectancy for us to follow; and (3) we look at the values we think others should hold, and go about teaching or persuading others in those directions. Raths et al. lists several ways in which we traditionally teach values. They are (1966, pp. 39-40):

1. *Setting an example* either directly, by the ways adults behave, or indirectly, by pointing to good models in the past or present.
2. *Persuading and convincing* by presenting arguments and reasons for this or that set of values.
3. *Limiting choices* by giving children choices only among values we accept.
4. *Inspiring* by dramatic or emotional pleas for certain values, often accompanied by models of behavior associated with the value.
5. *Rules and regulations* intended to contain and mold behavior until it is unthinkingly accepted as right, as through the use of rewards and punishments to reinforce certain behavior.
6. *Cultural or religious dogma* presented as unquestioned wisdom or principle.
7. *Appeals to conscience*, appeals to the still, small voice that we assume is in the heart of everyone, with the arousing of feelings of guilt if one's conscience doesn't suggest the right way.

Educational systems have always been charged with the responsibility of directing the learner into appropriate moral and social behaviors. Raths lists one of the primary components of teaching to be the teacher's responsibility to guide the development of values although some teachers clearly see it as more of the home's responsibility. Nevertheless, Raths contends that 75 percent of teachers accept it as an important component in their teaching assignment (1969).

Relevancy of value teaching at the prepuberty and postpuberty thinking stages is generally discussed by authors who feel that most preadolescents emulate and respect their teachers, a source of value learning confirmation as suggested by Thornburg (p. 169). Moving into adolescence, youths will begin to unfold their moral impulses in their peer associations and social life. The changing of values may occur here through the effective expression of behavioral and value alternatives.

Parental Discipline and the Child's Moral Development

MARTIN L. HOFFMAN AND
HERBERT D. SALTZSTEIN

Recent years have seen the accumulation of a body of findings relating moral development, especially internalization of moral values and the capacity for guilt, to parental practices. In a recent review of this research (Hoffman, 1963a) the following propositions received support: (*a*) A moral orientation based on the fear of external detection and punishment is associated with the relatively frequent use of discipline techniques involving physical punishment and material deprivation, here called power assertive discipline; (*b*) a moral orientation characterized by independence of external sanctions and high guilt is associated with relatively frequent use of nonpower assertive discipline — sometimes called psychological, indirect, or love-oriented discipline.

Several explanations of these findings have been advanced, each focusing on a different aspect of the parent's discipline. Thus, Allinsmith and Greening (1955) suggest that the significant variable may be the difference in the model presented by the parent during the disciplinary encounter (i.e., parent openly expresses anger versus parent controls anger). The importance of this factor may lie in the model it provides the child for channeling his own aggression. Where the parent himself expresses his anger openly, he thereby encourages the child to express his anger openly; where the parent controls his anger, he discourages the child from openly expressing anger and therefore may promote a turning of the anger inward which according to psychoanalytic theory is the process by which the guilt capacity is developed.

Another explanation of the difference between power assertive and nonpower assertive techniques is in terms of the duration of the punishment; that is, whereas nonpower assertive discipline may last a long

Reprinted from the *Journal of Personality and Social Psychology*, 1967, 5, 45-57, with permission of the authors and The American Psychological Association.

time, the application of force usually dissipates the parent's anger and thus may relieve the child of his anxiety or guilt rather quickly. A third possibility, suggested by Sears, Maccoby, and Levin (1957), is that punishing the child by withholding love, which is frequently involved in nonpower assertive discipline, has the effect of intensifying the child's efforts to identify with the parent in order to assure himself of the parent's love.

A still different formulation has recently been suggested by Hill (1960). According to this view, the crucial underlying factor is the timing of the punishment. Love-withdrawal punishment is believed more often to terminate when the child engages in a corrective act (e.g., confession, reparation, overt admission of guilt, etc.), whereas physical punishment is more likely to occur and terminate at the time of the deviant act and prior to any corrective act.

Finally, the important variable may be the information often communicated by nonpower assertive techniques regarding the implications of the child's deviant behavior. For example, Aronfreed's (1961) view is that such information can provide the cognitive and behavioral resources necessary for the child to examine his actions independently and accept responsibility for them.

Though varied, all but the last of these explanations assume the key ingredient for nonpower assertive discipline to be its punitive — more specifically, its love-withdrawing — quality. This hypothesis stems from psychoanalytic and learning theories that emphasize anxiety over loss of love as the necessary motivational basis for moral development.

In examining instances of nonpower assertive discipline, it became apparent that the amount of love withdrawal, real or threatened, varied considerably. In some cases, the love withdrawal aspect of the discipline seemed to predominate. In others it seemed totally absent, and in still others it seemed to be a minor part of a technique primarily focused on the harmful consequences of the child's behavior for others. This suggested that the effectiveness of these techniques might lie in their empathy-arousing capacity rather than, or in addition to, their love-withdrawing property. In the present study we accordingly made the distinction between two kinds of nonpower assertive discipline. One, called *induction*, refers to techniques in which the parent points out the painful consequences of the child's act for the parent or for others. In the second, called *love withdrawal*, the parent simply gives direct but nonphysical expression to his anger or disapproval of the child for engaging in the behavior. In a sense, by these latter techniques the parent points out the painful psychological consequences of the act for the child himself, that is, the withdrawal of love by the parent.

It is probable, of course, that the child experiences both these types of nonpower assertive techniques as involving a loss of love. However, as indicated above, the love-withdrawing component of the induction techniques is more subdued, and in addition they provide him with the knowledge that his actions have caused pain to others. By doing this the technique capitalizes on the child's capacity for empathy. In our view (see Hoffman, 1963b; Hoffman, in press; Hoffman & Saltzstein, 1960) it is this capacity for empathy which provides a powerful emotional and cognitive support for development of moral controls and which has been overlooked in other psychological theories of moral development. For this reason it was expected that *induction, and not love withdrawal, would relate most strongly to the various indexes of moral development.*

Affection has often been supposed to be a necessary condition for moral development. Measures of the parent's affection were therefore included for completeness. We expected, following the pattern of the previous research, that power assertion would relate negatively, and affection positively, to the moral indexes.

Method

The children studied were all seventh graders in the Detroit metropolitan area. The test battery was administered to groups of children in the schools during three sessions spaced about a week apart. Sometimes an individual class was tested in the homeroom, and sometimes several groups were tested together in the gymnasium or auditorium.

Data bearing on the various dimensions of moral development were obtained from over 800 children broadly representative of the population in the area. Because of the apprehension of some of the school officials, however, we were unable to obtain reports of parental discipline from about a fourth of these children, the loss being greater among the lower-class sample. In addition, children identified as behavior problems and those from nonintact families were screened from the sample. Further shrinkage due to absences, incomplete background information, and unintelligible or incomplete responses resulted in a final sample of 444 children. Included were 146 middle-class boys, 124 middle-class girls, 91 lower-class boys, and 83 lower-class girls.

Subsequently, interviews were conducted with a subsample consisting of 129 middle-class mothers (66 boys and 63 girls) and 75 middle-class fathers (37 boys and 38 girls). No interviews were conducted with parents of the children from the lower class.

Several different moral indexes were used — each tapping a different aspect of conscience. The two major indexes pertain to the degree to which the child's moral orientation is internalized. These are (a) the intensity of guilt experienced following his own transgressions, and (b) the use of moral judgments about others which are based on internal rather than external considerations. The other indexes pertain to whether the child confesses and accepts responsibility for his misdeeds and the extent to which he shows consideration for others. Identification, though not a direct moral index, was also included because of its relationship to moral development, as hypothesized by psychoanalytic theory and by recent researchers (e.g., Sears et al., 1957).

Guilt. Two semiprojective story-completion items were used to assess the intensity of the child's guilt reaction to transgression. The technique presents the child with a story beginning which focuses on a basically sympathetic child of the same sex and age who has committed a transgression. The subject's instructions are to complete the story and tell what the protagonist thinks and feels and "what happens afterwards." The assumption made is that the child identifies with the protagonist and therefore reveals his own internal reactions (although not necessarily his overt reactions) through his completion of the story.

The first story used here was concerned with a child who through negligence contributed to the death of a younger child. The story beginning was constructed so as to provide several other characters on whom to transfer blame. The second story was about a child who cheats in a swimming race and wins. In both stories detection was made to appear unlikely. In rating the intensity of the guilt from the subject's completion of the story, care was taken to assess first that the subject identified with the central character. If such identification was dubious, the story was not coded for guilt, nor were stories involving only external detection or concern with detection coded for guilt. All other stories were coded for guilt. For a story to receive a guilt score higher than zero there had to be evidence of a conscious self-initiated and self-critical reaction. Given evidence for such a reaction, the intensity of guilt was rated on a scale ranging from 1 to 6. At the extreme high end of the scale were stories involving personality change in the hero, suicide, etc. In coding the stories the attempt was made to ignore differences in sheer style of writing and to infer the feeling of the subject as he completed the story.

A departure from the usual practice was to assign two guilt scores to each story — one for the maximum guilt experienced by the hero, usually occurring early in the story, and the other for terminal guilt. In relating discipline to this and other facets of morality extreme groups were chosen.

In choosing the high- and low-guilt groups, attention was paid to both scores. That is, the high-guilt group included those who sustained a high level of guilt throughout the stories. The low-guilt group included children who manifested little or no guilt throughout the stories. Children who initially manifested intense guilt which was dissipated through confession, reparation, defenses, etc., were not included in the guilt analysis.

Internalized Moral Judgments. The moral judgment items consisted of several hypothetical transgressions which the children were asked to judge. These situations were of the general type used by Piaget, including moral judgments about persons committing various crimes, for example, stealing; choosing which of two crimes was worse, for example, one involving simple theft and the other a breach of trust; and judgments of crimes with extenuating circumstances, for example, a man who steals in order to procure a drug which he cannot afford and which is needed to save his wife's life. In each case the child's response was coded as external (e.g., "you can get put in jail for that"), internal (e.g., "that's not right, the man trusted you"), or indeterminate. The individual internal scores were then summed for all items, and the sum constituted the child's internalization score on moral judgments.

Overt Reactions to Transgression. Two measures were used to assess the child's overt reactions to transgression. The first was the teacher's report of how the child typically reacts when "caught doing something wrong." The categories included: "denies he did it"; "looks for someone else to blame"; "makes excuses"; "cries, looks sad, seems to feel bad"; "accepts responsibility for what he has done"; and "where possible tries on his own initiative to rectify situation."

The second measure was a questionnaire item asked of the child's mother, similar to the item used by Sears et al. (1957). The question was: "when ... has done something that (he) (she) knows you would not approve of, and you haven't found out about it yet, how often does (he) (she) come and tell you about it without your asking?" The mother was asked to check one of five alternatives, the extremes of which were "all the time" and "never."

Neither of these measures is ideal. The first has the disadvantage of asking for the child's reaction in the presence of an authority figure after detection. The second has the defect of being based on a report by the parent, who is the same person providing much of the discipline data and who is more likely to be influenced by "social desirability" than the teacher. Yet, the parent may well be the only person with enough background information and close contact with the child to make a knowledgeable estimate of how he acts before detection.

Consideration for Other Children. This measure was obtained from sociometric ratings by the children in the same classroom. Each child made three nominations for the child first, second, and third most "likely to care about the other children's feelings" and "to defend a child being made fun of by the group." The usual weights were used and the two scores summed.

Identification. Our major measure of identification was based on the child's responses to several items bearing on his orientation toward the parent: (*a*) admiration: "Which person do you admire or look up to the most?"; (*b*) desire to emulate: "Which person do you want to be like when you grow up?"; (*c*) perceived similarity: "Which person do you take after mostly?" Responses which mention the parent were coded as parent-identification responses and summed to obtain an overall identification score. It should be noted that this measure is designed to assess the child's conscious identification which the parents and not necessarily the unconscious identification of which Freud wrote.

Coding Procedure. The story completion and moral judgment coding were done by one of the authors (HDS). To avoid contamination, the procedure was to go through all 444 records and code one item at a time. Especially difficult responses were coded independently by both authors, and discrepancies were resolved in conference.

Before the final coding was begun, coding reliabilities of 82 percent for maximum guilt, 73 percent for terminal guilt, and 91 percent for internal moral judgment were attained by the authors. These figures represent the percentage of agreement in giving high (top quartile), low (bottom quartile), and middle ratings. There were no extreme disagreements, that is, no instances in which a child received a high rating by one judge and a low rating by the other.

Measures of Parent Practices

Two reports of each parent's typical disciplinary practices were available — one from the children who reported the disciplinary practices of both parents, another from the mothers and fathers who each reported their own typical disciplinary practices. The reports from the children were collected during the third testing session in the schools. The parents were interviewed separately by trained female interviewers. The interview typically lasted about an hour.

Assessment of parental discipline was made in the following way. Each respondent (the child or parent) was asked to imagine four concrete situations: one in which the child delayed complying with a parental request to do something, a second in which the child was careless and destroyed something of value, a third in which he talked back to the parent, a fourth situation in which he had not done well in school.

Following each situation was a list of from ten to fourteen practices. The respondent was asked to look over the list, then rate the absolute frequency of each and finally to indicate the first, second, and third practice most frequently used. These three choices were weighted, and the scores summed across the four situations. The practices listed represented our three main categories. The first category, *power assertion*, included physical punishment, deprivation of material objects or privileges, the direct application of force, or threat of any of these. The term "power assertion" is used to highlight the fact that in using these techniques the parent seeks to control the child by capitalizing on his physical power or control over material resources (Hoffman, 1960). The second category, *love withdrawal*, included techniques whereby the parent more or less openly withdraws love by ignoring the child, turning his back on the child, refusing to speak to him, explicitly stating that he dislikes the child, or isolating him. The third category, *induction regarding parents*, includes appeals to the child's guilt potential by referring to the consequences of the child's action for the parent. Included are such specifics as telling the child that his action has hurt the parent, that an object he damaged was valued by the parent, that the parent is disappointed, etc.

These lists were administered to each parent twice, once with instructions to select the techniques which he used at present and next to select those he remembers using when the child was about five years old. Reports of past discipline were not asked of the children because it was unlikely that they could remember parent practices used several years before.

The above measure of induction is a limited one in that it only included instances where the parent made references to the consequences of a transgression for the parent himself. To supplement this, an additional measure of induction was constructed. This dealt with the parent's reaction to two situations in which the child's transgression had harmful consequences for another child. In the first situation the child, aged five, aggresses against another child and destroys something the other child has built, causing the other child to cry. In the second situation the parent sees his child aged six to ten making fun of another child. The parent was asked what he would have done or said in such a situation, and his reaction was coded along a 3-point scale for the degree to which he (the parent) makes reference to and shows concern for the *other* child's feelings. The scores were summed to arrive at a measure of the parent's use of *induction regarding peers.*

Assessment of the parent's affection for the child was also obtained from the child and from the parent. The child was given a list of nineteen behaviors indicating affection, approval, criticism, advice giving, and participation in child-centered activities and asked to indicate along a

4-point scale how often the parent engaged in such behaviors. The affection score was a simple weighted sum for the affection and approval items.

A slightly different measure was used to obtain affection data from the parents. They were given a list of eight behaviors indicating affection, approval, qualified approval, and material reward and asked to indicate along a 4-point scale how often they engaged in such behaviors when the child "did something good." The affection score was a weighted sum for the affection items.

Background Information. The family's social class was determined from the child's responses to questions about the father's occupation and education. The distinction was basically between white collar and blue collar. In a few cases, families initially classified as middle class were later recategorized as lower class as a result of more accurate and specific information from the parent about the father's actual occupation and education.

Data Analysis. The data were analyzed separately for middle-class boys, middle-class girls, lower-class boys, and lower-class girls. The procedure for each of these subsamples was to form two groups — one scoring high and one scoring low on each moral development index — and then to compare these groups on the child-rearing-practice scores obtained in the child reports and (in the case of the middle class only) the parent interviews. In forming the comparison groups, the cutoff points were made as close as possible to the upper and lower quartile points within each subsample.

The test of significance used throughout was the median test.

Control on IQ. An important feature of this study, which was not true in the previous moral development research, was the control on intellectual ability which was instituted. Scores on either the California Test of Mental Maturity or the Iowa Tests of Basic Skills were found — with social class controlled — to relate positively to internalized moral judgments and consideration for others, negatively to confession, and negatively to parent identification. This suggested that some of the findings previously reported in the literature might be the artifactual results of a lack of IQ control. In forming the high and low quartile groups for these variables we therefore controlled IQ — to the point of making the high-low differences in IQ negligible. Since IQ did not relate to guilt, there was no need to control IQ in the guilt analysis.

Results and Discussion

To facilitate presentation of the results, the significant findings relating moral development indexes and parental discipline are summarized in Tables 5.2 and 5.3 for the middle-class sample and Tables 5.4 and 5.5 for the lower-class sample. Included in each table are relationships between each of the six indexes of moral development and each of the four measures of parental discipline: power assertion, love withdrawal, induction regarding parents, and induction regarding peers. Tables 5.2 and 5.3 are based on present discipline as reported by the child and present and past discipline as reported by the parent. Since the parent's report was not available for the lower-class sample. Tables 5.5 and 5.6 are based solely on the child's report of present parental discipline.

Middle-class Discipline. The overall pattern of the findings in the middle class provides considerable support for our expectations, at least with respect to the mother's practices. Thus the frequent use of power assertion by the mother is consistently associated with weak moral development. The use of induction, on the other hand, is consistently associated with advanced moral development. This is true for both induction regarding parents and induction regarding peers. In all, there are a large number of significant findings especially for the major moral indexes — guilt and internalized moral judgments.

In contrast to the mothers, few significant findings were obtained for fathers — for boys as well as girls — and those that were obtained did not fit any apparent pattern.

A further step in the analysis of induction was to combine all indexes of this category into a composite index. The results, presented in Table 5.6 were quite striking in the case of mothers for all the moral indexes. Significant findings, all in the expected direction, were obtained for boys on guilt, internal moral judgments, confession, and acceptance of responsibility; and for girls on guilt, internal moral judgments, and consideration for others. When both sexes are combined, the findings are significant for all the moral indexes. The findings on identification are significant only for boys, however.

In contrast to induction, love withdrawal relates infrequently to the moral indexes (see Table 5.2). Further, in most cases in which significant relations between love withdrawal and moral development do occur, they prove to be negative. Taken as a whole, the importance of the distinction between love withdrawal and induction has been clearly demonstrated by these findings.

In sum it is a pattern of infrequent use of power assertion and frequent use of induction by middle-class mothers which generally appears to facilitate the facets of morality included in this study.

There is, however, one major exception to this pattern. The peers' reports of the boy's consideration for other children is positively related to the mother's report of their present use of power assertion (Table 5.2). A possible explanation of this finding is that our measure of consideration is a poor one especially for the boys. In particular, there is no built-in provision to assure that the behavior is based on internal motivation. The motive behind such behavior in the case of boys might instead often be a need for approval by peers. Why this should be the case for boys and not for girls remains unclear. It should be noted, however, that consideration is a more deviant value for boys than girls. Evidence for this is provided from a measure of values administered to the children. The largest sex difference found was on the consideration item ("goes out of his way to help others"). The girls valued this trait more than the boys ($p < .001$). Thus consideration does appear to have a different meaning for the two sexes.

Lower-class Discipline. In discussing the lower-class findings the lack of parent interview data must be kept in mind. Nevertheless, there are several very apparent contrasts with the middle-class sample. Foremost among these is the general paucity of significant relationships between the child's moral development and his report of parental discipline. This is especially striking in the case of the mother's discipline. Furthermore, of those significant relationships that emerge, two are inconsistent with our expectations. First, as with the middle-class sample, the boy's consideration is related positively to the mother's use of power assertion. Second, in contrast with the findings for the middle-class boys, guilt is positively associated with the mother's use of love withdrawal, but unrelated to the mother's use of power assertion or induction. In summary, our expectations were not confirmed for the lower-class sample, and no general conclusion may be drawn.

The infrequent relationships between the child's moral development and the mother's discipline, compared to the middle-class sample, suggest that the lower-class mother's discipline may be less crucial and singular a variable. This in turn may be due to several factors. First, the mothers more often work full time in the lower than in the middle class. Second, the combination of large families and less space may result in the parent and child interacting with many other people besides each other. Third, according to the more traditional family structure usually found in the lower class (e.g., Bronfenbrenner, 1958), the father is more often the ultimate disciplining agent. In our sample, for example, boys more often reported that their mothers had the fathers do the disciplining ("says she'll tell your father") in the lower class than in the middle class ($p < .01$). Fourth, lower-class children are encouraged to spend more time outside the home than middle-class children. For all these reasons the socializing process may be more diffuse in the lower class; that is, it may be more equally shared by the mother with the father, with siblings, members of the extended family, the child's peers, and others.

Further research comparing the two classes needs to be performed. One might conjecture that because of the more diffuse socialization process in the lower class the basis of internalization may be quite different for children in the two classes, with consequent differences in the kind of morality that develops.

Affection. The relations between affection and the six moral indexes are presented in Table 5.7. The most notable features of this table are first, as expected, the relationships are positive; second, most of the findings, as with the discipline data, were obtained for middle-class mothers. It should also be noted that most of the findings are based on the child's report.

Role of the Father. Several studies of delinquency (e.g., Glueck & Glueck, 1950; McCord & McCord, 1958; Miller, 1958) suggest that the father is important in the development of internal controls. Our findings, especially in the middle class, seem to suggest that this is not so. Relatively few significant relationships were obtained between paternal discipline and the child's morality, and several were in a direction opposite to that expected.

Of course, it is possible that the role of the father is more important than indicated in this study. For example, the father might provide the cognitive content of the standards by direct instruction rather than by his discipline techniques. Lacking data on direct instruction, we could not test this possibility. Another possibility is that the role of the father is a less direct one. That is, he may affect the moral development of the child by his relationship to the mother and his influence on the discipline techniques chosen by the mother. This is indicated in a study of preschool children where evidence was found suggesting that women who are treated power-assertively by their husbands tend to react by using power-assertive discipline on their children (Hoffman, 1963c). It may also be that the father's role is ordinarily latent in its effects and only becomes manifest under exceptional circumstances such as those often associated with delinquency. That is, under normal conditions with the father away working most of the time and the mother handling most of the disciplining, as in our middle-class sample, the father's importance may lie mainly in providing an adequate role model that operates in the background as a necessary supporting factor. Under these conditions, the specific lines along which the child's moral development proceeds may be determined primarily by the mother's discipline. An adequate role model is lacking, however, in extreme cases as when there is no father, when the father is a criminal, or when the father is at home but unemployed, and this may account for the findings obtained in the delinquency research.

Methodological Issues. Any study of child rearing and moral development that relies on indexes of discipline and morality from the same source is open to the criticism that the relationships that emerge are due to the lack of independence of the sources. If that source is the child himself, the suspicion might be held that the child's report of parental discipline is simply another projective measure of the child's personality. It should be noted that in the present study the relationships between the child's morality and the parent's report of discipline were generally in the same direction as those involving the child's report of discipline. (We refer here to the middle-class-mother findings.) In addition, over half the significant findings for each sex involve relations between measures obtained from different respondents.

Further support for our findings comes from a recent review in which our threefold discipline classification was applied to the previous research (Hoffman, in press). Since most studies used a power assertive-nonpower assertive dichotomy, as indicated earlier, the raw data were examined (and recoded where necessary) to determine whether love withdrawal, induction, or some other form of nonpower assertion was responsible for the findings. The results were clearly consistent with ours. Since a wide range of theoretical and methodological approaches were involved in the studies reviewed, our confidence in the findings reported here is considerably strengthened.

A common problem also relevant to the present design is that no definitive conclusion may be drawn about causal direction of the relationships obtained. Any solution to this will have to wait upon application of the experimental method or longitudinal studies. Nevertheless, some support for the proposition that discipline affects moral development, rather than the reverse, may be derived from the fact that several findings bear on the use of discipline in the past. If these reports are assumed to be reasonably valid, to argue that the child's moral development elicits different discipline patterns (rather than the reverse) necessitates the further assumption that the child's morality has not changed basically from early childhood. This is an unlikely assumption in view of common observations (e.g., about the child's changing acceptance of responsibility for transgression) and the findings about the developmental course of moral judgments obtained by Piaget (1948), Kohlberg (1963), and others.

Theoretical Discussion. In this section we will analyze the disciplinary encounter into what we believe to be some of its most basic cognitive and emotional factors.

First, any disciplinary encounter generates a certain amount of anger in the child by preventing him from completing or repeating a motivated act. Power assertion is probably most likely to arouse intense anger in the child because it frustrates not only the act but also the child's need for autonomy. It dramatically underscores the extent to which the child's freedom is circumscribed by the superior power and resources of the adult world. This is no doubt exacerbated by the fact that power assertion is likely to be applied abruptly with few explanations or compensations offered to the child. (The empirical evidence for a positive relation between power assertion and anger has been summarized by Becker, 1964.)

Second, a disciplinary technique also provides the child with (*a*) a model for discharging that anger, and may provide him with (*b*) an object against which to discharge his anger. The disciplinary act itself constitutes the model for discharging the anger which the child may imitate.

Third, as much animal and human learning research has now shown, what is learned will depend on the stimuli to which the organism is compelled to attend. Disciplinary techniques explicitly or implicitly provide such a focus. Both love withdrawal and power assertion direct the child to the consequences of his behavior for the actor, that is, for the child himself, and to the external agent producing these consequences. Induction, on the other hand, is more apt to focus the child's attention on the consequences of his actions for others, the parent, or some third party. This factor should be especially important in determining the content of the child's standards. That is, if transgressions are followed by induction, the child will learn that the important part of transgressions consists of the harm done to others.

Fourth, to be effective the technique must enlist already existing emotional and motivational tendencies within the child. One such resource is the child's need for love. This factor depends on the general affective state of the parent-child relationship, the importance of which may be seen in the consistent relationship obtained between affection and the moral indexes (Table 5.7). Given this affective relationship, some arousal of the need for love may be both necessary for and capable of motivating the child to give up his needs of the moment and attend to (and thus be influenced by) the parent's discipline technique. Too much arousal, however, may produce intense feelings of anxiety over loss of love which may disrupt the child's response especially to the cognitive elements of the technique. All three types of discipline communicate some parental disapproval and are thus capable of arousing the child's need for love. But it is possible that only inductions can arouse this need to an optimal degree because the threat of love withdrawal implicit in inductions is relatively mild. Also, it is embedded in the context of a technique which explicitly or implicitly suggests a means of reparation. Inductions are thus less likely to disrupt the child's response — as well as his general affective relationship with the parent — than either love withdrawal which may arouse undue anxiety, or power assertion which arouses anger and other disruptive affects.

The second emotional resource, empathy, has long been overlooked by psychologists as a possibly important factor in socialization. Empathy has been observed in children to occur much before the child's moral controls are firmly established (e.g., Murphy, 1937). We believe that it is a potentially important emotional resource because it adds to the aroused need for love the pain which the child vicariously experiences from having harmed another, thus intensifying his motivation to learn moral rules and control his impulses. Of the three types of discipline under consideration, induction seems most capable of enlisting the child's natural proclivities for empathy in the struggle to control his impulses. As indicated in greater detail elsewhere (Hoffman, 1963b; 'Hoffman, in press; Hoffman & Saltzstein, 1960), we view induction as both directing the child's attention to the other person's pain, which should elicit an empathic response, and communicating to the child that he caused that pain. Without the latter, the child might respond empathically but dissociate himself from the causal act. The coalescence of empathy and the awareness of being the causal agent should produce a response having the necessary cognitive (self-critical) and affective properties of guilt.

It follows from this analysis that power assertion is least effective in promoting development of moral standards and internalization of controls because it elicits intense hostility in the child and simultaneously provides him with a model for expressing that hostility outwardly and a relatively legitimate object against which to express it. It furthermore makes the child's need for love less salient and functions as an obstacle to the arousal of empathy. Finally, it sensitizes the child to the punitive responses of adult authorities, thus contributing to an externally focused moral orientation.

Induction not only avoids these deleterious effects of power assertion, but also is the technique most likely to optimally motivate the child to focus his attention on the harm done others as the salient aspect of his transgressions, and thus to help integrate his capacity for empathy with the knowledge of the human consequences of his own behavior. Repeated experiences of this kind should help sensitize the child to the human consequences of his behavior which may then come to stand out among the welter of emotional and other stimuli in the situation. The child is thus gradually enabled to pick out on his own, without help from others, the effects of his behavior, and to react with an internally based sense of guilt. Induction in sum should be the most facilitative form of discipline for building long-term controls which are independent of external sanctions, and the findings would seem to support this view.

Love withdrawal stands midway between the other two techniques in promoting internalization. It provides a more controlled form of aggression by the parent than power assertion, but less than induction. It employs the affectionate relationship between child and parent perhaps to a greater degree than the other two techniques, but in a way more likely than they to produce a disruptive anxiety response in the child. However, it falls short of induction in effectiveness by not including the cognitive material needed to heighten the child's awareness of wrongdoing and facilitate his learning to generalize accurately to other relevant situations, and by failing to capitalize on his capacity for empathy.

The weak and inconsistent findings for love withdrawal suggest that anxiety over loss of love may be a less important factor in the child's internalization than formerly thought to be the case. Before drawing this conclusion, however, the possibility that love withdrawal is only effective when the parent also freely expresses affection, as suggested by Sears et al. (1957), should be considered. We were able to test this hypothesis by examining the relation between love withdrawal and the moral indexes within the group of subjects who were above and below the median on affection, and also within the upper and lower quartile groups. The results do not corroborate the hypothesis: the relations between love withdrawal and the moral indexes do not differ for the high- and low-affection groups.

In an earlier study with preschool children, however, love withdrawal was found to relate negatively to the expression of overt hostility in the nursery school (Hoffman, 1963b). It was possible to make a similar test in the present study since teacher ratings of overt hostility were available. Here. too. love withdrawal related negatively to hostility outside the home ($p < .05$). We also found that love withdrawal is used more when the child expresses hostility toward the parent than in other types of discipline situations. These findings suggest that the contribution of love withdrawal to moral development may be to attach anxiety directly to the child's hostile impulses, thus motivating him to keep them under control. Psychoanalytic theory may thus be correct after all in the importance assigned love withdrawal in the socialization of the child's impulses. Our data, however, do not support the psychoanalytic view that identification is a necessary mediating process. That is. we found no relation between love withdrawal and identification (Tables 5.2, 5.3, 5.4, and 5.6). It remains possible, of course, that a form of unconscious identification which may not be tapped by our more consciously focused measure serves to mediate between the parent's love withdrawal and the child's inhibition of hostile impulses – as suggested in psychoanalytic theory.

In any case, our data do tend to show that love withdrawal alone is an insufficient basis for the development of those capacities – especially for guilt and moral judgment – which are critical characteristics of a fully developed conscience.

Table 5.2
Statistically Significant Relations Between Child's Morality Indexes and Mother's Discipline Techniques: Middle Class

Morality Index	Power Assertion			Love Withdrawal			Induction Re Parent			Induction Re Peers[a]		
	Boys	Girls	Sum	Boys	Girls	Sum	Boys	Girls	Sum	Boys	Girls	Sum
Guilt (child's response)		$-p^b$	$-c^b$, $-n^b$, $-p^b$				$+c^b$	$+p^b$	$+c^b$, $+n^b$, $+p^b$	$+p^b$		$+p^c$
Internal moral judgment (child's reponse)		$-n^b$	$-c^b$		$-c^b$	$-c^b$		$+c^b$				
Confession (mother's report)	$-p^c$		$-p^c$				$+n^b$		$+c^b$			
Accepts responsibility (teacher's report)	$-c^b$	$-c^b$, $-n^b$	$-c^c$, $-n^c$		$+n^b$		$+c^b$, $+n^b$, $+p^b$		$+c^c$			
Consideration for other children (peers' ratings)	$+n^b$	$-p^b$		$-p^b$			$+p^b$	$+n^b$, $+p^b$, $+c^b$	$+c^b$		$+p^c$	$+p^c$
Identification (child's response)	$-c^b$	$-c^b$	$-c^c$		$-n^b$				$+c^b$			

Note. The data sources of the significant findings summarized in Tables 5.2, 5.3, and 5.5-5.7 are indicated as follows: c (child report), n (parent report of current practices), p (parent report of past practices).

[a] Data on induction regarding peers are incomplete since these data were obtained only from the parent reports of past practices.

[b] $p < .05$. [c] $p < .01$.

Table 5.3
Statistically Significant Relations Between
Child's Morality Indexes and Father's Discipline Techniques: Middle Class

Morality Index	Power Assertion			Love Withdrawal			Induction Re Parent			Induction Re Peers		
	Boys	Girls	Sum	Boys	Girls	Sum	Boys	Girls	Sum	Boys	Girls	Sum
Guilt (child's response)												
Internal moral judgment (child's response)		$-c^a$						$+c^a$				
Confession (mother's report)	$+p^a$		$+p^a$		$+c^a$		$-p^a$		$-p^a$			
Accepts responsibility (teacher's report)	$-c^b$		$-c^a$			$+c^a$						
Consideration for other children (peers' ratings)	$+n^a$		$+p^a$		$-c^a$			$+c^b$	$+c^b$			
Identification (child's response)												

^{a} $p < .05$. ^{b} $p < .01$.

[164]

Table 5.4
Statistically Significant Relations Between
Child's Morality Indexes and Mother's Discipline: Lower Class

Morality Index	Power Assertion			Love Withdrawal			Induction Re Parent		
	Boys	Girls	Sum	Boys	Girls	Sum	Boys	Girls	Sum
Guilt (child's response)				$+c^a$					
Internal moral judgment (child's response)								$+c^a$	
Accepts responsibility (teacher's report)									
Consideration for other children (peers' ratings)	$+c^a$							$+c^a$	
Identification (child's response)					$-c^a$	$-c^a$			

Note. Interview data were not obtained from the lower-class parents. Thus all entries in Tables 5.4 and 5.6 are based on child reports. For the same reason lower-class data on confession and on induction regarding peers were unavailable.

[a] $p < .05$.

Table 5.5
Statistically Significant Relations Between
Child's Morality Indexes and Father's Discipline: Lower Class

Morality Index	Power Assertion			Love Withdrawal			Induction Re Parent		
	Boys	Girls	Sum	Boys	Girls	Sum	Boys	Girls	Sum
Guilt (child's response)	$-c^a$								
Internal moral judgment (child's response)					$+c^a$				
Accepts responsibility (teacher's report)									
Consideration for other children (peers' ratings)									
Identification (child's response)	$-c^a$		$-c^a$				$+c^a$		$+c^a$

^{a} $p < .05$.

Table 5.6
Statistically Significant Relations Between Child's Morality Indexes and Parent's Composite Induction Score: Middle Class

Morality Index	Mother's Induction			Father's Induction		
	Boys	Girls	Sum	Boys	Girls	Sum
Guilt (child's response)	$+^a$	$+^a$	$+^a$			
Internal moral judgment (child's response)	$+^a$	$+^a$	$+^b$			
Confession (mother's report)	$+^b$		$+^c$			
Accepts responsibility (teacher's report)	$+^a$		$+^a$			
Consideration for other children (peers' ratings)		$+^b$	$+^a$			
Identification (child's response)	$+^a$					

^{a} $p < .05$.
^{b} $p < .01$.
^{c} $p < .005$.

Table 5.7

Statistically Significant Relations Between Child's Morality Indexes and Parent's Affection

Morality Index	Middle Class						Lower Class					
	Mothers			Fathers			Mothers			Fathers		
	Boys	Girls	Sum	Boys	Girls	Sum	Boys	Girls	Sum	Boys	Girls	Sum
Guilt (child's response)	$+c^a$		$+c^a$									
Internal moral judgment (child's response)		$+c^a$	$+n^a$			$+n^a$						
Confession (mother's report)	$+c^a$		$+c^a$			$+p^a$						
Accepts responsibility (teacher's report)		$+n^a$			$+n^a$							
Consideration for other children (peers' ratings)	$+p^a$	$+c^a$	$+c^a$	$+c^a$						$+c^a$		
Identification (child's response)	$+c^b$	$+c^b$	$+c^b$	$+c^a$								

^{a} $p < .05.$ ^{b} $p < .01.$

Behavior and Values
Consistency or Inconsistency
HERSHEL D. THORNBURG

The primary function of this paper is to conceptualize the development of a value system and its concomitant behaviors. In so doing the following positions are asserted:

1. The locus of the individual's initial value system is within the family.
2. During childhood there is a high degree of consistency between values and behaviors.
3. With growth discrepancies between values and behaviors may occur. This could result in:
   a. Values control behavior, thus behavior inconsistencies produce guilt, anxiety, shame, etc., or
   b. Behavior affects values, thus behavior inconsistencies produce value shift.
4. During adolescence maximum inconsistencies occur, an essential process in one's own value formation.
5. Well-adjusted adult functioning is facilitated by maximum value-behavior consistency.

Work in the areas of value or conscience development has been going on for some time with the first, most definitive work being Jean Piaget's *The Moral Judgment of the Child* in 1948. Piaget, being a developmental psychologist, interpreted corresponding intellectual and moral (conscience) growth. Two characteristics dominated his thinking, and several studies done since, which have attempted to replicate his work, are somewhat supportive of these two contentions: (a) Early in a child's experiences (such as preschool age) the child interprets the observable consequences of his behavior and forms such value judgments based on external evidence, and (b) As the child moves toward 9 to 11 years of age (within the defined range of preadolescence in this book), he begins to cognize, thus,

Reprinted by permission of the author and publisher from *Adolescence*, 1973, 8 (32).

internalize the rightness and wrongness of things. This behavior makes it possible to better confirm value indications within the child.

Aronfreed (1968) points to four characteristics which came out of Piaget's works. Briefly, they are (p. 258):

1. The young child at first judges the severity of transgressions with respect to their visible damage or harm. As the child becomes older, its judgments become more sensitive to the transgressor.
2. Younger children tend toward the perception of "imminent justice" — the perception that punishment is impersonally ordained in the very performance of a transgression. The older child becomes more perceptive of how punishment follows from principles which take into account the consequences of a transgression for other people.
3. The young child judges the appropriateness of punishment by its severity rather than by its relevance to transgression. Younger children seem to perceive that the expiation of a transgression is proportionate to the magnitude of external retribution. The older child is more likely to recommend that the transgressor make restitution or that punishment be tailored to have reciprocity with the transgression.
4. The child first interprets rules as having a fixed or absolute legitimacy that is given by external authority. Gradually, the child comes to see that the application of rules may be relative to people and situations, and that rules are established and maintained through reciprocal social agreements.

If evidences from Piaget's research are accurate, and they are thought to be so by several writers (Boehm, 1962; Kohlberg, 1964), then, it is appropriate to conceptualize as to the developmental nature of the consistency between values held by the child and behaviors expressed by him. Table 5.8 illustrates the developmental nature of the values and behavior systems. Emphasis is placed on the primary influence of each stage of development. Some readers may take exception to the specified

Table 5.8
From Consistency Through Inconsistency to Consistency

Primary Influences	Consistency Range	Stage	
Society	Behavior◄──────►Values	Adulthood (27-on)	Consistency
Peers/ Society	Behavior◄─ ─ ─►Values	Young Adulthood (20-26)	Toward Consistency
Peers	Behavior◄─────►Values	Adolescence (14-19)	Inconsistency
Parents/ Peers	Behavior◄─ ─ ─►Values	Preadolescence (9-13)	Toward Inconsistency
Parents	Behavior◄──────►Values	Childhood (1-8)	Consistency

age ranges. It should be pointed out that such ranges are approximate rather than inclusive ages. It is true, however, that with age variances, the developmental sequence is the same.

Family Influence

While it is true that we live in a more complex and influential society, it is equally true that the family still primarily influences one's values and behaviors throughout childhood. Parents are the child's interpreters of social and cultural systems and beliefs. In early childhood they represent most of the child's world. The basic concepts of right and wrong are usually taught as parents seek to develop appropriate behaviors within the child. Five ways to develop values in a child have been suggested by Calmes and Voight (1969). Briefly, they are:

A. The child learns consideration for others by being cared for, loved, and trusted by his parents.
B. Parents should serve as models of what they want their children to become.
C. Parents should be consistent in their behavior toward and demands of their children.
D. Parents should provide their children with realistic rationale as to why certain behaviors are appropriate.
E. Parents should use praise more frequently than blame or punishment to demonstrate the appropriateness of behavior.

The consideration of these five points as ways of teaching early values and behaviors also points to the hypothesized consistency between those things which a child believes in and those things he does. When such consistency occurs parents reinforce these behaviors. If a child's behavior brings parental approval, he feels more secure and is likely to learn that the behavior is not only acceptable to his parents but instrumental in satisfying the child's needs or feelings also. The strength of early parental influences is not only perpetuated throughout childhood but is also often carried into preadolescence (Petrich and Chadderdon, 1969).

Toward Inconsistency

By preadolescence values and behaviors of children are extremely diversified and increasingly unpredictable. This occurs out of several reasons: (1) The family as an influential unit is being severely challenged; (2) The preadolescent is increasingly concerned about the socialization process in school; (3) peers begin taking on importance; and (4) growth and development patterns cause the preadolescent to begin taking on a new view of self.

Several factors affect the family unit. Primary to change has been increased communication and technology. The mass media have become a major way of the preadolescent spending his time. More mothers are working, divorce is more common, mobility affects over 20 percent of all homes, and behavior alternatives are made more plausible. Families are encouraged to break away from traditional values and incorporate into the family unit the emerging societal values. This situation has been described by Mead as, "The present American family is caught between two images — the image the family people seem to think we once had, and that of a new, emerging one. In between the two there is a real family and it sometimes has a rather hard time (1955, p. 22)."

The preadolescent now often moves out of the mainstream of family influence toward more response to and acceptance of peer beliefs and behaviors. Upon entering this developmental stage the youngster brings with him the dominant values and behaviors of his family. Before leaving this stage, it is clear that peers have now become a strong influence (Havighurst, 1968; Thornburg, 1970). Thus, as conceptualized in Table 5.8, both parents (in the early stages of preadolescence) and peers (in the later stages) are primary influences. The solid line between behavior and values in the childhood stage represents consistency, a situation that is different as characterized by the broken line during preadolescence. It is appropriate to say that much of the preadolescent's behavior is consistent with values but to a lesser extent than during childhood.

Growing Value-Behavior Discrepancies

Upon moving out of preadolescence into adolescence, distinctive differences between behavior and values are prevalent. This period of repeated inconsistency is a natural outgrowth of the adolescent's need to emancipate himself and to begin determining those values which he wants to hold for himself. This may mean complete rejection of most parental and societal values or there may be little discrepancy evidenced. One factor involved here is how strongly parental values are within the system. Another value source is the strength of the influence of one's peers. It is clearly evident that the adolescent is quite involved with peers, especially in the behavioral realm. Many peer values also seem to be legitimate alternatives to existing values.

Two considerations are essential to this discussion. First, values may control behaviors and when the adolescent exhibits behavior that is contrary to values guilt might result. This is most likely if parental or religious influences have been a decisively strong determiner of one's values. The personality constructs become closed or restricted and, thus, when displaying differing behavior, the system cannot tolerate or accommodate such behavior. Guilt, remorse, anxiety, frustration, shame, or other comparable words describe the affective state of the behavior.

Second, behavior also affects values. It is possible that behavioral inconsistencies, after repeated incidents of the same behavior, will produce a value shift. Many youth initially experience behaviors which, because of their value discrepancy, produce guilt, only to find eventually that such a behavior is now part of their belief system. Perhaps most of our value shifts result from alternative behavior expressions. Through such action the personality learns to accept alternative behaviors, thus becoming more open and flexible.

During adolescence maximum inconsistencies occur. The dominant peer influence facilitates this. In fact, peers are often formed around value structures as well as behavior realms (Thornburg, 1971b). This organization means that differing behaviors may be (a) the same among youth but different from society or (b) different among youth and different from society. Therefore, adolescent subcultures may be formed because of behavioral differences or because of value differences. Unquestionably, with the myriad of beliefs and behaviors among youth, both reasons for peer affiliations can be demonstrated.

Toward Consistency

In the latter stages of adolescence social maturation is reaching completion (Dunphy, 1963; Thornburg, 1971a). With this maturation almost realized, social integration becomes an increasingly important task. It is fair to say that society probably influences social integration more than peers do. Thus, upon entering young adulthood most individuals carry into it the values and behaviors characteristic of one's peer group during adolescence. If the young adult remains in an educational institution, such as college youth, peer influence may still be more dominant than society's influence. Thus, social maturation is continued causing a prolongment of social integration. If, however, the young adult is beginning to find his way in the world, such as noncollege youth, society becomes the prevailing influence and social integration begins (Thornburg, 1971b).

The inconsistencies experienced within adolescence are instrumental in helping sort out the values held which may have been derived from parents, school, society, religion, or peers. As a young adult the move is back toward value consistency. It would be premature to assert that the value-behavior consistency model is restored here. First, many residual effects from adolescence are felt during this developmental stage. Second, it is unlikely that such consistency can be realized prior to successful attempts at social integration. It is, nevertheless, the period of time during which an individual realizes a high degree of value-behavior consistency.

The Functioning Adult

As an adult social maturation and social integration should both be realized. A high degree of consistency is now present. Adults find that well-adjusted functioning is better experienced when a minimum of internal conflict exists. While it is unlikely that anyone will ever reach perfect consistency between values and behavior it is true that operational consistency levels can be obtained. Such levels generally facilitate normal required functioning within one's self and his society. Society, of course, is the dominating external influence. It is desirable that an adult have self-acceptable reference points which direct his life.

In referring to Table 5.8, it may appear that the same ideology is proposed for the adult as was proposed for the child. The child, of course, exhibits value-behavior consistency because he knows little more than that which is directly taught him. He has neither the maturation nor experiences to challenge them. With the adult, the reverse is true. Every opportunity is given in the course of development to challenge both his basic beliefs and actions. If, as an adult, he emerges with an operational value-behavior consistency then the intellectual, emotional, and behavioral pursuits characteristic of preadolescence, adolescence, and young adulthood have served as learning experiences. Then as an adult it is possible to realize that value formation, while somewhat stabilized, is an ongoing process that is tested and considered with every behavior if the reason for behavior or the behavioral alternatives is known.

Values in Conflict
CHARLES A. GLATT

Many questions currently plague teachers. The unsettled and dynamic world in which we live refuses to let even the "self-contained classroom" exist apart from turmoil, conflict, and confusion. Established patterns and honored traditions lose their hallowed security, and a quicksand of uncertainty replaces them.

During the past few years, professional work has taken me from Quebec, Canada, to the Gulf Coast of Mississippi and from the Carolinas to California. Most of the travel has been related to two kinds of activities: 1) working with educators in the attempt to identify and to develop better ways of educating "unlucky kids" (sometimes labelled "deprived" or "disadvantaged"); and 2) working with school systems that are attempting to solve problems occasioned by the process of racial desegregation.

In spite of much that I have found unique about particular schools and school systems, at least one striking similarity exists, especially in the thinking that troubles teachers. The question most commonly asked in the workshops and institutes of which I have been a part is, "What can (or ought, or should, or must) we do about the conflict between the values we teach in the schools and opposing values that are being learned at home and in the neighborhoods?"

The question, of course, is not new. Nor is it easy to answer. One person's answer will not satisfy everyone. But the question can be answered, and ought to be.

Based on experiences born out of conflict in values, I am committed to the view that what teachers are searching for is not actually *an answer* to *a question* about that conflict. Rather, they are facing a problem and they

Reprinted with permission of the author and publisher from the *Pennsylvania School Journal*, 1970, 118 (3), 178-181; 201.

are wanting a defensible solution that can be translated into satisfying human behavior.

Customarily those of us who work especially in desegregation institutes pose a possible solution in terms of three causal factors: 1) the learning of values; 2) middle-classism *vs.* some alternatives; and 3) confusion related to stereotypes. These factors are important enough to merit some discussion here.

The Learning of Values

Several questions are often posed about the learning of values. For example, what is a value? How is a value taught? Can values once learned be unlearned? What ought to be the role of the school in teaching values? And, of course, when values conflict, how does one decide which is more desirable? Many other questions can be raised and need to be raised, but for the purposes of this investigation, we can at least start with these.

May the reader please mind, the attempt here is not to exhaust philosophical and sociological thought about a topic, but to examine a problem critically by means of philosophical and sociological analysis. A brief search that can result in behavioral differences sometimes offers the teacher advantages over larger treatises that often tend further to alienate theory and practice.

Values in common, ordinary language are guides for behavior. They are generally thought to be either intrinsic (built in) or instrumental (developed out of). When thought to be intrinsic, values sometimes lead to internal conflict for a person, especially if he detects conflict between the behaviors they prescribe and the ordinary behaviors that he enjoys or that others around him seem to engage in. On the other hand, when values develop from human transactions and become flexible tools by which man guides his activities, they can cause very disturbing problems for the person in whose world rigid standards are necessary.

Regardless of their origins, values are generally thought to be learned as an indirect result rather than a direct result of our teaching methods. They are not studied *per se.* Even though a teacher's lesson plan may have listed as an objective, "to teach children to be honest," the learning of honesty (as a set of behaviors) is most apt to be what Professor Kilpatrick used to call "concomitant." One learns to be honest or to be dishonest, we believe, as he chooses to pattern his behavior after models who appeal to his needs and wants.

Someone suggested long ago that by the time a child enters the first grade, he already knows half of all he will ever learn. Although the proportions may be inaccurate, the principle is sound. A child has learned a lot before his formal, institutional learning career begins. He knows quite well how to communicate by means of the language arts. A list of other learnings is not necessary here, but much of his future life has in a sense been determined by the values he already has learned previous to our getting him into the school.

If he has internalized respect for the rights of other persons and for property rights, for "telling the truth" and for not stealing, for neatness, for thrift, for punctuality, for sobriety, for fulfillment of responsibility, he most likely will fit our image of the good, solid American citizen throughout his life. If he has not, regardless of other factors, he probably will wear a label like "disadvantaged," "deprived," or "problem child," and in many ways always will have trouble adapting to society's expectations.

Most *unlearning* is difficult, as any cigarette smoker knows. All social systems have sets of folkways, taboos, mores, and laws to regulate behavior, but all societies also have found necessary the development of elaborate methods for dealing with deviant behaviors. Criminologists generally concede that attempts to rehabilitate prisoners have superficial results. The warden of Ohio's state penitentiary said recently in a recorded interview that the function of his institution is not to reform nor to rehabilitate, but to keep criminals away from society. (The very name, *penitentiary*, of course, suggests an institution where one unlearns former values and then learns new ones through repenting or becoming penitent.)

Values can be unlearned and can be replaced with alternate ones. But here, perhaps, is the Achilles' heel of learning theory. We have been so concerned with what are generally considered to be the primary purposes of education, cultivation of the intellect or transmission of heritage, that we have paid but scant attention to both the content and methodology of other learning. In fact, too few of our pedagogical spokesmen apparently have grave doubts about a deliberate role for the schools in the teaching of certain values, for example, as they relate to religion, to politics, to sex, to family life, to race, and to the consumption of alcohol and the use of drugs.

The policy making body of the National Education Association took a fairly firm stand on this issue several years ago (1951), but the uniqueness of America's educational systems seem currently to deter strong consensus on related issues today.

That some conflict in our commitment to basic sets of values does exist appears to be unquestionable. The 1968 national political scene certainly indicated that Americans differ greatly over the values we hold (or do not hold) relative to law and order in our society. When large portions of cities such as Newark and Detroit are burned by looters and rioters, white Americans shudder. When men such as Malcolm X, Medger Evers, Martin Luther King, and the two Kennedy brothers are murdered, black Americans tremble — both with fear and with rage.

Is one value system right or good or better or more effective and any others wrong or bad or worse or less effective? The answer is a confused one. But in our country we have geared our educational system to the answer that, until quite recently, seemed to be questioned only by kooks, crackpots, and traitors. Without bothering to confuse our thinking further by careful analysis and definition, we have labelled our answer "middle class values."

Middle-classism

America's greatest proponent of that answer currently is the longshore-man-philosopher, Eric Hoffer, whose defense of the middle class is at times magnificently stated (1967).

The middle class value system does not actually exist. But its myth, like Santa Claus and the Easter Bunny, does. The myth is about *a* value system; in reality there are many individual systems, all a lot alike, that are characterized by continuous (although usually slow) change.

These systems can be described in many ways, but the virtues they supposedly encourage are evidenced and taught, as they long have been, by terse and sometimes trite admonitions. These are common ones:

A penny saved is a penny earned (thrift).
A rolling stone gathers no moss (stability).
Don't kill the goose that lays the golden egg (loyalty).
A stitch in time saves nine (forethought).
A bird in the hand is worth two in the bush (contentment).
Look before you leap (caution).
Your sins will find you out (all of the virtues).
Opportunity knocks but once (preparation).

And the list goes on. . . .

What we often fail to recognize about middle class values is their sometimes inconsistency. How can "still water run the deepest" when still water does not run at all? And, of course, one must be honest and truthful, but not always. He must always be discrete. As the values are interpreted into human behavior, great conflicts develop. Double standards seem to be all right.

The point is, generally we conceive of a value system that permits or encourages certain behaviors, but which denies or discourages others. Specifically, however, we each want our individual actions to be evaluated not in general terms, but in view of all extenuating circumstances. And we are pretty good at justifying (thus excusing) ourselves.

This middle class citizen insists that in order to be an *acceptable* person, another must behave not as he, himself, behaves, but as he perceives himself behaving with his indiscretions all properly excused.

Of course, even the most exemplary behaviors that apparently manifest the most treasured values are only part of middle class exclusiveness. Many Negro professionals perceive themselves as belonging to the middle class, but that does not mean that in fact they do belong. Few whites with whom they associate would tell them so, but they certainly tell each other so. In many communities, like getting into Zen, the harder one tries to model after the stereotype the more likely he is to defeat his purposes.

Let's examine selected aspects of alternate value systems. For several years I worked for an engineering firm in the Southwest during the uranium boom. Trips were often taken onto the Navajo Indian Reservation. Since we knew something of the Navajo's reputation for being "thieving Indians," we were careful to take precautions against theft. Experience taught, however, that as long as a piece of equipment was *where it was supposed to be*, the fear of theft was wasted. *If*, on the other hand, a tool was left lying around in such a way as to suggest that it had been discarded, it likely would be taken. The value system was a highly ethical one. Stealing seldom if ever occurred. But discarded equipment soon disappeared.

Later, when I was teaching Navajo students in junior high school, this same value system was seen to operate. Bicycles properly belong in the stands provided for them, not scattered over the playing area. Some of the scattered ones disappeared.

The Navajo child, caught between cultures, often becomes what the behavioral scientist calls a "marginal person." Even though ignorance of the law is not ordinarily deemed a very good excuse, "involuntary" or "unpremeditated" crimes are usually met with justice tempered by more mercy than deliberate crimes are.

Another example: Our professional literature teaches us regularly that illegitimacy rates are much higher among Negroes than among whites. Statistics bear out the stereotype. Census data reveal, for example, that of 585 single women in Baltimore in 1960 with three or more children each, 575 were nonwhite (which may suggest any number of curricular implications from use of the pill to how to lie to a census taker). But what does the *white* middle class value system dictate when a single girl gets pregnant? Usually one of three choices. Either she enters into a forced marriage, has an abortion, or permits the child to be adopted. "Sinful" is thereby branded on the mother for all to see, and often "illegitimate" or worse is stamped on a document about the child if it is not aborted.

What does the supposedly inferior value system subscribed to by many Negroes dictate? The three alternatives listed above are not rare among Negroes, and perhaps are increasingly being chosen as more blacks attempt to move into the middle class. But traditional values where I grew up demanded that the best home and most love that adults can give to a child be given — by the mother, perhaps by a stepfather, often by aunts and grandmothers. And the child was not branded, except by white society which needed him as a statistic with which to prove inferiority of blacks.

Will middle class insistence on adherence to its own fictitious value system destroy the efficiency and humaneness of alternate systems? Is there an alternative to such potential destruction? I think there is.

We have learned a great deal from the behavioral sciences about introspection. We can get inside ourselves and find out what makes us "tick." As an alternative to forcing a system (whether it be mythical or just inadequate) on fellow Americans, we need social class introspection. This can perhaps best be accomplished as each of us examines our own values and questions their appropriateness as viable guides for human behavior.

Confusion Related to Stereotypes

The stereotypes we hold about other people are important. These stereotypes are often not deliberately taught, but they often are learned quite thoroughly.

Don't all Navajos steal?
Aren't all Negro men shiftless?
Haven't all of California's young people gotten hooked on LSD?
Aren't all Georgians and South Carolinians descendants of thieves and murderers?
Aren't all Negro women "loose" sexually?
Aren't all white women frigid?
Don't all Negro men have much greater sexual prowess than white men have?
Aren't all Polish women big dumb blondes?
Aren't all Jews wealthy?
Don't all physicians engage in fee-splitting, a form of white collar crime?
Don't all lawyers collude on cases at their clients' expense?
Don't all teachers feel that they would have good jobs if somehow they didn't have to put up with the kids?
Don't all principals spend most of their time counting dimes from Coke machines?
Don't all women of southern European extraction get fat and flabby after they start having children?
Don't all bankers foreclose mortgages on widows unmercifully?

The answer to each question, of course, is "no." But even as some smoke indicates some fire, stereotypes about human behavior usually have some basis in fact. We too easily substitute *all* for *some* and then behave as if *all* had been accurate originally.

Some of the most commonly mentioned among stereotypes I hear which supposedly indicate conflicting values between middle class youngsters and lower class youngsters are these (phrased in the negative tone about lower class children as they are said to me):

They have no aspirations or ambitions.
They don't care about the future.
They can't learn.
They won't take responsibility.
They can't read.
They have never known any security.
They are dirty.
Their language patterns are different.
They can't work verbal problems.
They don't respect themselves.
They steal.
They don't mix with the other kids.
Their parents take no interest in the schools.
Their parents won't come to P. T. A.
They misbehave.
They just don't care.

And the list continues.

Quite honestly, most of the teachers with whom I have worked perceive themselves as professionals, not as glorified babysitters. Or rather, they want desperately to be professionals, and resent bitterly the feeling that their jobs often resemble something other than what they want. "If I could just get rid of the ones who cause trouble, I could teach the rest. But all the new ones — ugh!"

John Dewey, among others, pointed out long ago that we not only structure new learnings in terms of previous experiences, but that current experiences cause us to restructure what we retain of previous learnings. Yet, we find this concept difficult to use as an intellectual tool.

Stereotypes, whatever their origins, have been learned by each of us through our experiences with others. Pragmatic learning theory suggests that much of what we "know" resides with us in the form of *prehensions*, or vague general beliefs that we have learned passively, not through active intellectual endeavor. In order to clarify, or correct, or supplant this "knowledge" we have to *apprehend* ourselves (literally, to stop whatever else we are doing), to become *at tension* (not pay attention) mentally, and discover. This process may never result in ultimate, unchanging Truth, but it can lead to a sounder basis for beliefs. Something then is added to our prehension (now *com*-prehension) — understanding, or literally *standing under*, since we assume learning to be upstairs in our heads.

Without this process of apprehension leading to or facilitating comprehension, stereotypes are perpetuated. They are inflicted on ourselves and our students, and they quite effectively block the learning of more accurate concepts. When this process is applied by a teacher to the kinds of stereotypes listed above, most of the supposed conflicts between the values we teach in the schools and opposing values being learned in the home and neighborhood simply do not exist.

But we hopefully do not live in a fool's world. Many white middle class children come from homes where they are taught to hate — especially to hate Negroes. Many black children have learned devious ways of surviving in an unfriendly world. In the Appalachian hills a lot of children learn to distill, to age, and to distribute corn whiskey illegally. Some of their teachers even buy it from them occasionally.

We likely will never solve all of our problems.

Value Conflicts and New Values

Up to this juncture I have described the problem of value conflict as one largely fictitious, but also quite real since we behave as if it were genuine. A basic assumption has underpinned most of the preceding remarks, that is, that what we are teaching in the schools as desired learnings are behaviors consistent with middle class values. That our language, our mannerisms, our materials, and our expectations reflect middle class orientation has been profusely documented in recent years. The "white Anglo-Saxon Protestant" ethic has been a popular topic for writers to elaborate. An accompanying assumption, at least partially denied here, insists that children from other than middle class homes have problems that arise from opposing values.

One further aspect of this entire discussion needs to be examined. If one assumes that certain values are learned at school and others learned elsewhere, he is likely to overlook a most important characteristic of contemporary American life — namely, that young people not only *learn* values, they also originate them. The generation gap so commonly mentioned today is not new, but it may be different from gaps that previously existed.

Not only are our young people questioning, they are also rejecting pat answers. They also are openly experimenting with a wide variety of human behaviors as they develop their own answers. Sex, politics, religion, race relations, hallucinatory drugs, and "the establishment" all seem to be open to their inquiring minds, and the bravery that motivates their investigations shocks the rest of us. The answers they develop, the knowledge they gain, the beliefs they structure, all influence the values they internalize. These values, in the long view, may be the most important of all.

The answers given here are perhaps at best intelligent guesses; but the world in which human behavior occurs demands that problems be analyzed and that answers be applied to real situations, for it is an unsettled and dynamic world. When we as adults fail to apply critical thinking to our tasks, the young people who are our responsibility suffer most.

Combined References for Chapter 5

Allinsmith, W., and Greening, T. C. Guilt over anger as predicted from parental discipline: A study of superego development. *American Psychologist*, 1955, 10, 320. (Abstract)

Aronfreed, J. The nature, variety, and social patterning of moral responses to transgression. *Journal of Abnormal and Social Psychology*, 1961, 63, 223-241.

Aronfreed, J. *Conduct and Conscience*. New York: Academic Press, 1968.

Becker, W. Consequences of different kinds of parent discipline. In M. L. and L. W. Hoffman (Eds.), *Review of Child Development Research*. Vol. 1. New York: Russell Sage Foundation, 1964. Pp. 169-208.

Boehm, L. The development of conscience: A comparison of American children of different mental and socioeconomic levels. *Child Development*, 1962, 33, 590.

Bronfenbrenner, U. Socialization and social class through time and space. In E. E. Maccoby, T. M. Newcomb, and E. L. Hartley (Eds.), *Readings in Social Psychology*. New York: Holt, 1958. Pp. 400-425.

Calmes, R. E. and Voight, R. L. The influence of rural America on the character of the nation. *Progressive Agriculture in Arizona*, 1969, 21(5), 18-19.

Dunphy, D. C. The social structure of urban adolescent peer groups. *Sociometry*, 1963, 26, 230-246.

Educational Policies Commission. *Moral and Spiritual Values in the Public Schools*. Washington, D.C.: National Education Association, 1951.

Glueck, S., and Glueck, E. *Unraveling Juvenile Delinquency*. New York: Commonwealth Fund, 1950.

Gordon, J. E., and Cohn, F. Effect of fantasy arousal of affiliation drive on doll play aggression. *Journal of Abnormal and Social Psychology*, 1963, 66, 301-307.

Grinder, R. E. Relations between behavioral and cognitive dimensions of conscience in middle childhood. *Child Development*, 1964, 35, 881-891.

Havighurst, R. L. The middle school child in contemporary society. *Theory into Practice*, 1968, 7(3), 120-122.

Hill, W. F. Learning theory and the acquisition of values. *Psychological Review*, 1960, 67, 317-331.

Hoffer, E. *The Temper of our Time*. New York: Harper and Row, 1967.

Hoffer, E. *The True Believer*. New York: Harper and Row, 1967.

Hoffman, M. L. Child-rearing practices and moral development: Generalizations from empirical research. *Child Development*, 1963a, 34, 295-318.

Hoffman, M. L. Parent discipline and the child's consideration for others. *Child Development*, 1963b, 34, 573-588.

Hoffman, M. L. Personality, family structure, and social class as antecedents of parental power assertion. *Child Development*, 1963c, 34, 869-884.

Hoffman, M. L. and Hoffman, L. W. (Eds.) *Review of Child Development Research*. Vol. 1. New York: Russell Sage, 1964.

Hoffman, M. L. and Saltzstein, H. D. Parent discipline and the child's moral development. *Journal of Personality and Social Psychology*, 1967, 5, 45-57.

Hoffman, M. L., and Saltzstein, H. D. Parent practices and the development of children's moral orientations. In W. E. Martin (Chm.), Parent behavior and children's personality development: Current project research. Symposium presented at American Psychological Association, Chicago, September 1, 1960.

Kohlberg, L. The· development of children's orientations toward a moral order. *Vita Humana*, 1963, 6, 11-33.

Kohlberg, L. Development of moral character and moral ideology. In M. L. Hoffman and L. W. Hoffman (Eds.), *Review of Child Development Research*. New York: Russell Sage, 1964, Vol. 1., pp. 383-441.

Kohlberg, L. Moral education in the schools: A developmental view. *School Review*, 1966, 74, 1-29.

McCord, J., and McCord, W. The effect of parental role model on criminality. *Journal of Social Issues*, 1958, 14, 66-75.

Mead, M. How fares the American family. *National Parent Teacher*, 1955, 49, 22.

Medinnus, G. R. Behavioral and cognitive measures of conscience development. *Journal of Genetic Psychology*, 1966, 109, 147-150.

Miller, W. Lower class culture as a generating milieu of gang delinquency. *Journal of Social Issues*, 1958, 14, 5-19.

Murphy, L. B. *Social Behavior and Child Personality*. New York: Columbia University Press, 1937.

Neagley, R. and Evans, N. *Dean Handbook for Effective Curriculum Development.* Englewood Cliffs: Prentice-Hall, 1967.

Petrich, B. and Chadderdon, H. Family beliefs of junior high school pupils. *Family Coordinator*, 1969, 18(4), 374-378.

Piaget, J. *The Moral Judgment of the Child*. Glencoe, Ill.: Free Press, 1948. (First edition: London: Kegan Paul, 1932).

Raths, L. E., Harmin, M., and Simon, S. B. *Values and Teaching*. Columbus, Ohio: Charles E. Merrill, 1966.

Sears, R. R., Maccoby, E. E., and Levin, H. *Patterns of Child Rearing*. Evanston, Ill.: Row, Peterson, 1957.

Steinberg, S. The language of prejudice. *Today's Education*, 1971, 60(2), 16.

Thornburg, H. D. Learning and maturation in middle school age youth. *Clearing House*, 1970, 45(3), 150-155.

Thornburg, H. D. *Contemporary Adolescence: Readings*. Monterey, Calif.: Brooks/Cole, 1971a.

Thornburg, H. D. Peers: Three distinct groups. *Adolescence*, 1971b, 6(21), 59-76.

CHAPTER 6 discipline and the preadolescent

Introduction

By the time the child reaches grade four, a definite trend away from the inner self toward the social self is unfolding. Throughout the intermediate grades, each student becomes increasingly aware of his social environment and of the importance to entertain beliefs and behaviors observed within it. With accompanying interest in one's peers and a gradual movement away from one's parents as the primary social and attitudinal source, this social movement is even more pronounced by the time the preadolescent reaches the middle school or junior high.

You will recall from the readings in Chapter One that the preadolescent has been characterized as a changing physical, intellectual, and social being. Lois Barclay Murphy has described the preadolescent in the following manner:

Between the ages of ten and thirteen or fourteen, typically the child goes through almost as great a transformation as that seen when a tadpole changes into a frog (1970).

Place this new-type individual with his emerging, seemingly inexhaustible energy in the classroom and often what is observed is a preadolescent who is somewhat restless, irritable, energetic, impossible, disinterested, withdrawn, ornery, or some other adjective which attempts to describe him. In short, for many teachers, the preadolescent is a *discipline problem.*

Because classroom management is a phase of teaching with which each teacher must contend, it is important to discuss ways in which the teacher can manage his classroom, the most common approach of which is discipline. Therefore, within this introduction and the three readings selected for this chapter, our attention will focus on aspects of the teaching-learning environment that are incorporated within the concept of discipline.

First, it should be remembered that the preadolescent is a changing emotional being as well as a changing being in other areas of his life. He will bring into the classroom attitudes which are important and relevant to him. His attitudes may focus on school in general, teachers in general, a specific subject, a specific teacher, other students, homework, the social environment, or other important concerns in his life. Attitudes may also be expressed at different levels by the preadolescent. This is best conceptualized within the classification of attitudes developed by Katz and Stotland (1959). They defined five attitudinal categories which are briefly stated:

1. Affective Associations. This is the simplest type of attitude, based on the degree of positive or negative influence in a situation. If an individual goes fishing and catches several large fish, he most likely will perceive the experience as pleasant and do it again. If all he catches is a rubber tire, the fishing outing might not seem so attractive next time. The degree of positive or negative attitude is dependent upon past association of the attitude situation. The persistence of an attitude position is related to the repeated pleasantness and unpleasantness of attitude behaviors.

2. Intellectualized Attitudes. This is an attitude containing a strong cognitive component. When an individual seeks to gain perspective within his environment, he exercises a cognitive attitude. If environmental situations are incongruous, one's attitude is modified or distorted in order to environmentally adapt. A person may be driving down the highway and observe huge billows of smoke pouring out of a factory's smokestacks. His immediate attitude might be one of contempt toward the company for polluting the air. Later, he might find out that while what he saw was upsetting, the company was in the process of installing an anti-pollution device on its smokestacks. This, he reasons to himself, is more acceptable, and, in fact, all companies should be doing the same thing. The basis for change of an intellectualized attitude is new or additional information that a person may cognitively handle.

3. Action-Oriented Attitudes. When we act toward objects we value as a way of satisfying our needs, we are expressing action-oriented attitudes. If we value social relationships with prestigious people, our action tendency will be able to create situations in which such a need can be satisfied. Similarly, there may be things we prefer to avoid as much as approach, i. e., negative action tendency.

4. Balanced Attitudes. Katz and Stotland describe a balanced attitude as one which has affective, cognitive, and behavioral components. Usually an individual seeks to reduce a drive or need when expressing a balanced attitude. A high school girl may join the homemaker's club (behavioral) because she feels strongly about allying with other girls (affective) and recognizes many basic benefits as a result of the affiliation (cognitive), i. e., learning how to sew, cook, design, create, etc.

5. Ego-Defensive Attitudes. This attitudinal force has the same components as the balanced attitude with only the source of origin being different. Ego defensive attitudes are generated from internal conflict. While external conditions may control the exercise of internal conflict, it does not lessen

the source of conflict. Typically, ego-defensive attitudes are unconsciously expressed such as rationalization, repression, scapegoating, projection, etc.

It may seem that undue stress is being placed on attitudes here. Nevertheless, it is a valid contention that the attitudes which the preadolescent has toward his school environment, or any specific aspect of it, may directly bear upon his behaviors and how a teacher views the preadolescent. Thus, if many of his behaviors are reflections of negative attitudes, he may be viewed as a discipline problem, whereas, if his behavior reflects degrees of positivism, he is often described as an "ideal student."

The question as to what teachers consider serious behavior problems in the classroom is not new, but it is one which bears continued analysis. A most recent discussion of this issue has been conducted by Rajpal (1972). In his study, data from a 1928 study (Wickman) was compared to a group of third through sixth grade teachers today. The results of the study are shown in Table 6.1.

In analyzing his data Rajpal makes an observation that is highly significant. "The rankings of 'unhappy' and 'un-social' behaviors are up from 22.5 to 2 and from 40.5 to 9 in seriousness respectively. In both cases, there seems to be greater awareness by classroom teachers in the current study of the feelings of children and their significance in the life of the child (1972, p. 592)."

It is appropriate to suggest that those teachers who see some classroom behaviors as serious, too deviant from the classroom norm, or intolerable, may invoke some type of disciplinary action. This, of course, can be problematic for several reasons. First, there is no common acceptable definition as to what discipline is and, therefore, disciplinary practices run the gamut from strict authoritarianism to high permissiveness. Second, teachers, either during their teacher training program or within their school district, have been given very little help or direction as to how they should handle discipline problems. Third, teachers often invoke discipline on children when the teacher is under some stress and thus, too emotionally involved to evaluate the situation with perspective. Fourth, many teachers out of lack of knowing what to do, adopt traditional methods of discipline, such as corporal punishment, locking classrooms, standing children in the corner, placing them in the hallway, etc. Finally, the impending lack of support often given to the classroom teacher by the administration and the community, causes a permissiveness of anti-social preadolescent behaviors to occur in the classroom.

The problem of discipline is a crucial one. The importance of the topic is reflected in the initial article in this chapter by David Ausubel. Hardly any writer has so cogently stressed the role and alternatives available to the

Table 6.1
Rank-Order of 50 Behavior Problems, Based on Ratings Made by Four Groups: Rankings of Teachers and School Psychologists in This Study in Comparison with Rankings of Wickman's Teachers and Mental Hygienists in 1928

Behavior Items	Wickman Teachers	Teachers in This Study	Wickman Mental Hygienists	School Psychologists in This Study
Tardiness	30	38	43	39.5
Truancy	6	5	23	17.5
Destroying school materials	10	3	45	4
Untruthfulness (lying)	5	4	23	10.5
Imaginative lying	42	28	33	34
Cheating	9	6	23	8.5
Stealing	2	1	13.5	4
Profanity	15	34.5	47	44.5
Smoking	18	34.5	49	46.5
Obscene notes, pictures, talk	4	23	28.5	34
Masturbation	3	45	41	46.5
Heterosexual activity	1	32.5	26	36
Disorderliness	20.5	46	46	44.5
Whispering and note writing	46.5	50	50	50
Interrupting (talkativeness)	43.5	48	48	49
Restlessness (overactivity)	49	47	41	42.5
Inattention	26	20	34	20
Lack of interest in work	14	14	25	8.5
Carelessness in work	24.5	24	37.5	24
Laziness	16.5	18	35.5	16
Unreliableness (irresponsible)	12	8	21	10.5
Disobedience	11	17	41	20
Impertinence (defiance)	7	21.5	37.5	28.5
Cruelty and bullying	8	7	6	4

Behavior Items	Wickman Teachers	Teachers in This Study	Wickman Mental Hygienists	School Psychologists in This Study
Quarrelsomeness	27	21.5	31	25.5
Tattling	46.5	42	28.5	39.5
Stubbornness (contrariness)	32.5	43	20	39.5
Sullenness (sulkiness)	35	27	12	22
Temper tantrums	13	13	17	14.5
Impudence, impoliteness, rudeness	16.5	19	32	28.5
Selfishness (unsportsmanship)	24.5	15	16	12
Domineering, overbearing	32.5	26	11	25.5
Shyness (bashfulness)	50	39	13.5	34
Sensitiveness	48	29.5	10	23
Unsocial, withdrawing	40.5	9	1	1
Overcritical of others	45	29.5	9	27
Thoughtlessness (forgetting)	38	32.5	39	32
Inquisitiveness, meddlesomeness	43.5	44	44	39.5
Silliness (smartness)	39	49	30	48
Unhappy, depressed	22.5	2	3	2
Resentful	29	12	4	7
Nervousness	20.5	16	18.5	14.5
Fearfulness	36	11	5	6
Enuresis	19	36.5	27	20
Dreaminess	40.5	41	18.5	37
Slovenly in appearance	34	36.5	35.5	42.5
Suspiciousness	37	25	2	17.5
Physical coward	31	40	15	30.5
Easily discouraged	22.5	10	7	13
Suggestibility	28	31	8	30.5

Reprinted by permission of the publisher from Rajpal, P. L. What behavior problems do teachers regard as serious? *Phi Delta Kappan*, 1972 (May), 591-592.

classroom teacher as well as Ausubel has. After considering the problem of discipline historically, Ausubel advanced the concept of democratic discipline. His attempt to find for teachers a workable definition of discipline without falling victim to extreme disciplinary practices or extreme permissiveness will provide the reader with tremendous insight as to the nature of discipline in the classroom. The problem of discipline is one of perspective, and, indeed, this article gives perspective.

Ausubel makes mention of attempts to make the study of discipline a scientific one, a notion that has to some extent been realized in the past decade. Many such notions have been subsumed under the term "behavior modification," a Skinnerian approach to classroom behavior that has been most strongly advocated by Albert Bandura (1969). This concept bears on the problem of attitudinal teaching, an idea that merits some discussion here.

Attitudinal Teaching

Attitudinal teaching techniques focus on the behaviors desirable for the student to learn. Attitudinal modification techniques focus on the behaviors which we desire to change within the student. Both focus on behavior — attitudinal or social. Teachers seem to be specifically interested in affecting two kinds of student behavior: (a) behaviors that interfere with learning and social adjustment, and (b) behavior which the student does not perform that should be performed. In this process, teachers may create either positive or negative attitude teaching-learning situations.

Each day the teacher faces a variety of student behaviors, from disruptive to aggressive to outstanding work. The manner in which the teacher is able to handle such situations provides social reinforcement for the student, thus shaping attitudes. To some extent, it is being suggested that student-initiated affective behavior will inevitably occur and seem quite appropriate to the student. Whether it is appropriate to the teacher or not depends on the situation. In gym class, a student learns that it is acceptable to yell to a teammate for the ball. Yet, the student also learns that it is unacceptable to yell at a classmate during math. Teachers should teach their students the various situations in which the same behavior may be appropriate or inappropriate. This makes it easier for positive attitudes to be maintained in the classroom (Thornburg, 1973).

Two social reinforcement techniques have proven quite useful in attitude learning. The first step of the social reinforcement technique is to define the behavior to be modified. Once this has been determined the teacher should be able to provide the student with an alternative behavior that is acceptable. By failing to reinforce the inappropriate behavior and sufficiently reinforcing the appropriate behavior, the teacher may be able to modify the student's response pattern. Consider the following illustration:

Ralph is a disruptive ten-year-old boy in the fifth grade. He is the third of three boys who have gone through the same elementary school. Both of his older brothers were described as ideal students, although none of the three would be considered high achievers. Ralph finds many things annoying to him in the classroom. Because of the teacher's constant attempt to "keep him under her thumb," Ralph finds ways to do little things that are upsetting to the teacher. Thus, he has been successful in expressing an undesirable classroom attitude and being reinforced for it by watching his teacher become upset.

The teacher determines that some measure must be taken to correct the situation. Because he has been a general annoyance to the teacher, the teacher has decided to observe Ralph's behavior very closely and determine which frequent disruptive behaviors can be identified. After a sufficient time period, the teacher devised the following list:

a. hits other
b. yells out in class
c. pushes children on the playground
d. meanders around the room during study time
e. crowds into lunch line

The teacher decides that each of these five behaviors are inappropriate. The alternative behaviors listed for Ralph were:

a. keep his hands to himself
b. raise his hand to talk in class
c. be cooperative on the playground
d. stay at his seat during study time
e. take his right place in lunch line

In order to use social reinforcement techniques, the teacher must be able to ignore the undesired behaviors and give attention to the desired behaviors. The procedure is very simple: (a) when Ralph is displaying any one of the five unacceptable behaviors he should not be rewarded for it; (b) when Ralph emits one of the five desired behaviors, the teacher should reinforce so that Ralph knows that the behavior he displayed is acceptable to the teacher. For example, the teacher may even facilitate the learning of acceptable behavior by letting Ralph be first in the lunch line sometimes.

These two processes of social reinforcement work. Often teachers become discouraged because they expect them to work instantaneously. It may take several trials to shift Ralph from just one undesired to one desired behavior. It may take weeks to shift all five behaviors. It may even be that some behavior will never be completely eliminated. But, through the process of attending to desired behaviors and ignoring undesired ones, the teacher increases the chance of Ralph learning those attitudinal and social skills which are most appropriate for him to use within the classroom.

Punishment

The suggestion that the teacher can effect teaching strategies that will bring about some behavioral change in the classroom leads us directly to the consideration of punishment. It can take two forms: (1) the infliction of something painful such as spanking, sarcasm, or ridicule; (2) taking away something the student likes, such as special privilege. In most cases, punishment has tended to develop aversive attitudes and often creates personality conflict problems between the teacher and the pupil being punished. It cannot be denied that punishment is the most traditional approach to discipline, but it is questionable whether it is the most effective. Several reasons are listed in support of not using punishment as a means of attitude teaching.

1. Punishment does not last. If the threat of punishment or actual punishment is severe enough, the student's behavior will be controlled for a while. However, when the punishment effect wears off, the behavior will likely appear again.
2. Punishment does not teach alternative responses. This is a most serious limitation of punishment. Often children do not have the skills to behave appropriately in the classroom. Will punishment teach them the new skills? In contrast, social reinforcing techniques are instrumental in learning new alternatives.
3. Punishment is upsetting. Most teachers find punishment upsetting, not only to the child being punished but to the teacher and the rest of the class as well. It intensifies the emotional climate of the classroom, often engendering feelings of anger, frustration, dislike, and hostility. When a child is punished it puts extreme strain on the social relationship between the child and the teacher. In similar fashion, it often makes the child socially ill at ease with the rest of the class through embarrassment and loss of face.
4. Punishment causes counteraggression. It is not uncommon for students to "get even" with a teacher because of the way they have been handled by the teacher. The child who sees a teacher, administrator, or school environment as punitive, and has no alternative but to remain in the situation, may strike out.
5. Punishment demonstrates punishment. If students can learn through modeling and imitation, then they can learn to be punitive by seeing it in their environment. We should not be disillusioned and believe that students imitate only the appropriate behaviors they see in their environment. If the teacher is going to use modeling as a theoretical position for affective learning, it must be done in a "do as I do" environment.

6. Punishment causes withdrawal. Students often withdraw from punishing persons or places where punishment is being given. The student may avoid coming to school, or, if he physically attends, he may academically and socially avoid interaction. If the student sees his teacher or his school as a punitive place, he may see his academic work as dull and boring. Even the teacher who is too demanding may be perceived as punishing by the children. Mr. Sauer was an eighth grade math teacher who insisted that all of his students should learn eleven algebraic equations overnight. When the students came to class the next day Mr. Sauer found that six boys did not know the equations. He immediately took them into the hallway and proceeded to give them three swats each. "Now maybe you will know your math tomorrow," he stated (Thornburg, 1973).

Alternatives to Punishment

The social reinforcement approach to attitude teaching offers alternatives to punishment. Two such alternatives have already been discussed, namely, ignoring inappropriate behavior and rewarding appropriate behavior. The teacher's sequence would be (1) when a student behaves in an unacceptable way, ignore him, (2) provide stimulus situations which will bring about the desired behaviors from the child, (3) once the child has displayed appropriate behavior, reward or reinforce him, (4) through a series of stimulus/reward situations, shape the student's behavior toward acceptable as opposed to unacceptable ways of behaving.

The ideas that have just been advanced regarding punishment are borne out to some extent in research that has been done. Because there has been considerable research, the second article in this chapter by Hermine Marshall is highly relevant to the previous discussion. Essentially Marshall's article is a review of the literature and reflects both supportive and nonsupportive ideas about punishment. Reading the article will increase one's awareness of the role of discipline, and how punishment affects it.

The problem of discipline is not always one which can be handled by the teacher. The preadolescent brings into the classroom some attitudinal and behavioral patterns which are direct reflections of parental teaching and the modification of such may be beyond the domain of the teacher. As Ausubel points out in his essay, "The child who is handled too permissively at home tends to regard himself as a specially privileged person. He fails to learn the normative standards and expectations of society, to set realistic goals for himself, and to make reasonable demands on others. In his dealings with adults and other children he is domineering, aggressive, petulant, and capricious."

In addition to parental teachings, the influence of one's society may also be felt by the child in the classroom. Therefore, many behaviors are not expressions of classroom problems but may come from other pressures on the child. The child's own aggression, of course, is another source of misbehavior. The final article in this chapter is by Fritz Redl and focuses on the different types of aggressive tendencies in the preadolescent. Because much classroom behavior is directly influenced by the individual's aggressive nature, it is an important topic to consider.

As you read through Redl's article, two strong points should stand out. First, Redl considers several different sources of aggression within the classroom. Second, the author expresses several different suggestions to teachers for coping with aggressive tendencies. The article is most helpful in putting potential disciplinary problems in perspective.

In conclusion, it is important to consider the fact that classroom discipline is a crucial problem for teachers, one which is somewhat confusing by lack of definition as to what constitutes disciplinary action, what action is most beneficial in modifying behavior, and what kind of social-emotional effects the exercise of classroom discipline will have on the preadolescent being disciplined and the other members of the class. A school board in a small Arizona town most recently received a request from its teachers that they may be given the authority to use corporal punishment as the primary means of discipline in the classroom. In response to this, one leading Tucson educator, who was interviewed by the press for her reaction to this request, stated, "Supposedly the teachers are a little smarter than the students (*Tucson Daily Citizen*, May, 1972)." This very well reflects the status and confusion surrounding the concept of discipline in the classroom.

A New Look at Classroom Discipline
DAVID P. AUSUBEL

A few years ago, in one of our better New England high schools, two members of the school's counseling staff happened to be walking in the building when their attention was drawn to sounds of a disturbance in an adjoining corridor. Investigating further, they found that two boys, surrounded by a knot of curious onlookers, were engaged in an all-out switchblade fight. One counselor quickly whispered to the other, "We'd better break this up in a hurry before there's bloodshed." The latter replied heatedly, "For heaven's sake leave them alone or you'll ruin everything! Do you want the kids to think we are *disciplinarians?*" Fortunately, however, the native common sense of the first counselor prevailed over the doctrinaire permissiveness of his colleague, and a near-tragedy was averted.

This true story is admittedly a bit extreme and unrepresentative of disciplinary attitudes in American public schools. Nevertheless, somewhat less extreme versions occur frequently enough to suggest that American teachers are more confused and disturbed about matters of discipline today than at any previous time in the history of our public school system.

It is true that superficial observation does not support this conclusion. On the surface, practically everything *appears* the same as it was ten years ago when, except in the so-called "Blackboard Jungles," these same teachers seemed supremely confident that the ideal of democratic discipline had been achieved in the American classroom. Substantially the same disciplinary philosophy is still preached in our teachers' colleges; and teachers, by and large, still practice the same kind of discipline they practiced a decade ago.

Reprinted by permission of the author and publisher from the *Phi Delta Kappan*, 1961, 43, 25-30.

To be sure, there is still an appreciable gap between the theory of discipline as taught in colleges of education, and discipline as it is actually conceived and practiced in the schools. For example, in a recent survey conducted by the National Education Association, 72 per cent of the responding classroom teachers favored the judicious use of corporal punishment in the elementary school. But the gap is no greater now than it has ever been. In everyday disciplinary practice, American teachers have never gone along completely with the more extreme ideas of educational theorists. Elementary and high school teachers, after all, have to be realistic in handling problems of discipline because they encounter them daily in doing their jobs. Unlike professors of education who rarely, if ever, have to cope with disciplinary problems in the classroom, they can ill afford to be starry-eyed about these matters.

Why then should teachers be suddenly confused and disturbed about issues of discipline? Closer scrutiny reveals that everything is not *really* the same as it used to be. One important factor in the situation has undergone significant change: Although educational theory in the field of classroom discipline has remained virtually unchanged over the past two decades, the pendulum of public opinion in recent years has been swinging further and further away from the formerly fashionable cult of permissiveness. As a result, a growing estrangement has arisen between the general public, on the one hand, and educational and psychological theorists, on the other — with the classroom teacher and the rank-and-file school administrator caught squarely in the middle. Teachers, of course, were also in the middle throughout the entire period of approximately 1935-1955 when American classroom discipline underwent a process of extensive democratization. But this middle position was decidedly more comfortable then than it is now, because all three groups — educational theorists, teachers, and the public at large — were moving toward the same culturally desirable goal of a less authoritarian classroom climate.

It is true that these three groups were moving toward this goal at quite different rates. Permissiveness, nondirective guidance, and the cults of extroversion, conformity, and social adjustment were much more extreme among child-centered educators, client-centered counselors and psychoanalytically trained child study experts than among American parents and teachers generally. By 1955, however, the entirely laudable objective of more democratic pupil-teacher relationships had been reached, and perhaps overreached. Public opinion began moving away from permissiveness, but educational and psychological theorists and professors of education, with few exceptions, stood their ground tenaciously. The same relatively extreme permissive doctrines of discipline are still dominant in teachers' colleges, even though educational philosophy in the post-Sputnik era has generally become less permissive in most other areas such as curriculum.

Now, it was one thing for teachers to swim in the middle of two streams moving in the same historically necessary direction, and to enjoy the approbation of both the general public and of their own professional leaders. It is quite another for them to be caught between two opposing streams, and to be faced with the problem of having to choose between the spirit of the times, on the one hand, and the historically obsolete ideological extremism of their former professors, on the other.

Historical and Cultural Perspective

Before examining how particular concepts and practices of discipline have gone astray, it might be profitable first to view the problem in historical perspective within a broader cultural context. The revolution in classroom discipline that swept American schools between 1935 and 1955 was as necessary as it was inevitable. Teacher-pupil relationships had to be brought into closer alignment with the general spirit of adult egalitarianism in American society; and a more desirable balance had to be achieved between the actual dependence of children on adult direction and their realistic capacities for exercising self-direction and self-discipline. It was inevitable, of course, that we should go too far in redressing the balance — in overdoing the permissiveness and in cutting back adult control and guidance too drastically. Much more serious, however, were the deplorable consequences of de-emphasizing certain other traditional American values in the enthusiasm of democratizing adult-child relationships.

Thus, in stressing the inherent right of children to receive the consideration to which they are entitled, we have neglected the equally valid claims of age and maturity. In debunking superficial and unilateral forms of etiquette, we have lost sight of the importance of genuine courtesy in human relationships. And in attacking despotic and abusive adult rule, we have failed to cultivate appropriate respect for just and rightful authority.

By respect for age I do not mean uncritical veneration or ancestor worship, but simply the consideration that is due all human beings at any stage in the life cycle. Yet our cultural attitude toward middle-aged and elderly persons tends to be patronizing and slightly contemptuous. Because they quite understandably lack the exuberance and venturesomeness of youth they are often cavalierly dismissed as "has-beens" or as bumbling, ineffectual "fuddy-duddies."

Courtesy is another of our most valuable cultural assets that was overlooked in the frenzy of extending democracy to home and school. It is fashionable in many quarters — not only among the younger set — to regard good manners and the more subtle amenities of interpersonal relationships as hollow formalities. But even the highly stylized bowing ceremony of the Japanese is far from being an empty gesture. It symbolizes deep and culturally ingrained respect for the dignity of the individual and genuine concern for his pride and feelings. Although bowing is obviously incongruous with our modern way of life, concern for the pride, feelings, and dignity of every human being is one of our most cherished American values. Hence, since courtesy is basically an institutionalized set of rules designed to safeguard and implement this legitimate cultural concern, those who sneer at courtesy, whether they realize it or not, sneer at nothing less than human dignity.

Finally, our culture has tended to put authority figures in an anomalous and untenable position, particularly in the school environment. We have assigned them the necessary and often distasteful task of authority figures the world over, that is, to enforce certain basic standards of conduct; but in too many instances we have failed to give them the respect, the authority, and the protection commensurate with this responsibility. When they conscientiously attempt to apply without fear or favor the community approved sanctions for violating these standards, we accuse them of being punitive, vindictive, and authoritarian. School administrators, of course, are not above criticism and reproach when they use poor judgment or exceed their authority; but society has an obligation to protect them from disrespect and abuse for simply doing their duty and exercising their just and necessary disciplinary prerogatives. In our present cultural climate, therefore, it is small wonder that many principals and superintendents of schools are more concerned with courting general popularity than with enforcing desirable norms of pupil behavior.

The Brighter Side of the Coin

In pointing out some of the failings of our recent approach to discipline, I do not mean to detract in any way from our genuine accomplishments. The latter are extremely impressive when compared with disciplinary practices in many other countries. I recently had an opportunity to study secondary schools in New Zealand, an English-speaking welfare state of British origin with a pioneering tradition not unlike our own. School discipline in New Zealand high schools connotes explicit subjection to authority and implicit habits of obedience that are enforced by a very heavy-handed set of controls and punishments. It implies a very identifiable atmosphere of classroom control which the teacher maintains with much deliberate effort − in much the same sense that he strives to have his pupils understand and assimilate the subject-matter he teaches.

By contrast, the American approach to discipline seems laudably incidental. Our teachers tend to feel that the cause of discipline is adequately served if pupils exercise sufficient self-control and observe a minimum set of rules with sufficient decorum to enable classroom work to proceed in an orderly, efficient manner. They do not, in other words, strive deliberately for discipline as an explicit goal in its own right. They assume instead that good discipline is *ordinarily* a natural by-product of interesting lessons and of a wholesome teacher-pupil relationship; that the vast majority of pupils respond positively to fair and kindly treatment; that respect for the teacher is a usual accompaniment of the latter's superior knowledge, experience, and status as a leader, and does not have to be reinforced by such artificial props and status symbols as differences in clothing, mode of address, and fear of the strap. Hence they treat adolescents as maturing young adults rather than as unruly children, and implicitly expect them to respond in kind — which they usually do. And it was a very gratifying experience to discover that despite the absence of strict authoritarian controls, American high school students, on the whole, behave more decorously than their New Zealand counterparts — particularly when not under direct supervision.

Science or Opinion?

Discipline today is much less a science than a matter of opinion. It not only shifts in response to various social, economic, and ideological factors, but also manifests all of the cyclical properties of fads and fashions. Objective scientific evidence about the relative merits of different types of discipline is extremely sparse. Indeed it is highly questionable to what extent valid empirical data are obtainable and even relevant in matters of discipline. Whether or not particular disciplinary practices are appropriate depends, in the first place, on the particular values, institutions, and kinds of personal relationships prevailing in a given culture; and, second, any definitive empirical test of appropriateness would have to be conducted over such an extended period of time that its conclusions would tend to be rendered obsolete by intervening changes in significant social conditions. For all practical purposes, therefore, the choice of disciplinary policy involves taking a rationally defensible and self-consistent position based on value preferences, relevant considerations of child development, and on individual experience and judgment.

The fact that discipline cannot be placed on a largely scientific basis, however, does not mean that one position is as good as another or that no public policy whatsoever is warranted. Society is continually obliged to resolve issues of much greater moment with even less objective evidence on which to base a decision. Under the circumstances all we can reasonably expect is greater humility and less dogmatism on the part of those engaged in formulating disciplinary policy. Thus, the most disturbing aspect of the entire problem is not the fact that there is precious little scientific evidence to support the disciplinary doctrines expounded in our colleges of education and educational journals and textbooks, but rather the ubiquitous tendency to represent purely personal opinions and biases as if they were incontrovertibly established findings of scientific research.

The Definition and Functions of Discipline

By discipline I mean the imposition of *external* standards and controls on individual conduct. Permissiveness, on the other hand, refers to the absence of such standards and controls. To be permissive is to "let alone," to adopt a laissez-faire policy. Authoritarianism is an excessive, arbitrary, and autocratic type of control which is diametrically opposite to permissiveness. Between the extremes of laissez-faire permissiveness and authoritarianism are many varieties and degrees of control. One of these, to be described in greater detail below, is democratic discipline.

Discipline is a universal cultural phenomenon which generally serves four important functions in the training of the young. First, it is necessary for socialization — for learning the standards of conduct that are approved and tolerated in any culture. Second, it is necessary for normal personality maturation — for acquiring such adult personality traits as dependability, self-reliance, self-control, persistence, and ability to tolerate frustration. These aspects of maturation do not occur spontaneously, but only in response to sustained social demands and expectations. Third, it is necessary for the internalization of moral standards and obligations or, in other words, for the development of conscience. Standards obviously cannot be internalized unless they also exist in external form; and even after they are effectively internalized, universal cultural experience suggests that external sanctions are still required to insure the stability of the social order. Lastly, discipline is necessary for children's emotional security. Without the guidance provided by unambiguous external controls, the young tend to feel bewildered and apprehensive. Too great a burden is placed on their own limited capacity for self-control.

Democratic Discipline

The proponents of democratic classroom discipline believe in imposing the minimal degree of external control necessary for socialization, personality maturation, conscience development, and the emotional security of the child. Discipline and obedience are not regarded as ends in themselves but only as means to these latter ends. They are not striven for deliberately, but are expected to follow naturally in the wake of friendly and realistic teacher-pupil relationships. Explicit limits are not set routinely or as ways of showing "who is boss," but only as the need arises, i.e., when they are not implicitly understood or accepted by pupils.

Democratic discipline is as rational, nonarbitrary, and bilateral as possible. It provides explanations, permits discussion, and invites the participation of children in the setting of standards whenever they are qualified to do so. Above all it implies respect for the dignity of the individual, and avoids exaggerated emphasis on status differences and barriers between free communication. Hence it repudiates harsh, abusive, and vindictive forms of punishment, and the use of sarcasm, ridicule, and intimidation.

The aforementioned attributes of democratic classroom discipline are obviously appropriate in cultures such as ours where social relationships tend to be egalitarian. This type of discipline also becomes increasingly more feasible as children become older, more responsible, and more capable of understanding and formulating rules of conduct based on concepts of equity and reciprocal obligation. But contrary to what the extreme permissivists would have us believe, democratic school discipline does not imply freedom from all external constraints, standards, and direction, or freedom from discipline as an end in itself. And under no circumstances does it presuppose the eradication of all distinctions between pupil and teacher roles, or require that teachers abdicate responsibility for making the final decisions in the classroom.

Distortions of Democratic Discipline

Many educational theorists have misinterpreted and distorted the ideal of democratic discipline by equating it with an extreme form of permissiveness. These distortions have been dogmatically expressed in various psychologically unsound and unrealistic propositions that are considered sacrosanct in many teachers' colleges. Fortunately, however, most classroom teachers have only accepted them for examination purposes – while still in training – and have discarded them in actual practice as thoroughly unworkable.

According to one widely held doctrine, only "positive" forms of discipline are constructive and democratic. It is asserted that children must only be guided by reward and approval; that reproof and punishment are authoritarian, repressive, and reactionary expression of adult hostility which leave permanent emotional scars on children's personalities. What these theorists conveniently choose to ignore, however, is the fact that it is impossible for children to learn what is *not* approved and tolerated, simply by generalizing in reverse from the approval they receive for behavior that *is* acceptable. Even adults are manifestly incapable of learning and respecting the limits of acceptable conduct unless the distinction between what is proscribed and approved is reinforced by punishment as well as by reward. Furthermore, there is good reason to believe that acknowledgment of wrong-doing and acceptance of punishment are part and parcel of learning moral accountability and developing a sound conscience. Few if any children are quite that fragile that they cannot take deserved reproof and punishment in stride.

A second widespread distortion of democratic discipline is reflected in the popular notion that there are no culpably misbehaving children in the classroom, but only culpably aggressive, unsympathetic, and punitive teachers. If children misbehave, according to this point of view, one can implicitly assume that they must have been provoked beyond endurance by repressive and authoritarian classroom discipline. Similarly, if they are disrespectful, then the teacher, by definition, must not have been deserving of respect. It is true, of course, that much pupil misconduct *is* instigated by harsh and abusive school discipline; but there are also innumerable reasons for out-of-bounds behavior that are completely independent of the teacher's attitudes and disciplinary practices. Pupils are also influenced by factors originating in the home, the neighborhood, the peer group, and the mass-media. Some children are emotionally disturbed, others are brain-damaged, and still others are aggressive by temperament; and there are times when the best behaved children from the nicest homes develop an irresistible impulse — without any provocation whatsoever — to test the limits of a teacher's forbearance.

Both of the aforementioned distortions of classroom democracy are used to justify the commonly held belief among educators that pupils should not be reproved or punished for disorderly or discourteous conduct. I have, for example, observed classrooms where everybody talks at once; where pupils turn their backs on the teacher and engage in private conversation while the latter is endeavoring to instruct them; and where pupils verbally abuse teachers for exercising their rightful disciplinary prerogatives. Some educators contend that all of this is compatible with wholesome, democratic teacher-pupil relationships. Other educators deplore this type of pupil behavior but insist, nevertheless, that punishment is unwarranted under these circumstances. In the first place, they assert, reproof or punishment constitutes a "negative" and hence axiomatically undesirable approach to classroom management; and, secondly, the misbehavior would assuredly have never occurred to begin with, if the teacher's attitudes had been less autocratic or antagonistic. I have already answered the second group of educators, and to the first group I can only say that I am still sufficiently old-fashioned to believe that rudeness and unruliness are not normally desirable classroom behavior in any culture.

When such misconduct occurs, I believe pupils have to be unambiguously informed that it will not be tolerated and that any repetition of the same behavior will be punished. This action does not preclude in any way either an earnest attempt to discover why the misbehavior occurred, or suitable preventive measures aimed at correcting the underlying causes. But, by the same token, the mere fact that a pupil has a valid psychological reason for misbehaving does not mean that he is thereby absolved from moral accountability or rendered no longer subject to punishment.

Still another related distortion of democratic discipline is reflected in the proposition that it is repressive and authoritarian to request pupils to apologize for discourteous behavior or offensive language. However if we take seriously the idea that the dignity of the human being is important, we must be willing to protect it from affront; and apology is the most civilized and effective means mankind has yet evolved for accomplishing this goal. In a democratic society nobody is that important that he is above apologizing to those persons whom he wrongfully offends. Everybody's dignity is important – the teacher's as well as the pupil's. It is no less wrong for a pupil to abuse a teacher than for a teacher to abuse a pupil.

If apologies are to have any real significance in moral training, however, it is obvious that, even though they are explicitly requested, they must be made voluntarily, and must be reflective of genuine appreciation of wrong-doing and of sincere regret and remorse. Purely formal and mechanical statements of apology made under coercion are less than worthless. Apologies are also without real ethical import unless their basis is reciprocal, i.e., unless it is fully understood that under comparable circumstances the teacher would be willing to apologize to his pupils.

A final distortion of democratic classroom discipline associated with the extreme child-centered approach to education is the notion that children are equipped in some mysterious fashion for knowing precisely what is best for them. Empirical "proof" of this proposition is adduced from the fact that nutrition is adequately maintained and existing deficiency conditions are spontaneously corrected when infants are permitted to select their own diet. If the child can successfully choose his diet, runs the argument, he must certainly know what is best for him in *all* areas of development, including curriculum and classroom management.

This doctrine, however, has even less face validity than the three other distorted concepts of school discipline. Because the human being is sensitive in early childhood to internal cues of physiological need, we cannot conclude that he is similarly sensitive to complex intellectual and moral needs, or that he has sufficient experience, perspective, and judgment to make intelligent decisions in these latter areas. Even in the field of nutrition, self-selection is a reliable criterion of need only during early infancy. The current interests and opinions of immature pupils can hardly be considered reliable guideposts and adequate substitutes for seasoned judgment in designing a curriculum or in formulating rules of classroom behavior. Hence, while it is reasonable to consider the views of pupils in these matters, teachers and school administrators cannot abdicate their responsibility for making the final decisions.

What Needs To Be Done

In seeking to correct these undesirable permissive distortions of classroom democracy, it would be foolhardy to return to the equally undesirable opposite extreme of authoritarianism that flourished in this country up to a quarter of a century ago, and still prevails in many western nations. Democratic school discipline is still an appropriate and realistic goal for American education; hence there is no need to throw away the baby with the bath water. It is only necessary to discard the aforementioned permissivist doctrines masquerading under the banners of democracy and behavioral science, and to restore certain other traditional American values that have been neglected in the enthusiasm of extending democracy to home and school.

More specifically, we first have to clear up the semantic confusion. We should stop equating permissiveness with democratic discipline, and realistic adult control and guidance with authoritarianism. Permissiveness, by definition, is the absence of discipline, democratic or otherwise. We should cease instructing teachers that it is repressive and reactionary to reprove or punish pupils for misconduct, or to request them to apologize for offensive and discourteous behavior.

Second, we should stop misinterpreting what little reputable evidence we have about discipline, and refrain from misrepresenting our personal biases on the subject as the indisputably established findings of scientific research. The available evidence merely suggests that in our type of cultural setting, authoritarian discipline has certain undesirable effects — *not* that the consequences of laissez-faire permissiveness are desirable. As a matter of fact, research studies show that the effects of extreme permissiveness are just as unwholesome as are those of authoritarianism. In the school situation a laissez-faire policy leads to confusion, insecurity, and competition for power among pupils. Assertive pupils tend to become aggressive and ruthless, whereas retiring pupils tend to withdraw further from classroom participation. The child who is handled too permissively at home tends to regard himself as a specially privileged person. He fails to learn the normative standards and expectations of society, to set realistic goals for himself, and to make reasonable demands on others. In his dealings with adults and other children he is domineering, aggressive, petulant, and capricious.

Third, we should stop making teachers feel guilty and personally responsible for all instances of misconduct and disrespect in the classroom. We do this whenever we take for granted, without any actual supporting evidence, that these behavior problems would never have arisen in the first place if the teachers involved were truly deserving of respect and had been administering genuinely wholesome and democratic discipline.

Finally, teachers' colleges should terminate the prevailing conspiracy of silence they maintain about the existence of disciplinary problems in the public schools. Although discipline is the one aspect of teaching that the beginning teacher is most worried about, he receives little or no practical instruction in handling this problem. Colleges of education, as pointed out above, rationalize their inadequacies in this regard by pretending that disciplinary problems are relatively rare occurrences involving the disturbed child, or more typically the disturbed teacher. Due respect for the facts of life, however, suggests that prospective teachers today not only need to be taught more realistic propositions about the nature and purposes of democratic discipline, but also require adequately supervised, down-to-earth experience in coping with classroom discipline.

The Effect of Punishment on Children
A Review of the Literature
and a Suggested Hypothesis
HERMINE H. MARSHALL

The purpose of this paper is to explore the research on the effect on children of punishment or negative reinforcement. An important distinction must first be made between what has been called "punishment training" and "avoidance training." In punishment training, the subject performs a particular act (R) for which he is subsequently "punished" with a negative reinforcer (S). That is, a particular response is followed by the aversive stimulus (R–S). In contrast, in avoidance training, the aversive stimulus occurs first, causing the subject to perform a particular response (S–R). It is on punishment training that this paper focuses. Those punishment situations that have been utilized in research with children include such negative reinforcers as blame, reproof, failure situations, and the word "wrong," as well as the removal of positive reinforcers: e.g., candy and trinkets.

The importance of research findings on the effects of punishment on children for the fields of child rearing, socialization, and education are obvious. The lasting effects of punishment on personality (particularly regarding the oral, dependency, and aggressive aspects of behavior) have been pointed out by Sears (1950); by Sears, Maccoby, and Levin (1957); and by Whiting and Child (1953). The ineffectiveness (over the long run) of punishment as a manner of handling behavior as compared with nonpunitive techniques has been noted in several field studies: e.g., in Sears *et al.* (1957); and in Crandall, Orleans, Preston, and Rabson (1958). Whiting and Child (1953) and Seward (1954) have considered the detrimental effect of severe punishment on the process of identification and on the gaining of parental affection. Although all of these field studies emphasize the harmful effects of

Reprinted by permission of the author and publisher from the *Journal of Genetic Psychology*, 1965, 106, 23-33.

punishment, particularly of severe punishment – at least one source is inclined to believe that punishment of *specific* acts has the desired effect. What, then, is the consensus of more controlled studies done in the laboratory or in the classroom? That is the question to which we now turn.

Effectiveness of Punishment

Of those studies comparing (*a*) the effects of administering punishment – either alone or in combination with a reward – with (*b*) the effects of no punishment or of reward alone, by far the greatest proportion show the former condition to be superior.

In a classroom setting, Hurlock (1924) found that those third-, fifth-, and eighth-grade children who had been either praised or reproved improved significantly more than the control group on a group intelligence test. However, reproof was more effective than praise for the fifth grade, for children of superior intelligence, and for those rated superior by their teachers. Brenner's study (1934), which utilized the learning and retention of spelling words at the third-grade level, was also carried out in a classroom situation. Brenner concluded that, in learning and recall, blame was a more powerful incentive than praise, and that blame sustained its influence longer than any other incentive. (Although he found "delayed control" to be the most effective condition, the superiority of that condition over blame and praise cannot be analyzed as the study does not make clear just what was said to the control group.) Potter (1943) found that reproved groups improved their performance on an arithmetic reasoning test at the sixth-, ninth-, and twelfth-grade levels, as contrasted with the control groups. But the effect of reproof at the higher grades was slight, and it impaired performance at the third-grade level. Although Potter related this finding to age difference, a more satisfactory explanation might be in terms of task difficulty, which difficulty was not controlled in this experiment. Because the Otis Arithmetic Reasoning Test was constructed for children age 8 and older, one might hypothesize that this test is too difficult for the third graders and too easy for those in grades nine and 12. Therefore, only at the most appropriate age – grade six – was the effect of reproof significant. This hypothesis regarding the importance of task difficulty might also serve to explain the results of the second part of Potter's study in which the reproved group, at the third- and sixth-grade levels, improved more than the control group in a motor task, but the reverse was true at grade nine. The superiority of blame over praise for general performance in the classroom is supported also by Forlano and Axelrod (1937), although they used a cancellation test instead of academic materials.

In studies in which the punishment was administered not toward the situation in general but for specific responses, the results also tend to support the beneficial effect of punishment. Stevenson, Weir, and Zigler (1959) found that five-year-olds learned a discrimination problem faster if they were penalized for their errors by having to relinquish a reward object than those who were not penalized. These results are substantiated by Brackbill and O'Hara's study (1958) in which those kindergarten boys who were rewarded with candy for each correct response and punished by having to return their candy for each incorrect response learned a discrimination problem more rapidly than those who received the reward alone.

Similarly, in those studies utilizing verbal punishment, combinations that included stating the word "wrong" after each incorrect response — whether correct responses were rewarded with "right" or not — led to faster learning than those in which the incorrect response was not thus negatively reinforced (Curry, 1960; Meyer and Offenbach, 1962). Combinations including the word "wrong" were also superior to a condition in which a buzzer followed correct responses and nothing followed incorrect responses. In the learning series, no significant difference was found between those groups in which each response was followed appropriately with either "right" or "wrong" and those groups in which only incorrect responses were termed "wrong" and nothing followed correct responses. However, when an extinction series was carried out (Meyer and Seidman, 1960, 1961) the nothing-"wrong" group showed little decrement in performance. The explanation that "wrong" is a stronger negative reinforcer than "right" is a positive reinforcer was suggested. However, "nothing" paired with "wrong" acquires the value of a positive reinforcer; and because, in extinction, nothing is said after either a correct or an incorrect response, nothing continues to reinforce positively. This acquired reinforcing value of the "nothing" side of the condition may account satisfactorily for the superiority of the "nothing"-"wrong" combination over the "right"-"wrong" combination during extinction — without hypothesizing a difference in strength between the reinforcing values of "right" and "wrong."

Although Penney and Lupton's results (1961) are in general agreement with the preceding studies concerning the effectiveness of punishment alone and conditions including punishment over reward alone, Penney and Lupton's study with grade-school children showed that the groups who were punished with an intense tone and received no reward learned a discrimination problem faster than those who received a candy reward in addition to the punishing tone. They account for the superiority of the punishment-only group in terms of possible additional frustration received by the punishment-only groups. They hypothesize the source of this frustration to be the unfulfilled expectation of receiving candy, after having seen their peers return with candy. They hypothesize that this frustration increased the motivation level in this group and thereby caused them to perform better.

Using a very small number of six-year-olds, Baer (1961) found that the withdrawal of a positive reinforcer (movie) as a punishment led to more rapid extinction and to less spontaneous recovery in the use of a toy "peanut machine" than in the control group the members of which did not receive the punishment. The punished subjects also played more with toys other than the peanut machine than did the control group. Although caution needs to be exercised in applying these findings (due to the small number) they are in the predicted direction.

Despite the large amount of research that shows the superior effect of negative reinforcement, there are a number of studies the results of which are not in complete agreement. Anderson (1936) found that performance with a hand dynamometer showed a precipitate drop under failure conditions. In this experiment, "failure" was manipulated by E so that each attempt in the series, no matter how successful, was described to the subject as a failure. Hence, these results may not be directly comparable to those in which only incorrect responses were negatively reinforced or with those experiments in which general performance was reproved after the completion of the task and the effect of the reproof was subsequently measured.

Terrell and Kennedy (1957) found that those children rewarded with candy learned a discrimination task significantly more rapidly than those punished by reproof. In this experiment, the other conditions in rank order of effectiveness, though at a nonsignificant level, were praise, token to be exchanged for candy, reproof, and control. However, each group (including the control group) was reinforced by a light flash following correct responses. Thus, the candy, praise, and token groups received two sources of positive reinforcement; the reproof group received only one positive reinforcement and one negative reinforcement; and the control group received only one positive reinforcement. The discrepancy between these results and those previously reported might be accounted for by this additional source of reward in all groups but the control group. The double positive reinforcement may have caused better performance. Comparison of the reproved group with the control group, which group received only one source of positive reinforcement, reveals that the reproved group was superior to the control.

The studies by Hurlock (1924), by Potter (1943), and by Meyer and Seidman (1960) did not uniformly support the superior effects of punishment conditions. Hurlock found that eighth graders, children with inferior intellectual ability (*IQ* below 90), and rated average or inferior by their teachers did better following praise than following blame. However, the impaired performance following reproof at the third-grade level (indicated by Potter) has already been noted and explained on the basis of uncontrolled task difficulty. Also, Meyer and Seidman's finding (1960) that preschool children performed better under conditions of both "right"-"wrong" and of a buzzer for correct responses and nothing for incorrect responses was not substantiated by their later study and was accounted for by the higher achievement motivation of the children in the former study compared with a more representative sample in the latter.

Thus, the discrepancies in all of the studies that do not completely support the superiority of the effects of punishment (except Hurlock's), can be accounted for, so that basic substantiation of the beneficial effect of negative reinforcement remains. A hypothesis regarding Hurlock's results will be elaborated later.

Relation of Punishment to Other Factors

A number of experiments have been concerned not only with the effectiveness of punishment itself, but also with the way other variables contribute to the effect of negative reinforcement. Meyer and Offenbach's study (1962) investigated the effect of task complexity by controlling the relevant and irrelevant dimensions in a discrimination problem. Their results, noted earlier, showed that combinations including "wrong" were superior to reward alone for tasks involving at least two irrelevant dimensions. There was no significant difference for tasks involving just one irrelevant dimension. As Postman (1962) noted, in most experiments there is only one correct response but several incorrect responses. Therefore, the subject has to learn positively only one item while eliminating several incorrect ones from a rather homogeneous series. When each of the incorrect responses is negatively reinforced, one might expect performance to be better. Meyer and Offenbach's results tend to lend support to this writer's hypothesis accounting for the discrepancy in Potter's results (1943) in terms of uncontrolled task difficulty.

Stephens (1941, 1944) hypothesized that symbolic reward would strengthen weak connections more than symbolic punishment would weaken them, but that symbolic punishment would weaken strong connections more than symbolic reward would strengthen them. Investigations by Stephens and his associates (1941, 1944) on high-school students confirmed this hypothesis. In addition, it was found that a delay in reinforcement increased the influence of "wrong" on strong connections, but had little effect on weak ones (1944). Because the amount of time for review was controlled, they explained that this condition (and that of weak but right) was the only one susceptible to such enhancement. Brenner's investigation (1934) of the effect of the delay of reinforcement showed immediate blame and delayed blame to be equally effective with spelling words — when presumably there was no appreciable difference in strength of connections.

Stephens and Baer also showed that wrong associations were avoided more for the group receiving specific instructions regarding the importance of avoiding wrong associations on the retest than the noninstructed group.

The experiment by Stevenson *et al.* (1959) investigated the effect of pre-experimental satiation on punishment, by varying the number of reward objects given before the experiment. They found that the amount of pre-experimental satiation made a significant difference in the effectiveness of the penalty of relinquishing reward objects.

Forlano and Axelrod (1937) studied the influence of a personality variable on the effectiveness of blame. Using the extroversion inventory from Pintner's Personality Test, they found that introverts who were blamed increased their performance more than the introverts in the control group after both the first and second applications; whereas extroverts increased their performance only after the second time they were blamed.

An elaborate experiment by Schmidt (1941) investigated the influence of praise and blame on junior-high and high-school students in a code-substitution test. His results showed that praise was more effective for one tester (a male), and that blame was a better incentive when used by the other tester (a female graduate student); thus pointing to the importance of the experimenter as a variable.

A related conclusion was reached by Kipnis (1958) who had a group leader manipulate the atmosphere. In an attempt to induce fifth and sixth graders to change their preferred comic heroes, he found that under the threat of punishment (removal of a promised movie pass) more subjects accepted the leader's influence attempt in the groups to whom the leader lectured; whereas the groups — also under threat of punishment — which participated with the leader in a discussion resisted the attempt and were unwilling to change their standards. Under both participation and lecture leadership, the subjects held a lower affective evaluation of the leader if they had been threatened by punishment than if they had been promised only the reward.

A final dimension investigated is the generalization of preference following negative reinforcement. Starting with N. E. Miller's assumption that the avoidance gradient is steeper than the approach gradient, Gewirtz (1959) had first and second graders learn formboard puzzles arranged along a dimension of shape similarity. However, this hypothesis was confirmed only for the group negatively reinforced by failure, reproof, and the withholding of a prize. In accounting for the partial substantiation, she notes that a considerable number of subjects in the **positively reinforced** group were unaffected by the experimental conditions of success, approval from the experimenter, and a material reward. She attributes this result to the high-achievement motivation of the sample. The negatively reinforced subjects were equally **achievement oriented**. Nevertheless, Gewirtz suggests that the external motivation from negatively reinforcing conditions was sufficiently more powerful than the positively reinforcing conditions to overshadow the internal achievement motivation, so that the results for this group reveal the effects of this experimental condition. The influence of something akin to achievement motivation or intellectual level has also been noted in the results of the studies by Hurlock (1924) and by Meyer and Seidman (1960).

That so few studies into the effects of punishment on children have considered and controlled for these additional variables: e.g., task difficulty, achievement orientation, and personality factors is a striking fact. In addition, no experiments considered the relation of ego involvement and level of aspiration. All of these factors might be taken into account to explain variations in experimental results.

Learning Theories and
Explanations of Punishment

The research reported in the literature seems to support the contention that punishment or **negative reinforcement** helps rather than hinders learning in children and that there are a number of other variables related to its effectiveness. We turn now to the question of whether learning theories predict this conclusion and to the explanations that are postulated to explain the conclusion.

Although Thorndike revised his **Law of Effect** so that it stated that punishment only indirectly weakened **S-R** connections, Skinner and Estes found that punishment had a temporary or depressing effect upon learning in animals (Hilgard, 1956). Baer's conclusion (1961) that punishment reduced the number of responses in extinction tends to bear out this effect with children. An important point here, however, is that the punished children played more with other toys. In other words, while punishment reduced the number of nonreinforced responses, it also caused the subjects to shift their activity to something else. It led to more varied behavior. This follows from Thorndike's revised law. As Postman (1962) points out, the educative value of this variability of behavior depends upon what the "something else" is that the subjects do.

The main theoretical issue seems to center on this change in behavior: on the question of whether punishment serves as a motivator — instigating and arousing the subject to action — or whether this motivational concept is superfluous and the change in behavior can be explained by referring simply to the cue or to the informative value of the negative reinforcement, or whether both concepts are necessary.

According to Postman (1962), Hull regards a punishing state of affairs as an instigator of behavior and the cessation of punishment as reinforcing. Guthrie sees punishment as facilitating learning because it arouses the subject to varied action and provides a multiplicity of cues — thereby utilizing both concepts. Likewise, Tolman includes (*a*) a "Law of emphasis" — the perceptual impact of cues, (*b*) a "Law of motivation" to maximize rewards and minimize punishment, and (*c*) a "Law of disruption." Brown (1961) assumes that punishment produces frustration and frustration increases drive or motivation. On the other hand, from his work with animals, Dinsmoor (1954, 1955) criticizes recourse to "acquired drive" in explaining punishment, but accounts for the effect of punishment through the conditioning of discriminative stimuli so that the stimuli that precede the punished response acquire an aversive power and function as would a "warning signal" in avoidance training. Regarding the effect of punishment in terms of discriminative stimuli may be considered analogous to the cue or informative function referred to by Guthrie and Tolman. Farber (1955) emphasizes the importance of distinguishing between what he calls the "purely motivational (D) effects" of negative reinforcement and the informative aspects, in addition to its distraction aspects. He also notes that if the negatively reinforcing instructions are applied to performance in general, rather than to specific responses, there is likely to be a decrement in performance.

Hypothesis

By carrying this reasoning further, one might hypothesize that negative reinforcement of *specific* responses has discriminative or informative and therefore beneficial value; whereas negative reinforcement applied to the situation in general may have a motivational function. Whether the increased motivation leads the subject to be more aware of appropriate cues or whether its effect is disruptive may depend on other factors in the situation: e.g., strength of negative reinforcement, task difficulty, achievement orientation. According to this hypothesis, one might predict that reinforcing each response would be informative and hence more beneficial. On the other hand, if negative reinforcement after a series or after the situation serves as a motivator, its beneficial or detrimental effects would be likely to depend on other factors in the situation. For example, the Yerkes-Dodson Law might apply here, so that as motivation increases, subjects would be expected to perform better on simpler tasks. Thus, one might expect less consistent results from experiments where negative reinforcement, administered after the situation, acts as a motivator.

Table 6.2 classifies the studies reviewed as to (*a*) whether the punishment was administered after each response or after the situation and (*b*) whether the punishment improves performance. Of those experiments in which each response was reinforced, only two do not completely support the hypothesis. However, as has been noted, Meyer and Seidman's later study (1960) did not substantiate the effectiveness of the buzzer-nothing combination over a combination including the word "wrong."

Table 6.2
Classification of Studies
According to Time and Effect of Reinforcement

REINFORCEMENT AFTER EACH RESPONSE	REINFORCEMENT AFTER SITUATION
Punishment beneficial	
Stephens and Baer (1944)	Hurlock (1924)
Brackbill and O'Hara (1958)	Brenner (1934)
Stevenson *et al.* (1959)	Anderson (1936)
Curry (1960)	Forlando and Axelrod (1937)
Meyer and Seidman (1960)	Schmidt (1941)
Meyer and Seidman (1961)	Potter (1943)
Penney and Lupton (1961)	
Meyer and Offenbach (1962)	
Punishment detrimental	
Terrell and Kennedy (1957)	Hurlock (1924)
Meyer and Seidman (1960)	Brenner (1934)
	Anderson (1936)
	Schmidt (1941)
	Potter (1943)

And the discrepant results of the Terrell and Kennedy study have been explained to be the outcome of a double source of positive reinforcement. When negative reinforcement is compared with one source of positive reinforcement, the hypothesis is supported.

Examination of those experiments in which negative reinforcement was given after the series (or after the situation) indicates that five of the six studies carried out under this condition are listed as evidencing both the helping and the hindering effect of punishment. Hurlock's divergent results fall into this category and are related to grade level, intellectual level, and teacher ratings. Anderson found that a change from success to failure conditions as well as a change from failure to success conditions served to increase performance, but that continued failure led to a drop in perform-ance. Schmidt indicates that whether blame had a beneficial or detrimental effect depended upon the experimenter. Potter's results were related to task difficulty. Brenner showed immediate and delayed blame (though both occurred after the test) to be superior to other conditions except for "delayed control." It was noted that the latter condition was not explained sufficiently to warrant comment. Forlano and Axelrod indicated that blame was even more effective for introverts than for extroverts.

In general, the hypothesis that negative reinforcement of specific responses has an informative and therefore beneficial effect, whereas the effect of negatively reinforcing the situation depends upon the action of other factors appears to have been supported by the available research. This conclusion is in agreement with the belief expressed by Sears *et al.* (1957) regarding the desired effect of parental punishment of specific acts as opposed to the negating effect of general parental "punitiveness."

Summary

A review of the research on the effect of punishment on children reveals that, in general, negative reinforcement tends to improve performance.

Other factors found to influence the effect of punishment include intellectual and achievement level, task complexity, strength of association, delay of reinforcement, pre-experimental satiation, instructions, subjects' personality, experimenter, and atmosphere. The possible effects of ego involvement and level of aspiration have not been considered in the experimental literature.

Suggested and supported by the available research is the hypothesis that negative reinforcement of specific responses has an informative and therefore beneficial effect, while the effect of negatively reinforcing the situation depends upon the action of other factors in the situation.

Aggression in the Classroom
FRITZ REDL

There's plenty of minor aggression in the classroom that nobody objects to. The real problem is the aggression that prevents good teaching and good classroom life. This aggression comes primarily from three areas.

First, it is an input from the home or from the community. A teenager gets hopping mad at his old man, but he doesn't dare let off steam until he gets to school. Now, the teacher didn't produce the aggression, but it's there and he's got to handle it.

Second, is the discharge from within. Some youngster sits there daydreaming, and all of a sudden during a wild fantasy, he thinks of something that upsets him and he conks his neighbors on the head. None of them have done anything to him, and the teacher hasn't either. Something just burst out from within. (If youngsters are seriously disturbed, most of the aggression comes from way within, and neither they nor anyone else knows why.)

Third, the aggression is engendered right there in the classroom. It may be triggered either by what the teacher does that's right but that doesn't happen to fit the kid, or by God knows what — the kid's reaction to the group or to other kids, or to something that maybe the teacher wouldn't have done if he had stopped to think. But anyway, it's reactive to something in the environment at the moment.

Now, if I were a classroom teacher, I would like to know how much of which of those three packages is exploding before me, because it makes a difference in terms of long-range planning. It also makes some difference in terms of what to do at the moment. Most of the time we are not sure, but different sources of aggression smell different when we are confronted with them. Experienced teachers develop an uncanny skill at sensing "This is something the kid brought with him. I've got to help him recover from it before he acts it out." The outsider, though, wouldn't know.

Reprinted by permission of the author and the National Education Association from *Today's Education*, 1969, 58, 29-32.

Some aggression does not affect us directly because certain youngsters may be model pupils in the classroom, but then after school they may go out and rape or murder someone. So a youngster may be full of sick aggression without being a classroom problem.

On the other hand, there may be a great kid sitting over there who's bored stiff. He likes you a lot, but he gets mad at the fact that you bore him stiff. Finally, he's just had it, and he runs out and slams the door. A normal youngster like that whose aggression is classroom-produced is our problem. Too often, an article on aggression in the classroom concentrates on a few examples of youngsters who should have been in a mental hospital for the last 10 years anyway and ignores all the other kids who bother us.

The term *aggression* is so overused now, you've got to watch out for it. Don't ever let anybody trap you into discussing aggression without first asking him: "Listen, brother, which aggression are you talking about? What actually happened?" Because aggression has a wide range — all the way from reacting to boredom to wrestling at the wrong time in the wrong place with another pupil.

Discharge of surplus energy or of displaced needs from the home or neighborhood; loss of control in the face of seductive equipment like a slingshot or a knife or whatnot; personal battles with adults, other kids, the group, or the teacher — all these fall under the heading of aggression.

The way Joe or Jane expresses aggression, while not the end of what we're looking for, certainly should be the starting point. Unless you know what lies behind their behavior, you will have trouble knowing how to handle it. Sometimes you may understand perfectly well how come. So the question then is what do you do to help him, which is a separate matter from knowing what was cooking to begin with.

I want to give special warning here not to make aggression synonymous with violence. The two are not the same, although they are obviously related. There is a theme in violence that we can legitimately call aggression. On the other hand, not all violence comes from aggressive drives. The behavior is aggressive, but the basis may be quite different. Let me give a few illustrations of violence that does not spring from aggression.

Panic coping. A kid may get scared stiff, so scared that he doesn't know what to do anymore. So he does something violent; he tears something apart. The fact that the behavior is violent is important. But this child is not hyperaggressive; he is frightened and desperate.

The need to be heard. A frequent source of violence is the feeling that nobody listens. The child finally concludes that the only way to get someone to listen is to be violent enough. So when other avenues are blocked off, violence is a substitute for verbal and nonverbal communication.

The desire to display guts. If a kid is supposed to be tough, how can he show it? Who is going to believe it? "I'd better not let them know I'm scared. So I've got to find ways to show I'm brave." In order to do this in a peaceful life, he's got to create problems.

Demonstrating loyalty to the group code. This source of violence is not originally meant to be aggression for aggression's sake. ("If the rest of my gang thinks school is no good, I'd better show that I'm with them. So I put a thumbtack in the teacher's chair. I don't hate the teacher; too bad it's her rear that gets stung. But I'm a regular guy and I'm going to prove it.")

Risk taking – to study survival skills. For instance, how can a boy know if he can run fast enough to outrun the cop, unless he swipes something first? Or else picks a rat out of an ash can, swirls it by the tail, throws it in somebody's first-story window, and then hops over the garage roof fast before they can catch him? A kid has to know how good he is in handling a dangerous assignment.

The stink and the dust produced in the decay of group psychology. If a group suddenly gets anxious or panicky or wild or disorganized or elated or mad at each other, you get a lot of behavior that involves violence but that did not start as aggression. Although Joe and Jane may be doing something, they're not doing it as Joe and Jane but as members of a group.

Last on my list of violence that does not start with aggression but is secondary to it is, of course, *an invasion of societal turmoil from the outside.* Someone or something in the community ties a package of emotional TNT to the back of a kid and it blows up in the classroom. The kid responsible wasn't originally aggressive; he carries the whole load of community or neighborhood or subgroup aggression. As his teacher, you're just an innocent bystander. What he does has nothing to do with the way you taught him or whether you bawled him out or flunked him.

In short, there is some relationship between violence and aggression, but not a simple one. For teachers it's very important to begin to sense the difference between Joe's being loaded with personal anger at what you just did and the explosion that results when his TNT package goes off at a given time. They are different problems.

Now let me give you a few abbreviated hints of what to do about various kinds of child behavior – hints that are not fancy enough to be written up much in books.

First, you sometimes need to get kids off the hook. The aggressive behavior is beginning but without having really been planned, and if you get pupils off the hook *now*, they don't have to continue. Another way of putting it is that you sometimes need to cut a contagion chain without making a big deal out of it. And in most cases knowing how to do this is very important in dealing with a normally well-behaved child as well as with a wild one.

Take Joe, for example. He's sitting over there shaking imaginary dice, and at the moment you're not too bothered. You catch his eye and he stops, but only momentarily. After a while everybody else gets interested. You want to cut that contagion chain now, because if you wait another five minutes, you'll have a mass problem on your hands.

If you interfere too early, everyone thinks you're a fusspot, a dope, or chicken, and you only aggravate things. If you don't interfere at the right time, you'll have trouble. Getting Joe off the hook at the right moment will stop his behavior without a big scene, and the rest of the group will not be too heavily afflicted. This skill of cutting contagion chains without making too much of a mess is, I think, one of the most important for anybody who deals with groups.

A second important technique for the practical handling of aggression in the classroom is signal interference. Signal interference in time saves nine. Very often teachers underestimate the possibility of stopping minor forms of misbehavior quite casually before the kid gets too carried away by it. They don't take the behavior seriously, because it isn't bothersome enough. So they wait until it does get bothersome enough, and by that time the situation is tense, the kid is already off his noodle, and anything they do now will have an explosive effect.

The big problem is that most teachers lack a good inventory of preaggression signals for their pupils. In some youngsters, the signals are easy to spot. Others apparently go aggressive all of a sudden from nowhere. That's because the teacher's radar doesn't pick up their signals. But if the teacher works at it, after a while he begins to get the messages from all around the room. One kid, for example, gets glassy-eyed and sits there quietly in a certain rigid position. If the teacher goes over and taps him on the shoulder, he'll go up like a rocket. Two minutes ago, if the teacher had gone around and said, "Come on, let's start working," that would have been fine.

A good many teachers — particularly those who are new to the classroom — do not know enough about the physiological and gestural signals that indicate the work-up to aggressive behavior. Everybody with experience understands them, but conveying this understanding to the other guy is hard. Apparently we don't think it's important because we don't have any fancy lingo for it, but if I were a beginning teacher, that's the kind of information I would like to have.

If you send me a kid with an unknown aggression work-up potential, I'd like to get to know that kid and figure out what he looks like before he goes off the handle. After that, I can tell at a glance that this is the moment to go over to him.

In observing classrooms and watching teachers with disturbed youngsters, I am constantly amazed at the terrific skill people with experience develop, and they can't ever explain it. What's more, they don't even mention it. They think it isn't worth discussing.

Let me describe one incident I observed:

A kid is sitting stiffly at his desk, obviously determined that he "ain't gonna do *nothing.*" The teacher walks over to him, pats him on the shoulder, and says: "Now, how about it? You don't feel so good, huh?" And he doesn't say anything. What does she do then? She says: "OK, I'll come back in a while. Maybe by then you'll be feeling better." That's all. She doesn't push him. ("Why don't you . . . ? What's the matter with you? What kind of family do you come from, anyway?")

She uses her judgment, and sooner or later he's over the hump. His face clears up; his posture is relaxed. Then she comes over and puts the pencil in his hand and he starts working.

Now, number three: Watch out for the choreography of the dare. In our present society we all have an insatiable, unquenchable thirst for tribal rituals. We still perform tribal dances. Take this scene:

We have what looks like a relatively normal classroom at the moment. Here is Joe back there, who wishes I'd leave him alone. But he knows I'm a nice guy, that I've got to make a living, after all. And I'm pretty harmless, though a little crazy, maybe.

Still, somehow, the noise gets too loud, and I finally say: "Listen, you, you'd better stop that now." Then maybe things get worse, and maybe by this time I'm angry, too. So I say: "All right, now, if you can't be quiet here, why don't you go out and cool off?"

Let's assume I'm relatively lucky in my diagnosis, and the youngster gets up and moves to the door, but on the way he mumbles something under his breath. If I ask him what he said, he probably feels he has to lie — so I make a liar out of him. Or if he is decently honest, I have to send him to the principal.

The foregoing is one way the scene can be played. But it also can be played differently. If Joe is sensitive of his prestige in the group, and I happen to have adults looking over my shoulder, then both of us become involved in a tribal dance. He has to say, "Make me," and I have to say, "All right. I'll make you." So either I try to bounce him or I call the principal or whatnot. Then for three weeks, lots of procedures go on — all nonsensical and having nothing to do with the original issue. Joe's become a discipline case, almost.

What I've described here is a personal interaction, a limit-setting process of a very simple nature, really. Most of the time it works like a charm, but in the second instance it became a tribal dance. If I were a principal assigning teachers to study halls or other large groups, I would like to know how vulnerable they are to the tribal dance routine, because in a dare situation the pressure is terrific. If you send me a kid who is tough, I don't mind. But I would like to know how involved this kid is in a tribal dance.

You see, some kids who are plenty tough don't fall for that kind of nonsense. In fact, some of my best delinquents would never be so stupid as that. If I really challenged them, they would think: "All right, so let the guy have his little victory for a change. So what! So I go out. I'm tough enough. Nobody will think I gave in." If, however, the youngster isn't really tough enough, but has to pretend he is, then he has to do the tribal dance in order to impress the others with his plumage, or whatever.

This is a big danger. And many a teacher could avoid many a large discipline problem if he were able to recognize the first drum beats of a tribal dance. Very often we push relatively tough kids who mean well into tribal dances because we are unaware of the position they are in. At other times, we do not interfere when we should because we are too afraid we'll provoke a tribal dance when actually we wouldn't.

So the tribal dance is a whole phenomenon — separate from the usual problem of discipline — that is a rather deep psychological problem.

Number four: Watch out for the subsurface effect. Whatever I do also has a side effect, and it is not always visible right now. If we are aware of what else happens besides the immediate effect of what we do, we won't simply say, "Because I blamed him for being noisy or because I praised him for being quiet, everything is hunky-dory right now."

So it's important to look with one eye to the possible nonvisible side effect. I can do something about it afterwards, but only if I'm on the lookout for it. Like that boy we've been talking about. Let's say he leaves the room and doesn't start the tribal dance. In that case, I'll want to make sure we have a brief get-together afterwards to tell him that I appreciate his doing what I asked and that I'll defend his reputation with the rest of the kids. I'll say that there are no hard feelings; it was just that I couldn't let him get so loud in class. That's all; nothing more.

If you have to live with aggression, at least try not to breed it. We breed it, of course, by exposing even otherwise normal boys and girls to experiences, to space arrangements, to life situations that invariably produce inner frustration.

For instance, if I bore a youngster, I expose him to frustration. Or, if I have to delay giving help that is needed — say, a boy over there is stuck in the middle of a long division problem, and I can't get to him for a while because I have to be over here with the others. Sooner or later he's had it, and he gets mad.

Or I may breed aggression if I intervene with too little sympathy. If a youngster is doing something interesting, something he likes, do I say, "Get going this minute. Do you want to be late again?" when I could just as well say, "Look, I'm sorry to have to break that up, but you know we've got to get out now."

One final point: Don't forget that from time to time, your own aggression will start showing. As you probably are aware, your hostile feelings and how you deal with them make a story no less complex and touchy than the one just presented. That your anger may be righteous and justified is not the only issue. You must ask yourself some questions: How does my anger make me behave in the classroom? Which (if any) of the behaviors it produces in me seem helpful in reducing youngsters' aggressive feelings, and which ones just make matters worse? Figuring this out requires clear thinking and real objectivity, but it is worth the effort. Your professional obligation is to handle your own aggression in such a way that the individual pupil or the class can manage the spillover effect.

Combined References for Chapter 6

Anderson, H. H. Motivation of young children: Further studies in success and failure, praise and blame. *Child Development*, 1936, 7, 125-143.

Baer, D. M. Effect of withdrawal of positive reinforcement on an extinguishing response in young children. *Child Development*, 1961, 32, 67-74.

Bandura, A. *Principles of Behavior Modification.* New York: Holt, 1969.

Brackbill, Y., & O'Hara, J. The relative effectiveness of reward and punishment for discrimination learning in children. *Journal of Comparative Physiological Psychology*, 1958, 51, 747-751.

Brenner, B. Effect of immediate and delayed praise and blame upon learning and recall. *Teachers College Contributions to Education*, 1934, No. 620.

Brown, J. S. *Motivation of Behavior.* New York: McGraw-Hill, 1961.

Crandall, V. J., Orleans, S., Preston, A., & Rabson, A. The development of social compliance in young children. *Child Development*, 1958, 29, 429-443.

Curry, C. Supplementary report: The effect of verbal reinforcement combinations on learning in children. *Journal of Experimental Psychology*, 1960, 59, 434.

Dinsmoor, J. A. Punishment: I. The avoidance hypothesis. *Psychological Review*, 1954, 61, 34-46.

Dinsmoor, J. A. Punishment: II. An interpretation of empirical findings. *Psychological Review*, 1955, 62, 96-105.

Farber, J. E. The role of motivation in verbal learning and performance. *Psychological Bulletin*, 1955, 52, 311-327.

Forlano, G., & Axelrod, H. C. The effect of repeated praise or blame on the performance of introverts and extroverts. *Journal of Educational Psychology*, 1937, 28, 92-100.

Gewirtz, H. B. Generalization of children's preferences as a function of reinforcement and task similarity. *Journal of Abnormal and Social Psychology*, 1959, 58, 111-118.

Hilgard, E. R. *Theories of Learning* (2nd ed.) New York: Appleton, 1956.

Hurlock, E. B. The value of praise and reproof as incentives for children. *Archives of Psychology.* New York, 1924, 11, No. 71.

Katz, D. & Stotland, E. A preliminary statement to a theory of attitude structure and change. In S. Koch (Ed.) *Psychology: A Study of a Science.* New York: McGraw-Hill, 1959, Vol. 3, pp. 423-475.

Kipnis, D. The effects of leadership style and leadership power upon the inducement of an attitude change. *Journal of Abnormal and Social Psychology*, 1958, 57, 173-180.

Meyer, W. J. and Offenbach, S. I. Effectiveness of reward and punishment as a function of task complexity. *Journal of Comparative and Physiological Psychology*, 1962, 55, 532-534.

Meyer, W. J. and Seidman, S. B. Age differences in the effectiveness of different reinforcement combinations on the acquisition and extinction of a simple concept learning problem. *Child Development*, 1960, 31, 419-429.

Meyer, W. J., & Seidman, S. B. Relative effectiveness of different reinforcement combinations on concept learning of children at two developmental levels. *Child Development*, 1961, 32, 117-127.

Murphy, L. B. Enjoying preadolescence: The forgotten years. *Childhood Education*, 1970, 46, 178-180.

Penny, R. K., & Lupton, A. A. Children's discrimination learning as a function of reward and punishment. *Journal of Comparative & Physiological Psychology*, 1961, 54, 449-451.

Postman, L. Rewards and punishments in human learning. In L. Postman (Ed.), *Psychology in the Making*. New York: Knopf, 1962.

Potter, E. H. The effect of reproof in relation to age in school children. *Journal of Genetic Psychology*, 1943, 63, 247-258.

Rajpal, P. L. What behavior problems do teachers regard as serious? *Phi Delta Kappan*, 1972, 591-592.

Schmidt, H. O. The effects of praise and blame as incentives to learning. *Psychological Monographs*, 1941, 53, Whole No. 240.

Sears, R. Ordinal position in the family as a psychological variable. *American Sociological Review*, 1950, 15, 397-401.

Sears, R., Maccoby, E. E., & Levin, H. *Patterns of Child Rearing*. Evanston, Ill.: Row Peterson, 1957.

Seward, J. P. Learning theory and identification: II. The role of punishment. *Journal of Genetic Psychology*, 1954, 84, 201-210.

Stephens, J. M. The influence of symbolic punishment and reward upon strong and weak associations. *Journal of General Psychology*, 1941, 25, 177-185.

Stephens, J. M. & Baer, J. A. Factors influencing the efficacy of punishment and reward: The opportunity for immediate review and specific instructions regarding the expected role of punishment. *Journal of Genetic Psychology*, 1944, 65, 53-66.

Stevenson, H. W., Weir, M. W., & Zigler, E. F. Discrimination learning in children as a function of motive-incentive conditions. *Psychological Reports*, 1959, 5, 95-98.

Terrell, G., Jr., & Kennedy, W. A. The discrimination learning and transposition in children as a function of the nature of the reward. *Journal of Experimental Psychology*, 1957, 53, 257-260.

Thornburg, H. D. *School Learning and Instruction*. Monterey, Calif.: Brooks/Cole, 1973.

Whiting, J. W. M., & Child, I. L. *Child Training and Personality: A Cross-Cultural Study*, New Haven, Conn.: Yale University Press, 1953.

Wickman, E. K. *Children's Behavior Problems and Teachers' Attitudes*. New York: Commonwealth Fund, 1928.

transitional
introduction

Transitional Introduction

In Chapter Five it was established that one of the characteristics of preadolescence was the growing inconsistency between youths' behavior and their values. Increased physiological maturation, greater intellectual aware-ness, and more involvement in social behaviors cause greater unpredictability in the individual's behavior than was characteristic of early childhood. This introduction and the articles in Chapters Seven and Eight, on drugs and sexuality, focus on common behaviors of the preadolescent.

A rather pointed stance on preadolescent and adolescent behavior is taken by this author. Behaviors do not occur in a vacuum. *There are causative factors behind all behavior whether they are apparent to the observer or not.* To ascertain the scope of preadolescent behaviors without considering their source of origin is incomplete and will most likely lead to erroneous conclusions. Therefore, overt behaviors must be explained within the life style or value structure of the behaving organism. The relevancy of preadolescent behavior is found within the following contexts:

1. The developing preadolescent often expresses the need to be antisocial, the manifestation of which is sometimes a delinquent behavior.
2. Smoking is one of the first norm-violating behaviors experienced by preadolescents. This is often the result of peer pressure and the easy access to cigarettes although some preadolescents use smoking as a form of rebellion.
3. The use of alcohol is another common preadolescent behavior. This too may result from peer pressure or rebellion. Incidences of use have been found to be more frequent among delinquents than among nondelinquents.
4. Drug usage is a more common social behavior among preadolescents. Chapter Seven represents several aspects of the problem. The implications for drug education are significant.
5. Today's preadolescent often uses sex as a behavioral alternative in which heavy involvement with the opposite sex may occur. Such behavior is usually a result of peer pressure, increasing curiosity, and perhaps as rebellion against authority. The articles in Chapter Eight center on various aspects of preadolescent sexuality.

Preadolescent Delinquency

Significant longitudinal research on delinquency has been done by Glueck and Glueck (1950, 1968). Using a matched sample of 500 each delinquent and nondelinquent boys, the Gluecks studied them to determine initial causative factors in delinquency as well as patterns of persistence in delinquent or criminal behaviors over a twenty-year period. Table A, taken from Glueck and Glueck's initial report (1950), points to the age at which delinquent behavior began with the group they studied.

Table A
Age at Onset of Misbehavior of 500 Juvenile Delinquents*

	Delinquents	
AGE	NUMBER	PERCENT
Under 5 years	20	4.0
5-7 years	222	44.4
8-10 years	196	39.2
11-13 years	53	10.6
14-16 years	9	1.8
TOTAL	500	100.0

M. = 8.35 years
S.D. = ±2.39 years

*Reprinted by permission of the Harvard University Press.

Preadolescent ages have been defined as 9 to 13 within this book. Following that criteria it is easy to see that almost all delinquents began anti-social behavior either before or during preadolescence. Specifically, 48.4 percent engaged in delinquent behavior before age eight; 49.8 percent before age fourteen, and only 1.8 percent beyond the age range of preadolescence. Furthermore, the average age of first court appearance was 12.4 years and first conviction at 12.5 years. Over 28 percent of the boys appeared in court before they were eleven.

It is not enough to simply establish the fact that most delinquency occurs prior to adolescence. One must look for its causes as well. Most delinquency is explained in terms of one's socio-cultural environment. This has been true especially in cases dealing with the culturally disadvantaged delinquent. Unquestionably, distinct social disadvantages may precipitate delinquent behavior. This is especially true when frustration is generated from the discrepancy between the lower-class goals, ambitions, and values and the middle class goals to which he is constantly exposed (Kvaraceus and Ulrich, 1959). While this explanation may hold true for many lower-class preadolescent delinquents, it is not a satisfactory explanation for the rising incidence of middle class delinquency. Further, Glueck and Glueck (1968) found that the nondelinquents in their study have comparable environments and gathered in comparable social settings with the delinquents. Such evidence points to other factors which may be delinquency sources.

The cause of delinquency is the "totality of conditions sufficient to produce it (Glueck and Glueck, 1968, p. 172)." This statement, of course, means that several causes go into delinquent behaviors, although the causes of delinquency found in one preadolescent do not necessarily mean that another delinquent's behavior results from the same causes. This may be illustrated by the trait "defiance" which was found in 50 percent of their delinquents. Obviously, defiance could not be an explanation for delinquency in the 50 percent where no such trait was evidenced.

Glueck and Glueck did find different family characteristics in studying delinquents and nondelinquents. Some such characteristics are indicated in Table A. The authors considered physical ailments and mental disability as strong genetic influences on delinquent behaviors. The psychological home environment is somewhat affected by the high degree of emotional disturbance, drunkenness, and criminality with the delinquents' mothers and fathers. The fact that 45 percent of the mothers and 66 percent of the fathers of the delinquent boys were involved in delinquent behaviors themselves must be regarded as a strong determiner of potential delinquency within their children. It is likely that Glueck and Glueck are correct in stressing the nature of the family in the early years of the identified delinquent's life as a primary causative source of preadolescent and adolescent delinquency.

Glueck and Glueck looked for delinquency causes within the individual. This doesn't mean, however, that they discount social and cultural factors that may be potential causes or precipitators of delinquency. Within their 1968 book a rather clear, yet concise, analysis of causations to delinquency is presented. In part, they said:

In emphasizing that our findings tend to confirm the view that delinquency involves both the biological make-up of the individual offender and his immediate forbears, and the family drama in which he and his parents play leading roles, especially during the first few years of life, we do not mean to ignore certain ideas which have been stressed by some sociologists. For example, we have in the past noted the influence of culture conflict in stimulating violation of social norms in some cases. Again, we recognize the special influences that are involved in the recent rise of delinquency in middle-class and upper-class regions. But such influences – rapid social mobility, conflicts in values and standards, weakening of middle-class and upper-class value systems so that they no longer guide behavior as much as in

Table B
History of Serious Physical Ailments, Mental Retardation, Emotional Disturbances, Drunkenness, and Criminality of Father and Mother

CONDITION	MOTHER				Difference	P
	Delinquents		Non-Delinquents			
	NUMBER	PERCENT	NUMBER	PERCENT	PERCENT	
Serious physical ailments	243	48.6	165	33.0	15.6	<.01
Mental retardation	164	32.8	45	9.0	23.8	<.01
Emotional disturbances	201	40.2	88	17.6	22.6	<.01
Drunkenness	115	23.0	35	7.0	16.0	<.01
Criminality	224	44.8	75	15.0	29.8	<.01
	FATHER					
Serious physical ailments	198	39.6	143	28.6	11.0	<.01
Mental retardation	92	18.4	28	5.6	12.8	<.01
Emotional disturbances	220	44.0	90	18.0	26.0	<.01
Drunkenness	314	62.8	195	39.0	23.8	<.01
Criminality	331	66.2	160	32.0	34.2	<.01

NOTE. The numbers in this table represent *minimal* incidence; percentages are based on totals of 500.

Reprinted by permission of the Harvard University Press.

the past — are two, three, or more stages removed from the immediately and intimately operative ones. For, as previously pointed out, the influences of the culture, and of exposure to another, are *selective*. Individuals react differently to the impact of cultural standards. That is why such general etiologic theories as the "delinquent subculture," or the working-class or middle-class subculture, or the "interstitial area," or the slum or "ghetto," or the process of "differential association" and other nondiscriminative, all-embracing general theories, do not adequately account for the operative facts in etiology.

Despite the many unwholesome and antisocial features of our culture — its excessive materialism, its stress on "success," its recent overwhelming assaults on values by various mass-communication media, its encouragement of the spread of "literature" of pornography and violence, the weakening hold of the church and formal religion — the majority of people are, in normal times, relatively law-abiding. In the research of which the present study is an extension (*Unraveling Juvenile Delinquency*), we had no difficulty in finding 500 nondelinquent boys living in underprivileged and high-delinquency areas of greater Boston.

In other words, antisocial aspects of culture are only *potential* or *possible* causes of delinquency. Persons of varied innate natures and differing early parent-child relationships respond in different ways to those elements of the culture which they wish, or are impelled, to *introject*, some of them transforming such cultural elements into antisocial motives. Environment can play no role in conduct unless and until it is, as it were, emotionally absorbed, becoming a part of the motivating force for or against the taboos and demands of the prevailing culture, its values, and its norms. For this reason it is indispensable to study individuals as well as broad social dynamics. Whatever future research may yet disclose about the causes of delinquency in the affluent segment of our society, as regards delinquency among the underprivileged, the emphases suggested by our analyses in the present and in prior works are supported by the facts.*

Smoking

The use of cigarettes is often an outcome of the preadolescent's growing interest in adultlike behaviors and an increasing curiosity to experience. Limited research has been done in the area of preadolescent smoking. It is reasonable to say that it is considered inappropriate by most adults. The adult intolerance is usually felt by restrictive and punitive measures levied against the preadolescents who get "caught." It is not this author's prerogative to make value judgments as to the morality of such behavior in youth. Four points may be helpful to individuals who are concerned about this type of behavior. They are:

---

*By permission of the Harvard University Press.

1. Many preadolescents smoke out of their natural curiosity toward a behavior they constantly see within their environments. This does not mean that the experimenter will become a habitual smoker or a delinquent "kid." Greater adult understanding about such behavior may prohibit severe problems in this behavioral domain if it is viewed as an experimental behavior rather than as an immoral behavior.
2. The recent anti-smoking campaign launched by the federal government is a widely publicized effort that has caused many children and adolescents to give serious thought to its use. It is quite possible that television and other advertising media can do a more effective job of persuading youngsters not to use tobacco than can parents or teachers.
3. Peers become increasingly important during preadolescence, and much of this behavior is conformity to peer pressure rather than individual initiative.
4. Anti-smoking programs should be based on logic and reasoning. School programs should educate preadolescents about smoking, and, indeed, it should be done in a positive, nonthreatening manner. Youth do not accept scare techniques at face value.

Many educational institutions have strict rules about students smoking on the school grounds. Typically, the apprehended student is paddled, given detention, or suspended from school for a few days. An experimental program in Illinois evolved out of the belief that these ways of handling such behavior were ineffective. As an alternative to suspension, these students were given the opportunity to attend four two-hour seminars designed to inform students about the consequences of smoking. The primary goal of the sessions was to reduce the incidence of cigarette smoking on campus (Herzog, 1970).

Using teaching materials from the Tuberculosis Institute, the American Cancer Society, and the Heart Association, the four seminar sessions focused on (a) the respiratory and circulatory systems, (b) what physiologically and bio-chemically happens when you smoke, (c) cancer and emphysema, and (d) the psychology of cigarette advertising. Herzog (1970) reported that of 198 students followed-up after the course, 12 percent stopped smoking, 85 percent said they significantly reduced smoking, and after five months the now nonsmokers had an increased lung capacity. Much controversy could focus around this program as a school function. However, it is important to point out that this school district saw a problem in their school environment and constructively and objectively attempted to correct the situation by showing the students who were part of the problem that some behavioral alternatives did exist.

Alcohol Use

There are few deterrents to the use of alcohol within our society. Research shows that almost three-fourths of the adults in our society have drunk alcohol at one time or another (Mulford, 1964). There are relatively few anti-drinking programs within our society, especially in comparison to anti-smoking and anti-drug campaigns. In spite of the fact that there are over seven million alcoholics in America, that it is a leading cause of death, and that over half of all traffic accidents are attributable to drinking, its use is not only socially acceptable but often reinforced. Our value structure has accepted drinking as a normal social behavior. Its use has been purported to be tension-reducing as well as facilitating interpersonal relationships (Dinitz et al., 1969). In essence it has become an integral part of the life style of many people in the Western world.

It is similarly true that many American youth are alcohol users. One could hardly expect anything different considering its prevalence in society. The inconsistency in its use is not in adults and adolescents alike using alcohol, but in the adults' intolerance in youth regarding its use and the expectancy among adults that adolescents should accept the adults' use of it. Research repeatedly indicates that adolescents are less prone to accept this difference and, thus, participate in its use without feeling anti-social about it. There are many youth who do use alcohol as a form of rebellion or delinquency. MacKay et al., (1967) found that 86 percent of the delinquency-prone and 71 percent of the nondelinquent junior and senior high school students in a New England state had used alcohol at one time or another. The average age when drinking first began was twelve to thirteen years.

Alexander (1964, 1967) and Alexander and Campbell (1967) have done extensive research on alcohol among youth. They found that (a) youths are quite likely to drink if their best friends drink, (b) they are highly vulnerable to peer pressure, (c) drinking is a form of rebellion against parental authority, and (d) drinking is an expression of personal independence. If one's best friend drinks this is the overriding determiner of adolescent drinking, thus peer pressure is felt. If one's best friend does not drink, the absence of peer support generally indicates defiance of parental authority as the cause for drinking (Alexander, 1967). In addition to the four reasons for drinking given by Alexander and Campbell it is likely that youth also drink out of their curiosity about alcohol and because of its widespread societal use.

First Drinking Experience

Most preadolescent drinking begins between eleven and thirteen years of age by consuming beer. In the early drinking stages beer and wine tend to be the primary beverages used by youth (MacKay, 1967, Pearce and Garrett, 1970). Toward middle adolescence (fifteen or sixteen) there is an increasing use of hard liquor.

The sources and places of drinking may be crucial factors in the continued use and need for alcohol. The study of these factors was undertaken by

Pearce and Garrett (1970) in Western United States. Comparing delinquent and nondelinquent drinking behaviors the following points are supported by their research:

1. 68.8 percent of the delinquents studied initially drank without parental permission compared to only 25 percent of the nondelinquent youths.
2. Most delinquents first drank in the home of a friend whereas most nondelinquents took their first drink in their own home.
3. Most delinquents obtained their first drink from friends while most nondelinquents had their parents as the initial source of alcohol.
4. Delinquents tended to drink at an earlier age than nondelinquents.

Alcohol as a Drug

Alcohol is a depressant of the central nervous system. Its action upon the body is the release of an inhibiting mechanism. This makes some individuals more jovial, perhaps sexually more permissive, and often aggressive and boisterous. With inhibitions depressed, an individual's behavior is often quite different and unpredictable as compared to the time when one is not under the influence of alcohol.

Alcohol is also addicting although it is more likely to be habituating. It is often consumed for emotional reasons. Excessive quantities can impair one's thinking and psychomotor coordination. Occasionally, normally reserved people become aggressive, often violent. The social drinker is a good example of a vulnerable alcohol user. He does not consider himself an alcoholic and has no emotional reasons for using alcohol. Yet, he is occasionally drunk, occasionally aggressive, and tends to consume alcohol without having a need for it. Such practices often serve as a model for behavior among our youth and encourage indiscriminate practices of alcohol.

It is difficult to conclusively state that there is a cause and effect relationship between alcoholic usage and subsequent drug use among youth. Studies do tend to show that drug users typically begin with alcohol and may even use the two simultaneously. Suchman's research (see Table C) points to the stronger usage of alcohol than either marijuana or LSD, a more favorable attitude toward alcohol, and more peer pressure to use alcohol. Certainly the availability of alcohol in society enhances the opportunity for its use. The preadolescent is aware of such opportunities. His growing desire for experiencing leads him into the area of alcohol, usually beer, as he moves toward independent behaviors, anti-authority behaviors, or peer conformity behaviors.

Table C
Comparison of Drugs According to
Use, Attitudes, and Pressures

Questions	Type-Drug		
	Alcoholic Beverages	Marijuana	LSD
Use[a]			
Frequently	47.2	14.1	1.2
Occasionally	36.9	24.5	8.8
Seldom	10.0	18.9	16.9
Never	2.4	30.7	53.8
Don't know	3.5	11.8	19.3
Attitude[b]			
Strongly approve	11.4	5.6	1.2
Approve	59.2	29.5	3.6
Undecided	22.2	31.5	20.9
Disapprove	5.2	20.1	25.7
Strongly disapprove	2.0	13.3	48.6
Pressure[c]			
A great deal	12.9	3.0	2.8
Some, but not much	38.2	16.5	2.0
Very little	47.0	78.1	92.6
No answer	1.9	2.4	2.6
Total percent	100.0	100.0	100.0
Total cases	497	497	497

[a]Question: "How frequently do most of the students you know do the following?"

[b]Question: "How strongly do you approve or disapprove of students doing each of the following?"

[c]Question: "How much pressure do you feel to engage in any of the following?"

Reprinted by permission of the publisher from Suchman, E. A. The "hang-loose" ethic and the spirit of drug use. *Journal of Health and Social Behavior*, 1968, 9, 146-155.

References

Alexander, C. N., Jr. Consensus and mutual attraction in natural cliques: A study of adolescent drinkers. *American Journal of Sociology*, 1964, 69, 395-463.

Alexander, C. N., Jr. Alcohol and adolescent rebellion. *Social Forces*, 1967, 45, 542-550.

Alexander, C. N., Jr., and Campbell, E. Q. Peer influences on adolescent drinking behaviors. *Quarterly Journal of Studies on Alcohol*, 1967, 28, 444-453.

Dinitz, S., Dynes, R. R., and Clark, A. C. *Deviance.* New York: Oxford Press, 1969.

Glueck, S. and Glueck, E. *Unraveling Juvenile Delinquency.* Cambridge, Mass.: Harvard University Press, 1950.

Glueck, S. and Glueck, E. *Delinquents and Non-Delinquents in Perspective.* Cambridge, Mass.: Harvard University Press, 1968.

Herzog, M. Seminar or suspension? Education or punishment for teenage smokers? *Clearing House*, 1970, 45, 146-149.

Kvaraceus, W. C. and Ulrich, W. E. *Delinquent Behavior: Principles and Practices.* Washington, D.C.: National Education Association, 1959.

MacKay, J. R., Philips, D. L., and Bryce, F. O. Drinking behavior among teenagers: A comparison of institutionalized and non-institutionalized youth. *Journal of Health and Social Behavior*, 1967, 8, 46-54.

Mulford, H. A. Drinking and deviant drinking, U.S.A., 1963. *Quarterly Journal of Studies on Alcohol*, 1964, 25, 634-650.

Pearce, J. and Garrett H. D. A comparison of the drinking behavior of delinquent youth versus non-delinquent youth in the states of Idaho and Utah. *Journal of School Health*, 1970, 40(3), 131-136.

Suchman, E. A. The "hang loose" ethic and the spirit of drug use. *Journal of Health and Social Behavior*, 1968, 9, 146-155.

CHAPTER 7 **drugs and the preadolescent**

Introduction

The use of drugs has made interesting inroads into our society. Incidence of drug usage have been found in: children, preadolescents, adolescents, young people, and adults; upper-class, upper-middle-class, middle-class, and lower-class; elementary educated people, high school dropouts, high school graduates, college graduates, graduate college students; black, white, Indian, Chicano, Puerto Rican, etc.; rural and urban. The use of drugs in America knows no barriers or cultural restraints, thus approximating a universality of appeal.

Among children drug usage commonly starts with sniffing solvents, more generally known as glue sniffing. The objects typically inhaled are glue, gasolines, lighter fluids, paint thinner, cleaning fluids, and similar volatile hydrocarbons (Kaplan, 1970; Strack, 1968). The sniffing of such substances will produce a state similar to alcohol intoxication. Its use among preadolescents is common. Kaplan describes its effects as follows:

> The sniffer will probably exhibit the same behavior as in the first stages of alcohol intoxication. In the first half hour or so, blurring of vision, ringing in the ears, loss of coordination, slurring of speech, and perhaps hallucinations will occur. Drunkenness is the typical symptom. A sense of floating or spinning is often experienced. Marked changes of mood can occur. After this follows a let-down period. Drowsiness, stupor, perhaps nausea, and sometimes unconsciousness are exhibited. This period is frequently blanked-out to memory after recovery (1970, pp. 20-21).

Tolerance for solvent sniffing develops but physical dependence does not occur. It is highly possible for psychological dependence to develop, usually in children or young adolescents. This activity, in fact, is the preadolescent's counterpart to marijuana or stimulants in the older adolescent. One of the most hazardous results of glue sniffing is the suffocation which often occurs during administration. Intoxication is commonly achieved by placing glue in a plastic bag. Several deep breaths bring on a rapid exhilaration. In addition, gasoline sniffers usually inhale fumes directly.

Glue sniffing is being stressed here because it is the most common form of drug use among preadolescents (Chapel and Taylor, 1970). It is also important to dispel the popular idea that it really isn't that dangerous anyway. Brozovsky and Winkler (1965) point out that its practice is often carried out in the restrooms of elementary and high schools. Chapel and Taylor (1970) note that its use is so well established in some users that intoxication is enhanced by drinking wine or beer between sniffs. It is appropriate to observe that the problem is common enough and potentially hazardous enough to educate our preadolescents regarding its nature, its use, its effects, and its corollary to subsequent use of additional drugs.

Marijuana

This drug, technically classified as hallucinogen, is the most commonly used drug in youth. It is uncertain how much use is within the preadolescent age range but it is the most likely drug to be used within the ten to fifteen year old age range. It is the most controversial drug because of its common use, the ease of obtainment, and its relatively harmless effect on the user.

Marijuana is a plant which grows wild in most temperate zones. It produces an active resin known as tetrahydrocannabinol (THC) which is capable of effecting hallucinatory states within the user. It is ordinarily inhaled through a cigarette (joint, joy stick, reefer, smoke, solid, spliff). Generally it produces a delightful, euphoric state in which distortion of time and space occur. Like alcohol, it tends to break down inhibitions and often creates assertive, self-confident behaviors in the user. It is often used in combination with an amphetamine or alcohol which most likely will lead to more intense reactions within the user than if used in isolation (Chapen and Taylor, 1970).

The preadolescent is attracted to marijuana out of curiosity or peer pressure and out of the conviction that it is harmless, in fact, less harmful than alcohol or tobacco. Pot parties have replaced beer busts. The relaxed, uninhibited disposition that characterizes many users is seen as a way to "be one's self" and is sought after by many users as a momentary utopia. During the normal four to six hours that the drug influences the user, a sense of lightness and tranquility is enjoyed.

It is the apparent harmlessness of marijuana expressed by most users that has caused its proponents to advocate its legalization. They contend that prohibiting its free use only reflects the absurdity of our social and legal laws (Fort, 1968; Johnson and Westman, 1968). In fact, a study conducted by the American Medical Association stated that it is a relatively harmless drug (Dependence, 1967). This attitude is not reflected in its individual membership, as 85 percent of some 28,000 physicians polled in 1969 were opposed to the legalization of the drug. Their primary reason was that marijuana often leads to addiction to more dangerous drugs (Modern Medicine, 1969).

These physicians were not pointing to a cause-and-effect relationship as much as the fact that the use of marijuana gives you an attitudinal predisposition and susceptibility to more harmful drug usage. One very recent study, for example, reports that among marijuana smokers, (a) 83 percent had also smoked tobacco, (b) 91 percent had used amphetamines, (c) 90 percent had tried alcohol, (d) 82 percent had used barbiturates, (e) 62 percent had tried LSD, and (f) 11 percent had tried heroin (Drugs, 1971). It is the kind of evidence that suggests an attitude toward drugs and causes professionals to seriously question the legalization of marijuana.

Drug Classifications

Each of the known drug categories, the trade names for the drugs, and the popular or slang drug names are presented in table form as a general classification of the commonly used drugs among youth.

Drug Users

One of the most cogent writers on the drug problem in contemporary America is David Smith. Some of his work is reprinted here as article one in Chapter 7. Focus is placed on the user. Smith contends that regardless of the drug taken, it is impossible to effectively help the user unless one is aware of the motivation behind such drug usage. Smith categorizes users four ways: (a) experimental, (b) recreational, (c) compulsive, and (d) ritualistic.

Smith's article is slanted toward the medical profession and his discussion of the diagnosis and treatment of the drug user may seem to be irrelevant to some readers. Obviously, by virtue of its inclusion in the book, it seems highly relevant to this author. The manner in which Smith describes the real problem of dealing with a youth under the influence of drugs can increase our understanding of the nature and cruciality of the problem.

Drug Education

The two articles in Chapter Seven, in addition to Smith's, focus on the nature of the drug problem and the manner in which we may educate and influence youth against drug use. The article by Vogl takes us into several different geographical sections of the United States to inform us of what

Table 7.1
The Common Names of Drugs*

Depressants
  Opiates
  opium · pen yan, hop, tar, black stuff
  morphine · M, white stuff, hard stuff, hocus, morpho, morphia, emsel, unkie, Miss Emma
  heroin · diacetylmorphine, H, boy, horse, white stuff, Harry, hairy, joy powder, scot, doojee, junk
  codeine
  meperidine · Demerol

  Barbiturates
  Nembutal · yellow jackets, yellows, nimbie, nimby, nemmies, phenobarbital sodium
  Amytal · blues, blue heaven, blue birds, blue devils, amobarbital sodium
  Seconal · reds, red birds, red devils, seggy, seccy, pinks, secobarbital sodium
  Tuinal · rainbow, double trouble, tooies, amobarbital plus secobarbital
  Luminal · Luminal, purple hearts, phenobarbital, pentothal, truth serum
  sodium thiopenthal

  Alcohol · Booze, bubbly, corn, hooch, juice, liquor, moonshine, mountain dew, pick-me-up, poison, red eye, sauce, suds, white lightning, etc.

Stimulants
  Cocaine · coke, C, Cecil, Corine, Carrie, Cholly, happy dust, heaven dust, dust snow, star dust, girl, Bernice, Burnese, Bernie's, flake, gold dust

  Amphetamines
  Benzedrine · bennie, benzies, peaches, roses, hearts, cartwheels, amphetamine sulphate
  Dexedrine · hearts, organes, dexies, footballs, dextroamphetamine sulphate
  Methedrine · Desoxyn, Norodin, Syndrox, speed, businessman's trip, bombitas, meth, methamphetamine hydrochloride

Hallucinogens

LSD	D-lysergic acid diethylamide, LSD-25, lysergic acid diethylamide, acid, cubes, wedding bells
mescal, mescaline	mescal, button, Anhalonium, mescal beans, hikori, hikuli, huatari, seni, wokawi, peyote
STP	dom, serenity—tranquility—peace
psilocybin, psilocin	tryptamine
DMT	dimethyltryptamine
DET	diethyltryptamine
marijuana	pot, weed, hemp, grass, hash, rope, kif, stuff, etc.

Vapors

glue, ether, chloroform, gasoline, lighter fluid, refrigerants, carbon tetrachloride, paint thinner, shellac, kerosene

*Reprinted by permission of the publisher from Einstein, S. *The Use and Misuse of Drugs*. Belmont, Calif.: Wadsworth Publishing Company, 1970.

various agencies are doing to combat the drug problem. Vogl focuses on the role that physicians, police officials, clergymen, teachers, and ex-drug addicts play in the educative process. Perhaps the most effective approach is organized groups which are generated out of community concern about drugs. Vogl asserts that specially organized groups are often more effective in communicating with their youths than already established groups, i.e., the school and church, about the drug problem. The author cites instances of special group effectiveness in reducing the drug problem in several different communities.

Most drug education programs focus on the legal and medical aspects of drug use, although there is a shifting emphasis toward the drug user (Weissman, 1969). Among reasons commonly given for drug usage are: (a) rebellion against parents, (b) reduction of inadequate feelings, (c) boredom, (d) thrills, and (e) escaping responsibility (Hollister, 1969). Peer pressure is very strong and recent research shows varying amounts of drug participation in high schools, ranging from 12 percent marijuana use in Utah, 20 percent in Maryland and Wisconsin, 24 percent in suburban New York City, to 43 percent in San Mateo County, California (Weiner and Elkind, 1972).

An extensive program in Connecticut has been under the direction of Marlin Dearden. In the five school systems in which he has worked, preliminary data suggest that drug use is not on a precipitous decline, but the decline has been effective enough to warrant continued effort and expansion of the program. Dearden makes the following observations about student use of drugs (1971, p. 10):

1. Drug use among students is a social phenomenon. The smoking of marijuana and the use of most other drugs, except heroin, usually occurs in groups.
2. The need for recognition and acceptance is high among drug using students, and their verbal activity and occasional aggressiveness in small groups is one means of gaining the attention they seek.
3. Factual knowledge about drugs among non-drug-using students is considerably less than among users. Knowledge about drugs among drug users, however, is primarily experiential and "grapevine" information, which is frequently distorted or incomplete.
4. Many students who use drugs share their drugs and do not push them. They do not actively promote or sell the idea of using drugs to those students who do not use them.
5. Students have shown a reduction in the use of drugs or a discontinuance of their use when made to feel accepted and respected by peers, teachers, and parents.

Dearden (1971) also found that most drug users incriminated the schools, contending that the curriculum was irrelevant and teachers were insensitive to and unconcerned with the students. Other writers have contended that the drug problem has evolved out of an inadequate society (Keniston, 1969). This author, while recognizing weakness within societal and school environments, contends that the drug problem is probably more individualistic and, therefore, attempts to control the drug problem should focus on the peculiarities of each individual user (Thornburg, 1971).

The final article on drugs which is reprinted here is written by Janice Pearce about drug education. She points to certain societal problems as well as discussing several dimensions of man. She advances the concept of the total person and the drug curriculum. Out of Pearce's article should come a philosophical and working conceptualization of the nature of the drug user. While many people would prefer a "cookbook" approach to drug education, Pearce's conceptualization of the problem is ultimately more helpful in understanding drugs and youth, and it is more adaptable to the varying needs of different communities regarding drug education.

The Trip There and Back
DAVID SMITH

Editor's Note:

One of the more realistic approaches to the drug dilemma within today's society is expressed in Smith's article here. His cogent discussion on both drug classifications and drug users lends objectivity to an issue that often is overridden by emotion. To illustrate, Smith's comment of "How can you treat an adolescent who's smoked one marijuana cigarette out of curiosity? There's nothing to treat," recognizes the seriousness of parental concern, the potential threat to a preadolescent through continued use, and the fact that the "curiosity" behavior may be symptomatic of some underlying reasons for using marijuana, although there is not yet any medical basis for treatment.

Consider the possibility that most preadolescents who use drugs fall within Smith's experimental user stage. What do you think is the likelihood that any preadolescent would be a compulsive drug user? Can you see Smith's point in attempting to assess underlying causes for drug use as well as different stages of user involvement? Which type of drug user appears to be the most likely target for drug education?

H.D.T.

Any day now, wherever you are, whatever kind of medicine you practice, somebody's likely to come into your office in the midst of a bad trip on drugs — from cough syrup to LSD. It's an old problem, but it's getting commoner all the time, and the victim is likely to be almost anyone. He may be carried in in a coma or he may arrive in a delirium. He may be severely depressed or somewhere beyond euphoria. He may be on the edge of violence or he may be filled with fear. Whatever his outward appearance, he's in bad shape and he needs your help. How you give that help may be one of the

Reprinted by permission of the author and publisher from *Emergency Medicine*, 1969, 1 (11), 26-41.

most difficult and delicate decisions you have to make in your practice. In the more commonplace medical emergency, such as an auto accident or heart attack, the patient is a more or less innocent victim of circumstances. What happens to him is a specific incident that has little to do with him as a person or his life style. The victim of drug abuse is not personally so isolated from his acute injury, and the doctor who treats him must consider more than the injury at hand and the agent that caused it. In medical school, we're not taught about drug abuse, and what we do get of pharmacology focuses entirely on chemical agents and their effect on the various body systems. The chemical factor — the pharmacological effect of a specific drug at a particular dosage — *is* one of the variables to consider in treatment, but only one.

The Users

The point I want to emphasize is that you cannot understand drug reactions — and you cannot effectively treat them — unless you understand that any pattern of drug use and abuse is a complex interaction between the chemical factors, the personality of the drug user, and the environment in which he takes the drug.

If you ask what effect marijuana or LSD or the amphetamines or any other psychoactive drug has, the only reasonably honest answer is, "It depends . . . ." What it depends upon is the user's personality and environment and, to some extent, his previous drug experience. A particular dosage of LSD, for example, may have a certain effect in one individual and an entirely different effect in another individual with a different personality structure or a different attitude toward the drug experience. It can even have different effects at different times in the same individual, depending on his attitude and environment at the moment. Or a good trip can turn bad if something or someone — a sound, for example, or a policeman — turns a safe environment into a threatening one. And since we're speaking of treatment, it's important to note that you can also manipulate environment to turn a bad trip into a good one.

I have been asked — and probably with complete sincerity — whether a physician *should* attempt to take the bumps out of a bad trip. Isn't a patient more likely to keep away from drugs in the future, the reasoning goes, if he has a bad trip the first time out? Certainly there *may* be some truth in this, but it's also true that an untreated panic reaction to LSD or other psychedelic drugs can lead to severe long-term psychological problems. There's also a very good chance of another residual effect. You've probably heard of "flashbacks" — the recurrence of the LSD experience days, weeks, or even months afterward without further use of the drug. These are primarily an aftereffect of a bad trip, and one of the principal reasons why proper treatment of an acute reaction to LSD or any of the other psychedelic drugs is so important.

Ethically, I think it's very questionable to let moral judgments influence the management of any emergency. In other areas of social disease – alcoholism and VD, for instance – this concept of humane, nonjudgmental treatment has been emphasized and is now generally accepted. But currently, the concern with increasing use of drugs, with their role in the youth culture of today, with their relationship to a generalized rebellion against the mores and practices of past generations, may obscure the point about proper medical practice as it applies to the acute drug reaction.

Even apart from the fact that the physician has a responsibility to do the best he can to help anyone who needs medical attention, you can do a better job in counseling the drug abuser about his long-range problems if you've taken care of him when he needed you.

When a patient has had a bad reaction to a drug and you've helped him through it, you've gone a long way toward gaining his trust, and you'll never find him more receptive to your advice and counsel. It would be naive of me to tell you that he'll now buy what you have to say one hundred percent of the time, but he will listen while you point out – not sermonize on – the dangers of drug use and the problems he can get into, and suggest alternatives to a potentially destructive life style.

Another common counseling situation arises less out of the user's reaction to the drug than the parent's reaction to the use. What often happens now is that a parent finds that a child has smoked marijuana and rushes him down to the family physician and says, "Treat him." How can you treat an adolescent who's smoked one marijuana cigarette out of curiosity? There's nothing to treat. What you can do is warn him about the potential dangers of drug use if he goes on, and – perhaps more realistically – advise him of the severity of the drug laws and the danger he runs of getting arrested. Family therapy, involving the treatment of parental anxiety or hostility, may be very much in order.

In considering the personality factors in drug use, it's important to recognize that people use drugs for reasons. And these reasons differ. They differ from individual to individual, and they may be different in the young from what they are in older adults. They range from curiosity to pleasure seeking to psychological need to desire for a religious experience. To be more precise about it, we've classified drug users into four categories: the experimental user, the periodic or recreational user, the compulsive user, and the ritualistic user.

The experimental user is the beginner. In our research, we've found that the primary motivation in the early teens is curiosity and group conformity. These kids want to know what "being high" is. Their friends are using drugs, so they decide that they want to try them. The trouble is that the experimental user is very often unsophisticated about what a high is. He'll try anything he's heard will give him one, and sometimes it isn't even a real high, it's just a toxic reaction.

They begin young. We've seen one patient at the Haight-Ashbury Clinic who was addicted to barbiturates at age 10 and another who had aplastic anemia from sniffing glue at age 7. These are the drug users you're most likely to see with an acute drug reaction.

For the second category, I prefer the term "periodic" to "recreational" for the simple reason that the experimental user may also be out to have fun. The periodic user, however, has gone beyond the thrill of trying a new sensation and has settled into a pattern of use, not for pathological reasons but just to have a good time. His attitude is much like that of the social drinker, and like the social drinker, he may occasionally overindulge. But he knows what the consequences will be and when they come, he gets through them without any help or with the help of his friends, because he's usually part of a subculture in which recreational drug use is as accepted as the cocktail party in the dominant culture. So you're not so likely to see the periodic user in your office.

But like the social drinker, he's also in some danger of passing into the next category. The compulsive drug user is the one who has gone beyond periodic or recreational use and feels a need for the drug, whether it's a true physical dependence or a psychological need. Usually he acquires a tolerance for his drug and begins increasing the dosage. This is when the acute reactions are likely to occur. But these patients are less likely than some of the other types of user to seek treatment because they are more concerned with concealing their compulsive use of drugs or because they don't recognize their use as compulsive. And you may fail to recognize it too.

In this group you may find the housewife or the businessman who takes off in the morning on two or three diet pills to create a kind of maintenance euphoria to counteract the boredom or tension of the day's tasks, and then comes down at night with barbiturates or a few drinks. Both patients and physicians often have a stereotyped vision of the drug abuser: He has long hair, he's a radical, and that's what a dope fiend is. It's hard to accept the fact that middle-class Mrs. Jones is also a dope fiend.

The ritualistic drug user takes drugs because he believes that they help him find some spiritual or religious experience. These users are not really germane to the discussion here because they don't usually have a drug abuse problem. Very often the ritualistic user eventually goes beyond drugs, stops taking them altogether, and develops a very personal, nonchemical turn-on.

These categories are by no means mutually exclusive. Obviously every drug user was once an experimental user. And those who use one drug periodically or compulsively may continue to experiment with other drugs. The individual who smokes pot occasionally for kicks may be compulsive in his use of amphetamine, and there is always the danger that either experimental or periodic use may lead to compulsive use.

The Drugs

These patterns of use are determined partly by the personality factor and partly by the agent itself. Some people have personality characteristics that predispose them to compulsive use of almost any agent. But drugs have characteristics, too, and a drug is increasingly dangerous in proportion to its innate tendency to produce a compulsive pattern of use.

Every physician knows about the abuse potential of the opiates, and because of the very rapid development of physical dependence, I think most of us realize that the barbiturates have a high abuse potential. But many of us are much less aware of the dangers of other sedative-hypnotic agents. We've been told that meprobamate is a minor tranquilizer and that glutethimide is a non-barbiturate sedative. These descriptions suggest that these drugs are somehow milder and lacking the abuse potential of the barbiturates, but the implication is false. You can become addicted to either one and you can have convulsions on withdrawal.

The young are often more knowledgeable about these things than many of their elders. If you ask an adult what the major drug problem is in this country, he'll probably say marijuana. But a drug-oriented teenager will tell you it's "speed" — the amphetamines — and he's right. This difference between what we tell them and what they know is one of the things that makes meaningful communication about the problem so difficult. I've suggested an approach to counseling the young experimental user, but I'd like to emphasize further that it doesn't help to try to scare them. That's been tried too often, and it only becomes a barrier. The young drug user knows what marijuana is and what it isn't. He's resentful of what even many adults see as the excessively stiff penalties imposed on a relatively mild agent. He observes the overreaction of the dominant culture to the use of marijuana, which is actually a minor problem in the drug area, and feels that he's being lied to, and his natural reaction is: "Why should I believe anything you tell me about any drug?"

The most rapidly increasing problem, and the most dangerous, is amphetamine abuse. The amphetamines and barbiturates have become the major agents of abuse both in the drug subculture, like that of Haight-Ashbury, and in high schools all over the country. In recent years, experimentation with these drugs in Bay Area high schools has gone from an estimated 5 percent to 8 percent up to about 15 percent or 20 percent.

It usually begins with dropping diet pills, either for kicks or to keep awake while studying for exams or some such reason. The user soon develops the dependence on the pills that I've already mentioned. This is the low-dose oral maintenance pattern of amphetamine abuse, and it's bad enough, but unfortunately it doesn't stop there. The real problem now is a different kind of pattern, the high-dose intravenous pattern. Black market speed labs have sprung up to synthesize and sell methamphetamine, which is injected rapidly into the bloodstream.

What the user is after in this pattern of abuse is not the maintenance euphoria, but the initial euphoric flash that follows the injection. This is often described as a whole-body orgasm. So naturally the speed freak injects himself repeatedly to get repeated flashing. The record, I think, may be held by one young girl in Haight-Ashbury who injected herself one hundred times in a single day.

The dosage can get up to anything from 1000 mg. to 5000 mg. of amphetamine per day. When you consider that a diet pill contains from 5 mg. to 15 mg., you can see that young people who get heavily into this situation are injecting a potentially lethal dose with each shot. They develop tolerance, of course, so it doesn't usually kill them — not directly anyway — but the problems it produces are very different from those of the "upper-downer" syndrome produced by diet pills and barbiturates. Or rather, they represent a traumatic accentuation of the speed cycle.

The user, flashing repeatedly, may stay up for three or four days at a time. He doesn't sleep, he doesn't eat, he's continually excited and hyperexcitable, continually on the go. This is the action phase, and eventually — either from running out of drugs or simple lack of sleep — he goes into an exhaustion phase, called "crashing" in the world of speed, and may sleep for as long as 24 to 48 hours straight. He wakes up with a ravenous appetite, but once he's satisfied that, he goes into a prolonged depression that can last days, weeks, or even months.

Because of the unpleasant aftereffects, the speed freak comes to fear the crash, and he'll push the action phase as far as he can to avoid it. Eventually, of course, he has to come down. But in the absence of treatment facilities, or perhaps because he doesn't want to seek treatment, he's likely to begin flashing again as soon as he wakes up in a frenzied effort to treat the depression himself.

Barbiturates are often added to the speed cycle, either sequentially or in graded doses along with the amphetamine — a lot of speed and a little barb — to smooth the trip. They don't always work or after a while they don't work as well as they did, and the user begins to increase the dosage until he's become a barbiturate addict as well.

There's another possible effect. With prolonged abuse, the amphetamine user develops a paranoid psychosis and becomes very prone to violence. Since it's known that a barbiturate can produce irritability if you don't go to sleep after taking it, barbiturates taken along with amphetamine may reinforce the violent behavior pattern.

In general, the drugs we're concerned with fall into four categories, with varying potentials for abuse, even within the same category. These are the sedative-hypnotic drugs, the narcotics, the central nervous system stimulants, and the psychedelic drugs. Actually, this doesn't begin to be a comprehensive list of all the things that drug takers have found to take. There's almost nothing ingestible or injectable that a determined experimenter won't try if he thinks it'll give him a high. But since the point I want to make about treatment is that you treat the reaction and not the drug, it would only be confusing to try to give even a partial list. So we'll stick to the commoner agents.

The sedative-hypnotic drugs include both the true barbiturates and such barbiturate-like drugs as glutethimide and meprobamate. Like alcohol, which is also classified as a sedative-hypnotic, they have a high potential for abuse, based on the three factors of high potential for psychological and physical dependence and the production of tolerance leading to increasing dosage. In very high doses, these drugs produce coma.

Tranquilizers, on the other hand — such as chlorpromazine, prochlorperazine, trifluoperazine, and reserpine — have little potential for abuse since they produce only minimal psychological dependence and no physical dependence or tolerance. They're also unlikely to cause acute reactions.

The most notorious of the sedative-hypnotics is *Cannabis sativa*, better known in this country as marijuana. It also comes in other forms such as charas, ganja, bhang, hashish, kif, and dagga. It produces neither tolerance nor physical dependence but sometimes some psychological dependence and thus has a moderate potential for abuse. Acute reactions are relatively rare, usually nothing more serious than nausea and vomiting, but occasionally there are panic reactions, particularly when the user is unfamiliar with the effects of the drug.

The narcotics include such drugs as opium, heroin, morphine, codeine, and their derivatives, and also meperidine, and various proprietary codeine-containing cough syrups. For all these agents the factors of psychological and physical dependence and tolerance are all positive and the abuse potential is high. Although chronic dependency is the primary concern, heroin addicts do occasionally get an overdosage with an acute reaction leading to coma.

The most widely used of the CNS stimulants are nicotine and caffeine, and caffeine, at least, has a relatively low potential for abuse. Antidepressant drugs are also in this category and also relatively harmless.

Considerably less harmless are the notorious product of the coca leaf, cocaine, and the more respectable but hardly less dangerous amphetamines. Though none of these drugs are considered to have any potential for physical dependence, they do produce tolerance and a high degree of psychological dependence and are frequently abused. Probably the most striking acute reaction is toxic psychosis, usually after long-term use.

The last category is the psychedelic or hallucinogenic drugs. I prefer the term psychedelic because the visual imagery is usually perceived as an illusion — what we call a pseudohallucination — an effect of the drug, rather than reality. LSD is the best known of these drugs, along with the natural but less potent substances, psilocybin and mescaline. But the category also includes the psychotomimetic amphetamines, MDA and DOM (called STP on the street, for "serenity, tranquility, and peace"), and the active ingredient in cannabis, tetrahydrocannabinol or THC, which is much more potent than marijuana. Actually, there's no THC available at all on the street, but its reputation is so great that a number of other drugs, in particular the veterinary anesthetic PCP, are sold under the name of THC.

The psychedelics produce minimal psychological dependence and no physical dependence, but the user does acquire a tolerance, so they have a moderate potential for abuse. Acute reactions include anxiety and panic as the hallucinations become more real and frightening — the classic bad trip. The panic reaction is more common with STP than with LSD because the effects are longer lasting.

A fringe drug in this area, because it does cause hallucinations, is *Sominex*, a nonprescription medicine for sleep, which contains the atropine-like substance scopolamine. It isn't a true sleeping pill though at low doses it does produce sedation. Where sleeping pills produce coma at high doses, *Sominex* produces delirium. The acute reaction is like a bad trip with the psychedelics, only worse. You can't become addicted to it because it's such an unpleasant experience.

The Diagnosis

As with anything else, the first step in treating drug overdosage is diagnosis. And the obvious first step here is to ask questions. You can ask the patient, if he's conscious and not too far out of it. Or you can ask his friends or his family or whoever brought him in if he didn't come alone.

While you're doing this, remember that the patient has probably come reluctantly. To him, you represent the dominant culture that nearly all drug users — whether initiates or confirmed addicts — are somewhat at odds with, and he expects disapproval. Try to make him feel as comfortable as possible. Show him by your manner as well as your words that you're concerned, that you're not just pumping him but trying to get information that will help you to help him.

If you can get an accurate idea of the drug that was taken by questioning, you're that far ahead. But it's not always that easy. Some patients are reluctant to talk, and there's nothing to be gained by persisting, especially if the patient is agitated or hostile.

If you haven't had much experience with drug users, the street language can be a broad barrier when the patient or his friends do talk. In Haight-Ashbury, there's a new drug marketed almost every week, and you get them talking about the peace pill, the pink wedge, the purple wedge, the paisley cap, the green dot, the purple dot. The point is that a patient may come in and say, "I've dropped three red barrels," and you're supposed to begin treating him for an overdosage of LSD. Or there's the patient who doesn't know what he took, or the one who *says* he knows but is wrong. A lot of drugs sold on the street just aren't what they're advertised to be.

If I've made the situation sound impossible, it isn't that difficult either. Taking the history is an important part of diagnosis, but in acute drug reactions, physical examination, simple observation, and eventually laboratory tests may be more important. What you've got to know is not so much the specific agent as the type of reaction the patient is having. That's why the drug classifications are useful. You can get into the habit of thinking, "This is a drug reaction of the sedative-hypnotic type, or the narcotic type, or the hallucinogenic type, or the CNS stimulant type," and treat it accordingly.

The results can be disastrous if you respond only to what the patient says, or what you think, he took. For example, there was a lot of underground publicity recently about THC — you weren't going to have to smoke marijuana any more, you could just take the active ingredient directly. Naturally, something called THC soon began appearing on the street — a white powder that sold for about $2.50 a cap — and naturally every kid on the street had to try it at least once.

Now it takes a seventeen-stage synthesis to manufacture THC and it costs about $50 to synthesize a psychoactive dose. Furthermore, it's stable only under liquid nitrogen, and the finished product is very difficult to get down because the taste is foul and you can't make it soluble and put it into a pill. So the underground manufacturers had either come up with a major breakthrough or it wasn't THC — and of course it wasn't.

Nevertheless, one physician saw a patient who was overdosed with what the doctor was told was THC. He had read that high doses of THC produce hallucinations, so he gave the patient a large dose of a tranquilizer. The phenothiazines *are* of value in treating adverse LSD reactions, but this patient hadn't had LSD and he certainly hadn't had THC, and he wasn't hallucinating. He'd gotten phenylcyclohexylpiperidine, or PCP, the veterinary anesthetic also known as sernyl or the peace pill, which was then the agent most commonly sold as THC. In short, he's already been overdosed with a depressant and the physician gave him another one. He went into coma and respiratory arrest and died.

The mistake the physician made was in basing his treatment on the history rather than the reaction he saw in front of him. The patient was obviously intoxicated, ataxic, and disinhibited. If he had come in with an acute drug reaction of unknown etiology, the physician would have recognized it immediately as acute intoxication of the sedative-hypnotic type and treated it accordingly.

The Treatment

The real point, perhaps, is that there is so much concern about the problem of drugs today that the uninitiated physician faced with a drug reaction *feels* that he's come up against something he knows nothing about. This simply isn't true as far as the medical aspects go. If you look at the reaction and don't worry too much about what caused it, you'll probably *know* what to do. It's in the area of the patient's personality and the nature of his underlying problem and your interaction with these factors that the difference lies.

Another point is that it isn't necessary, or even desirable, to give a large dose of medication to every patient with an acute drug reaction. This is a particularly good thing to remember with two types of patient that doctors often ask about — the patient who's taken a combination of drugs and the solo, unconscious patient.

Combinations like speed and LSD, or speed and barbiturates, or alcohol and barbiturates or tranquilizers can cause tremendous problems. You have to be very cautious not only about the type of medication you give but the quantity and the rapidity of administration. Even though the reaction appears to be of one type — say hallucinogenic — if you know that the patient has also taken barbiturates, you probably don't want to give him a sedative or one of the phenothiazines.

Whenever you're in doubt, don't do anything. Just watch the patient and when something needs to be done, you'll know it. If he stops breathing, you know you've got to treat him for a depressive reaction no matter how many kinds of drugs he's taken. If he's bizarre and noisy on a combination of seven different kinds of drugs, why then he's bizarre and noisy, and you use supportive psychotherapy and keep him in a nonthreatening environment. But don't give him any more drugs.

When a patient is brought in unconscious and there's no one with him to tell you what happened, you can still be pretty sure that it's either a narcotic or a barbiturate overdosage. You wouldn't get this kind of reaction with the amphetamines or the psychedelics. A very common practice with the unconscious patient, of course, is to take urine and blood samples and send them off for an emergency toxicological analysis, which will tell you exactly what you're dealing with. In the meantime, you give him whatever supportive treatment seems indicated and leave the drug to metabolize itself. No specific medication is required. As in any comatose patient you focus on maintaining an airway and, if necessary, assisting respiration.

Even though the individual case of drug overdosage in our context is not standard, I don't mean to put down standard methods of poison control when they're appropriate. If a patient comes in who's just overdosed himself with a barbiturate, you're perfectly correct in using a stomach pump and possibly gastric lavage, even if he is a regular drug user.

But an acute reaction in a drug user isn't always a pure poison control matter. It makes no sense to pump the stomach of a patient who comes in hallucinating on LSD. The drug is already out of his stomach into the blood stream and affecting his mind. And putting a tube through the nose and into the stomach of a patient who's hallucinating or one who's high on amphetamines can really freak him out. Yet I've known of cases where this was done. "They're putting a snake in me!" cried one patient.

Even in the standard methods, there are few specific antidotes for any dangerous drug. You do, of course, have nalorphine (*Nalline*, Merck, Sharp & Dohme), a narcotic antagonist for use in cases of heroin overdosage. But it's no good at all against cocaine, marijuana, barbiturates, or psychedelics.

In a drug reaction of the sedative-hypnotic type — which means primarily barbiturate overdosage — you may see a patient who is severely intoxicated but conscious or one who is already in a coma. If the patient is still conscious, you want to keep him up and moving, keep him stimulated, though we don't usually find it necessary to give stimulant drugs, even if the patient has to be hospitalized.

If the patient is unconscious, give him general supportive treatment to maintain an airway and keep him breathing. Begin electrocardiographic monitoring to watch for cardiac arrhythmias and potential cardiac arrest. If these appear, stimulants may be necessary.

The patient's blood pressure may drop sharply, and this is treated by the standard method of rapid administration of intravenous fluids. Since secondary lung infections can develop in a patient with depressed breathing, give antibiotics if his temperature rises or there are other signs of pneumonia.

Narcotic overdosage can also lead to coma, and the treatment is essentially the same as for barbiturate overdosage. But you have the additional possibility of giving nalorphine to counter the effects of most — but not all — of the narcotics.

Acute psychiatric reactions to amphetamine range from acute anxiety to full-blown psychosis, including paranoia, if the patient has been abusing the drug for some time. The anxiety-ridden patient can be given a sedative or a phenothiazine tranquilizer. This treatment may also be useful for the patient going into the exhaustion phase to help him sleep it off. But be sure to keep the dosages low. Even though a patient seems still to be in the action phase of the speed cycle, he may be on the verge of going into the reaction or exhaustion phase, and you don't want to give him a high dose of a depressant drug just when he's about to go into a deep sleep anyway.

A very high overdosage of CNS stimulants can also produce a hypertensive crisis. And death from amphetamine overdosage is usually a result of hyperpyrexia and convulsions. I've seen physicians treat an acute reaction to amphetamine and forget completely to watch the patient's temperature. You've got to keep the temperature down as an essential part of the emergency treatment of acute reaction to amphetamine overdosage.

There are a whole host of secondary medical problems with amphetamine abuse, such as hepatitis, malnutrition, skin problems, some acute respiratory distress, and occasionally gastric distress. The treatment of these differs from that in nondrug patients only insofar as the condition is complicated by the other manifestations of amphetamine overdosage or abuse.

Again I must warn you that the often violent and paranoid amphetamine abuser is the most dangerous of all the drug users to handle – the only one in fact who is likely to be dangerous. Your best course is to approach him calmly in a nonthreatening environment, but the talk-down, which is the most effective treatment for acute psychedelic reactions, doesn't work with amphetamine users. If a toxic psychosis persists, the best treatment is temporary hospitalization and administration of antipsychotic medication, such as one of the phenothiazine tranquilizers. But the paranoid aspects of amphetamine psychosis may make this treatment easier for me to suggest than for you to institute.

The acute anxiety reaction, or what is often diagnosed as a "nervous breakdown," can often occur as a result of amphetamine abuse in patients you don't think of as drug addicts. In an area like Haight-Ashbury, where all of our patients use illegal drugs, the diagnoses we sometimes miss are nondrug conditions. But in more normal areas of medical practice, I find that the physician with little experience with drug users often fails to consider a drug etiology in his differential diagnosis. He may even fail to get a drug history.

The patients themselves – and they may be either adolescents or adults – may fail to recognize their use of amphetamine diet pills as the cause of their symptoms or of family problems. Or they may be unwilling to recognize it. The amphetamine abuser is prone to conceal his abuse, but the patient's own attitude toward his drug use is not what determines whether he's a compulsive user or not. That's a diagnosis you have to make. And evasion or denial of any drug problem is often a clue to the diagnosis.

Despite widespread use — and widespread concern about the use — of marijuana, you're not going to see very many acute reactions to it in your office. That's because the worst acute reaction to overdosage — smoking too much — is simple nausea and vomiting. The user just sleeps it off and no more thinks of going to a doctor than a drinker with a hangover.

There is, however, a rare panic reaction that you may see. At high dosages, marijuana can cause perceptual alterations, a loss of immediate memory that the kids call being "spaced." Most users find it funny and enjoy the experience. But the effect may be alarming to an experimental user or someone with a negative set toward the drug or with a pre-existing personality disturbance, and particularly to older users who are less able than the young to tolerate changes in their perception of reality. They may think they're losing their minds. The effect will pass, and the best treatment is simply to let them sleep it off. If a patient becomes really agitated, you can give him one of the phenothiazines, and I would stress the use of a tranquilizer rather than a sedative.

As the drug is used in this country, virtually no organic effects are associated with marijuana. There is a form of chronic toxicity, however, which I would describe as a motivational syndrome. Some young people do become potheads. They smoke large quantities primarily for psychological reasons and remain somewhat stoned all the time. As you might expect, this does impair motivation and social performance. You're most likely to see this when a mother comes in because she's concerned about her boy's deteriorating performance in school. But I want to emphasize that it's an entirely reversible condition. When the user stops smoking pot, either because of psychotherapy or his own volition, he usually returns to his pre-drug level of functioning.

Acute reactions to LSD are also usually handled in the community, although they are much more serious than reactions to marijuana. But you may see them occasionally, especially in areas away from the drug subculture. I've described the effects of LSD as pseudohallucinations rather than true hallucinations, but what can happen in an acute reaction is that the user forgets that what is happening is a drug effect, and in that sense the visual imagery becomes a true hallucination. Instead of responding positively to the *illusion* that his body is changing colors or shapes, he is terrified by the *belief* that he has actually become purple. Or sometimes the doors of his subconscious have opened and he recalls, or reexperiences, the loneliness he felt at the age of seven or being locked in a refrigerator at the age of two or feelings of homosexuality he had at thirteen. It's like a nightmare, but he's awake and he knows it. That's what a bad trip is.

You have to be particularly careful what you do with a patient like this because his altered perceptions will color everything you do. You can do or say anything you want to a comatose patient. But a gruff manner may send a patient on LSD into a screaming panic, or a sympathetic manner may be treatment enough. Even with the most severe cases of LSD intoxication, we've been able to turn a bad trip back to a good trip with nothing but the talk-down. And then they're all right.

We get the patient into as pleasant an environment as possible and try to make him comfortable. If he's got sympathetic friends with him, keep them around, and then just talk. Try to find out what is actually causing the panic — whether it's a bad body trip or an environmental trip or memories that he thought he'd forgotten. Keep emphasizing that all these things are effects of the drug and that they'll pass.

Very often you may want to use a tranquilizer, too — you can give about 50 mg. of *Thorazine* orally to begin with and then repeat it every three or four hours depending on the patient's anxiety — but the psychological support is more important. If he's been using one of the other hallucinogens, such as STP or MDA, I would recommend that you use a sedative in place of *Thorazine.* The intoxication can last much longer than that caused by LSD — some users hallucinate actively for as long as 24 hours on STP — and the phenothiazines, especially in high doses, seem to prolong the period of disability.

The approach I've outlined is not only the best emergency treatment for an acute psychedelic reaction, but it's the best way to prevent flashbacks. These are almost exclusively an aftereffect of a bad trip, and particularly a bad trip that's been handled badly — throwing a boy on a bad trip in jail, for instance, or giving him a massive dose of *Thorazine* and leaving him to himself.

Belladonna and the atropine-like drugs can also have a very unpleasant hallucinogenic effect. This, too, may last up to 24 hours. The talk-down can be used here, too, but you must avoid the phenothiazines because they have atropine-like side effects. So for belladonna overdosage use a sedative like *Librium* or phenobarbital or pentobarbital — and again, in low doses, because a massive dose of belladonna, unlike the true psychedelics, can take the user through an excitation phase into respiratory arrest.

Belladonna intoxication is usually easy to recognize by the widely dilated pupils, the dry mouth, and rapid pulse rate. Other acute drug-induced psychotic reactions, however, may be difficult to tell from a nondrug psychosis. Often, careful observation and the history, if you can rely on it, will be your only clue. This will probably be your most difficult diagnostic problem, much more difficult than differentiating one drug from another. I'd also like to emphasize that with a highly agitated patient it's important to distinguish between the violence of the amphetamine abuser and the terror induced by an acute LSD reaction. They require very different appoaches.

Drug reactions are most common in the experimental user, but they can occur with any pattern of use. It's vital that you don't direct your attention solely to the acute problem — remember that it may be a sign of a chronic problem, and we all know the dangers of treating symptoms and overlooking the underlying causes.

Sometimes the dangers can be very immediate. In one case, a girl was brought in after having injected 1200 mg. of a barbiturate in an apparent suicide attempt. In spite of the dosage, she was only groggy when she was brought into the emergency room, and after observing her for a while, the doctor on duty determined that she was not, in fact, in any immediate danger and discharged her. The next day she went into convulsions.

What the physician overlooked was the obvious fact that anyone who can take that much barbiturate in a single dose without ill effect has a substantial tolerance to the drug and is almost certainly addicted. And when you withdraw from a high-dosage addiction to barbiturates, you have convulsions. Actually, I think, the girl's apparent overdosage was a cry for help with her much more serious long-term problem. An acute reaction in a compulsive user often is. And an acute reaction in a periodic user may be a warning sign that his drug use is beginning to get out of hand.

What Comes After

I don't think any acute drug reaction of this kind should ever be treated and then forgotten. You should follow the patient up just as vigorously as he will tolerate.

If you're not able to follow the case yourself, you should have it handled by a psychiatrist or psychologist or some facility where the patient can be seen at least one more time. The compulsive user, and often the initiate as well, usually has severe underlying psychiatric problems, and it's almost impossible to break a pattern of abuse without treating these problems. Also, the follow-up may be the only way to determine whether an acute reaction is a sign of a chronic problem.

If the patient is in fact addicted to one of the drugs which produce severe withdrawal symptoms — heroin or the barbiturates — you'll want to try to put him into withdrawal treatment, with methadone for heroin addiction and with long-acting phenobarbital for addiction to one of the short-acting barbiturates. After psychedelic intoxication, there is always the possibility of flashbacks, greater with STP than with LSD, but still possible with either.

And a final reason for keeping in touch with the patient: The drug user is often most receptive to your counsel when he's been hurt and you've helped him. There's no guarantee that you'll get results, but he'll probably listen, and you'll at least have the opportunity to keep experimental or periodic drug use from becoming compulsive abuse.

Influencing Kids Against Drugs: What Works?
A. J. VOGL

The battle cry is raised: "We've got to educate our kids against drugs." The battle is joined by teachers, doctors, police officials, clergymen, ex-addicts, and community groups. A crash program is mounted, and the crash is resounding: Almost overnight there are panels and lectures and courses, something for everybody.

While all this may be gratifying to adults, how effective is the program for their youngsters? Drug abuse certainly *looks* vulnerable to a crash program because adults see it in terms of black and white, good and evil. In reality — the youngsters' reality — drug abuse has as many gray areas as sex, and it is quite as loaded. Tough questions outnumber easy answers. As with sex education in the schools, the would-be educator's good intentions are not enough.

The limits of good intentions are reflected in the remark of a high school sophomore, after listening to a discussion of drug abuse by a panel composed of a doctor, a psychologist, the local chief of police, and a teacher: "I can't get mad at them because they mean well," he said, "but they want to talk *about* the problem, while I want to talk *with* somebody about it, somebody who'll listen to me instead of thinking what to say next to grind his own ax."

This is not to say that youngsters don't respect knowledge or strong convictions or personal experiences; they simply demand that their viewpoints and sophistication about drugs also be taken seriously. Twisting the truth to make a point is still the most irretrievable error an "expert" can make. "If 20 per cent of the students in a classroom of fifty have used a drug," the National Institute of Mental Health points out, "there are at least ten students carefully measuring the teacher's words against empirical

Reprinted by permission of the publisher from *Medical Economics*, April 20, 1970, Special Issue.

knowledge. At least thirty students will know the ten are users and be briefed by them. With forty of the audience of fifty in good position to judge the accuracy of a teacher's statements about a drug he probably never has tried, any discrepancies will be quickly noted and used to breed distrust of the total presentation."

Distrust will also be bred if the youngster feels his generation and "his" drugs are being singled out for condemnation. The harmful potential of alcohol and tobacco should not be ignored; neither should the fact that "straight" society is dependent on drugs to alleviate tension, anxiety, insomnia, depression, and other painful psychic states; our children have watched too many television commercials — and looked too often into their parents' medicine cabinets — to believe otherwise. Because of what seems to them inconsistency, youngsters will ask pestering questions: What's the difference between getting drunk on New Year's Eve and getting high on grass at a rock concert? What's the difference between drug *use* and drug *abuse*? Is there any way marijuana can be *used*? Am I *abusing* marijuana if I turn on only on weekends, and otherwise fulfill my obligations to myself, my parents, and my community?

In a confrontation characterized by such questions, it takes more than truisms and "a good platform manner" to be effective.

Who's effective?

Physicians? Yes, if they know what they're talking about and don't try to preach or judge. "I'd say the average eighteen-year-old has been exposed to much more nonmedical drug use than most doctors," observes Dr. Warren Gadpaille, a Denver psychiatrist. "There's nothing wrong with that if we admit it. But kids will stop listening if we try to gloss over our ignorance. I let youngsters teach me."

Police officials? In a time when "law and order" has become a euphemism for repression, the policeman bears a considerable handicap as an educator of the restive young. Furthermore, at least as concerns marijuana, the police are responsible for enforcing laws that many youngsters — including non-users of drugs — consider unjust.

Clergymen rarely fill the bill either, according to Dana L. Farnsworth, director of Harvard University Health Services: "Most clergymen have been unable to take any constructive approach to the problem of drugs. Many already feel out of touch with the younger members of their congregation, and are further handicapped by their lack of knowledge concerning the different drugs. Thus a clergyman may inveigh against all drugs as 'dope,' and young people, knowing better, are confirmed in their opinion that the clergyman does not know what he is talking about." Younger clergymen, those who are in touch with younger members of the congregation, are likely to be casual about drugs to the point of toleration.

The same is true of some younger teachers. U.C.L.A. psychiatrist J. Thomas Ungerleider notes: "It is rare that I speak at a high school without some adult taking me aside and informing me that 'our school has ten (or twenty or thirty) teachers who use marijuana regularly.' " Such teachers, of course, constitute a very small minority. Most of the others are conscientious people but ignorant about drugs. For the older teachers, just as for today's parents, drugs are "something else," something that has played no part in their growing up. To remedy their ignorance, special seminars have been held to acquaint teachers with the basic facts and issues.

If ignorance of drugs is the problem, then it would seem that the ex-drug user or addict should make an ideal teacher. His understanding of drugs and the drug life is drawn from firsthand experience, which youngsters respect. But not any old ex-addict will do. "While they were quite knowledgeable about drug abuse, some of the ex-addicts who spoke to our high school students weren't effective in changing attitudes because the kids couldn't relate to them," reports Vito A. Giordano of the Youth Services Division in White Plains, N.Y. "They were stereotyped as ex-Dead End kids, and they got involved with drugs for reasons different from those that impel our middle-class youth." Dr. Judianne Densen-Gerber, the lawyer-psychiatrist who heads Odyssey House in New York City, is aware of the problem: "The kids must be able to identify with the ex-addict. So we'll be sure to send a girl to a girls' school, for instance, or a Catholic to a Catholic school, or a black to a black school."

Many of these ex-drug users on the "speaking circuit" are not so sure of their effectiveness. "I think they see me as either super-straight or super-freak," one explains. "I've been there and come back. They're pleased that I've returned, but they don't think they'll ever be where I was. Nobody believes drugs can control his life until his life is controlled."

Despite such reservations, a study at two Los Angeles schools found that students exposed to ex-addicts tended to acquire more accurate information about drugs than from the usual programs, and also emerged with attitudes that were closer to those health educators sought to produce. Moreover, there seems little doubt that youngsters usually and understandably prefer the ex-addict speaker. At East Hampton, N.Y., for example, high schoolers were asked to rate a panel composed of a doctor, a clergyman, an attorney, a policeman, and an ex-addict. "The ex-addict came out on top," reports Lucian F. Capobianco, a G.P. who is active in the town's program against drug abuse.

Whatever else it accomplishes, rating the speakers is a way of involving the students in a drug abuse program, so that it becomes more than the voice of the Establishment. This is a very real problem, as Dr. Capobianco concedes: "We have to bridge the gap between us and them, and there's no question that a gap exists. To that end, we have an advisory council of five teen-agers that acts as a liaison between our narcotic guidance council and the youth of the community."

As part of the DOPE STOP program in Maricopa County, Ariz., that liaison has been broadened by assigning high school students direct responsibility for explaining the dangers of drugs to grade schoolers. Every "Teen Counselor" is assigned a specific class that he stays with until he graduates; he visits the class once a month and is available for individual consultation between visits. More than 1,000 students are reportedly involved in the Teen Counselor program.

Some drug abuse programs go even further, to the point of letting youngsters run the whole show. This, in fact, is the stated purpose of a nonprofit organization based in Hollywood, Calif., called Smart Set International, Inc., which goes out of its way to avoid letting it appear that the school or any other Establishment group is sponsoring its program. In its handbook, Smart Set advises that the program should be presented to eight or ten of the school leaders, who should then be left to carry the ball. The teen-agers themselves are supposed to set up speaking panels, show films, distribute posters and decals, and otherwise support Smart Set's campaign theme that *not* taking drugs is the smart and fashionable thing to do. Conversely, taking drugs is attacked as square and stupid. This kind of rationale, Smart Set believes, protects the youngster against charges of being "chicken" or "out of it" if he refuses to go the drug route.

Smart Set advises that its program stands its best chance of success in the grade and junior high schools "where the teens have not committed themselves to the drug scene," and today Smart Set reports over 1,500 programs in operation.

While on the surface the Smart Set program seems rather superficial and contrived, there is evidence that it works. Robert Racine of Bristol, N.H., an attorney, first heard of the program when it was described on the "Dragnet" television show. "We started in Bristol last year," he recalls, "and 40 per cent of the local students enrolled within eight weeks; three months later, we had about 500 students from thirty schools in New Hampshire. The best reception is from elementary (fifth grade and up) and junior high school students. The seniors have made up their minds one way or the other, and they're too big to be involved."

The biggest problem attorney Racine and New England teen-agers face is the indifference, or even antagonism, of adults. "A girl from Connecticut wrote that she asked her principal's permission to put up posters and start the program, " Racine says. "He refused, saying there was no drug problem in the school — a ridiculous response considering she'd just told him that girls were smoking marijuana in the restrooms. He then confessed that he was afraid of the reaction he'd get from kids who were using drugs."

Mark Braley, the teen-ager who started Smart Set in Bristol, reports that such fears are not imaginary: "One of the reasons we know the program works is that it does bother the drug users. In Bristol, two kids were beaten up, and all the officers of our local group got threatening phone calls. And, of course, the drugheads kept tearing down our posters. One reason our program bothers the user is that it reverses the usual roles. One of us who's asked to take a drug will ask in turn, 'Why?' The drug users have to come up with an answer, and they don't like it."

Braley has also had problems with the parents in his community. "When we began the program in Bristol last year," he explains, "I had over twenty-five phone calls from parents saying I was out of my mind, that I was using Smart Set as some sort of cover-up, and that they wouldn't let their kids join. At the first meeting at my house, parents called the police department saying we were showing kids how to use drugs."

According to U.C.L.A. psychiatrist Ungerleider, who is an authority on the psychedelic drugs, the overzealousness of Smart Set groups in ridiculing drug use and users tends to backfire. "Wherever the program goes," he asserts, "among bright and hitherto uncommitted youngsters the rate of drug use goes *up*."

Dr. Ungerleider's own youth program — considerably smaller than Smart Set — is called D.A.R.E., for Drug Abuse Research and Education. It consists of about seventy-five teen-agers who have never used drugs. The group is less interested in directly attacking drug use than in convincing adults that long hair and an interest in psychedelic art and music aren't the exclusive marks of a drug user.

"D.A.R.E. youngsters accompany me on lectures and speak from the audience during question and answer periods," Dr. Ungerleider recounts. "Initially, the audience is hostile and even calls the D.A.R.E. kids 'dopers' because of their long hair and vividly colored psychedelic outfits. When these very verbal youngsters finally respond with conviction that they've *never* 'turned on,' it startles the adults. Then, if we're really communicating well, some local crew-cut football player type will get up and admit that he uses dope. The audience gets very anxious then — for if the 'long-hairs' don't use drugs and local 'short-hairs' do, what is one to believe?"

Most of the approaches discussed so far are aimed at keeping youngsters from starting to use drugs. But what about those who are "into" drugs past the experimental stage? Here, too, peer programs seem to offer considerable promise.

An organization named Encounter, based in New York City and only four years old, is already a veteran leader in the field of treating what it calls the "pre-addict" — the youngster who may have been using "soft" drugs for two years, who is still functioning, and is not yet a "hard-core" narcotics addict.

Encounter aims not only to get the youngster off drugs but also to help him mature so that he won't return to drugs upon re-entering society. The Encounter pre-addict continues to live at home but must spend about 30 hours weekly with the organization, including attendance at three group therapy sessions. The therapy, much like that used in residential communities for hard-core addicts, is led by ex-drug users, and zeroes in on the problems that caused the youngster to turn to drugs.

"We don't just provide therapy but an entire social life," says Brendan Sexton, who heads Encounter. "Belonging to Encounter means giving up all drug-using friends and making new friends here." Most of the Encounter youngsters, Sexton continues, never learned to cope with the problems of growing up. "Let's face it," he says, "the average fourteen-year-old guy has trouble talking to girls, getting along with his parents, and figuring out what he wants to do with his life. But while the average guy works out these problems, or at least muddles his way through, the kids we see here haven't been able to do that. They're trapped in adolescence unless they do something to break out of it."

They may also be bound for harder drugs if no intervention occurs. "In comparing the scores our kids make on the Minnesota Multiphasic Personality Inventory against the scores of hard-core addicts, we find no real difference at all," Sexton says. "Both have virtually the same problems. The only difference is that we're getting them at an earlier age, before their entire lives revolve around drugs." Encounter is supported by small foundation grants, donations, and whatever its members can make from speaking engagements.

Awareness House is modeled on the Encounter pattern, and demonstrates that drug abuse is not just a city problem. Located in Fort Bragg, Calif., a town of 5,000, it was established after the town learned that a large percentage of the local school's 550 students were on drugs. In addition to formalized encounter therapy, Awareness House offers the community's youth a place to hang out and learn about "turning on without drugs." The staff is also training selected ex-addicts as drug specialist counselor-aides under a grant from the U.S. Office of Education, and has helped Sonora and Yuba City, Calif., and Tucson, Ariz., to set up Awareness House programs of their own.

A relatively new development in the area of youth-directed programs is the telephone counseling service. One such, called Terros, is in Phoenix, Ariz., sponsored by the Community-wide Organization for Drug Abuse Control (CODAC). Terros received 723 calls during its first month of operation, 608 of them from people with drug-related problems, reports Dr. Eugene Ryan, CODAC's chairman.

Terros (not an acronym but a misspelling of terra) occupies a big, white, two-story house in downtown Phoenix. The staff, composed of six students who serve at nominal pay, live upstairs and youngsters visit them downstairs. Most of Terros's work, however, is done by phone. "It's not unusual to talk to somebody on the phone for two hours," says Bill Thrift, a staffer who is an electrical engineering student. "Usually the kid is really scared: Little ugly people are walking up his chest, about to bite his neck, or bugs are coming out of the walls. We try to convince him that the little people and the bugs have been created by the drug, and they'll go away when the drug wears off. He may also be receptive to the suggestion that he lay off drugs for a while to let his head clear out."

"Afterwards, the same kid may come down to see us and say: 'Man, you guys sure helped me. What can I do to help?' And we say, 'Man, that's very nice of you, but as long as you're doing dope, there's nothing you can do to help.' We make them understand that, while we'll love them as people no matter what they do, they'll have to change in a few ways before we'll respect them as helpers."

Often young drug users phone to complain about the emptiness and futility of their lives. "The heads talk a lot about their disappointment with people," reports Lanny Lindtiegen, the graduate student who supervises Terros. " 'People are so plastic,' they'll say, or 'relationships are so meaningless,' and they'll usually conclude by saying that the only people worth anything are those who do drugs. Then I hit them between the eyes by asking: 'How many dopers do you know that can really love — especially when they're on dope?' They know there aren't any drugs under which you can honestly love your fellowman. They just know it.

"Then I say: 'O.K., baby, if you really want to be useful and extend some love and help your friends, how are you going to do it when you're high? You say relationships are meaningless. Well, here we are. What are you going to do about us? We're friends. We're Terros. Are you going to put your mind where your mouth is? We're the kind of people you say you want, but you can't really have us and dope at the same time.' "

Terros even receives calls from non-users, illuminating the vast gap it is trying to bridge between lonely youngsters and a world they never made. "We even had a thirteen-year-old girl call and ask how to act at her first dance!" Lindtiegen exclaims. "She couldn't get up the nerve to ask her parents because they were very cool people who never had time to listen to her problems."

For all these "bummers" (a term that originally meant a bad LSD trip, but now has been extended to mean any kind of emotional upset), Terros offers its own alternative: "grooving on people." Explains Lindtiegen: "It's hard to put into words, but it means getting out and interacting with people, interchanging feelings and ideas, really loving people. One reason the drug subculture attracts teen-agers is that it professes love, which is something all kids need. After a while I think they realize they've been gypped in the drug world, too, and they're out in the cold again without any love. Well, love is what we try to offer here."

Consider, by contrast, the communities of Clifton, N.J., and Smithtown, N.Y., where the school board and a citizens committee, respectively, were recently proposing to ferret out young drug users by subjecting public school students to periodic urine and saliva tests. Or consider the Grossmont High School District near San Diego, which in the two years past has automatically expelled 342 students found guilty of drug use. From such panicked or authoritarian adult minds, the drug scare has apparently driven all memory of the lessons taught by Prohibition — as well as memories of their own youth.

Unlike adult-sponsored programs that attack the drug user, or even those that merely attack the drug problem's symptoms, Terros, Encounter, and other youth-directed programs are primarily concerned with *why* a youngster turns to drugs and how he can be helped to overcome those problems. For youngsters, to help each other find their own reasons to shun drugs may well be the single most effective way of tackling the drug abuse problem. Adults can give encouragement, support, information, the fruits of mature experience — and, perhaps even more important, good example. But each new generation can find fulfillment only through its own efforts to shape the world closer to its heart's desire.

The Role of Education in Combating Drug Abuse
JANICE PEARCE

It is obvious by now that the solution to the drug problem does not lie with any single agency or discipline. It is a multi-faceted problem and as such requires a multi-faceted approach. Thus, if we are to find solutions to the dilemma which faces us, a cooperative effort is essential, beginning in the home with the parents and extending to the medical profession, pharmaceutical profession, government and law enforcement agencies, social agencies, and to the schools. In focusing on the aspect of prevention, however, the home and the schools can serve as the primary agencies for control. As President Nixon (Brown, 1970, p. 3) recently noted, "The long-term solution to the nation's drug problem does not rest with law and order techniques alone, but rather with education." The purpose of this presentation, therefore, is to consider the role and responsibility of education in coping with the drug phenomenon facing the American people.

An intelligent approach to the drug problem must be based on the awareness that widespread drug abuse is not an isolated phenomenon. It is the product of a complex society — a by-product of changing cultural patterns and a variety of personality stressors. Thus education must deal with the drug phenomenon within the social and cultural context in which it has developed. Consequently, this investigation of the role of education will focus first on the socio-cultural factors which have contributed to our present problem and secondly on teacher behaviors which attempt to generate communication as a basis for the development of socially constructive behaviors.

Reprinted by permission of the author and publisher from the *Journal of School Health*, 1971, 41 (2), 83-87.

The Changing Scene

Societies constantly change, but usually at a rate that is almost imperceptible when viewed from a single point in time. The American society today, however, is undergoing change at a phenomenal rate, and we are experiencing an upheaval in traditional social structures and value patterns. We have undergone, during this century, a prolonged industrialization accompanied by radical shifts in population from rural settings to urban, with resultant areas of high population density and with the social and health problems which characteristically accompany high population density. We have experienced a technological explosion in which it is said we have doubled, in a twenty year period, the knowledge that had been accumulated in the thousands of years of human habitation that preceded us. The affluence we enjoy is unprecedented and some industries flourish on creating new ways for the public to use its buying power.

Today's youngsters have grown up in a world of television, nuclear power, and wars of rather dubious value which have produced intense ideological conflict. They have grown up in a world where family structure has undergone a change that has modified traditional family ties. They have grown up in a world of heightened mobility where occupational progress may necessitate frequent movement from city to city, or from one geographical area to another. Traditional values have been assaulted, and if not uprooted, certainly shaken. Thus this generation has developed in a world that is increasingly characterized by an impersonal, mechanistic technology and a materialistic, consumer-oriented society; it has developed with what columnist Max Lerner (Brown, 1970, p. 5) has described as ". . . a basic rootlessness that has stripped a whole era, and not only a generation, of the sense of belonging that earlier eras had in America. The prevailing symptom is a desperate feeling of emptiness, and with it the yearning to fill the emptiness with anything — kicks, adventures, bizarre cults, drugs . . . ."

Concomitant with these developments has been a literal explosion in the pharmaceutical field, and a plethora of drugs are now available for modifying physiological and psychological processes. As a result, it is possible to cure countless diseases which took a significant toll in human life not too many years ago. In addition some control can be maintained over fluctuating blood pressures, the seizures of epilepsy, the tragedy of leukemia, and the depressions frequently precipitating mental illness. However, many of the same drugs which are used for the cure or control of these diseases are also used to facilitate recovery from a hang-over (which has also been drug induced), to keep us driving beyond our normal limits, to get us through examinations, to make us feel better by either pepping us up or calming us down, and to achieve what is claimed to be a euphoric bliss — the chemical cop out! To further complicate the situation, almost everyone is a drug user at one time or another, and the distinction between drug use, mis-use, and abuse is sometimes indistinct; yet that distinction is vital to the positive concepts on which constructive behavior is based.

As children spend more time out of the home and away from the family, the school inherits greater responsibility for the transmission of attitudes, beliefs, practices, and values from one generation to the next. To facilitate this task educators have sought effective instructional innovation, and in recent years both students and teachers have experienced curriculum reform, team teaching, programmed learning, flexible scheduling, and computer-based-instruction. Thus a university student can now learn chemistry via a computer. In order to develop a particular solution the student decides which compounds to mix and feeds the appropriate terms into the computer. If the problem is correctly solved the computer gives the desirable reinforcement through immediate feedback and the student proceeds to the next problem. If there is a failure to select the proper compounds, however, the computer may respond with large, ominous letters across the screen, "You have just had an explosion!"

While the "mechanistics" of learning have moved forward, the "humanistics" — the personalized, caring, feeling elements of learning have failed to make equal progress and at times seem to have become almost extinct. Thus on one college campus the feeling toward education was aptly expressed by the following piece of poetic creativity (May, 1969, p. 61):

The word has come down from the Dean
That with the aid of the teaching machine,
King Oedipus Rex
Could have learned about sex
Without ever touching the Queen.

It is proposed, therefore, that education is allowing itself to fall into the same patterns that characterize society — an increasingly mechanized, computerized, de-humanized modus operandi. Rollo May (1969) stated in the book, *Love and Will*, that we have become afraid of feeling, of close relationships, of meeting one another with openness. May described what he termed, "schizoid man," as man cold, aloof, detached, avoiding close relationships — essentially apathetic. "Schizoid man," according to May, is not an infrequent occurrence, but rather a "general condition of our culture" and a "natural product of the technological man." In addition, May wrote that the current obsession with sex in our society, and with sexual technique, is symptomatic of a lost ability for caring. "It is an old and ironic habit of human beings to run faster when we have lost our way; and we grasp more fiercely at research, statistics, and technical aids in sex when we have lost the values and meaning of love."

Maslow (1967) discussed essentially this same type of behavior which he characterized as a defense mechanism used extensively by the youngster of today. These youngsters have become doubtful and suspicious of the existence of values and virtues. They have little respect for their parents who, being confused themselves about values, have transmitted their confusion and hypocrisy. As a result, according to Maslow, these young people "have learned to reduce the person to the concrete object and to refuse to see what he might be or refuse to see him in his symbolic values, or to refuse to see him or her eternally (p. 287)."

Although adolescents reject any attempt at having adult values imposed upon them, many are nevertheless basically idealistic and searching for ways to establish their own values as behavioral guidelines. It is contended, however, that education has failed to help them significantly in this search. We, as educators, have been fully aware that adolescents and preadolescents will not allow us to make decisions for them, so we have based programs in the decision-making areas on providing scientifically accurate information and avoiding classroom concern with values, morals, or spirituality on the premise that knowledge will, hopefully, assure personally and socially wise decisions. There are two fallacies in this approach in regard to drug education. First, teachers often know less about drugs, their effects, and the personal and social implications of drug abuse than a good portion of the students whom they are teaching. Second, when the scientific facts of drug use have been imparted, such facts have been of little value in changing attitudes or behavior. In essence, then, it is proposed that the educational setting is becoming a reflection of the de-personalized and technologically oriented society, and that drug education in this setting is, to a large extent, ineffective.

On the other hand, today's child is one who is difficult to reach; one who may turn the teacher off at the slightest hint of Establishment clichés; who, in proclaiming the need for and virtues of individuality, is perhaps more of a conformist to peer pressure than previous generations. Exactly who are the children in today's schools? Are they the "spoiled brats" of the too permissive home? Are they the aggressive, violent revolutionaries we read about in newspaper headlines? Or are they, beneath the defense of the impersonal, the idealistic in search of values and direction?

The Five Dimensions of Man

Homel (1969a,b) has proposed what could be termed a teaching-learning model based on the total person concept. He has suggested that as teachers we tend to look at the Johnnys and Marys seated before us in the classroom and see essentially the physical entity — the biological dimension of the individual. But it is with what teachers do not see that Homel is predominantly concerned. What is it teachers may not see? What does Johnny see when he looks at himself that a teacher may fail to see? If we were to ask Johnny who he is, we would probably receive a response to the effect that, "I am me," and only with further probing would Johnny relate that the "me," aside from the physical fact, is a myriad of ideas, feelings, social relations, and beliefs. And in these intangibles exist the other dimensions of Man — the intellectual, emotional, social, and spiritual facets of every individual.

It seems that as teachers we tend to base our knowledge of students on the biological dimension and focus our efforts on the intellectual. Yet it is rarely the physical aspects of problems that bother a child. For example, a child develops diabetes. The disease presents definite biological problems. It is diagnosed and appropriate treatment is established. The biological component has been controlled. However, many of the child's problems remain, are perhaps intensified, by the reactions of parents, siblings, and peers to the diabetic condition.

A more common example is the child who wears glasses in the elementary grades. Parents may feel great concern, but their concern is not essentially because they feel the visual problem cannot be corrected, but with how Johnny's friends will react to his glasses, how Johnny will subsequently come to perceive himself. Undoubtedly many of you who have had to wear glasses through childhood, or who have had children wearing glasses will agree that the biological aspect of the situation is not nearly as pervasive as the social and emotional implications.

To what extent, then, should the teacher direct efforts beyond the biological and intellectual dimensions of students and become involved in attempting to help them structure their beliefs and values? In reacting to such a question, Homel (1970) may in turn ask what happens to the biological being when proper nourishment is not provided. It is, of course, merely a matter of time until anemia develops. He may then ask if it is not likewise possible to have *five different types of anemia?* The implication is obvious — without proper nourishment anemia, atrophy, disease — whether spiritually, socially, emotionally, intellectually, or physically. With proper nourishment, each dimension will tend to grow.

The Total Person Concept and the Drug Curriculum

Which aspect of the drug abuse problem should we as teachers be more concerned with: the physiological effects of marijuana on the body processes, or behavior that may lead to drug dependent personalities? It might be questioned how uptight teachers can legitimately become when students involve themselves with one or two experimental episodes with marijuana *if* this action is viewed from a strictly biological point of view. It is still not certain if there are detrimental biological effects from infrequent marijuana use. Yet, there is more than adequate justification for concern if we consider that each episode may be establishing the foundation for future methods of reacting to stress, of confronting personal problems, or of searching for excitement.

Consider for a moment the typical drug curriculum. Is it not based primarily on the pharmacology of drugs, the physiological effects of drugs, and drug laws? Judging from the widespread and increasing abuse of drugs, it is doubtful that these are the critical elements on which students base behavioral decisions. On the other hand, how often is there an attempt to systematically investigate, in dialogue with the student, the social implications of drug use or the value judgments implicit in drug decisions?

Salisbury and Fertig (1968, p. 38) cite the case of a drug researcher who talked with teachers in an urban school about marijuana use in order to help them communicate better with students concerning the drug problem. He was surprised to learn that most of the teachers did not want to counsel students or engage in dialogue concerning behavioral decisions. The teachers' main concern was "to learn how to identify the smell of marijuana and the symptoms of the users so they could report them to the police." In my opinion, this is an abdication of educational responsibility. It is an example of an educational cop-out that may be as serious in its ramifications as the chemical cop-out.

Providing educational nourishment for each of the five dimensions of man is not an easy task. A teacher can feel much more secure presenting a lesson on the physiological aspects of drug use than in probing social ethics. The lesson can be current, scientifically accurate, punctuated with colorful, eye appealing visual aids, and it can proceed in a carefully structured sequence with the teacher in complete control. In this manner one can give the students the facts, allow them to make their decisions on the basis of those facts, and believe that the educational responsibility has been met.

It is a far less secure position for a teacher to attempt to lead a discussion, to create meaningful dialogue concerning the allegation, for example, that "Drugs expand your mind," or that, "Drugs engender love and facilitate communication." A teacher can't be certain what the students will come up with in such a discussion, and the pat answer may not be readily available. Such teaching necessitates a shift from the traditional conceptualization of the teacher as a giver of information to the teacher as a participant in a process. Wolk (Brown, 1970, p. 15) stated, "When discussing the topic of drugs, the teacher must be a student in his own class, a participant-observer, a guide or a facilitator . . . ."

To reach the total person, communication is vital and the teacher must establish a classroom climate in which there can be a free exchange of ideas with tolerance and without recrimination. This does not imply that values must be compromised or behavior condoned that is illegal or detrimental to the individual or society. But there must be a willingness to listen to various points of view and to investigate rationally the possibilities of various behavioral decisions. A few years ago members of a college health class were discussing the relative merits of drug use when an antagonistic polarity developed between students who advocated the benefits and values of indiscriminate drug use and the Establishment-oriented majority. There was a great deal of verbal exchange between the groups, but appallingly little meaningful communication. There was no attempt for either group to understand the motivation or belief system of the other. This was a disappointment since it is believed that students should investigate, both intellectually and emotionally, the pros and cons of drug use and not rely on standard arguments they have heard or read and are projecting without really internalizing. If the reasons for the intelligent use of drugs and the rejection of abusive practices cannot stand up under intense scrutiny in a classroom, it is feared they may not withstand the subtle and pervasive pressures of a social situation.

Maslow's (Krech, 1962, p. 77) personality theory is based on a hierarchy of needs, beginning with the physiological and progressing successively through the need for safety, for belongingness and love, for esteem, and ultimately ending with the need for self actualization. The basic or lower level needs must be satisfied before higher level needs can be attained. The rather complex concept of self actualization is, somewhat simplistically, a process of functioning to one's fullest potential, with inner direction, and with harmony between one's beliefs and values and one's actions (Maslow, 1967).

In former years much of an individual's youth and early adulthood focused on fulfilling physiological and safety needs. More recently food has been plentiful for the majority in this country, shelter available, parents have showered children with material goods, and a permissive attitude has made sexual needs somewhat more obtainable. This generation has been relieved of the necessity of spending the major part of each day in attaining basic survival needs. The resultant freedom has enabled adolescents to become preoccupied with needs for belonging and love and for self esteem, as well as with the search for self actualization. This phenomenon plus the availability of drugs may, therefore, have been major factors in the development of the drug sub-culture, for an inherent part of that sub-culture has been the search for values, for spiritual meaning through an expanded consciousness, and for belonging through a group commitment.

It is proposed that education has not adequately capitalized on an awareness of adolescent needs in the development of drug curricula. The focus has been basically negative, with emphasis on harmful physiological effects of drugs, dire social consequences, and threatening legal implications.

A positive approach to the study of drug use should include concepts such as social ethics, human relationships, personal values, and the meaning of life. It could include discussions of civics, mental health, consumerism, and community identification and contribution. The objective should not be to eliminate the use of drugs, but to teach an appreciation of their potential as a positive and constructive influence on human life. A positive drug curriculum could be based on developing an appreciation of the drugs which are available and investigating ways in which they can alter man's functions — not just the biological, but intellectual, social, emotional, and spiritual functions as well.

Peer pressure has been found to be a significant cause of drug experimentation. It is an interesting paradox that while placing a high value on freedom and non-conformity, the youth culture exerts tremendous pressures for conformity. It implies that teenagers, in initially identifying with the drug culture, are not as interested in the "up" or "down" achieved with pills and needles, as they are with the need to be accepted, to be popular, and to prove oneself. It means that education must deal with the conformity phenomenon by preparing students emotionally for making behavioral choices on the basis of their beliefs. Maslow (1967) wrote that one part of self actualization is daring to be different and maintaining internal honesty whether or not it engenders popularity or peer approval.

A second implication of the conformity phenomenon is that education must create among youth an acceptance for the point of view of another individual and a responsibility for avoiding the employment of coercion tactics exemplified by the derisive phrase, "Don't be chicken!" In essence, education must help youngsters develop a sense of responsibility and integrity in human relations.

Summary

It is contended that education has abdicated a part of its responsibility to youth. Educators have been primarily concerned with the tremendous reservoir of information confronting them and with the mechanics of facilitating the transferral of that information. It is proposed that to meet the challenge of the current drug phenomenon it will be necessary to humanize, in a sense, the approach to youth, to aim with curricula and methodology at the social, emotional, and spiritual dimensions of the individual as well as at the biological and intellectual dimensions.

It is a responsibility of teachers to show the youth culture that we can value and develop creativity and sensitivity without drugs; that we can investigate the cosmic questions without the use of drugs; that we can transcend the immediacy of the here and now and move into a world of shared beliefs and ideas without drugs; and that perhaps such experiences without drugs may be more enduring than the transcience of their drug induced experiences.

Combined References for Chapter 7

Brown, B. J. (Ed.) *A Time Guide to Drugs and the Young.* Time Education Program, 1970.

Brozovsky, M. and Winkler, E. Glue-sniffing in children and adolescents. *New York State Journal of Medicine*, 1965, (Aug.), 1984-1989.

Chapel, J. L. and Taylor, D. W. Drugs for kicks. *Crime and Delinquency*, 1970, 16(1), 1-35.

Cohen, Y. A. *Social Structure and Personality.* New York: Holt, Rinehart & Winston, 1966.

Dearden, M. H. Observations about student use of drugs. *School Management*, 1971, 15(5), 10.

Dependence on cannabis (marijuana). *Journal of the American Medical Association*, 1967, 202, 47-50.

Drugs and Drug Abuse Education Newsletter, Washington, D.C.: Scope Publications, 1971, 2(9), 4.

Einstein, S. *The Use and Misuse of Drugs.* Belmont: Wadsworth Publishing, 1970.

Fort, J. Youth: How to produce drop-ins rather than drop-outs. *Research Resume No. 38.* Burlingame, Calif.: Proceedings of the 20th Annual State Conference on Educational Research, 1968, pp. 53-64.

Glueck, E. Cultural conflict and delinquency. *Mental Hygiene*, 1937, 21, 46-66.

Hall, C. S. and Lindsay, G. *Theories of Personality.* New York: John Wiley, 1957.

Hollister, W. G. Why adolescents drink and use drugs. *PTA Magazine*, 1969, 63, 2-5.

Homel, S. R. Invitations to understanding through dialogue. *Pediatric Clinics of North America*, 1969a, 16, 505-525.

Homel, S. R. The need to grow and mature as the basis for education. *Pediatric Clinics of North America*, 1969b, 16, 379-393.

Homel, S. R. Presentation made at the University of Utah, June, 1970.

Johnson, F. K. and Westman, J. C. The teenager and drug abuse. *Journal of School Health*, 1968, 38, 646-654.

Kaplan, R. *Drug abuse: Perspectives on Drugs.* Dubuque, Iowa: Wm. C. Brown, 1970.

Keniston, K. Students, drugs, and protests. *Current*, 1969, No. 104, 5-25.

Krech, D., Crutchfield, R. S., and Ballackey, E. L. *Individual in Society*. San Francisco: McGraw-Hill, 1962.

Maslow, A. H. Self-actualization and beyond. In J. F. T. Bugental (Ed.) *Challenges of Humanistic Psychology*. San Francisco: McGraw-Hill, 1967.

May, R. *Love and Will*. New York: W. W. Norton, 1969.

Modern medicine poll on sociomedical issues: Abortion — homosexual practices — marijuana. *Modern Medicine*, 1969, 37(22), 18-25.

Salisbury, W. W. and Fertig, F. R. The myth of alienation and teen-age drug use: Coming of age in mass society. *California School Health*, 1968, 4, 29-39.

Strack, A. E. Drug use and abuse among youth. *Journal of Health, Physical Education, and Recreation*, 1968, 39, 26-28; 55-57.

Thornburg, H. D. *Contemporary Adolescence: Readings*. Monterey: Brooks/ Cole, 1971.

Weiner, I. B. and Elkind, D. *Child Development: A Core Approach*. New York: Wiley, 1972.

Weissman, R. Teens and drugs: Monkey on our backs. *Arizona Teacher*, 1969, 57, 10-13.

CHAPTER 8 **sexuality in preadolescence**

Introduction

Out of Freud's concepts of infant sexuality, one stage, the latency period, characterized the age group of preadolescence. The developing child's behavior was completely nonsexual which Freud theorized was a normal developmental characteristic of humans, thus, tied to one's biological system rather than one's cultural system. Because it described the typical behavior of the six to twelve year old it became a fact of life in America. Conflicting evidence has since been advanced by anthropologists who have found that boys and girls progress from absentminded fingering of the genitals to systematic masturbation by age eight. This finding, and other contradictory evidence, dispelled the idea that latency was a biological process. Rather, latency is tied to cultural expectancies.

The research by Ramsey in 1943 with preadolescent boys indicated considerable sexual behavior by age eleven. He found that 53 percent of the boys had masturbated, 27 percent had homosexual play, 52 percent had sex play with girls, and 26 percent had tried or achieved intercourse. The Kinsey studies (1948, 1953) indicated increased sexual play between ages five and nine. Kinsey defined sex play as heterosexual and homosexual activity involving more than one person, as in self-exploration or masturbation. His findings were comparable with the Ramsey study. Evidences of the nature of preadolescent sexual activity are discussed in the first article in Chapter 8. The authors, James Elias and Paul Gebhard, associates of the late Alfred Kinsey, report heretofore unpublished research data on the nature of sexual activity in children ages four through fourteen. The data clearly establish the idea that latency, as defined by Freud, does not hold true anymore and, is, in fact, highly affected by one's culture. The authors conclude their article by pointing to the implications for education as a result of known sexual activity in the preadolescent.

Sexual Knowledge

Sexuality has its basis in man's biological makeup; with development the preadolescent gains increased sexual feelings and urges. Much sexual knowledge and behavior is molded by the social influences of parents and peers.

Combined with the increasing commercialization and portrayal of sex at a consumer level, our preadolescent youth are (a) pressed into sexual behavior earlier, (b) exposed to sexual language earlier, (c) moving toward learning the basic sexual concepts earlier, and (d) demand to carry on sexual conversation at an earlier age. The question is whether such preadolescents are really more informed today than in previous generations.

There is little question but that preadolescent youth know the sexual terminology relevant to them, especially the slang expressions. Both Bell (1938) and Ramsey (1943) provided evidence that the twelve-year-old was well acquainted with many sex terms. A study by Thornburg (1970) found that the average age of sexual information on eleven basic terms was 12.4 years. Table 8.1 shows which terms were asked, and what were the peak ages for first learning about them.

The age of sexual information only points to the strong need for considering what the sources of the information are. It is usually thought that parents should be the primary source of sex information although numerous

Table 8.1

Peak Age for First Sex Information Source

Sex Concept	Peak Age	Percent Known 1970 (n = 88)	1973 (n = 99)
Origin of Babies	7-10	77	60
Menstruation	7-10	60	37
Petting	12-14	52	60
Prostitution	12-14	43	50
Intercourse	12-14	39	42
Contraception	13-15	50	55
Nocturnal Emissions	13-15	42	63
Ejaculation	13-15	39	45
Masturbation	13-15	33	47
Venereal Disease	14-16	65	52
Homosexual Activity	14-16	44	53

From Thornburg, H. D. Ages and first sources of sex information as reported by 88 college women. *Journal of School Health*, 1970, 40, 156-158. Actual samples drawn Fall 1967 and Fall 1973 respectively.

studies in the past thirty-five years show parents as a relatively infrequent source of information. A summary of these studies indicates:

1. Bell (1938) found that 78 percent of the white males and 47 percent of the white females received information from peers. This was also true for 91 percent of the black males and 69 percent of the black females.
2. Ramsey (1943) found that just over 45 percent of all information in his preadolescent male sample learned from their peers.
3. Lee (1952), in studying 400 9th graders, found that both boys and girls obtained over 40 percent of their information from peers with boys slightly more dependent than girls on their companions.
4. Angelino et al. (1958) studied 266 black students finding that among males, peers account for over 35 percent of all information and female peers provided about 32 percent of all information.
5. Thornburg (1972) found, in studying almost 400 students, that 38 percent of sex information came from peers.

Each of the above studies focused on first sources of sex information, and with the exception of Lee's study, were not concerned with the accuracy of information. Lee (1952) found that girls thought mothers, teachers, and other adults were the most reliable source although boys prefer their peers. A major study which did focus on the accuracy of information was conducted by Schwartz in 1969. By referring to Table 8.2 it can be observed that most information gained by this ninth grade sample was poor or inadequate. It is somewhat disturbing that menstruation and masturbation were the areas of the greatest distortion. Since both sexual concepts are outcomes of normal development, this study reflects the fallacy of depending on one's peers for information.

In analysis, the following statements could be made regarding the preadolescents' sources of sex information. Each of them point to a more systematic, reliable way of providing information to youth.

a. Most preadolescents already have considerable knowledge about sex by age eleven although in many cases their knowledge is in the vernacular.
b. Most preadolescents rely on peers as their primary sex information sources.
c. Most information gained during preadolescence is poorly defined or totally inaccurate.
d. There is increasing sexual participation with others at the preadolescent stage.

Sex Education

Several factors must be considered in discussing the controversy over sex education. The first, obviously, focuses around the popular knowledge youth have about sex regardless of its source or accuracy. Taking insufficient or erroneous knowledge into many social-sex situations can be distressing and anxiety-producing.

Table 8.2
Ratings of Populations' Responses to Each Question on Sex Information Schedule
N = 87

Category and Question	Excellent Information	Adequate Information	Poor Information	Distorted Information	No Information	Total
1. Male Anatomy			86	1		87
2. Female Anatomy		4	82	1		87
3. Nocturnal Emission		5	48	19	15	87
4. Menstrual Cycle	1	3	55	25	3	87
5. Conception	1	27	45	11	3	87
6. Birth of Baby	1	1	78	4	3	87
7. Sexual Intercourse		27	59		1	87
8. Contraception	5	43	34	3	2	87
9. Venereal Disease		8	39	18	22	87
10. Masturbation		3	51	33		87
Total	8	121	577	115	49	870
Percent	0.9%	13.9%	66.3%	13.2%	5.6%	99.9%

From Schwartz, M. S. A report of sex information knowledge of 87 lower class ninth grade boys. *Family Coordinator*, 1969, 18 (4), 361-371. By permission of the publisher.

Second, we must consider the influence of the mass media. Motion pictures, television, and much literature all allude to sexual behavior. The excitement, thrills, and naturalness of sex are portrayed at the consumer level. Most sexual behaviors are presented in a way that suggests sexual play without consequences. The effect of this constant exposure has not been fully ascertained although, without question, such exposure represents powerful sources for adolescents to learn ideas about sex (Thornburg, 1969).

It is now known that by the time children enter school they probably have watched 4,000 hours of television. Studies have demonstrated that the image of male-female relations projected on the screen is not one of pleasure or human fulfillment, but, rather, of joylessness, hostility, tension, and sexual frustration. This is an influence over which parents, teachers, and youths themselves have little control. Its ultimate effect is to confuse the preadolescent about human sexuality (Sex Education, 1969).

Third, most parents believe that discussions about sex are a matter between parent and child. To delegate the responsibility for teaching about human sexuality outside the home is to deny the home natural functions. It is true that the home is the natural place for conversation about sex. It is not true, however, that the home has carried on such discussions. In fact, outside of the teaching of menstruation, the home has been found to be a limited source of sex information (Lee, 1952; Thornburg, 1972).

One final consideration is the role of the school in teaching sex education. The movement toward such teaching met with violent resistance in the late 1960's, and it has not returned to such teachings on a wide-scale basis yet. Much of the concern for teaching sex education in the schools was what educators saw as a growing dilemma in their preadolescent and adolescent students when thrown into social-sex encounters with an insufficient understanding of appropriate sexual behavior. Therefore, numerous school districts planned and incorporated programs in family life and sex education into the curriculum to give youth accurate and complete information in hopes of reducing their vulnerability and naivete about sex. It is important for all individuals concerned with youth to consider that the school was not trying to usurp the authority of the home or church but was trying to focus on sexual dilemmas of our youth and hoping that they would emerge with a practice code of sexual conduct.

Three real issues face any school interested in sex education: (a) who will teach it; (b) when is it to be taught; (c) what is to be taught. Analysis of these factors should provide a better understanding.

The Teacher. A study done by this author (Thornburg, 1968) revealed that 84 percent of the school administrators surveyed felt that they did not have teachers qualified to teach sex education. This is a real problem and one the schools must face before moving headlong into a sex education program. The teacher's own orientation and commitment to such a subject in the classroom is usually ambiguous and lacking. The second article in Chapter 8 (by Thornburg) is an analysis of sex education for the preadolescent and the teacher's role in it. Focus is on the teachers' roles and the basic knowledge they must have to effectively implement a program. The functions of the teacher as a provider of sex education materials is presented in a way that points to the feasibility of sex education in the schools.

How soon? Most proponents feel that various sexual concepts should be taught prior to the preadolescent's actual involvement in or encounter with sexual issues. Jones et al. contend that "a girl should know the facts regarding menstruation and breast development in advance of the actual events (by age nine) so that she will not be frightened or embarrassed when they occur which may be as early as age ten. A boy should similarly know about erection, seminal emission, masturbation, and ejaculation by age ten, to prevent his feeling frightened or guilty at the time they occur (1969, p. 146)." If actual behavior is an indicator of when it should be taught, then Broderick's research (1968) convincingly supports preadolescence. He found, in a sample of 1000 preadolescent boys and girls, that 15 percent of the boys had attempted intercourse with a girl and 30 percent of the girls had experienced heterosexual play by age twelve. Similarly, this author found that first information about sex peaked in most youth by age twelve (1970, 1972).

There has been strong reaction to teaching sex education by fifth or sixth grade. One psychiatrist views ages nine through twelve as asexual, with a concomitant aversion to sex information. "Sex education in those years upsets the psychic balance and is just as real a seduction as an encounter with a child molester — and worse, because the seducer is his teacher, a parent substitute (Sex Education, 1969, p. 28A)." Furthermore, the possibility exists that this premature catapulting into a sex information world may accelerate, thus producing abnormality in the normal biological expression of sex which unfolds throughout adolescence. This point, of course, is a very real problem, but one cannot help but wonder if most youth are not already to some extent prematurely catapulted into sexual behavior as a result of living in our society.

Sex Education: A Societal Concept

The final article in Chapter 8 is written by Mary Calderone and in it she discusses sex education for the whole society. It is presented here because it returns our thinking back to the nature of man. It is quite possible that discussion over sex education in the past ten years has focused upon several segmented issues, that, in it we have lost sight of the philosophy behind providing our youth with systematic and accurate information about sex.

Calderone draws our attention back to the role of sexuality in the development of man, the relationship between sexuality and genitality, the continuing nature of sex education from birth, the primary role of the family in sex education, the morality of sex, and the role of the schools. By re-evaluating the total concept of human sexuality, a fairer judgment can be made as to the nature of preadolescent sexual involvement and their need for systematic instruction about human sexuality.

Sexuality and Sexual Learning in Childhood
JAMES ELIAS AND PAUL GEBHARD

The turn of the century saw an awakening interest in sexuality and sexual learning among children. The most significant work of this period was Freud's theory of infantile sexuality, which directed the attention of the world to sexuality in early childhood and its importance for the future adult role. A somewhat neglected work, by Moll (1909), was overshadowed by the Freudian wave; but Moll's observations on the sexual life of the child were the first comprehensive writings done in this field. In an earlier study, Bell (1902) examined childhood sexuality through the study of the activities of children.

Research Since 1917

Numerous studies resulted from this increased interest in childhood sexuality. Among them were Blanton (1917), looking at the behavior of the human infant during the first thirty days of life; Hattendorf (1932), dealing with the questions most frequently asked by pre-school children; Isaacs (1933), studying the social development of young children; Dudycha (1933), examining recall of pre-school experiences; and Campbell (1939), writing on the social-sexual development of children. Conn (1940a, 1940b, 1948) has done a series of studies dealing with various phases of sexual awareness and sexual curiosity in children. Other important studies were made by Halverson (1940), on penile erection in male infants; Conn and Kanner (1947), on children's awareness of physical sex differences; Katcher (1955), on the discrimination of sex differences by young children; and Ramsey

Reprinted by permission of the authors and publisher from *Phi Delta Kappan*, 1969, 50, 401-406.

(1950), on preadolescent and adolescent boys. Sears, Maccoby, and Levin (1957) present a discussion of labeling and parental sanctioning of sex behavior, and Bandura and Walters (1959) examine parental response to sex information questions.

Current research has tended to move away from direct studies of infant and childhood sexual behavior. Sexuality has its roots in man's biological makeup, and the development of gender role or sex differences has become one of the main focuses of present research (Sears, 1965). Since the molding forces, or socializing agents, are the family and the peer group (among others), sexuality is being pursued as a form of social development. Receiving special emphasis are the development of the male and female role — for example, the part aggression plays in developing an aggressive adult male sexual role and the concomitant emphasis on nonaggressiveness in the development of an adequate female role. Other areas of current research are found in the work of John Money and Joan and John Hampson, on the ontogeny of human sexual behavior (1955).

The Kinsey Data

This discussion utilizes previously unpublished data from the Institute for Sex Research, taken from case histories of pre-pubescents interviewed by Alfred Kinsey and his co-workers. These histories are somewhat outdated (before 1955), but the information contained in them provides one of the few sources of actual interview information on pre-pubescent children. Questions were asked regarding sources of sexual knowledge, extent of knowledge, homosexual and heterosexual prepubertal play, and masturbatory activity, all of crucial importance for any educator, counselor, doctor, or other professional who deals with children. Some of the critical problems encountered in preschool counseling find their source in the sexual area. Educators recognize that differences between males and females, ethnic groups, and socioeconomic status groups are essential for an understanding of the attitudinal and behavioral patterns that children exhibit. Adequate sexual adjustment in early childhood is a prime factor in later adult sexual adjustment, as healthy attitudes toward self and sexuality are the foundations of adult adjustment.

Partly through necessity, many school systems are presently moving into education programs with a maximum of speed and often a minimum of preparation regarding the specific needs of the population the particular program is to serve. Sex research can offer some aid to the educational community by providing information about critical factors in the lives of children and how these factors affect later adjustment.

The Sample

The sample consists of 432 pre-pubescent white boys and girls ranging in age from four to fourteen. There are 305 boys and 127 girls in the study, and they are grouped by occupational class (social class) and age. The occupational classifications originally used in the work at the Institute for Sex Research have been combined in order to increase the number of cases and to provide social-class categories. The occupational classifications consist of: 1) unskilled workers who are labeled as lower blue-collar, 2) semi-skilled and skilled workers who comprise the upper blue-collar, 3) lower white-collar workers, and 4) business and professional men, here termed upper white-collar. A mean age is given for the children in each social class to make explicit the unequal age distribution.

The sexual behavior of younger children often lacks the erotic intent attributed to similar adult activities, raising the question, in some cases, of the validity of labeling some childhood activities as sexual. This research does not label childhood behavior as sexual unless it includes one of the following: the self-manipulation of genitalia, the exhibition of genitalia, or the manual or oral exploration of the genitalia of or by other children. Of course, many of these activities could be motivated by mere curiosity concerning a playmate's anatomy.

The term "sex play" as used here includes those heterosexual and homosexual activities involving more than one person which occur before the onset of puberty. Among the males, 52 percent report homosexual prepubertal activity and 34 percent report heterosexual prepubertal activity. These percentages seem accurate when we compare them with the self-reports of adults in the earlier Kinsey volumes. Adult males recalled homosexual experience in their preadolescent period in 48 percent of the cases, just four percent less than is reported by these children in their preadolescence (1948). The adult males also indicated that heterosexual preadolescent activity occurred in approximately 40 percent of the cases, but the reports of the children indicate only about 34 percent of prepubescent males engage in heterosexual experiences. However, many of the children in this study have not reached the average age at which these experiences first occur. The average age among males for homosexual play is 9.2 years and for heterosexual play, 8.8 years.

Among female children, 35 percent report homosexual prepubertal sexual activity and 37 percent report heterosexual prepubertal experiences. The incidence of homosexual activity in the females is much less than that reported by males, but is very close to the percentage recalled by adult females in the 1953 Kinsey volume (33 percent). The adult females recalled heterosexual preadolescent activities in 30 percent of the cases, and the reports of the children show 37 percent with such experience.

Table 8.3
Study Sample for Prepubescent Sex Knowledge

		Males		Females	
Social Class		N	Mean Age	N	Mean Age
Blue-Collar	Lower	59	11.2	21	9.5
	Upper	79	11.5	17	10.1
White-Collar	Lower	115	9.9	53	6.9
	Upper	37	7.2	35	6.6

This table presents the number (N) of boys or girls in each category and the mean age of that category.

The blue-collar–white-collar distinction provides an excellent indication of social level *vis-à-vis* the occupational level. The association between occupation and education (used in the original Kinsey publications) is very close. See p. 328, *Sexual Behavior in the Human Male.* Philadelphia, Pa.: Sanders, 1948.

One of the noteworthy findings coming from this analysis of the case histories of preadolescents is the surprising agreement between prepubertal report and adult recall. Another important finding is the lack of any consistent correlation between socio-sexual activity and parental occupational class. The percentages do vary, but in no meaningful way.

Masturbation

Masturbation is most often described as self-stimulation leading to sexual arousal and usually to climax or orgasm, accompanied (after puberty) by ejaculation on the part of the male. Some writers prefer to believe that prepubertal children do not masturbate but simply fondle their genitals. These present data concerning prepubertal masturbation are not derived from reported "fondling of the genitals" but rather from deliberate activity done for pleasure and often accompanied by pelvic thrusts against an object (e.g., a bed) or manual manipulation. Sometimes a state of relaxation or satisfaction comparable to the postorgasmic state is achieved; in other instances indisputable orgasm occurs.

More males than females masturbate in childhood, as is the case later in adolescence and adulthood. Among prepubescent males, 56 percent report masturbatory activity, while only 30 percent of the females do so. In comparison, information received from adults in self-reports indicates preadolescent masturbation in 57 percent of the cases. These actual childhood reports are within one percentage point of the recall data from adults as reported in the earlier works.

Looking at age groupings and social class, one finds that the blue-collar classes contain the highest percentages of boys who have masturbated – 60-70 percent. The majority of those in the blue-collar and lower white-collar classes who masturbate are in the eight to ten-year age group. The upper white-collar class has the lowest percentage of those who have masturbated (38 percent), with more beginning in the three to seven-year age group than at any subsequent time. The mean age for first masturbation is as follows: Lower blue-collar, 8.6; upper blue-collar, 8.8; lower white-collar, 7.8; and upper white-collar, 6.0. The probable explanation for the lower mean age, lower percentage of those who have masturbated, and lower average age at first masturbation for upper white-collar boys is the fact that their average age at interview is 7.2 years, while the average ages for the boys of other social classes are two to four years older.

Fewer girls tend to masturbate than boys, and only 30 percent of the girls report that they have masturbated. The highest percentage is among the lower blue-collar females (48 percent); the other three classes have lower and quite similar figures (between 25 and 29 percent). The average age of masturbation for girls is lower than that of the boys. By class, it is: lower blue-collar, 7.5; upper blue-collar, 7.4; lower white-collar, 5.7; and upper white-collar, 6.7.

Masturbation has been designated in the past as the prime cause of mental illness, low morals, and stunted growth, among other things. These stigmas are for the most part behind us, but tradition dies slowly and many children are still being told "old wives' tales" concerning the alleged effects of masturbation. This is unfortunate for in early childhood masturbation might influence the child to accept his body as pleasureful rather than reject it as a source of anxiety. Society has progressed to a point where few parents punish their offspring for masturbating, but it is noteworthy that fewer still encourage it.

Sexual Knowledge

In this study, additional measures are taken of current knowledge while controlling for child's age and occupation of father. The occupational level is dichotomized into lower (blue-collar) and upper (white-collar) classes for purposes of analysis. Presence or absence of knowledge about the following topics is examined: intercourse, pregnancy, fertilization, menstruation, venereal disease, abortion, condoms, and female prostitution. In general, the white-collar class surpasses the blue-collar class in all sex knowledge categories. Of special interest to the educator are some of the differences in learning which occur on the part of the children in these two groups. For example, while 96 percent of the blue-collar boys have an understanding of sexual intercourse by ages thirteen to fourteen, only 4 percent have any knowledge concerning the "coming together of the sperm and the egg" — fertilization. Twenty-seven percent of the upper white-collar group in the same age range understand the concept of fertilization, and this nearly seven-fold difference is indicative of the language level and sources (hence quality) of information for the two groups. Blue-collar boys learn about intercourse, abortion, condoms, and prostitution earlier than do other males, especially by age eight to ten. These words and activities become a part of the sex education of lower-class boys much earlier than of boys whose fathers are employed in higher-status occupations, as a result of most sex information being provided by peers on the street.

This earlier and more extensive knowledge of coitus is reflected in pre-pubescent heterosexual activity, wherein nearly three times as many blue-collar boys have, or attempt, coitus than do white-collar boys. Interestingly enough, more blue-collar males know of intercourse than know of pregnancy (except in the four to seven-year-old group) and just the reverse is true for the white-collar males. The white-collar male surpasses the blue-collar male in sexual knowledge in later age groupings, perhaps indicating that many of the more formal aspects of his sex education come from his mother, with peers "filling in the gaps" concerning some of the more sensitive areas, such as methods of birth-control and prostitution.

The pattern for girls stands in marked contrast to that for boys. Pre-pubescent girls, unlike boys, are not inclined to discuss or joke about sexual matters. Also, the girl eavesdropping on conversation by adult females is less apt to hear of such matters than is the boy listening to adult males. Lastly, there is reason to believe that the lower-class mother is more inhibited about, and less capable of, imparting sex education to her daughter. Consequently, the lower-class girl generally lags behind her upper-class counterpart in sexual information. Thus, for example, in age group eight to ten, not quite half of the lower-class girls know of coitus, whereas close to three-quarters of the upper-class females have this knowledge. This gap is found even with regard to menstruation, a thing sufficiently removed from overt sexual behavior that one would expect it to escape from taboo. On the contrary, at lower social levels, menstruation is often regarded as dirty and somehow shameful. The result is that among the eight to ten-year-olds roughly a quarter of the lower-class and nearly three-quarters of the upper-class girls possess this inevitable knowledge.

On more technical matters the lower-class girls are equally or even more disadvantaged. For example, none of them grasp the concept of fertilization: the idea that pregnancy is the result of the fusion of an egg and a sperm.

Among upper-class girls from age group eight to ten on, the knowledge of pregnancy is universal, whereas many of their lower-class counterparts are unaware of where babies come from. Indeed, in age groups eight to ten and eleven to twelve, more lower-class girls know of coitus than of pregnancy. This situation, so incongruous to an upper-class reader, is explicable. Thanks to their contact, both physical and verbal, with lower-class boys (a substantial number of whom have attempted coitus), more lower-class girls hear of or experience coitus than hear of pregnancy. Note that while a boy may attempt to persuade a girl to have coitus, it is most improbable that he will defeat his aim by informing her of the consequence.

Lastly, the differences in knowledge between upper- and lower-class girls hinge to some considerable extent on literacy and on communication with parents. The upper-class girl, more prone to reading, and in a milieu where books and magazines with sexual content are available in the home, will educate herself or ask her parents to explain what she has read. The upper-class parent, having been told by innumerable magazine articles and books on child-rearing of the desirability of sex education, is far more likely to impart information than is the less knowledgeable and more inhibited lower-class parent. This statement will be substantiated in the following section on sources of sexual knowledge.

Sources of Sexual Knowledge

By looking at the sources of sexual learning for children, one can see the origin of sexual "slang" terms and sexual misinformation frequently unacceptable to the middle-class teacher. Though a large portion of this mislabeled and often incorrect information is the product of children's "pooled ignorance," the problem is only confounded by adult noncommunication.

The main source of sex education for most boys is the peer group — friends and classmates. Nevertheless there are important differences, depending on the child's social class (measured here as father's occupation). The peer group is overwhelmingly important as a source of information for all the boys from blue-collar homes: From 75 percent to 88 percent of them report other boys as their major source. The boys of lower white-collar homes seem a transitional group, with 70 percent so reporting, while the boys whose fathers are lower white-collar men find their mothers as important as their peers with respect to information. The boys from upper white-collar homes derive little from their peers, most from their mothers, and a relatively large amount from combined educational efforts by both parents. These figures are in striking contrast to those of the blue-collar boys: only eight percent cite peers as the main source, 48 percent report the mother, and 24 percent both parents. This inverse relationship between parental occupation and the importance of peers as an informational source is one of the major, though anticipated, findings of this study. As the occupational level of the home increases, the child's mother plays a growing role in the sex education of her son, rising to nearly half of the cases for males whose fathers are upper white-collar men. For all occupational levels, the father seems to play a marginal role as a source of sex information for boys, and when he does play a role in his boy's sex education, it is mainly when both parents act as a team. While we can only speculate on the basis of our data, the mother is probably the "prime mover" of the parental educating team. Other sources as major channels of information (e.g., siblings, other relatives, simple observation, etc.) are statistically unimportant, never exceeding four percent.

Some children report that their sources of information are so evenly balanced that they cannot name one as the major source. Boys reporting this situation are more common (20 percent) in homes of lower blue-collar fathers. The percentages tend to decrease progressively as parental occupational status increases, but this trend is unexpectedly reversed by the boys from upper white-collar homes. This reversal is probably not the result of small sample vagary, since the same phenomenon is to be seen among girls. No explanation is presently known.

Teacher Unimportant as Source

It is interesting to note that the teacher is not mentioned by any of the children as the main source of sex education. In fact, throughout the study the contribution of the teacher and the school system to the child's information about sex is too low to be statistically significant. However, with the current proliferation of formal sex education programs in some of our nation's school systems, the role of the teacher and the school has no doubt increased in importance since the time these interviews were conducted, before 1955.

When looking at the main source of sex knowledge for girls, we see similar trends. Peers provide the main source of sex information for 35 percent of the girls whose fathers are lower blue-collar men and for 25 percent of the girls whose fathers are upper blue-collar workers. By contrast, only 9 percent and 4 percent, respectively, of the girls whose fathers are white-collar men report the peer group as their main source of sex education. The mother's importance as a source of sex education increases with increased occupational status, being the major source for 10 percent of the daughters of lower blue-collar workers up to 75 percent of those whose fathers are upper white-collar men.

For girls, fathers provide very little sex education, and then only as a member of a father-mother combination. It is interesting to observe that significantly more girls than boys report no main source of sex education, especially those girls from homes in which the father has a lower-status occupation. For example, 45 percent of the daughters of lower blue-collar workers report no main source of sex education, as compared to 20 percent of the boys whose fathers are at this occupational level. Other possible informational sources, such as siblings and printed material, are inconsequential.

Nudity

The general level of permissiveness regarding nudity in the home, a sex-related phenomenon, also varies in relation to the occupational level of the family. As a rule, boys are allowed more nudity than girls, except in homes where nudity is a common practice — in which case the girls report a higher incidence of nudity. Differences between occupational groups are great, with 87 percent of the lower blue-collar workers never allowing nudity among their sons, as compared to only 28 percent of upper white-collar men. Again for boys, 40 percent who come from upper white-collar families report nudity as very common, compared to only 3 percent whose fathers are lower blue-collar workers. Among girls, we find the same patterns emerging, with 44 percent of the girls from upper white-collar families reporting nudity as very common, and none of the girls from lower blue-collar families reporting nudity as usual in the home. Thus nudity in the lower-class home is more the exception than the rule for both girls and boys; in the upper-class home almost the reverse is true. This upper-class permissiveness regarding a sex-related behavior, nudity, fits nicely with our finding that upper-class parents communicate more freely on sexual matters with their offspring.

Implications for Education

The main implication of the reported data for those in the field of education is the need for educators to be aware of the differences in information and experience which exist between boys and girls, between different occupational and socioeconomic groups (and though not treated in this article) the differences which may occur between ethnic groups. An apparent problem regarding these differences still evident in much of our educational system today, is an often inflexible adherence to the "middle-class yardstick."

The sexual experiences and the sexual vocabulary of the heterogeneous student population, especially the pupil who has not come from the same socioeconomic, occupational, or ethnic background as his teacher, create definite problems in expectations, understanding, and communication between teacher and pupil. An adequate knowledge of the sources of sex education, types of experiences, and the vocabulary and attitudes of these students will enable the teacher to gain a wider understanding of some of the problems of pupils regarding sexual matters and to modify his or her teaching accordingly.

Counseling the child in the school system raises some of the same problems encountered by the classroom teacher in an even more intense, personal situation. The counselor should have some idea of differences in preadolescent sexual activities and knowledge, enabling him to aid the child and his parents more intelligently as they deal with questions and problems of sexuality. If the average age for preadolescent homosexual experiences, for instance, is around nine years, this activity should be recognized as possibly a part of normal sexual development rather than as a sexual aberration. There is great danger of confusing activities accompanying normal sexual development with pathological behavior.

It is also apparent from the data presented here that many lower-class children will probably experience problems in learning and adjustment because of the lack of accurate information from informed sources. Neither the teacher nor the parent will completely replace peer-group influence in the process of providing sexual information, especially in the lower class, but the educator has the opportunity to provide programs to meet the needs of children otherwise inadequately prepared to cope with sexuality because of restraints imposed by social-class position. Therefore education should continue to initiate programs which will help fill this void created either by peer misinformation or by similar misunderstanding and reluctance on the part of parents.

Educating the Preadolescent About Sex
HERSHEL D. THORNBURG

The controversy that raged in the late 1960's over the teaching of sex education in the schools directly involved the consideration of preadolescent youth since many of the programs advocated teaching human sexuality to the nine to thirteen year old. In many respects this focus on the preadolescent was an indication that parents, educators, physicians, and psychologists viewed the preadolescent as a changing sexual being now subjected to earlier interests in the opposite sex as well as facing social pressures for heterosexual involvement.

Elsewhere, this author (1973) has stated that there exists a *social puberty* today which precedes the physiological puberty known to most twelve to fourteen year olds. Social puberty may be defined in this sense as the direct involvement with individuals of the opposite sex in some manner prior to the developmental physiological basis for such interaction. It may very well be encouraged by the highly suggestive social stimuli that these youth confront within their daily environment. The exposure of the preadolescent to different sexual behaviors is quite common through the media of television, motion pictures, literature, music, and advertising. Because of its materialistic value, sex is generally presented in an enticing, luring, get-involved way. The naturalness of sexual involvement and the consequences (either positive or negative) of it are rarely realistically presented. In short, the preadolescent, as well as the adolescent, is encouraged to show interest in sex behaviorally with little regard to concomitant emotional involvement.

Also published in the *Family Coordinator*, 1974, 23, 35-39.

Preadolescent Heterosexual Involvement

"In the selection of my friends my mother did let me make my own decisions. One time, though, she was quite perturbed when, in sixth grade, I turned down my first date offer because I felt I was too young to accept."

"I shall never forget one Christmas party I attended when I was in seventh grade. There were only couples there. We ate and danced for a while and then everyone sat on the couch with the lights out and kissed. I was so embarrassed and confused at such activity that I left the party early, went home, and cried. I hated that boy from then on and refused to go any place with him."

"Eighth grade was when I began kissing a boy with some affection. Parties used to be just 'make out' parties. It all seems so silly now: the parents would take us to the party; we would go to the basement and neck; and then our parents would take us home again."

The above three anecdotes come from a research study about sexual behavior among 700 middle class adolescents in Minnesota (Martinson, 1968). It provides some first hand accounts of the early demands felt by preadolescent youth to become heterosexually involved. The nature of the involvement, and its lack of meaning to the total sexual being, caused confusion and embarrassment, indications of inadequate emotional coping skills.

Dating back to the Kinsey Reports (1948, 1953) the incidence of preadolescent sexual involvement was assessed. Among preadolescent boys, Kinsey found the average age for first homosexual play was 9.2 years and for heterosexual play, 8.8 years. An analysis of additional Kinsey data by Elias and Gebhard (1969) indicates that 52 percent of the preadolescent boys sampled reported homosexual prepubertal play and 34 percent prepubertal heterosexual play. The incidences of sexual play in the female are somewhat lower in the Elias and Gebhard study showing 35 percent homosexual and 37 percent heterosexual prepuberty play.

More recent studies have been conducted by Broderick which indicate considerable incidences of heterosexual play among preadolescents. Broderick not only has investigated 32 anthropological studies which establish that in other cultures and societies prepubertal children are sexually responsive, but he has conducted wide-scale research in the United States that indicates the same thing.

Broderick and Rowe (1968) studied 1029 ten to twelve year olds in Pennsylvania and 610 ten to twelve year olds in Missouri to determine the amount of sexual interest that boys and girls might have in each other. In the Pennsylvania sample the researchers found that 71 percent of the girls and 56 percent of the boys had a boyfriend/girlfriend. In addition, 51 percent of the girls and 47 percent of the boys attested to having been in love. In responding to date preferences for a movie, 39 percent of both the boys and girls chose seeing a movie with the opposite sex. In addition, 22 percent of the girls and 24 percent of the boys had had a date.

Drawing a completely independent sample from Missouri, the findings were basically the same as in the Pennsylvania study with the exception of dating. In the Missouri sample the incidence of dating was considerably lower, 11 percent girls and 19 percent boys, a finding that may be attributable to the fact that 93 percent of the sample was Protestant. The authors interpret their findings as a complex of behaviors preparatory to relating socially to the opposite sex in adolescence. While they recognized that many of the boys' or girls' love objects were more imaginary than actual, they were felt quite seriously by the preadolescent who described an 'in love' feeling toward some individual. This feeling allowed the preadolescent to eventually single out one individual for companionship such as going to a movie or other types of dating.

Preadolescent Sex Knowledge

There have been repeated evidences that the primary source of sexual information and knowledge is among one's peers (Elias and Gebhard, 1969; Lee, 1952; Ramsey, 1943; Schwartz, 1969; Thornburg, 1970, 1972). In addition, such studies show that most sexual information comes during preadolescence (Elias and Gebhard, 1969; Ramsey, 1943; Thornburg, 1970) as well as being incorrect (Elias and Gebhard, 1969; Schwartz, 1969).

Elias and Gebhard found that upwards from 75 percent of sexual information came from peers, a finding comparable to the studies done by Bell in 1938. Other studies show peers to be the dominant influence although the percent of influence is lower. Table 8.4 is reprinted from the study by this author (Thornburg, 1972) and it indicates that peers are important information sources, especially in the behavioral domain.

One study by this author (1970) shows the peak age for first information about sex occurs during preadolescence. Since petting and intercourse are two of the heaviest heterosexual involvements among youth, it is interesting that such information was well known by late preadolescence. Elias and Gebhard find, in fact, that information about sexual intercourse was known by 50 percent of the lower-class girls in their study and 75 percent of the upper-class girls by age ten. Similarly approximately 75 percent of both class groups knew about menstruation by age ten.

In addition to the idea that (1) sexual knowledge is learned rather early, and (2) it is generally provided by peers, a third problem is its accuracy. Perhaps one of the better assessments of this was done by Schwartz. Schwartz's studies considered anatomical information, developmental information, behavioral information, and preventive information. In brief,

Table 8.4
A Comparative Analysis of Initial Sex Information Sources

	Arizona N = 191	Oklahoma N = 190	Total	%
Mother	382	406	788	19.3
Father	23	20	43	1.8
Peers	688	829	1517	37.9
Literature	461	360	821	20.6
Schools	377	213	590	14.8
Minister	20	13	33	.8
Physician	12	9	21	.5
Street talk/ experience	62	107	169	4.3
Unanswered	76	133	209	–
Totals	2101	2090	4191	100.0

Schwartz found that .9 percent of the preadolescents in his study had excellent information, 13.9 percent adequate information, 66.3 percent poor information, 13.2 percent distorted information, and 5.6 percent no information. Knowledge about masturbation, venereal disease, nocturnal emissions, and menstruation was the poorest.

Educating the Preadolescent

The impingements of environmental sexual stimuli, the early incidence of preadolescent sexual involvement, and the sources and inaccurateness of knowledge about sex all point to the fact that a more systematic and accurately informative presentation of the concepts of human sexuality should be afforded our youth. Since preadolescents have such ongoing exposure to sexual stimuli and a concomitant curiosity as to what it is all about, it is necessary to give students sound factual information and knowledge necessary for their development throughout preadolescence and adolescence into healthy, well adjusted adults.

It is also necessary to explore emotional problems facing the developing preadolescent. Most of his behavior will be determined by his reaction to parental, teacher, and social pressure, although a growing interest in peers will cause a gradual shift toward them as the primary behavior stimulus. Therefore, upon entering preadolescence, emotional development may still stem from basic parental influences, although by the end of this period peer influence may dominate. Nevertheless, in learning to work sexual values through emotionally, it is important for the preadolescent and adolescent to have an awareness of parental opinion on sexual behavior. Kimbrough found in analysis of a sex education program in Albany, Georgia that one of the more positive outgrowths as reflected by the students was the suggestions given on how to control one's emotions (1966).

It is also quite likely that any systematic program for educating youth should include helping students develop a sense of personal moral responsibility for the sexual actions. In many cases, this means the preadolescent must know the mores of his social group, the reasons why such standards exist, and the consequences of violating them.

Many controversial opinions surround the implementation of sex education within a school. Setting aside emotional appeals and reactions, it is true that to teach, adequate resources for the teaching, qualified personnel to teach sex education, and the morality of sexual behavior are basic problems that must be confronted and resolved before successfully incorporating a sex education program (Thornburg, 1969).

Table 8.5, which is drawn from curriculum guides in two different parts of the United States, gives some idea as to the teaching concept, its appropriate grade level, and the topic or activity which a teacher might do in order to help the students more systematically learn about human sexuality and their role and response to it.

Table 8.5
The Teaching of Social Concepts to Middle
School Age Youth*

Grade Level	Concept	Teaching Topic or Activity
4	We live in a family unit and associate with peers. How we see and understand ourselves is important to our growth.	Functions and roles within a family. Various types of family groups. Family relationships, i.e., parental and children's roles.
5	Puberty, a time of change.	Male and female growth spurts, i.e., development of skeletal and muscular systems as well as growth of the sex organs.

Grade Level	Concept	Teaching Topic or Activity
6	The menstrual cycle is a natural event indicating the body has reached one area of maturity.	Select and show film on menstruation. Prepare class for film and provide for discussion and follow-up. Present the process of menstruation to boys as a separate group.
6-7	An individual learns to accept his own sexuality and that of the opposite sex.	Discuss peer groups, the difference between belonging or being on the outside. Discuss dating — purpose, types, etiquette, how to choose a date.
7	Maturity involves physical as well as personality changes.	Examine the causes for change in physical appearance in moving toward adolescence. Describe and discuss the changes that take place during adolescence.
8	The many physical changes occurring in our bodies, as well as the intellectual, emotional, social, and spiritual, are processes for preparing the individual for parenthood.	Pre-test to evaluate class knowledge of human reproduction. Relate physical changes to accompanying changes in behavior.
7-9	Several infectious diseases can be transmitted during sexual contact.	Present appropriate film on venereal disease. Discuss syphilis and gonorrhea — causative agents, modes of transmission, incidence of infection, treatment, cure.

*This table reflects teaching on family life and sex education as represented in *Health Education Course*, Curriculum Guide, K-6, Los Alamos Schools, 1968 and *Conceptual Guidelines for School Health Programs in Pennsylvania*, Pennsylvania Department of Education, 1970.

In summary, it would be well if we remember the following points:

1. Naivete is an expensive price that many of our preadolescent and adolescent youth pay for being thrust into sexual behavioral roles with limited and inaccurate sexual information.

2. The influence of the mass media is powerful and cannot be disregarded by the adult sectors of our society. The excitement, thrills, and naturalness of sexual involvement is made highly attractive to our emerging and vulnerable youth.

3. No one can legitimately disregard the social impact of the peer group, a phenomenon which begins during preadolescence and extends into young adulthood. Considering that they are the most frequent source of information, and that for the most part, they are inaccurate in what they share, we must consider giving our youth adequate, consistent, and formative information. They need more than just their reference group to emerge with an understanding of human sexuality.

Sex Education for the Whole Society
MARY S. CALDERONE

Editor's Note:

In 1964, a public health physician, Mary Calderone, established the Sex Information and Education Council of the United States (SIECUS) in order to establish man's sexuality as a health entity. Throughout the past decade she and many of her colleagues have brought to the United States a broader, more complete understanding of the naturalness of human sexuality and its subsequent expression. In addition, she has become the primary target for the reactionaries to sex education in the United States, even to being charged of establishing through SIECUS a Communist-inspired plot for the moral decay and degeneracy of America.

In the article by Dr. Calderone reprinted here, she has addressed herself to the idea that sex education is a societal concept and suggests ways in which we could better apprise ourselves of issues central to a total societal understanding of human sexuality and its behavioral expressions. Regardless of the reactionaries, however noted they may be (or claim to be), it is difficult to discount the logic and clarity with which Dr. Calderone attempts to make man aware of himself sexually in order to ultimately be a better total individual.

H.D.T.

At the outset I should like to point out quite categorically that there is no other aspect of man's life and health that has, throughout the centuries, been so continuously at the mercy of mythology, superstition, bigotry, exploitation, and just plain ignorance as has man's sexuality. Today we see a

Reprinted with permission of the author and publisher from the *North Central Association Quarterly*, 1971, 45 (4), 342-348.

recrudescence of these attitudes, coupled with a campaign of fear and hate about sex education that is deliberately designed to spread seeds of suspicion and dissension in community after community throughout the country.

Thus this aspect of our being that is as universal to all of us as the fact that we breathe, instead of serving to fulfill and enlarge our lives and therefore our human relationships, and to provide us with perhaps our most electric moments of feeling alive, has been used by man in such various ways as to degrade and exploit his fellow humans, to fill himself with guilt, shame, and often disgust, and most of all to separate him from those who should be closest to him. As a result the medical and behavioral sciences recognize that, in our society, to experience some kind of sex-related problem during one's lifetime is unfortunately the norm.

Conceptual Errors About Sex

It has become clear that, given the tremendous diversity of sexual attitudes and behaviors that we see in the United States society, some unification is needed regarding knowledge and attitudes about human sexuality. We ought all to learn to speak the same language about it, share the same knowledge as it becomes available, understand the same basic concepts, if we are to identify goals that we might hold in common as desirable and move towards them with our young people. This makes it inevitable that many of our tenaciously held, quite rigid concepts about human sexuality must now be recognized as untenable:

Sex education . . . is not just sex instruction. To use the latter term is not appropriate, since sex *instruction* is not concerned with sexuality at all, but merely with the technique of propagating the species — a small but incidentally very useful bit of knowledge. Sex *education* embraces much more (Meyer, 1970).

This is a direct quote from Rev. John Meyer, of the Family Life Apostolate of the Newark Archdiocese in an article by him on Sex Education and Psychological Readiness, in the U.S. Catholic Conference Guide for Teachers in Sex Education. What sex education embraces I hope to make clear.

A further error in our concepts was to equate *sex* and *reproduction* when these are actually not only separable but dual functions of the same sets of organs. We have also erred in presuming that the erotic or physical aspects of sex were the totality of sexuality. In other words we tend to judge every human being, at any age, by whatever of his erotic *acts* we become aware of.

Another serious error was the concept that sexual morality meant no sexual feelings or expression of *any* kind permissible until marriage, as if it were desirable or even possible or "normal" to go through childhood, adolescence, and adulthood as a neuter, a sexual blank until the marriage ceremony.

Sexuality and Identity

I shall be using two terms, but not interchangeably, and therefore want to define them at the outset: 1) Sexuality is the totality of the human being at any age, as male or female, with all of his personality traits, behavior and acts as they relate to this; 2) Sex, aside from indicating gender, I use to denote primarily the erotic or genital component of sexuality. Thus, sexuality relates to *gender identity* and *gender role behavior* while sex relates to erotic *acts*.

There are many pieces of evidence that lead scientists today to the thesis that the making of a man or a woman should no longer be left to chance and parental instincts alone. Society has an obligation to ensure that, by the age of three, a child's core gender *identity* be firmly set to conform with his given sex at birth as shown by his chromosomes and anatomy, and should be able to say with certainty as well as accuracy that he is a boy or she is a girl.

Just as important, between the ages of three and fourteen the structure of his gender role *behavior* should have been set up to conform with this core gender identity. I repeat then — gender identity is not merely a matter of being born with certain organs and hormones, but is the result of a long psychodynamic process, a learning continuum that begins at birth and that we can call *sexualization*. And so we have to recognize that sexual behavior is learned behavior and that, therefore, both heterosexuality and homosexuality are not born but made.

We find more and more professional people using the word *sexuality* as well as the phrase *education for sexuality.* In other words, *education consciously planned by the best minds of a society to support the process by which the infant, small child, preadolescent and adolescent develops his sexual identity as male or female, to conform with his "given" anatomical sex, learns to understand himself and others as sexual beings and learns to live with and manage his genitality and his reproductivity in responsible ways.* This whole area embraces not merely knowledge but all attitudes and feelings about sex and reproduction, all of which will ultimately control the individual's own sexual behavior in adult life.

I mentioned reproductivity and genitality. We have to understand all of these terms before we can understand what planning for secure gender identity and gender role behavior might consist of. *Reproductivity* relates merely to the capacity of the individual to impregnate or to be impregnated and its onset is signalized by menstruation and ejaculation.

The process of reproductive maturation is absolutely automatic, *will* happen regardless, but our great error has been to equate it with total maturation and is one of the bases for the confusion of behavior exhibited by many adolescents. A girl is not a little woman when she first menstruates, nor does ejaculation mean that a boy has become a man — far from it. In any case, responsible use of the reproductive function is now recognized as one absolute requirement for every person today and education about this responsibility, that is, *family planning*, should be a part of the education of every young person. We must hold every individual accountable for his reproductivity not only in terms of numbers (population) but in terms of total responsibility for his offspring's well-being and development.

Sexuality and Genitality

Genitality is the capacity to localize sex sensation at the genital level culminating in the sharply defined experience called orgasm. Genital maturation or genitalization is also automatic in the male, for by definition the ejaculation that appears at puberty should not take place without orgasm. By the age of eighteen essentially one hundred percent of males have experienced orgasm, that is have completed their genitalization, but a large percentage of these began genital response long before, usually in early infancy or childhood with masturbation. Masturbation is so almost universal a phenomenon that it is now looked upon as a norm to child development.

In females genitalization follows a different and non-automatic pattern, far fewer females than males experiencing genital sensation in youth. By the age of eighteen 60 percent according to Kinsey's figures had *not* experienced orgasm, even though a number of them had experienced intercourse. Of the 40 percent who had experienced orgasm, many did so quite young in masturbation. Although these figures may be changing because of the change in cultural attitudes regarding female sexuality, the largest group of females still experience first orgasm in the late teens or considerably later, this bearing no relation at all to the onset of reproductive maturity as it does in the male. Furthermore, the female's genital response is less physically oriented than in the male, and is a learned rather than a spontaneous experience. The point to remember, especially with the young female, is that the experience of intercourse does not guarantee the experiencing of orgasm.

Another major difference arises in later life for, once established in the female, her capacity for sexual response tends to rise and remain at its peak intensity throughout most of the rest of her life cycle, whereas the male's, having reached its peak intensity in the late teens or early twenties, tends thereafter gradually to diminish. It is estimated that by the age of seventy perhaps 30 percent of males have lost the capacity for erection. With Masters' and Johnson's newest findings, however, this 30 percent may turn out to be needlessly high (Masters and Johnson, 1970).

The Concept of Sexuality

Now I will come back to the error we make of tending to look upon reproductivity and genitality as the whole of sex, for this is a trap of modern society. The concept of sexuality *as the totality of expression of the individual's entire self as male or female is the essence of the purpose for which SIECUS was established.* Father John L. Thomas, a Jesuit, during his term on the SIECUS Board wrote in one of the SIECUS Newsletter's lead articles that we must keep ourselves firmly and constantly oriented to the concept of *sexuality as part of the total personality* (Thomas, 1970).

Over the years since SIECUS was established the term sexuality has been brought into common usage. Where formerly the tendency was to give it a connotation of off-color eroticism or even of animalism, now it is being widely used and understood in identifying the whole human being, at any age as male or female, with all of his attributes, his relationships, his actions, behaviors, thoughts, joys, achievements, as such — all included in the concept of sexuality as well as, *from time to time*, the erotic feelings and genital behaviors that are clearly the *norm* to being human.

Human Sex Not Animalistic

In point of fact, to behave sexually in the way that human beings do behave is human and *not animal.* For the lower mammals sex and sexual expression are delimited by various external factors: age, climate, length of day, state of nutrition, etc., and the sexual behavior when it occurs *as controlled by these factors* is usually a clear precursor to reproduction of the species. Certainly with animals the psychological aspects of sexual behavior are, as far as we can tell, non-existent.

Not so with humans. Human beings behave sexually in a kaleidoscopic variety of ways that are seldom geared specifically and intentionally to reproduction of their species. Rather, the sexual behaviors, whether genital or non-genital, usually include many psychological factors and occur as intrinsic facets of human life itself that can and should be made clearly subject to human choice, decision, and again, accountability.

Sex Education From Birth

What Father Thomas and Father Meyer, a committee of the Group for the Advancement of Psychiatry (1965) and other social scientists today are drawing our attention to, is that the sexual education of the child and young person *is going on continuously* from birth; attitudes, behaviors and relationships of the men and women in his life, *especially of his parents*, constitute his earliest and most potent sex education — without any words at all. The way the father and mother see and treat each other as man or woman, their self concepts of themselves as male and female — these are powerful non-verbal sex education, but negative or distorted if their attitudes to and treatment of each other are cold, unloving, hostile, or brutal. Furthermore the way the father or mother treats the blossoming sexual feelings and curiosities of the child — masturbation or childish sex play for instance — can be reflected years later in difficulty or success in achieving a mature heterosexual adjustment.

Remember too that the average pre-school child today experiences 4,000 hours of television viewing and much of this is of comics or soap operas with extremely negative sexual messages. Certainly afternoon and early evening programs constantly beam the message that the only way men and women can relate to each other is in anguish and hostility. Thus the child actually comes into kindergarten with a great deal of powerful sex education already, much of it distorted or fearful, and even though he can easily observe sex to be of obsessive concern to adults, he himself is never free to speak or inquire about it, and he has been given little help in understanding his own sexual feelings which are the norm even in preadolescence.

Parental Role is Primary

It is easy to see why so many parents are confused and unable to comprehend much less carry out their roles as sex educators. They have never been helped to the realization that sex education is far, far more than impartation of the simple facts of reproductivity, as Father Meyer reminded us.

This leads us to return to some of the basic questions I considered earlier, but with a different emphasis. How can parents best be helped by the society to do their double job: 1) Make it possible for each of their children to achieve solid gender identity and develop gender role behavior in conformity with each child's given anatomical/chromosomal/hormonal configuration? 2) Make it possible for the child and young person to develop and manage appropriately, the erotic drives and behaviors that, appearing as they do spontaneously during childhood and adolescence, are *givens* to being human?

The methods that parents use to accomplish these two goals should be so non-traumatic and nondistortive that ultimately the marriages of their children will be sexually fulfilled instead of, as presently, so often grossly deprived. Masters and Johnson estimate that 50 percent of all marriages go stumbling along for ten to twenty years in the face of the miseries of one or another of the primary sexual inadequacies (frigidity, impotence, premature ejaculation, etc.).

The small organization that is SIECUS has in a few short years succeeded in leading the major professional disciplines that deal in various helping ways with human beings to become aware of how little they know about sexual functioning. Indeed, if the health professions knew as little about urinary or cardiac or digestive or reproductive functioning as they do about sexual functioning they could not obtain their professional degrees! People moreover are increasingly and more openly coming with their sexual problems to physicians, clinical psychologists, social workers, clergymen, lawyers, and others. And, of course, professionals themselves have lived with sexual problems in their own lives, for our professions do not immunize us from the ills common to mankind. The children of clergymen or doctors experience about the same rates of out-of-wedlock pregnancy, homo-sexuality, or venereal disease as in the general population. We are humans, male and female, before and after we become professionals.

SIECUS was not formed for, and was never primarily interested in, formal programming of sex education for school children. We have never ourselves produced a program in or even guidelines for a program, or films, or books for use in the school room. The primary demand came to us spontaneously *from* the schools in overwhelming numbers, so SIECUS met these by serving as best we could in a *consultant* capacity only, leaving full and final decision on planning and programming within each community where it belongs.

Our goal is and always has been *the recognition of human sexuality as a primary field of scholarship by every professional discipline.* This is why the SIECUS Board has consistently included about 20 percent representation from the various fields of medicine, the rest from the behavioral sciences, from social work, the three religious faiths, education, the law, nursing, communications media — all professional areas dealing directly with people of all ages. This is why we are widely recognized as an informational resource by the American Medical Association, by major Protestant denominations, the teaching and medical professions, etc. This is why I can now postulate that no professional in the helping disciplines will be considered prepared to practice his profession without adequate training in this new field of scholarship: human sexuality.

Where does this leave the lay person, the average parent, with his perfectly "normal" questions regarding what he should be doing in the sexualization and education of his child?

Parental Role Needs Support

Hopefully, more and more parents are coming to realize that the efforts of the various professions now being officially made in this field are not for the purpose of usurping their rights, or replacing their prerogatives as parents, but rather of supporting these. Until parents are willing to study the new knowledge on their own, along with the professionals, to re-examine their own attitudes and feelings, to read widely and to discuss what they read under trained leadership, they will require much help on behalf of their children in a very confused world. This is being increasingly recognized by the various religious faiths and denominations which are themselves producing excellent sex education materials for parents and for their own church schools. Educators too are training themselves in summer workshop courses to accept whatever responsibilities a community wishes to place on them in sex education programs for all ages.

Moral Values Are Crucial

The question of moral values is crucial and has been included in the considerations of the SIECUS Board in various of its published materials available to adults and professionals. It seems clear that schools should and do teach moral values constantly, in basic ethical terms even if not in a specific religious context. In any case it must be agreed that surely there are no moral values special for sex – the same ones should govern all of our acts and relationships.

There are scientific findings here too that can help the churches and the parents, especially the significant research work of psychologist Lawrence Kohlberg of Harvard University, on how children, and indeed whole societies no matter how diverse, move through identical stages of moral reasoning. He identifies six stages common to a number of different cultures, although not all people or all cultures move to the highest or sixth stage of moral decision-making – that is, the stage of moral autonomy based on self-chosen ethical principles (Keniston, 1970). Here again, it is useful to quote Father John Meyer:

Sex education ... is one aspect of the aim of education in general: the guidance of children to maturity. ... It should aim at encouraging the child to grow into an adult who thinks, judges, and acts for himself. It should not aim to turn out an obedient robot relating by heart the wisdom (or lack of wisdom) imparted by its teachers. ... Authoritarianism in the area of sex education can be as damaging as authoritarianism in any other area of education – perhaps considerably more damaging. By its very nature it retards the growth of the child, keeps him from developing to sexual maturity. And it exists and does this because of the personal sense of weakness of the one in the position of authority. But the temptation to be authoritarian is great, particularly in the case of those persons whose attitude towards their own sexuality is inadequate – and this is true whether the person in question happens to be a parent or a teacher. I feel that it is in this area that our major difficulty lies.

The Role of Secondary Schools

Secondary Schools have a prime role and primary responsibility in education for responsible, mature sexuality. The evidence of emotional and sexual difficulties and problems in this age group is overwhelming, not alone in terms of pregnancies, forced marriages, venereal diseases, and increasing numbers of teenage abortions. Deeper and more haunting are the questions and anxieties indicating the need for knowledge and straight facts by our youth — evidence not only of an appalling lack of knowledge but also of mature attitudes.

An outstanding study that should be read by parents, administrators, and teachers of young people was carried out by the Department of Education of the State of Connecticut (Byler, 1969), which collected the questions of 5,000 children K-12 on many aspects of health — smoking, drugs, venereal disease, alcoholism, and sex. The questions in all areas are moving and revealing as to how early the thirst for true knowledge in these different areas is identified.

The high school young people recommended that sex education be started in kindergarten, but be concentrated at the seventh and eighth grade levels "before it's too late."

Opportunity for Redress

It's never too late. In fact, the secondary schools seem to me to have the great opportunity to redress the lacks and gaps. Because some social scientists may be advancing the hypothesis that adolescence could provide, in its own right, a new period of sensitivity to imprinting, parents and educators might seize on such a possibility as a great chance not only to offer factual information at a moment when the child himself perceives the need for it and wants it, but almost more important, to provide the opportunities for discussion and dialogue *with peers* that might serve as a basis for re-programming faulty attitudes. Kohlberg has shown that one critical factor in helping an individual move from a less advanced (conventional) stage to more advanced (post-conventional) stages of capacity for moral reasoning is exposure to other moral value systems than his own. This would reinforce what secondary school teachers have found — the growth value of small group discussions on great moral issues of the day, in helping young people to crystallize out and internalize elective moral attitudes about these issues. The rap sessions young people inevitably move into on their own will be more valuable if they are accompanied by some sessions under skilled leadership — and Father Meyer's injunctions against authoritarianism as blocking evolution of moral reasoning power applies particularly to these sessions.

The rejection of authoritarianism by adolescents should be seen as an effort to move to a more mature level of moral autonomy rather than a rejection of morality itself. That the struggle by adolescents to move toward a system of moral values established by themselves rather than by outsiders appears often confused is natural, and is explained by Kohlberg as follows: An adolescent who is trying to move away from the stage of being a robot repeating moral values enunciated by his parents and others towards establishing his own, will not only rebel against his parents, but also against that portion of himself that up to that time had accepted unthinkingly the moral values of his parents. If he can be helped to verbalize this conflict in an unthreatening group situation, the chances are high that he will emerge with the very values that he had so fiercely rejected, but this time because they are internalized by himself rather than unthinkingly accepted, they will be his own and he will be able to defend them as well as live by them. It is certainly congruent with these findings that major Protestant denominations and the Roman Catholic Church are recognizing the importance of adolescence as a testing and proving-ground for adolescence values.

So it's never too late. The high schools and colleges have the challenge and opportunity to meet the stated needs of the young people that may well not have been met by home and elementary school, and this before they leave school for the wider freedoms of college, job, or armed services. Only a relative few of the colleges are presently recognizing that a sexually naive freshman is only a few weeks removed from the sexually naive high school senior, and that in today's sexually open society it is knowledge that protects and ignorance and naivete that render vulnerable.

Education for responsible, mature, fulfilled sexuality is not only a field of scholarship to recognize, but a trust to be recognized by every community element — home, school, church.

If the secondary schools play their roles by recognizing and meeting the need, the lies about the methodology and true goals of sex education will be put to rest. As knowledge increases, fear decreases. In the end, not only young people but all of us will benefit by better understanding of ourselves and others as the sexual human beings we were created to be.

Combined References for Chapter 8

Angelino, H., Edmonds, E. R., and Mech, E. V. Self expressed "first" sources of sex information: A study of 266 Negro students. *Psychological Newsletter*, 1958, 9, 234-237.

Bandura, A. & Walters, R. *Adolescent Aggression*. New York: Ronald, 1959.

Bell, H. M. *Youth Tell Their Story*. Washington, D.C.: American Council on Education, 1938.

Bell, S. A preliminary study of the emotion of love between the sexes. *American Journal of Psychology*, 1902, pp. 325-354.

Blanton, M. G. The behavior of the human infant during the first thirty days of life. *Psychological Review*, 1917, pp. 956-983.

Broderick, C. B. & Rowe, G. P. A scale of preadolescent heterosexual development. *Journal of Marriage and the Family*, 1968, pp. 97-101.

Byler, R. V. (Ed.) *Teach Us What We Want to Know*. New York: Mental Health Materials Center, 1969.

Campbell, E. H. The social-sex development of children. *Genetic Psychology Monographs*, 1939, p. 4.

Conn, J. H. Children's reactions to the discovery of genital differences. *American Journal of Orthopsychiatry*, 1940a, pp. 747-754.

Conn, J. H. Sexual curiosity of children. *American Journal of Diseases of Children*, 1940b, pp. 1110-1119.

Conn, J. H. Children's awareness of the origin of babies. *Journal of Child Psychiatry*, 1948, pp. 140-176.

Conn, J. H. & Kanner, L. Children's awareness of sex differences. *Journal of Child Psychiatry*, 1947, pp. 3-57.

Dudycha, G. J. & Dudycha, M. M. Adolescent memories of preschool experiences. *Pedagogical Seminar and Journal of Genetic Psychology*, 1933, pp. 468-480.

Elias, J. & Gebhard, P. Sexuality and sexual learning in childhood. *Phi Delta Kappan*, 1969, 50, 401-406.

Freud, S. Three essays on sexuality. In *Standard Edition of the Complete Psychological Works*. London: Hogarth, 1953, pp. 135-245.

Group for the Advancement of Psychiatry. *Sex and the College Student*. New York: G.A.P., 1965.

Group for the Advancement of Psychiatry. *Normal Adolescence*. New York: G.A.P., 1968.

Halverson, H. M. Genital and sphincter behavior of the male infant. *Journal of Genetic Psychology*, 1940, pp. 95-136.

Hattendorf, K. W. A study of the questions of young children concerning sex: A phase of an experimental approach to parent education. *Journal of Social Psychology*, 1932, pp. 37-65.

Isaacs, S. *Social Development of Young Children: A Study of Beginnings.* London: Routledge, 1933.

Jones, K. L., Shainberg, L. W., & Byer, C. O. *Sex.* New York: Harper & Row, 1969.

Katcher, A. The discrimination of sex differences by young children. *Journal of Genetic Psychology*, 1955, pp. 131-143.

Keniston, K. Student activism, moral development, and morality. *American Journal of Orthopsychiatry*, 1970, 40(4).

Kimbrough, R. T. SOS for junior high students. *Clearing House*, 1966, 41, 45-48.

Kinsey, A. C., Pomeroy, W. B., & Martin, C. E. *Sexual Behavior in the Human Male.* Philadelphia: Saunders, 1948.

Kinsey, A. C., Pomeroy, W. B., and Martin, C. E. *Sexual Behavior in the Human Female.* Philadelphia: Saunders, 1953.

Kohlberg, L. *Stages in the Development of Moral Thought and Action.* New York: Holt, Rinehart & Winston, 1970.

Lee, M. R. Background factors related to sex information and attitudes. *Journal of Educational Psychology*, 1952, 43, 467-485.

Maccoby, E. (Ed.) *The Development of Sex Differences.* Stanford: Stanford University Press, 1966.

Martinson, F. M. Sexual knowledge, values, and behavior patterns of adolescents. *Child Welfare*, 1968, 47, 405-410.

Masters, W. H. and Johnson, V. E. *Human Sexual Inadequacy.* Boston: Little, Brown, 1970.

Meyer, J. Sex education and psychological readiness. In J. McHugh (Ed.) *Sex Education: A Guide for Teachers.* Washington, D.C.: U.S. Catholic Conference, 1970.

Moll A. *The Sexual Life of the Child.* New York: Macmillan, 1923.

Money, J., Hampson, J., & Hampson, J. L. Hermaphroditism: Recommendations concerning assignment of sex, change of sex, and psychologic management. *Bulletin of Johns Hopkins Hospital*, 1955a, pp. 284-300.

Money, J., Hampson, J., & Hampson, J. L. An examination of some basic sexual concepts: The evidence of human hermaphroditism. *Bulletin of Johns Hopkins Hospital*, 1955b, pp. 301-319.

Ramsey, C. V. The sex information of younger boys. *American Journal of Orthopsychiatry*, 1943, 13, 347-352.

Ramsey, C. V. *Factors in the Sex Life of 291 Boys.* Madison, N.J.: Published by the author, 1950.

Schwartz, M. S. A report of sex information knowledge of 87 lower class ninth grade boys. *Family Coordinator*, 1969, 18(4), 361-371.

Sears, R. Development of gender role. In F. A. Beach (Ed.) *Sex and Behavior.* New York: Wiley, 1965.

Sears, R., Maccoby, E., & Levin, H. *Patterns of Child Rearing.* Evanston, Ill.: Row, Peterson, 1957.

Sex Education. *Medical World News*, 1969, 10(40), 25-28d.

Thomas, J. L., S.J. Sexuality and the total personality. *SIECUS Newsletter*, 1970, 5(2).

Thornburg, H. D. Administering a sex education program. *Arizona Teacher*, 1968, 57(2), 18-20.

Thornburg, H. D. *Sex Education in the Public Schools.* Phoenix: Arizona Education Association, 1969.

Thornburg, H. D. Ages and first sources of sex information as reported by 88 college women. *Journal of School Health*, 1970, 40, 156-158.

Thornburg, H. D. A comparative study of sex information sources. *Journal of School Health*, 1972, 42, 88-91.

Thornburg, H. D. *Adolescent Development.* Dubuque, Iowa: W. C. Brown, 1973.

Thornburg, H. D. Sex information sources. Unpublished data, 1974.

CHAPTER 9 **toward adolescence**

Introduction

Up to this point in the book our discussion has focused around the changing biological, intellectual, and social nature of the developing preadolescent. As he continues to move toward adolescence, each of these developmental areas shifts toward a more accelerated, often complex, level of involvement. This chapter, and the three articles presented herein, is designed, not so much to tie the preceding eight chapters together, as to show that as a result of preadolescent changes, there is a new, continued growth period known as adolescence for which the preadolescent period provides readiness. The most conclusive evidence that adolescence is about to begin comes through physical development. With the new physical characteristics that emerge, comes the adolescent's awareness of change.

It is generally thought that youth today are a different breed than in any previous generation. Most advocates of this position point to industrialization, technology, mobility, urbanization, and the influences of the mass media as producing such change. Nevertheless, all of these changes point to different stages of societal growth, rather than individual growth, and perhaps the uniqueness of today's youth lies in their interaction with society rather than within the changing nature of the youths themselves.

An adolescent's reactions to his own developmental traits are usually acceptable if he develops within the normal range of his peers. If accelerated growth patterns or late maturation patterns prevail, they may affect the adolescent's perception and acceptance of himself as a normal maturing individual. The adolescent's primary criterion for self-evaluation is anticipated peer reaction. In addition, he is affected by social and cultural expectancies and his ability to approximate sex-appropriate behaviors. As a result of his growth spurt, changes in height and weight as well as the emergence of secondary sex characteristics are instrumental in affecting the emerging self-image.

To some extent, the adolescent's self-perceptions, which began in preadolescence, are affected by important people in his environment. In the first article of this chapter, William Looft points to the changing perception of important information sources from the time of preadolescence throughout adolescence. It is interesting that the predominant reference to parents while a preadolescent drastically changes to peers by adolescence. Looft's article is helpful in seeing the changing perceptual nature of youth. The relative importance of peers and parents throughout the entire life span is a significant result of his research.

In Chapter Five, the article by Thornburg pointed to the movement from parents to peers as the primary influence of behaviors. Underneath such changes, however, there may very well persist beyond preadolescence a strong complex of parental values. To some extent, associations throughout adolescence are based on value communalities as well as behaviors. The second article in this chapter looks at peer values as a basis for peer group affiliation. Thornburg cites evidence which indicates that there have most likely emerged in our culture three distinct peer groups, namely, high school youth, noncollege youth, and college youth. Upon reading the article, it will become clear that most high school youth are still heavily involved in resolving developmental tasks basic to their development. Working through physical, cultural, and personal changes which have occurred through the continuing growth from preadolescence on accounts for the primary interests of high school youth.

There is a large portion of our youths that do not extend their education beyond high school. In describing these youth, it is observable that while they may have undergone some behavioral differences from parental standards during adolescence, their basic value structures are the same. This is quite a contrast with the evidences which support college youth as having a distinctly different set of behaviors and values from parents or from their noncollege youth counterparts. Undoubtedly, the different value complexes began emerging in childhood and may have caused some behavioral discrepancies during preadolescence. Still, research evidence is not conclusive as to what point in time a child may begin developing distinctly different values from those held by his parents.

The final article in the book is by William Lowry and Robert Reilley and it focuses on the problems and interests of adolescence in several different social-emotional dimensions. Their study is a follow-up to a study originally done in 1935, and by comparing youth problems in 1969, they are able to see how many concern areas have maintained themselves and how many are different.

The authors analyze fifteen issues considered by youth as problems. Interestingly enough, money has been the most serious problem and interest of youth through the thirty-five year span. Study habits, personal and moral qualities, personal attractiveness, and philosophy of life have also been high ranking interests of youth over the years. A decisive increase in sex adjustments and mental hygiene was found by the authors. With increasing social emphasis during a prepubertal time, these areas of concern are perceived earlier, thus providing the motivation for many behaviors and values in emerging adolescents.

In analysis, this book has focused first on the physiological determinants of preadolescent growth and behavior. After that, discussion extended to the social-cultural milieu in which the preadolescent not only finds himself but must find some way to adjust to and live with. Finally, attention focused on the behavioral domains of preadolescent youth points to the fact that from nine to eleven, the emerging preadolescent becomes an active, exploratory, and vulnerable social being who may exercise a wide range of anti-social behaviors which may persist well beyond the point of preadolescence. Overall, the preadolescent can be viewed as a distinctly dynamic individual who gathers unto himself the necessary impulses, emotions, and teachings in his striving to be a total individual.

Perceptions Across the Life Span of Important Information Sources for Children and Adolescents

WILLIAM R. LOOFT

Introduction

Many observers of the contemporary social scene (Looft, 1971; Morison, 1967) have commented that the family is rapidly diminishing in importance as a source of basic information for the developing individual. Assumedly other institutions or agents, such as the school and television, are taking over educational and socializing tasks that historically have been the prime responsibility of parents. It thus may be that young boys and girls no longer view their parents as important sources of knowledge. Their fundamental expectation, though perhaps not a conscious one, is that they will learn about the world and how to get along in it from persons and places other than the parents and the home. As McLuhan (1967) has said, the level of information inside the family circle is much lower than that outside.

That parents are insignificant sources of information with regard to sexual matters has long been acknowledged and verified. Studies (Angelino and Mech, 1955; Elias and Gebhard, 1969; Juhasz, 1969; National Schools, 1969; Thornburg, 1970) have consistently demonstrated that most young people receive their sex education from peers and from printed materials. Perhaps because parents are unable or unwilling to provide their offspring the needed information regarding the business of sex, it may be that in the eyes of their children they also lack credibility as reservoirs of knowledge in other critical areas. The dramatic changes in life styles in recent years in this society may contribute to these attitudes about parents as educators. Accordingly, the present investigation addressed these questions:

Who is *perceived* to be the most important single agent in providing a child the basic kinds of information he will need to be a functional adult in this society? Is this same agent also perceived to be the most important informational source for the adolescent? Do persons of all ages agree on the relative importance of various informational sources for children and adolescents?

Reprinted by permission of the author and the Journal Press from the *Journal of Psychology*, 1971, 78, 207-211.

Method

During the summer and fall of 1970 interviewers were stationed along the sidewalks of the business district of Madison, Wisconsin, in order to obtain data for the study.[1] The interviewer approached an individual and said the following: "Hello, I'm representing the Department of Educational Psychology at the University of Wisconsin, and I wonder if you would answer four quick questions? OK? I guess everybody agrees that we are living in difficult times. Children and adolescents have a great deal to learn if they are going to make it as happy and successful adults. (*a*) Who or what is the principal agent from whom the child − a school-age child − learns about the world and how to get along in it? That is, who is the most important transmitter of knowledge to children? (*b*) Who or what is the principal source of knowledge about how to get along in the world for the adolescent, or teenager? (*c*) Who or what are some other important agents in helping our children and youth to grow into happy and well-functioning adults? (*d*) And your age is_____? Thank you for your cooperation."

A total of 236 persons were interviewed. The breakdown of age groups was done in hopes that the data analysis would be sensitive to changing perceptions across the life span. Accordingly, seven groups resulted: 10-14 years (early adolescence), $n = 24$; 15-17 (late adolescence), $n = 31$; 18-25, $n = 35$; 26-30, $n = 49$; 31-40, $n = 28$; 41-50, $n = 36$; 51-75, $n = 33$.

Results

Table 9.1 presents the nominations across age groups of the agent or institution perceived to be most important for children (only the first-named agent was recorded). Clearly, all age groups perceived parents to be most important for the individual at this time of life. A *chi*-square contingency test for parents *vs.* all other nominations across age groups was highly significant ($\chi^2 = 48.6$, $df = 6$, $p < .0001$).

Table 9.2 presents the nominations across age groups of the agent deemed most important for the adolescent. It is clear that other agents, particularly peers, were perceived as most significant at this time of life. However, parents were still nominated frequently by all age groups except the late adolescent/ young adult groups. The contingency *chi*-square test for parents *vs.* other nominations was highly significant ($\chi^2 = 58.1$, $df = 6$, $p < .0001$), indicating that parents were far less frequently perceived to be important informational sources in comparison to other kinds of agents.

---

[1] The author is grateful to the following persons, who served as interviewers for this study: Marc D. Baranowski, Deborah Foster, Susan Nitzke, and Les Posdamer.

Table 9.1

Perceptions Across the Life Span of the Most Important Informational
Transmitter for Children

	Percent nominated (first choice)						
Source	Ages 10-14	Ages 15-17	Ages 18-25	Ages 26-30	Ages 31-40	Ages 41-50	Ages 51-75
Parents	75	37	46	68	61	69	49
Peers	17	33	17	16	14	3	12
School, teacher	4	13	11	2	14	22	18
Church	0	0	0	2	0	0	3
Media, TV	0	4	17	2	11	3	0
Other, no response	4	13	9	8	0	3	18

The third question allowed the interviewees to nominate other agents they thought to be of secondary yet still considerable importance. The responses to this question were generally confined to the school and/or teachers, various forms of mass media, and the church. The school was mentioned most frequently to this question by the 10-14, 26-30, and 31-40 age groups. The 15-17, 18-25, and 51-75 groups mentioned media most often, and the 41-50 group was alone in nominating the church most often in response to this question.

Discussion

Despite contemporary observations by many that the family is declining in importance, it is clear from this research that, at least for children, the parents are still perceived by all age groups to be the single most notable transmitter of information. For adolescents, the power of the peer group ascends in importance, at least in the eyes of the perceiver. It is of interest that only the 41-50 age group perceived parents to be more important for adolescents than peers (see Table 9.2). Perhaps people in this age group are most likely to be the parents of the current adolescent generation, and therefore they may perceive themselves to be more influential than their offsprings' friends.

The perceived diminutive importance of parents as sources of knowledge for adolescents (and to some extent for children, see Table 9.1) is striking in the late adolescent/young adult groups. Speculation allows for perhaps one or both of two possible explanations for this finding: it may indeed be true that parents are insignificant informational sources for these young people; on the other hand, these data may reflect the unwillingness of this generation to recognize the continuing importance of their parents in their lives, and thus these data may reflect rejection or rebellion.

Another notable aspect of these findings concerns what was *not* mentioned: i.e., the absence of nominations for other feasibly important agents or

Table 9.2
Perceptions Across the Life Span of the Most Important Informational Transmitter for Adolescents

Source	Percent nominated (first choice)						
	Ages 10-14	Ages 15-17	Ages 18-25	Ages 26-30	Ages 31-40	Ages 41-50	Ages 51-75
Parents	25	7	3	14	25	39	24
Peers	38	61	66	55	53	28	33
School, teacher	8	0	6	12	11	19	27
Church	0	0	0	4	0	0	3
Media, TV	8	3	0	0	7	6	3
Self	0	6	11	4	0	3	0
Books	0	0	11	0	0	0	0
Other, no response	21	23	3	11	4	5	10

institutions. Organized religion was seen as first in importance by only a very small number of persons. Only one subject nominated siblings as premier in importance, and no mention of grandparents was made at all, even for a position of lesser importance. Educational institutions were given first place votes by a small proportion of people, although schools seemed to grow in importance with advancing age of those interviewed. Various forms of mass media, though frequently mentioned in response to question three, were very seldom mentioned as first in importance.

It is important to emphasize that this study reports *perceived* importance of informational sources; the data cannot be said to indicate where a young person obtains various kinds of necessary information in actuality. Despite recent dramatic changes in American society, the present findings suggest that, in general, persons of all ages still hold the traditional views regarding sources of information for young people: parents are most important for children, and peers are most important for adolescents.

Summary

Persons in age samples extending across the major portion of the life span were interviewed regarding whom they perceive to be the most important transmitters of information to children and to adolescents. Parents were perceived to be most significant for children, and peers were most significant for adolescents, although the importance of parents for adolescents was also a frequent response category. Agents perceived to be of somewhat lesser importance included the mass media, schools or teachers, and churches. The late adolescent/young adult samples attributed importance to parents less frequently than did any other age group.

Peers: Three Distinct Groups
HERSHEL D. THORNBURG

Adolescents have vital concerns about the individuals and situations that affect their development. Of primary importance to each adolescent are (1) his society and his peers, (2) gaining self and social identity, and (3) social maturation. Most behavioral scientists agree that these factors are essential to the successful development of adolescents. They also recognize that these factors are worked out mostly within one's own world — among one's peers.

An article by Smith and Kleine (1966) reviews the literature about the adolescent and his world. The conflicting propositions are presented that (1) adolescents are an emphatically strong subculture and that (2) adolescents' values do not differ significantly from their parents'. In an extensive study of middle-class families, Elkin and Westley (1955) found very little difference between adult and adolescent values. Research among rural youth has reflected the same findings (Bealer, Willits, Maida, 1964). Yet, Coleman's studies (1961) show quite distinctly that there is an adolescent subculture which is the primary influence in adolescent social maturation. Research studies since Coleman support his findings (Strom, 1963; Cawelti, 1968; *Generations Apart*, 1969).

While controversy may surround the subculture vs non-subculture issue, most likely the proposition could be advanced that there is often too much emphasis being placed on the issue that might be no more than a natural rebellion of the adolescent and be less conflict — and anxiety — oriented if less were being said about it. Bandura (1964) expressed it in an article he wrote, "The stormy decade: fact or fiction?".

Bandura's article focuses primarily on various sources of adolescent mythology. He attributes adolescent rebellion to superficial signs of nonconformity. He cogently parallels adolescent fad behavior with adult fad behaviors.

Mass media's ability to sensationalize adolescent behavior, especially deviant ones, is another perpetuation of the myth of significant adolescent-adult differences. Such a statement was attested to in the recent CBS report which asked college and noncollege youth, "What scene stands out most vividly in your mind from the TV coverages you saw of the Vietnam war

(*Generations Apart*, 1969, p. 34)?" Thirty-eight percent of the college youth and 42 percent of the noncollege youth answered "killing and bodies."

Other statements and research evidence in Bandura's article make one aware that more could be done than is being done to minimize adolescent conflict and accentuate more positive aspects of social development.

Some type of group behavior, i.e., cliques and crowds, is contributory in the pursuit of social maturation. The most recent investigation of adolescent social structure was done by Dunphy (1963) in which he found that nearly 80 percent of our youth are involved in some form of group behavior. The accompanying chart illustrates Dunphy's stages of group development in adolescence (1963, p. 236).

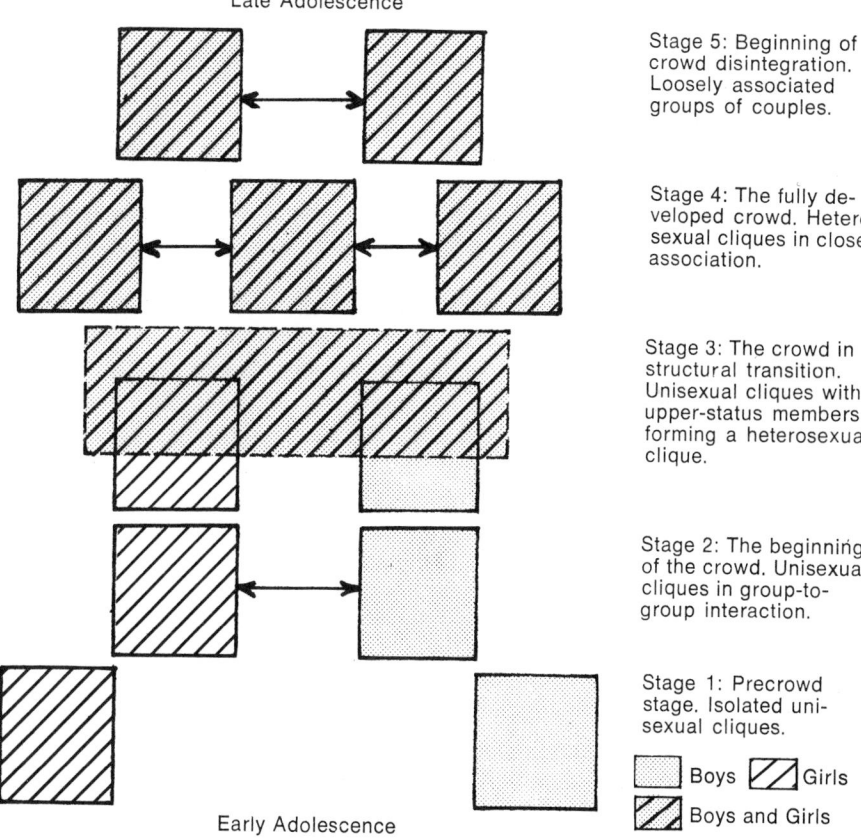

Late Adolescence

Stage 5: Beginning of crowd disintegration. Loosely associated groups of couples.

Stage 4: The fully developed crowd. Heterosexual cliques in close association.

Stage 3: The crowd in structural transition. Unisexual cliques with upper-status members forming a heterosexual clique.

Stage 2: The beginning of the crowd. Unisexual cliques in group-to-group interaction.

Stage 1: Precrowd stage. Isolated unisexual cliques.

☐ Boys ▨ Girls
▨ Boys and Girls

Early Adolescence

Stages of group development in adolescence. Reprinted by permission of author and publisher, from D.C. Dunphy, "The social structure of urban adolescent peer groups," *Sociometry*, 1963, 26, 236.

There are several reasons why group identification is so important to developing youth. One reason is to help youth in the process of emancipation. While Bandura (1964) suggests that most of youth's emancipation from parents has been more or less completed rather than initiated at adolescence, most writers believe that throughout adolescence there is a continuing emancipation process which is aided by peer association (Douvan and Adelson, 1966).

Group identification also spurs competition. Most adolescents spend much time in active competition. It serves an important developmental purpose when adolescents exercise their social maturation in spontaneous competition. Yet, not all adolescent competition is a result of growing up. Much of today's competition is affected by, sometimes even promoted by, the adult world since it is part of a society where so many attainments are necessary to success. However, the method of attainment can result in unhealthy competition. If adolescent competition is abused, it can produce lasting effects; it can become part of the individual's life style.

A third aspect of group identification is conformity, about which psychologists are in considerable disagreement. Adolescent group identity may be linked to one's values; one's needs for acceptance or one's fear of rejection. Others identify because of a need to escape loneliness. Regardless of the reason, many adolescent groups do conform. Studies indicate that peer activity has the dominating effect on adolescent behaviors (Brittain, 1969; Cawelti, 1968; Coleman, 1961; Friesen, 1968; Musgrove, 1966). These studies do not preclude the fact that adults have significant effects on their youth (Meissner, 1965), but they do point out that peer influence is quite strong during adolescence.

Smith and Kleine (1966) observe that adolescents, just like adults, form smaller social units or reference groups, and these groups may vary in activities, sentiments, and behavioral norms. Such reference groups manifest their behavior through clique and gang-member activity. Youth does belong. Such is the process of social maturation.

Three Types of Peer Groups

There is increasing evidence that some distinct peer groups with varying attitudes and value references have emerged. The three groups are: (a) high school youth, (b) noncollege youth, and (c) college youth. The differences are due to (1) distinctly different types of individual adolescent physical and intellectual functions, (2) the particular social and cultural milieu in which each adolescent develops, and (3) the attitudes and values of each adolescent peer affiliation.

High School Youth

Today, high school youth has basically the same type of peer relationships that earlier generation youth had. Most high school youth spend their time in breaking infantile ties, developing friendships, participating in high school activities and considering future plans. Parental, school and peer influences assist in this process. While there are many high school youth involved in student activism, drugs, and sex, they do it primarily as a means of identifying with some individual, clique, or gang. This results in some high school youth having stressful experiences. Yet, the primary focus is the continued resolution of developmental tasks (Garrison, 1966; Havighurst, 1952; Thornburg, 1970). Sherif and Sherif have stated, "Adolescents will find kicks in any activity – whether socially desirable or undesirable – that lets them act together on their own (1965, p. 6)." While this may very well apply to many high school youth, it is not the same type of motivation that triggers noncollege and college youth behavior.

Noncollege Youth

We have a majority of noncollege youth. In fact, certain surveys place the proportion of noncollege youth at around 80 percent (Braham, 1965). Yet little is heard of this group and few studies have been done in which noncollege youth were the primary focus. What are the values and attitudes of these youth? How do they differ from the high school youth? From college youth? From adults?

Noncollege youth compared to college youth, in addition to the amount of education, are characterized by a stronger work orientation. They also tend to hold middle-class values, to be politically conservative, to be middle-income blue collar workers, to be religiously oriented (*Generations Apart*, 1969). Their life style is so much like their parents' that one could strongly suggest that for this group, the generation gap is a myth. The impression is that today's problem may be a "fitting-into-society gap" – something that is far more difficult for college than noncollege youth.

In April, 1969, CBS News undertook a study of the generation gap. It was conducted by the Daniel Yankelovich research firm. The survey, originally the subject of a series of television shows, has since been released as *Generations Apart* (1969). The sample consisted of 2,881 noncollege youth and 723 college youth (seventeen to twenty-three years old); 310 noncollege youth parents and 362 college youth parents. Parts of the youth profile will be reported here. The following summary statements will indicate differences existing between noncollege and college youth and their parents.

(a) Question: Hard work will always pay off (percent that believe yes)

     Answer: Noncollege   College
                  Youth   79   Youth   56
                  NCY parents* 85   CY parents   76

(b) Question: Everyone should save as much as he can regularly and not have to lean on family and friends the minute he runs into financial problems (percent that believe yes)

     Answer: Noncollege   College
                  Youth   88   Youth   76
                  NCY parents 98   CY parents   90

(c) Question: Belonging to some organized religion is important in a person's life (percent that believed yes)

     Answer: Noncollege   College
                  Youth   82   Youth   42
                  NCY parents 91   CY parents   81

(d) Question: Competition encourages excellence (percent that believe yes)

                  Noncollege   College
                  Youth   82   Youth   72
                  NCY parents 91   CY parents   84

*NCY stands for noncollege youth.

Noncollege and college youth were asked which of the following changes they would welcome:

	Category	Noncollege Youth (percent)	College Youth (percent)
(a)	Less emphasis on money	54	72
(b)	More emphasis on law and order	81	57
(c)	More emphasis on self-expression	70	84
(d)	More sexual freedom	22	43
(e)	More vigorous protests by blacks and other minority groups	9	23
(f)	More respect for authority	86	59

The statements and responses thus far have focused on traditional value statements. The survey indicates that noncollege youth are more likely to agree with traditional value statements than college youth. Data also indicate that noncollege youth values are more like parent values than are the college youth. If there is a significant difference between noncollege youth and college youth values then it should reflect itself in areas in addition to traditional value statements. The following selected responses report the attitudes of noncollege youth and college youth on society's institutions and restraints:

(a)   Question: Having an abortion is morally wrong (percent agreeing)

  Answer: Noncollege   College
            Youth   64   Youth   36
            NCY parents   66   CY parents   50

(b)   Question: Relations between consenting homosexuals are morally wrong (percent agreeing)

  Answer: Noncollege   College
            Youth   72   Youth   42
            NCY parents   79   CY parents   63

(c)   Question: Premarital sexual relations are morally wrong (percent agreeing)

  Answer: Noncollege   College
            Youth   57   Youth   34
            NCY parents   88   CY parents   74

(d)   Question: Extramarital sexual relations are morally wrong (percent agreeing)

  Answer: Noncollege   College
            Youth   77   Youth   77
            NCY parents   92   CY parents   90

Additional questions were asked about restraints imposed by society which could or could not be accepted.

	Category	Accept	Noncollege Youth	College Youth
(a)	Abiding by laws you don't agree with	easily	34	15
		reluctantly	55	74
		reject	11	14

	Category	Accept	Noncollege Youth	College Youth
(b)	Conforming in matters of clothing and personal grooming	easily reluctantly reject	54 26 19	33 29 38
(c)	Prohibition against marijuana	easily reluctantly reject	72 11 17	48 20 31
(d)	Prohibition against LSD	easily reluctantly reject	79 7 13	73 11 13
(e)	Power and authority of the police	easily reluctantly reject	78 27 4	48 42 10
(f)	Being treated impersonally in a job	easily reluctantly reject	21 39 39	9 35 57

The statistics shown represent less than 10 percent of the total questions asked by the CBS News and do not include a political profile on youth presented in the report. But even in the questions not represented here, the noncollege youth still indicate more significant differences in attitudes and values from the college youth. In summary, it could be said, as compared to college youth, that noncollege youth are (1) more conservative, (2) more prone to traditional values, (3) more religious, (4) more respectful, (5) more work-oriented, (6) more money-oriented, (7) more patriotic, (8) more concerned about moral living, (9) more conforming, (10) more accepting of the draft and war, (11) less activism-oriented, (12) less sympathetic with activists, (13) less drug-prone, and (14) less sexually permissive (*Generations Apart*, 1969).

The behavior of noncollege youth is not like that of high school youth. For the most part they are now involved in social integration more than social maturation. Their world is here. The responsibility they encounter to self and others makes them aware that it is here. It is not the idealism of high school youth or the world of the college youth. Many are married, most have jobs. The responsibility for maintaining a home and rearing a family is common. Life decisions are made on what they know and what they think is most appropriate at the time. Life is the ever-present daily experience of the noncollege youth and his peers.

College Youth

Perhaps the most unique and certainly the most controversial group of youth today are college students. These youths are characterized by their various institutional challenging behaviors in which student activism, sexual freedom, and drug use are accentuated.

Most significant of their behaviors is the challenge they are presenting to the traditional conservative structure of life. As has been indicated by contrasting the noncollege student with college youth, today's college student is less likely to adopt traditional standards and it is among this group that the generation gap, if any, most likely exists.

New ideas are emerging in college youth today. Some of these are ideas that focus on the educational institution. The challenges are based on the idea that college is not relevant to the needs of today's youth or society. R. W. Carry (1968) has suggested five emerging trends in attitude and thought about rules, education and youth. They are:

1. Trend one is away from the traditional view that it is the individual's responsibility to make the education offered him relevant. The emerging view is that it is the educational institution's responsibility to make its offerings relevant to the individual (Coleman, 1965)
2. Trend two is away from the traditional view that a rule is a rule, and right or wrong, it must be obeyed.
3. Trend three is away from the traditional view that rules were made for the purpose of insuring essential controls or for making a better educational environment. There is an emerging suspicion that many rules are made for the convenience of educators (Goodman, 1968).
4. Trend four is away from the traditional view that modern youth "never had it so good" with so few demands and rules, to the emerging view that laws and processes purportedly protecting youth actually discriminate against them (Friedenberg, 1959).
5. Trend five is away from the view that we have adequate processes available to bring about changes in laws and rules in time to meet social pressures in a rapidly changing world. An emerging view is that riots or other less violent forms of confrontation are more effective in bringing about needed changes and that traditional methods are inadequate.

Perhaps it is the very college experience itself that these youth are having that has caused them to look for new definitions to replace old imperatives. Certainly, there is nothing wrong with youth expressing their concerns about contemporary issues and problems – and, many things within our society are "bugging" our youth.

The focus of attention is on drugs, sex, the war, politics, hypocrisy, civil rights, police brutality, and the generation gap (Fort, 1968). Not much has been said about education, occupations, marriage, or other basic issues which endure far beyond a drug stage or a war stage.

Yet, in a recent survey, 94 percent of the college students said their college experience had the greatest effect on their life and values. Other events, i.e., the death of John F. Kennedy, Vietnam, and civil rights, have had significant effects, but not to the extent that college itself does (*Generations Apart*, 1969). Two research studies conducted by Thornburg (1969, 1971) in which youth were asked to express problems, issues, and concerns confronting them, education was the most frequently mentioned. The CBS report found that college youth identified more with other students (88 percent) and other people of their own generation (83 percent) (*Generations Apart*, 1969). Therefore, it is hypothesized that (1) education is the most crucial factor in the college student's life and (2) the establishment of peer groups or subcultures at the college level is an essential part of college experience.

Gottlieb and Hodgkins (1963) have attempted to define the college student subculture by categorizing students into four areas: (1) the academic subgroup composed of students who want a good education and are willing to study in order to obtain it, (2) a vocational subgroup composed of those students pursuing primarily the same vocational choice, (3) a nonconformist subculture which concentrates on life and the issues of life, using the university setting as an avenue for their expression, and (4) the collegiate or the social group on campus, who are interested in social activities, athletic, sorority and fraternity functions, and the like.

A research article written by Lionel Lewis (1969) has looked at the value of college to these four different subcultures. Students falling within these subcultures were asked various questions about (1) intellectualism, (2) intellectual association, (3) autonomy, and (4) idealism. Students belonging to the academic subculture show strong interest in education, knowledge and understanding. Most of their leisure time was spent in intellectual or musical activities. In contrast, those belonging to the collegiate subculture spent most of their time in extracurricular and social activities. They also preferred courses where there was competition with other students for a final grade. Students in the vocational subculture were more practical-oriented. Their primary reason for being in college was to obtain a degree. Extracurricular and social activities meant very little to them. On idealism they had the lowest humanitarianism score of any of the four subcultures. (It may very well be that this particular subculture closely parallels the values of noncollege youth.) Lewis found the nonconformist subculture to be interested in intellectual association and they also stated that an important reason for being in college was to develop the resources necessary to become an autonomous person.

Lewis has been able to advance the hypothesis proposed by Trow and Clark (1960) and Gottlieb and Hodgkins (1963) through analyzing basic values of various student groups. Within these subcultures there are a common set of ideals and behaviors. One group, the collegiates, primarily identifies with their school. Characteristic of this group is a "social activities and minimal studying" philosophy. This group represents more accurately the social life and activity of the college campus. Within this group are strong peer attachments. Research by E. Jackson Baur focuses on such student peer groups and their academic development.

Baur's findings (1967) were categorized around (1) campus life, (2) relations with faculty, (3) studying, (4) the classroom, (5) student sub-cultures, and (6) honor students.

Baur found socialization to be the primary objective of both dormitory and Greek groups. Most activities were within their living groups, with Greeks emerging as the majority (87 percent) of campus-wide student leaders. While academic pursuits were not the main activity, interestingly, in most cases, in-group status was given to the persons with the highest grade-point average. Baur's analysis of social and academic life gives the reader a concise picture of campus life and its relation to peer affiliations and academic pursuits.

In conclusion, it must be remembered that while ideally adolescence is the time in which the young make decisions about themselves, it is often difficult to do so in a changing society. Therefore, many of the attachments made are with other adolescents who also seek answers amidst change, violence and affluency. In the process of identity-searching some seek out adults; others seek only their own. Some adults will seek out youth; some will be rejected for doing so. But, whether it is high school youth, noncollege youth, or college youth, each will seek out that which best accommodates his needs system. Some will conform; some will alienate themselves; some will find their place in society; and some will continue to allude to the generation gap.

Life Problems and Interests of Adolescents
WILLIAM H. LOWRY AND ROBERT R. REILLEY

To American educators, the problems and interests of adolescents have been frequent topics of discussion and concern, but only occasionally the subject of careful study. Among the advantages of an objective determination of any major characteristics of any group at a particular time and place is the opportunity thus provided for observing differences in the characteristics associated with other times and other places. This study investigated such changes in the problems and interests of American adolescents. The major hypothesis to be tested in this type of research was suggested by Harris' statement: "Change society and economic conditions, and you change the emphasis adolescents give to various problems and interests" (1959).

In 1935, Symonds submitted to high school students in New York City and Tulsa, Oklahoma, a list of fifteen areas of human concern (1936). The items as well as the words in which they were expressed were taken from interviews with young people. Students were instructed to rank the items first, in order of being the individual's greatest personal problems, and second in order of interest — topics the student would most like to read about, discuss, or hear discussed.

The study was replicated in 1957 by Harris (1959). He used the same list and directions with high school students in Minnesota. Following is the list of fifteen areas of human concern in the order and form employed in these studies.

1. *Health* — eating, drinking, exercise, posture, sleep and rest, air and temperature, sunlight, clothing, bathing, care of special parts, cleanliness and prevention of disease, excretion and elimination, use of drugs.
2. *Sex Adjustment* — love, petting, courtship, marriage.

Reprinted by permission of the authors and publisher from the November, 1970 issue of *The Clearing House*.

3. *Safety* – avoiding accidents and injuries.

4. *Money* – earning, spending, saving, etc.

5. *Mental Hygiene* – fears, worries, inhibitions, compulsions, feelings of inferiority, fantasies, etc.

6. *Study Habits* – skills used in study, methods of work, problem-solving.

7. *Recreation* – sports and games, reading, arts and crafts, fellowship and social activities, hobbies.

8. *Personal and Moral Qualities* – qualities leading to success, qualities of good citizenship.

9. *Home and Family Relationships* – living harmoniously with members of the family.

10. *Manners and Courtesy* – etiquette.

11. *Personal Attractiveness* – personal appearance, voice, clothing.

12. *Daily Schedule* – planning 24 hours in a day.

13. *Civic Interests, Attitudes, and Responsibilities.*

14. *Getting Along with Other People.*

15. *Philosophy of Life* – personal values, ambitions, ideals, religion.

It was the purpose of the present investigation to compare the rankings obtained by Symonds in 1935 and Harris in 1957 with rankings of the same items obtained from high school students in 1969. Comparisons were also made between the two groups of adolescents used in this study – one group from an all Negro high school; the other from a predominately white high school.

Procedure

Both groups of students in the present study were asked to rank the items in Symonds' list in order of greatest personal problems and in order of interest. Each subject was supplied with the list of fifteen areas of human concern and a second paper on which to record responses. As far as possible, materials and directions duplicated the original 1935 study.

The population for this study consisted of students in grades nine to twelve of two East Central Texas high schools. One of these high schools with a total enrollment of 330 students is an all Negro school located in an all Negro district of town. The median family income is well below the poverty level of $3000 as defined by the U.S. Government. The second high school involved is predominately white with an enrollment of 650 students. Parents of students attending this school are largely professors or employees of a nearby university with a median family income of $7000. The two high schools are located within ten miles of each other and in the same metropolitan area. Both are comprehensive high schools accredited by the Texas Education Agency and offer instruction in both college preparatory and vocational courses. A total of 692 students participated in the present study. The "Negro" school provided 220 subjects while 472 students from the white school took part. Group testing procedures were employed during the 1969 spring semester.

To allow comparison with the earlier studies, the same statistical methods were employed in determining the mean rank of each item for the two 1969 groups. No attempt was made to subdivide responses by grade or sex. In addition to finding the mean rank for each issue, the correlations between problems and interests and between the results of the 1969 and earlier studies were determined. Rank order correlation methods were used for this purpose in the present study (Snedocor and Cochran, 1967). Symonds and Harris utilized Kendall's W statistic for similar comparisons (1948).

Results

(1) *Comparison of 1969 results with earlier studies*

Tables 9.3 and 9.4 provide a comparison of the 1969 results with the earlier studies. Similarities and differences between findings for the total 1969 group and the two earlier studies can be noted. Money was rated high as a problem in all three studies. It has first place in 1935 and 1969 and second in 1957. Study Habits were also ranked high in all three studies, with fourth in 1935, first in 1957 and second in 1969. Personal Attractiveness continued dropping, from third in 1935, to fourth in 1957, to seventh in 1969. Personal and Moral Qualities were ranked fifth in 1935, third in 1957, and fourth in 1969. Health, after being ranked 2nd in 1935 and 12.5 in 1957, was given a rank of ninth in 1969. Mental Hygiene was even more of a problem in 1969 than in 1957 or 1935. Having a rank of eleventh in 1935, and 5.5 in 1957, it rose to a ranking of third in 1969. Sex Adjustment also showed a considerable rise from fifteenth in 1935, to 12.5 in 1957, to eighth in 1969. Manners and Courtesy continued to decrease in importance as problems as did Getting Along with Other People and Recreation. Other issues showing a slight increase in rank as problems were Daily Schedule, Civic Interest, Attitudes and Responsibilities, and Home and Family Relationships.

In ranking the items as interests, Money and Sex Adjustment showed the greatest change in rank. Money, from seventh in 1935, to ninth in 1957, to second in 1969. Sex Adjustment moved from thirteenth in 1935, to seventh in 1957, to first in 1969. Health continued to rank high as an interest with second in 1935, first in 1957, and third in 1969. Recreation dropped from first in 1935, to third in 1957, to 6.5 in 1969. Manners and Courtesy, Philosophy of Life, Getting Along with Other People, Safety, and Study Habits also showed a lower rank in 1969 than in 1935 or 1957. Remaining of least interest was Civic Interest, Attitudes, and Responsibilities with the same ranking of fourteen for 1935, 1957, and 1969 and Daily Schedule with a consistent ranking of fifteen. Showing a slight increase in rank as an interest was Personal Attractiveness with third, sixth and fourth in 1935, 1957, and 1969 respectively.

(2) *Comparison of two 1969 groups*

In comparing the ranks given to the fifteen issues as problems by students in an all Negro high school to the ranks given by students in a predominately white school, a correlation coefficient of +.707 was obtained. For the same issues ranked as interests the correlation coefficient was +.564. The number one problem for both groups was Money. Study Habits was ranked second by both groups. The greatest difference was noted in the ranking given to Safety, which was ranked sixth by the Negro group and thirteenth by the predominately white students. Another issue ranked considerably different by the two groups was Home and Family Relations, which was ranked eleventh by the Negro students and fifth by the white students.

In ranking the issues as to interest, the Negro students ranked Health as first, while the white students gave Health a ranking of fourth. Money was ranked second by both groups, while Sex Adjustment received a ranking of three by Negro students and a rank of one by the white students. Issues being of less interest to white students than to the Negro students include: Health, Safety, Manners and Courtesy, Personal and Moral Qualities, Home and Family Relationships, and Study Habits. Those issues being of more interest to white students than Negro students include: Personal Attractiveness, Philosophy of Life, Getting Along with Other People, and Sex Adjustment. Both groups ranked Civic Interests, Attitudes, and Responsibilities as fourteenth and Daily Schedule as fifteenth.

Discussion

This study supported most of Harris' earlier observations (1959). For example, he questioned Symonds' suggestion regarding the ranking of Money as the number one problem in 1935 as being due to the depression years. Harris reported Money ranked number two in 1957, and today, in the era of greatest affluence ever experienced by a nation, Money was ranked the number one problem.

Another item of concern to Symonds was the rank given Sex Adjustment — fifteen (1936). He ascribed this to "repression." Harris, on the other hand, hypothesized that social patterns influenced its low rank in 1957 — 12.5. In 1969, the rank given to Sex Adjustment was eight, a considerable rise. This might be explained by the increased emphasis on sex in the present culture, and to greater frankness in discussing the problem.

Mental Hygiene rose even higher in rank, from eleven in 1935, to 5.5 in 1957, to third in 1969. Harris attributed the 1957 increase to social change (1959). This would seem to be a plausible explanation in both instances.

Study Habits ranked as the number two problem and eleven in interest. This represents a change in rank as interest — from eleven in 1935, to thirteen in 1957, and to eleven again in 1969. Symonds concluded that "school is important but uninteresting" (1959). Harris concluded the change was due to "pressures exerted by parents and teachers." While these two conclusions certainly have merit, even today, a much more influential factor is pressure exerted by society itself. Education is generally recognized as much more important in today's society than it was 35 years ago.

Interpreting these data in larger context, one might search for the changed conditions that are associated with observed differences in results. Perhaps even more pertinent for some of the findings of this investigation would be a search for ways to explain consistency of results when apparently great differences in significant conditions exist. While additional study is necessary to evaluate the role of these variables, some of the varying conditions in these investigations should be noted and discussed.

Neither Symonds nor Harris reported any socioeconomic data on the young people participating in their studies. Although the matching of samples on this basis might be questionable, it is possible for socioeconomic status to be an influence that affected the responses of the students. In the 1969 study, it may have been the most powerful influence.

Cultural differences are another set of influences that often affected the responses of individuals. Cultural differences associated with geography probably had some effect on results, since the students of Symonds' study lived in Oklahoma and New York, those of Harris' lived in Minnesota, while those for the present study lived in Texas. Another cultural influence was that associated with race. While Symonds and Harris made no mention of race, it is almost certain that neither study was conducted with a sample containing a large number of students from an all Negro high school.

Table 9.3
Fifteen Issues Considered as Problems

	1935		1957		Negro School 1969		White School 1969		Total 1969	
	Mean Rank	Rank of Mean	Mean Rank	Rank of Mean	Mean Rank	Rank of Mean	Mean Rank	Rank of Mean	Mean Rank	Rank of Mean
1. Money	6.5	1	6.4	2	5.27	1	5.84	1	5.60	1
2. Health	6.61	2	8.9	12.5	7.35	5	8.35	9	8.03	9
3. Personal Attractiveness	7.0	3	7.3	4	8.18	8	7.54	6	7.74	7
4. Study Habits	7.1	4	5.7	1	5.86	2	6.16	2	6.06	2
5. Personal and Moral Qualities	7.2	5	6.9	3	7.18	3	7.65	7	7.50	4
6. Philosophy of Life	7.5	6	7.6	5.5	8.46	9	7.15	4	7.57	5
7. Manners and Courtesy	7.9	7	8.1	8	9.53	15	9.42	14	9.45	14
8. Home and Family Relationships	8.2	8.5	8.0	7	8.74	11	7.21	5	7.70	6
9. Getting Along With Other People	8.2	8.5	8.3	10	9.38	13	8.47	10	8.76	11
10. Recreation	8.3	10	10.1	15	9.45	14	10.17	15	9.94	15
11. Mental Hygiene	8.5	11	7.6	5.5	7.29	4	6.93	3	7.04	3
12. Safety	8.6	12	9.6	14	7.73	6	9.20	13	8.73	10
13. Civic Interests, Attitudes, and Responsibilities	8.7	13	8.2	9	8.93	12	8.99	11	8.97	12
14. Daily Schedule	9.2	14	8.5	11	8.72	10	9.13	12	9.00	13
15. Sex Adjustments	10.0	15	8.9	12.5	7.92	7	7.80	8	7.84	8

Table 9.4
Fifteen Issues Considered as Interests

	1935		1957		Negro School 1969		White School 1969		Total 1969	
	Mean Rank	Rank of Mean	Mean Rank	Rank of Mean	Mean Rank	Rank of Mean	Mean Rank	Rank of Mean	Mean Rank	Rank of Mean
1. Recreation	5.2	1	6.8	3	8.15	9	7.15	7	7.49	6.5
2. Health	6.1	2	6.7	1	5.48	1	7.05	4	6.52	3
3. Personal Attractiveness	6.8	3	7.0	6	7.95	8	7.14	6	7.42	4
4. Manners and Courtesy	6.9	4	8.6	10	8.72	11	9.60	12	9.30	13
5. Philosophy of Life	7.5	5	6.9	5	8.58	10	6.93	3	7.49	6.5
6. Getting Along With Other People	7.6	7	6.8	3	9.20	13	7.08	5	7.80	8.5
7. Personal and Moral Qualities	7.6	7	7.2	8	7.45	4	7.50	8	7.48	5
8. Money	7.6	7	7.4	9	5.62	2	6.12	2	5.95	2
9. Home and Family Relationships	8.4	9	6.8	3	7.68	6	7.86	9	7.80	8.5
10. Safety	8.5	10	9.5	12	7.56	5	9.62	13	8.93	12
11. Study Habits	9.0	11	9.6	13	7.89	7	9.23	11	8.78	11
12. Mental Hygiene	9.2	12	8.8	11	9.03	12	8.23	10	8.50	10
13. Sex Adjustments	9.3	13	7.1	7	5.71	3	5.07	1	5.28	1
14. Civic Interests, Attitudes, and Responsibilities	9.4	14	9.8	14	9.93	14	10.12	14	10.06	14
15. Daily Schedule	10.4	15	11.2	15	11.06	15	11.30	15	11.22	15

Combined References for Chapter 9

Angelino H. and Mech, E. V. Some "first" sources of sex information as reported by sixty-seven college women. *Journal of Psychology*, 1955, 39, 321-324.

Bandura, A. The stormy decade: Fact or fiction? *Psychology in the Schools*, 1964, 1, 224-231.

Baur, E. J. Student peer groups and academic development. *College Student Survey*, 1967, 1, 22-31.

Bealer, R. C., Willits, F. C., and Maida, P. R. The rebellious youth subculture — a myth. *Children*, 1964, 11, 43-48.

Braham, M. Peer group deterrents to intellectual development during adolescence. *Educational Theory*, 1965, 15, 248-258.

Brittain, C. V. Adolescent choices and parent-peer cross pressures. *American Sociological Review*, 1963, 28, 358-391.

Brittain, C. V. A comparison of urban and rural adolescence with respect to peer versus parent compliance. *Adolescence*, 1969, 4(13), 59-68.

Carry, R. W. Youth breaks the rules. *Research Resume* No. 38. Burlingame, Calif.: Proceedings of the 20th Annual State Conference on Educational Research, 1968, 124-125.

Cawelti, G. Youth assess the American high school. *PTA Magazine*, 1968, 62, 16-19.

Coleman, J. S. *The Adolescent Society.* New York: Free Press, 1961.

Coleman, J. S. *Adolescents and the Schools.* New York: Basic Books, 1965.

Douvan, E. and Adelson, J. *The Adolescent Experience.* New York: John Wiley, 1966.

Dunphy, D. C. The social structure of urban adolescent peer groups. *Sociometry*, 1963, 26, 230-246.

Elias, J. and Gebhard, P. Sexuality and sexual learning in childhood. *Phi Delta Kappan*, 1969, 7, 401-405.

Elkin, F. and Westley, W. A. The myth of adolescent culture. *American Sociological Review*, 1955, 20, 680-684.

Fort, J. Youth: How to produce drop-ins rather than drop-outs. *Research Resume*, No. 38. Burlingame, Calif.: Proceedings of the 20th Annual State Conference on Educational Research, 1968, 53-64.

Friedenberg, E. Z. *The Vanishing Adolescent.* Boston: Beacon, 1959.

Friesen, D. Academic-Athletic-Popularity syndrome in the Canadian high school society. *Adolescence*, 1968, 3(9).

Garrison, K. C. *Psychology of Adolescence*. New York: Prentice-Hall, 1966.

Generations Apart. New York: Columbia Broadcasting System, 1969.

Goodman, P. Freedom and learning: The need for choice. *Saturday Review*, 1968, 51(20), 73-75.

Gottlieb, D. and Hodgkins, B. College student subcultures: Their structures and characteristics in relation to student attitude change. *School Review*, 1963, 71, 289.

Harris, D. B. Life problems and interests of adolescents in 1935 and 1957. *School Review*, 1959, 67, 335-343.

Havighurst, R. L. *Developmental Tasks and Education*. New York: Longmans, Green and Company, 1952.

Juhasz, A. Mc. Background factors, extent of sex knowledge and source of information. *Journal of School Health*, 1969, 39, 32-39.

Kendall, M. G. *Rank Correlation Methods*. London: Charles Griffin, 1948.

Lewis, L. S. The value of college to different subcultures. *School Review*, 1969, 77, 32-40.

Looft, W. R. Sex education for parents. *Journal of School Health*, 1971, 41.

McLuhan, M. and Fiore, Q. *The Medium Is the Message*. New York: Bantam, 1967.

Meissner, W. W. Parental interaction of the adolescent boy. *Journal of Genetic Psychology*, 1965, 107, 225-233.

Morison, R. S. Where is biology taking us? *Science*, 1967, 155, 429-433.

Musgrove, F. The social needs and satisfactions of some young people: Part I — at home in youth clubs and at work. *British Journal of Educational Psychology*, 1966 (Part I), 36, 61-71.

National School Public Relations Association. *Sex Education in the Schools*. Washington, D.C.: The Association, 1969.

Sherif, C. and Sherif, M. Seeking thrills with the 'In Crowd.' *PTA Magazine*, 1965, 60, 5-6.

Snedocor, G. W. and Cochran, W. G. *Statistical Methods*. Ames, Iowa: Iowa State University Press, 1967.

Smith, L. M. and Klein, P. F. The adolescent and his society. *Review of Educational Research*, 1966, 36, 424-436.

Strom, R. D. Comparison of adolescent and adult behavioral norm properties. *Journal of Educational Psychology*, 1963, 54, 322-330.

Symonds, P. M. Life problems and interests of adolescents. *School Review*, 1936, 44, 506-518.

Thornburg, H. D. Student assessment of contemporary issues. *College Student Survey*, 1969, 3(1), 1-5; 22.

Thornburg, H. D. Age and first sources of sex information as reported by 88 college women. *Journal of School Health*, 1970a, 40, 156-158.

Thornburg, H. D. Adolescence: A reinterpretation. *Adolescence*, 1970b, 5(20), 463-484.

Thornburg, H. D. Environmental concerns: An assessment by youth. In H. D. Thornburg (Ed.) *Contemporary Adolescence: Readings*. Belmont, Calif.: Brooks/Cole Publishing, 1971.

Trow, M. and Clark, B. R. Varieties and determinants of undergraduate subcultures. Paper read at the annual meeting of the American Sociological Society, New York, 1960.

indexes

Index of Authors

354   Index of Authors

Subject Index